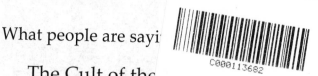

What people are sayi

The Cult of the

Janis Fry's endeavours to spread appreciation and reverence for ancient yew trees spans over four decades and is an inspiration to all of us who love trees. As one of the longest living life forms on our planet, the yew tree has rightly been celebrated as the Tree of Life. In this book, Janis takes us on a journey of discovery and wonder that skilfully weaves together the magic and history of trees.

Andy Egan, Director, Fellowship of the Trees and former CEO, International Tree Foundation

For those fascinated by the sacred power of the Yew, Janis Fry's book *The Cult of the Yew - Tree of Life, Mystery and Magic* offers a vast array of mythical connections to ponder and botanical wonders to marvel at, exploring not only the Yew's extraordinary physical qualities but also the archetypal and poetic truths at the heart of the tree's deeper mysteries.

It confirms that this most compelling and Otherwordly Tree of Life, Death and Rebirth is a phenomena to be valued, honoured and protected.

Eimear Burke, Chosen Chief of The Order of Bards, Ovate and Druids

Review of *The Cult of the Yew - Tree of Life, Mystery and Magic* by Janis Fry from Yew Shaman, Michael Dunning
I have always said that the yew mysteries are 'living mysteries,' representing the embodiment of an otherworldly wisdom-stream preserved from ancient times by the world's surviving ancient yew trees.

According to Janis Fry, the Cult of the Yew that was once

widespread in Britain, throughout mainland Europe and beyond, had its roots in ancient Mesopotamia. Fry also says that the yew was the original Tree of Life in ancient Egypt and traces it back to Heliopolis, some 15,000 years ago. From Egypt this special yew was transported to Eden and dispersed throughout that part of the world forming a bloodline of sacred yews – many of which are still alive today! As dramatic as these claims are, Janis Fry provides an abundance of multi-disciplinary evidence to convincingly back them up.

To a modern consciousness educated into a material culture, the mysteries of the cult of yew are highly elusive. Direct experience of the consciousness of an ancient yew is paramount and yet paradoxically such experience can only be gained through the adoption of perceptual principles as given by the yew herself!

In the ancient mystery schools, the initiate would be given the fundamentals of a mystery knowledge through which to develop a higher capacity for spiritual perception. Today and with regard to the mysteries of yew, it may seem that we have lost such a capacity. However, after 40 years of dedicated research and direct experience, Janis Fry surprises us by offering key elements of a mystery knowledge based on the yew – a knowledge that will become essential learning to all modern yew-enthusiasts and would be yew-initiates. Through this resuscitation of a mystery knowledge based around the yew as Tree of Life, Janis Fry also invites a radical re-evaluation and re-invigoration of the esoteric roots of Christianity, especially in relation to the British Isles. For example, we learn that some of Britain's ancient yews – mainly yews in Wales – were planted by holy hermits travelling from the Holy land – and that Joseph of Arimathea carried a yew branch from the Tree of Life into Britain and met with Silurian Druids in Wales. We also learn of the Armenian yew tribe that brought sacred yews to Devon and Dorset.

This book offers other astounding revelations concerning the

Golden Bough, the area of location of the Garden of Eden, the dragon-serpent yew god/desses, the bleeding yews of Nevern linking with the Roman Emperor Constantine, Jesus' use of a wand and the site of Arthur's burial on a Yew Isle.

At last – and thanks to the courageous work of Janis Fry – we can confidently claim the yew as the original Tree of Life and as the divinely incarnate guide to human evolution during ancient times and now reclaimed for the modern era.

Are you ready to step through the veil into the magic and mysteries of the Cult of the Yew?

Michael Dunning (America) www.yewmysteries.com

The Cult of the Yew

Tree of Life, Mystery and Magic

The Cult of the Yew

Tree of Life, Mystery and Magic

Janis Fry

**MOON
BOOKS**

Winchester, UK
Washington, USA

JOHN HUNT PUBLISHING

First published by Moon Books, 2023
Moon Books is an imprint of John Hunt Publishing Ltd., No. 3 East Street, Alresford
Hampshire SO24 9EE, UK
office@jhpbooks.net
www.johnhuntpublishing.com
www.moon-books.net

For distributor details and how to order please visit the 'Ordering' section on our website.

Text copyright: Janis Fry 2022

ISBN: 978 1 80341 153 8
978 1 80341 154 5 (ebook)
Library of Congress Control Number: 2021953214

A CIP catalogue record for this book is available from the British Library.

Design: Matthew Greenfield

UK: Printed and bound by CPI Group (UK) Ltd, Croydon, CR0 4YY
Printed in North America by CPI GPS partners

We operate a distinctive and ethical publishing philosophy in
all areas of our business, from our global network of authors to
production and worldwide distribution.

Contents

Previous Books

Warriors at the Edge of Time
ISBN 186163047-6

The God Tree
ISBN 1-86163-345-9978

The Name of the Yew

Invocation

Iber, ebor, eibe, yr
A gift of the gods is growing here.

Iva, iwa, iwe, eow,
First tree, first woman together grow.

Iur, iubhar, ywen, cis,
This tree I am, I am this.

If, an-t-iuchar, ivin, tis
The timeless changes never cease.

Eu, eihwaz, jeuen, yew
Eternally and always new.

Jehanne Mehta

Foreword

In *The Cult of the Yew - Tree of Life, Mystery and Magic,* Janis Fry has assembled an extraordinary amount of evidence – historical, archaeological, cultural, religious, mythological, folkloric, linguistic and scientific – and woven it into a compelling narrative. The central figure is, of course, the yew: a living being but one that is deeply mysterious, a biological avatar of immortality. Partly on that account, the yew has wound its way into countless myths and legends. At the same time, however, we have become bound up with its fate. So, this is a book about both trees and humans, distinct yet inseparable. And gods, since every intense experience of reality, such as the yew often induces, brings us into a divine presence.

Conversely, as Fry's account makes clear, the yew and its worshippers bitterest enemies have been men of the One God, located (when it suits them) off-planet, leaving the Earth and its non-human creatures desanctified. That has made matters much easier for, in the words of J.R.R. Tolkien, 'the destruction, torture and murder of trees perpetrated by private individuals and minor official bodies'. These enemies are godless in every sense of the word, and therefore oblivious to the divine in, and as, both trees and humans.

Experts in the various disciplines I mentioned a moment ago might quibble with Fry's borrowings from their fields of expertise. And even taking into account disciplinary territoriality, pedantry, and antiquarianism, they might sometimes have a point. But that is to miss the larger and more urgent point which rightly animates this book as a whole. A culture which fails to honour the yew, which cannot even see it as such, is doomed. The extinction of the yew and of humanity are inseparable, in a common Necrocene.

What, then, could turn this fate aside and bring the healing we all so need? It won't be information, important though that is; not even what abounds in these pages. No, it will, if anything, be *story*: the kind of story this book tells, infusing information with meaning, reawakening us to forgotten truths, reminding us of what really matters, and reweaving the torn fabric of our lives, human and nonhuman alike. And surely the ultimate story is that of life on Earth, which bore and sustains us all. So, we're not outside this story, merely reading it. (That really is a fantasy!) We're in it, living it, and part of it, although only one part. And among the people we are blessed to share it with is the yew: intractable, numinous, unique.

We are greatly in Janis Fry's debt.

Dr. Patrick Curry, July 2020,
Authority on J.R.R. Tolkien
Author of *Defending Middle Earth: Tolkien, Myth and Modernity*

Acknowledgements

Deepest thanks must go to Allen Meredith for his generosity and willingness to share and help with research and information and for inspiring an entire revival movement of our most iconic tree, the yew, in the 1980s. His work formed the basis for *The Sacred Yew* by Anand Chetan and Diana Brueton, published by Penguin in 1994 and produced the first book on the subject in a hundred years. I am proud to have contributed to that book, which formed the basis for all subsequent books on the subject, including this one. Despite grave personal problems and difficulties, Allen has dedicated his life to the yew and happily given of his time and resources in order to gain recognition and awareness of the ancientness and sacredness of this tree. Without him this book could not have been written.

Thanks also to:

David Bellamy,
David Shreeve, Libby Symon and The Conservation Foundation
The Tree Council,
The Woodlands Trust
John Scudamore
Patrick Curry
Heather Maling
Rob Mc. Bride
Val and Justin Gillings
Roberto Narayan-Tailor
Amber Woodhouse and Ron Cooper
Alison Goulbourne
Ian and Sandrine
Tom Beels
Andrew MacLean

Niall Bachuil
Pat Judson
Philip Carr Gomm
Paul Powlesland
Julian Hight
Sean Walters
Susan Elizabeth Hale
Lyndall Menzies
Maggie Wallis
Trevor Hails
Michael Dunning

Introduction

People sometimes ask me how I got involved with yew trees. In the late afternoon of a mellow autumn day in 1974, I was driving home with a friend. It was the weekend and we had spent the day in one of our favourite activities, exploring the area of West Wales we had both recently moved to. It was getting dark when ahead I saw some large iron gates at the side of the road slightly ajar and covered in brambles. It was just the kind of thing I found intriguing and so we stopped the car, and with difficulty made our way through the gates and up a long drive besieged with more brambles, lured by the darkened silhouette of an old country house. To the right of the house was what looked like a tall hedge. I went to investigate, imagining it was hiding another building but it seemed impenetrable till I found a gap in it just big enough to squeeze through. Without warning, I tripped and like Alice in Wonderland, fell headlong into another world. Above me tree trunks arched and interlocked with huge thick boughs in a network rather like a cathedral; a structure so complex you could not tell which tree a branch came from. I was in a tunnel that stretched in both directions. This was the Aberglasney Yew tunnel and I thought it was the eighth wonder of the world and so began my journey with the and the Tree of Life.

The legend of the Tree of Life is the most enduring story of all time, becoming more and more pertinent with each year that passes, as we come closer to the terrible possibilities of climate change and the enormity of what it may mean for us and all other life forms. Legends of the Tree of Life, the Babylonian Irkalla, the World Tree and the Norse prophecy of Ragnarök, the end of civilisation, are all bound up with this tree. This book traces the origins of the Tree of Life and the Cult of the Yew that surrounds it, as far back as it is possible to go before being lost in the mists of time. The book then traces its journey forwards to our time. The Tree of Life was a real tree, an extraordinary tree with powers of life, death and immortality. It originated with the gods and lent its powers to Pharaohs. It was too important ever to be lost and was transported great distances to sanctuaries in Britain and elsewhere where it still grows to this day.

The Cult of the Yew - Tree of Life, Mystery and Magic is something of a follow on from the previous book, *The God Tree*, published by Capall Bann in 2012 and although it can be read separately, some of the mysteries written about in the first book, actually reached resolution and conclusions in this current book as I continued to follow the trails. I am talking in particular of a place called Bernera which I now believe to have been the ancient, sacred, western isle sought by the Egyptians and referred to in the Pyramid Texts. This is how it is with the Yew and its mysteries and my involvement with this immortal tree has always been an exciting and ongoing quest of clues and synchronicities, delivering extraordinary answers. I will always be grateful for the great adventure of my life. Embarking on this journey to discover the secret and mostly forgotten history of the sacred yew as it was and continues to be, is a quest which once begun, will not allow the reader to remain indifferent. Either you will join me in this quest, be gripped by the unfolding story and the extraordinary importance of this sacred lost knowledge and the power of this ancient tree, or you will discard it. It is not for everyone. If your journey of discovery and meaning on the path of the yew begins and transports you, you will find there is no going back. The yew tree chooses its people and you are honoured and privileged if you are to be one.

The companionship that exists between humans and trees is a wonderfully close relationship that can be traced to humankind's first beginnings on earth. It is a relationship even more important than the relationship with our mothers. Trees fulfil all our practical needs for survival and the Tree of Life gives us our spiritual connection and claims our allegiance for the health and continuance of our civilisations and our planet.

The Cult of the Yew - Tree of Life, Mystery and Magic begins by discovering the earliest located sanctuary of this sacred tree before it moved to the Garden of Eden and traces its journey out into the world, with those who guarded, carried the sacred branch and planted it. It reveals the reasons why it was of the utmost importance for Druids, priests, saints and holy people to go to enormous lengths and personal sacrifice to preserve the Tree of Life and its bloodline and to protect the sacred knowledge that surrounded it, into the far distant future.

The people of the Yew took cuttings, pieces from the sacred tree to plant in new territory. Branches and roots were taken vast distances, sometimes with much ceremony, other times quietly, secretively, as dry staffs or sticks that no one would guess contained the lifeblood, the regenerative power of the sacred tree that would burst into life once more when planted at its destination. Often that destination was Britain and there was a long tradition of migrating tribes, ancient civilizations, pilgrims, saints, and holy people bringing sacred yews to these islands.

Long before the pyramids and the hieroglyphs, this tree had disappeared from Egypt and came to be recognised only by the Ankh symbol, which represents the branch of immortality. By the time of the early pyramids, the real meaning of the Ankh and the knowledge of which specific tree was the Tree of Life, was known by only a few and had become confused and lost. It is not difficult to see how this happened. Over time, as the life of mankind developed and wars, disasters, migrations, concerns, plans and ideas occupied our minds, people quite simply forgot that the tree was an actual real tree that lived in our world and not just in the Otherworld and thus the Tree of Life became a legend.

It seems that cuttings or branches were taken some 15,000 years ago, from a special Tree of Life yew, revered and growing at a temple in Egypt. These were taken and planted in sanctuaries elsewhere and out of the country. Later again, cuttings from the trees grown from these were taken in the form of staffs, particularly to Britain, the White Island, the final place of sanctuary, to await this time, and the return of such knowledge. This is the 'second coming', the return to a life lived as a sacrament to the natural world, in harmony with our environment. It is our final chance of renewal of the Earth and recognition of the Tree of Life.

The Cult of the Yew, the sacred tree, was to be found in one form or another, in all cultures of the Northern hemisphere. In the Christian world, common knowledge of the Holy Wood which derived from this tree only began to disappear fairly recently. Scratch the surface and it is all still there, re-emerging in this time when our survival or extinction is in the balance. The Tree of Life is both the Holy Grail and the Elixir of Life and still exists in our world. It is a special yew, guardian of our planet, which ultimately may decide the fate of the human race. The ancient hollow yew is nothing less than a portal to other worlds and other times.

What this book ultimately draws attention to is that the Tree of Life, the tree of immortality, the tree said by the ancients to be an ark, may well be in Britain, hidden in plain sight. I believe it is. From the sacred text of the *Bundahishn*, comes the information that the Tree of Life, known in that culture as the White Tree is requisite for the restoration of the universe and this may be the reason why the symbol of the White Tree, restated in JRR Tolkien's *The Lord of the Rings* resonates so deeply within us. The White Tree is the most ancient of sacred trees.

My wish is that Britain and in particular Wales should realise and celebrate its true importance in the world, of which it seems oblivious. 90% of the oldest trees in Europe are British yews. Wales has the highest concentration of ancient yews, being home to more than a quarter of them. Britain is therefore the country with the largest collection of ancient yews on earth. Yet in 2021 they still have no legal protection, an indication of how little our culture values them. This has to change. Those who own most of them see no need for it and are unable to believe that their days

4

in Britain are numbered and their land, on which these ancient yews stand, may become neglected or owned by those who do not care for this tree. As a result, our most precious trees, so valued by our ancestors now face an uncertain future.

This iconic tree is an immortal giant, King and Queen among trees, immeasurably old, a tree so unlike other trees there are those who would say it is hardly a tree at all but a mystical being with the extraordinary ability to regenerate itself, resurrect and renew itself after death, decay and destruction. The ancients, wiser than us, knew the yew tree as the flesh of the gods, the Immortal One.

Yews have been in Britain for hundreds of thousands of years as evidenced by Cromer Marshes and the Bristol Channel where fossilised remains have been found. Although the general opinion is that the Tree of Life was and is a yew tree, it is not to say that every yew is a Tree of Life. This title goes to a very special yew, a sacred yew whose bloodline this book attempts to trace. Only a DNA comparison can prove if it is found and due to vested interests, that is not forthcoming and indeed it is perhaps right that we are denied that certainty before we are fit to receive it. Human beings are complex and the truth can cause radical changes in reputations and established, accepted knowledge. Revolution and change is often resisted.

It is not the indigenous yews that particularly interest me but the sacred yews, Taxus Sanctus, those yews that were brought to Britain by various yew tribes, pilgrims and holy people who wished to preserve the bloodline and keep the tree with them as a deity and talisman. The reasons for bringing these trees to Britain and planting them, often in remote places, remains a mystery that continues to fascinate, occupy and make me question the reason why. These trees have special properties, of that I am certain. The fact that they are the source of a drug for treating cancer known as Taxol is an indication of what they are capable of but we may never know altogether what they are. The ancients knew though and at this point in our history I believe it is imperative that we regain what we can of their knowledge. However, we can only do so if we are responsible enough, care enough and have a pure enough heart to use that knowledge for good and so the issue is circular. One depends on the other. If we lose our sacred trees, allow them to be destroyed, or disregard and neglect them, we do so at our peril.

As we face climate change and one natural disaster after another in this time, the lesson we must learn is that Nature is in charge and we must abide by her laws of the web of life and support and protect her at all costs. The Yew is the seat of Nature's consciousness, the yew tree god/dess was known by the Hittites as 'Eya' and is the connector of consciousness on our planet and a register of our spiritual health. When we say the 'Tree of Life' we can now understand that in all its ways and characteristics, the yew fits the description of that eternal tree and was known as such in all the ancient cultures of the Northern hemisphere. It is a tree of great power, 'the double fatal tree', both a healing tree and a vengeful tree. It is the Tree of Life, Death and Resurrection and its religious significance is traceable back for millennia. If you wish to know the Yew better, there are now plenty of books on the subject. Still the most comprehensive is Fred Hageneder's *Yew: A History*. The purpose of this book, however, is not to replicate the work of others, (although some things necessarily overlap) but to re-establish a spiritual understanding of what the yew once was and still is. Much of the subject matter here you will not have come across before. The research is ground breaking. The phenomena known as 'Yew', is far more than a tree. It is a holder of wisdom, a keeper of knowledge and quite possibly a creator god and watcher of the human race. The Tree of Life, the Otherworldly tree, is a conscious entity, a tree that can bleed like a human, change sex and produce the enigma of the Golden Bough. It is inextricably linked with us and our future on this planet. The necessity for us to return to the respect and communication we once had with trees and the Yew in particular is as important as our return to the healthy relationship we once had with Nature.

Something I need to make clear from the start and reiterate from the statement made in *The God Tree* is that with this book, I am attempting to interpret things told thousands of years ago, attempting to understand symbols from the distant past made by people with a consciousness very different to ours. There are things here that will be criticised and questioned and there may well be mistakes made. I am dealing with things that have not been taken on seriously before and am sometimes attempting to reconstruct events, knowledge and beliefs from ancient manuscripts and half-forgotten texts. I won't have got it all right but this is a sincere attempt to re-establish the sacred knowledge of the Tree of Life and the natural laws of creation to which this tree is central. It is a knowledge that once underpinned civilisations and is the legacy left to us, if we can but recognise it, from people who were wiser than us and more responsible in their custodianship of the Earth. Without that knowledge we have no true understanding of our place on Earth and no map of life. It is this knowledge we must remember at this point in our history, return to and realign with if we are to live in harmony with Nature and regain a future for ourselves and all life on Earth.

Bon chance, good luck! The quest to restore this ancient sacred knowledge and an authentic way of life is a solemn and life-changing undertaking. It is not for the faint-hearted. The Yew will challenge you mentally, physically and spiritually. It will make you question all that you held dear and thought unshakeable. This book is nothing less than a book of revelations to augur a renaissance of spiritual understanding and wisdom. It is written with the hope of inspiring those who read it, to follow the Golden Bough, to a golden age of enlightenment and the restoration and rebirth of Nature.

Chapter 1

From Egypt to Eden

The earliest culture known to us, to have held the Tree of Life at its very heart, is that of Egypt. This sacred tree was central to that country's religion, rites and belief system, connected as it was with immortality, which was of the utmost importance to the Egyptians, amounting almost to an obsession.

According to Ralph Ellis, the yew tree was the Egyptians original 'Tree of Life', which featured prominently in Egypt's most sacred mystery school traditions and initiatory rites and was used as a symbol of death and also in underworld rites of rebirth. In *Eden in Egypt*, this author suggests 'the association between the yew and eternal life was an Egyptian as well as an Irish tradition.' The Egyptians had what is known as a 'step culture'; in other words, in its earliest time, it was in its most developed form and after that, it gradually deteriorated. This suggests that the culture had come from another civilization, perhaps transplanted by a natural disaster, as happened to Atlantis and may explain the fact that by the time of the pyramids, the sacred tree was already legendary, with no one living who knew what species it was. By the time of the pyramids the Egyptians, although still knowing the Tree of Life to be of enormous importance, had lost this knowledge but just because it had become a legendary tree does not mean it did not exist there at one time as a reality. Paintings in the pyramids and hieroglyphs, which were to do with the sacred tree and immortality, such as the Ankh and the Djed, were done from ancient memory and were likely to have been purely symbolic by then, for the detail surrounding these important things had been lost and forgotten and the original knowledge of the sacred yew may, in any case, have been privy only to the magi and the Egyptian priests. At one time, however, everyone would have been familiar with the Tree of Life, so familiar it would not have been deemed necessary to write it down but the day came when both the sacred tree and the yew trees no longer existed in Egypt, whether from climate change, excess demand for yew wood or for some other reason. Both the sacred tree and Taxus baccata disappeared entirely and records of it were either lost or had not been kept in the first place.

The Tree of Life is traceable back 15,000 years to Heliopolis which is the earliest place we can trace it to. Heliopolis is its Greek name, and it was probably renamed in Classical Greek times, as its Egyptian name was Iwni or Innu and somewhat tellingly, these names are also those of the yew tree goddess Anu, which we will come to later. The Tree of Life must have existed tens of thousands of years ago since Taxus baccata goes back 200 million but there is no real or documented way of telling about this powerful special sacred version of this tree and how it came into being. The Sun Temple of Atum Ra, in Heliopolis, dedicated to Ra, the Supreme Sun God, housed the sacred tree, the Tree of Life, which was also known as the Ished Tree, the Persea Tree or Phoenix Tree. Its fruit gave eternal life and knowledge of the divine plan, a kind of map of destiny. It is easy to see how these two functions or attributes, led later to the idea of there being two separate trees, one of Life and the other of Knowledge but at Heliopolis, these were embodied in one tree. This tree arose when Ra Atum, the Sun God, first appeared at Heliopolis and was connected with the creation myth and the nine gods of the Ennead of Heliopolis. Eating of this tree bestowed eternal life. Interestingly, all legends of the Tree of Life or sacred tree depict it as having creatures that guard it, and the Persea tree is no exception being the seat of the mythical Bennu Bird or Phoenix protected by a great cat. The Tree of Life was doubtless the most potent symbol of Ancient Egypt. According to Andrew Collins in his book *From the Ashes of Angels* 1996, this sacred tree may also be linked to the Tree of All Seeds said to have grown on an island in Lake Van.

Ancient cultures saw trees as gods and according to Mrs Philpot in *The Sacred Tree*, 1897, 'The most famous of Sycamores, the Sycamore of the South, was regarded as the living body of Hathor' and therefore was a tree looked upon as a god. It is no wonder the sacred tree was revered, kept and tended at the Temple of Ra. The sacred tree was connected with the sun and represented the lifeblood of the Egyptian spiritual life and the Temple of Ra at Heliopolis was symbolized by the Djed with the Ankh, denoting a branch of the Tree of Life and therefore also of immortality, above it. The circle of the Ankh denotes the continual circle of life and the cross below denotes the Tree. Eventually, in later Celtic times the cross was placed within the circle to denote the Tree of Life in its sacred enclosure. It was only through the Tree of Life that a person could be brought back to life or become immortal like the Tree itself and in the pyramids, the branch or Ankh is shown being presented to the nose of the Pharaoh. No ordinary mortal was allowed the privilege of immortality gifted by the Tree of Life. Through the branch, the Pharaoh is offered the breath of life and it stands to reason that whatever offers life, like the Tree of Life, should be worshipped as a god. In one of Harper's *Assyrian Letters* it is shown that smelling or breathing in the atmosphere of the magical and sacred plant is also of account. It is said that 'the king made us again alive, in that he laid the plant of life to our noses'. This is what we see depicted in the pyramids. We also see that many of the Egyptian gods were tree god/desses and in the pyramids, they are shown offering sustenance and therefore life, often as trays of food and drink.

Egyptian Pyramid painting of Tree goddess offering sustenance.

The tree was portrayed as a goddess that provided sustenance, in the pyramid paintings, showing not simply a person in the tree offering food and drink but the tree itself doing this. Similar ideas are found in other cultures and in Greece, the gods connected with Athena emerge from a hollow tree. Like the yews, the gods connected with them lived for thousands of years and were revered as having supernatural powers which derived from the sacred tree.

To avoid confusion, it must be stated that parallel to the reverence for the sacredness of a particular tree, is a separate but related issue. Yew wood was considered a precious wood, not only because it was related to the Tree of Life yew but perhaps as a result, there was a cult and belief that continued down the centuries and across continents, that pieces of the wood itself had certain divine, mystical or magical powers of protection, healing, prophecy and divination. As a result, yew wood was used for making the funerary goods, sarcophagi and temples of ancient Egypt to ensure its divine presence was with the dead on their journey into the afterlife. Almost as a separate but still related issue, it was valued for practical reasons as a good hard durable wood for building and making things and would have been an expensive commodity, a top-quality material. It was in much demand for practical purposes, across the whole of the region from Egypt to the Black Sea and inland across Mesopotamia and Persia. Temples made from it would last for centuries.

Later the yew wood which probably at one time grew in Egypt had to be sourced from elsewhere due to it becoming extinct in this country. Yew veneer was also used in ancient Egypt indicating it was a rare and precious wood. As in other ancient cultures, yew was used in royal tombs and mausoleums. Yew artefacts from ancient Egypt include grave furniture and sarcophagi and two busts of Queen Tiye, including a death mask which naturally needed to be made from a wood associated with immortality. The majority of yew artefacts occur in the 6th - 12th dynasties. In 1894, wooden planks from Egyptian coffins were sampled by Georges Beauvisage, the head of Botanics at the Faculty of Medicine in Lyons, France. Fred Hageneder in *Yew: A History* says:

> In the first microscopic investigation of wooden grave goods from ancient Egypt to that date, Beauvisage discovered - to everyone's surprise - that the sarcophagi had not been made of native wood or any other timber famously used in the ancient Orient but of yew...Beauvisage concluded that the coffins in questions probably belonged to the twelfth Dynasty (c. 2400 BCE) but admitted a possibly greater age.

Proletti et al (2011) found that the main wood species of

Egyptian sarcophagus was yew which was not native to Egypt. Dr A H Layard an English traveller, archaeologist, cuneiformist, art historian, draughtsman, collector, politician and diplomat, best known as the excavator of Nimrud and Nineveh also had wood from the remains of pillars from the Temple of Nineveh, said to be cedar wood from Lebanon, examined and found it was yew wood. This wood, hard as iron, was finally replaced with stone when the wood itself became more and more scarce and difficult to source and people realised stone was even more durable. It was thanks to this change in building technology that the remaining yews were saved.

Eventually the yew that grew in Egypt and the Holy Lands thousands of years ago either died out or was overused to the point of extinction and had to be sourced elsewhere. Ships would naturally have travelled along the coast to Lebanon to bring back the wood that grew there so prolifically and the yew trees of Lebanon were plundered until there were virtually none left and supplies were exhausted. At this point it would have had to be sourced from further north again, probably imported from Turkey and perhaps further west in North Africa. In *Trees beyond the Word* by Ian D. Rotherham, Christine Handley, Mauro Agnoletti and Tomasz Samajlik, 2012:

> King Solomon is reputed to have sent 30,000 workers to the Taurus Mountains of Southern Turkey to cut trees for his temple in Jerusalem and once the cedar forests in Lebanon were almost destroyed, the similar needs of countries in the eastern Mediterranean were provided by the Taurus mountains.

The Egyptians built a vast port and city at Heraklion on the Nile delta, where goods would have been transferred from sea-going vessels to fleets of cargo boats designed to travel up the Nile River and carry the yew wood otherwise known as almug to the destinations where it was needed, along with gold and precious stones. The yew wood would have come from not far inland because of the difficulty of transporting such heavy goods, which was most easily done by ship along the coast and rivers. Timber would have been taken on board or floated down river and the river Nile would have been ideal for this. There is more about the yews of Lebanon referenced from an ancient tablet from the 14th century BCE in the chapter on the Tree of Immortality in my book *The God Tree,* 2012. Only sound younger trees providing solid wood for the building of temples and sacred or funerary objects would have been taken, leaving those that were old and decayed behind as the only remaining evidence the yews were once there but yews, as we know, are capable of continuous regeneration and yews not chosen for making and building are still there in the mountains of Lebanon and Turkey.

Written records concerning the ancient city-state of Carchemish located in what is now southern Turkey, first appear in the Mari letters (royal archives of Mari, c.18th century BCE) and show that at that time, the city was a trade centre for wood, most likely involved in shipping Anatolian timber down the Euphrates. Carchemish survived the Sea People's attacks and continued to be the capital of an important neo-Hittite kingdom in the Iron Age. Yew wood or 'almug' would have been imported into Egypt not just from Lebanon but other places too. There were also stands of yew in Cilicia and the Taurus mountains. The word 'almug' is a word anciently used for yew but for a long time it was forgotten which tree this was. Linguistically the original word in several ancient documents is an Akkadian word and indicates a particular valuable timber from Lebanon. Even 3,000 years ago, the Biblical writers had no idea what almug was and assumed it meant cedar. This mistake was only discovered by Dr Layard and Professor Henslow (Botanist friend of Charles Darwin), in the last 100 years. This wood was in high demand in both Egypt and the Near East for temple building. Fred Hageneder says:

The old Hebrew word 'almug' is generally accepted to mean 'yew'...King Solomon would have been aware of the meaning of 'almug' and this might explain why he particularly requested some wood of this tree for his temple and why it is mentioned, not in league with other timber but in the same breath as gemstones.

Although Hageneder does not say why, it would imply that Algum wood was as precious as the gemstones and may have come from the same place, such as the area of Ophir, possibly the original Eden, which was described as a place where both were found. Solomon negotiated with Hiram, the King of Tyre (and hence ruler over the vast forests of Lebanon) after other kinds of woods had been brought from Lebanon for the temple construction, specifically for huge cargoes of Algum wood and precious stones. This wood was used for the pillars and for artefacts used in the temple and was therefore obviously considered to be special and was delivered separately from the other timber. Fred Hageneder goes on to say:

Another hint as to the natural distribution of yew in Lebanon comes from Nineveh. A palace inscription mentions 'cedar wood' from Lebanon as the material for the beams but a microscopic examination of a sample from one beam proved it to be yew wood. The Assyrian king Tiglath-Pileser I (11th century BCE), reports to have planted almug in his palace garden at Nineveh, together with cedar and the other trees of which he had collected specimens during his expeditions... According to Professor George Henslow in *Plants of the Bible*, almug is yew wood and as this whole area was a major source of yew wood, one wonders if almug was not a special kind of yew wood. In the Old Testament, an additional word for yew - smilax is used...

From *Wood* by Peter Ian Kuniholm, we read:

> Forests were exploited from the very beginnings of Near Eastern civilization... Extensive forest use has a history in this region of at least ten thousand years... In Egypt and Mesopotamia, good wood had to be imported by water. As far back as the Old Kingdom Egypt, timber was transported from Lebanon to Egypt in multiple shiploads. At all times, timber must have been floated down the Tigris and Euphrates Rivers to Mesopotamian cities...Cuneiform texts indicate that royal authorities were concerned about regulating timber cutting, setting timber prices and imposing taxes on timber.

It must be noted, that when the word for 'cedar' is used, Egyptologists do not agree this was the wood meant and they thought that it may simply mean a better quality conifer. Hundreds of temples were being built in countries of the Near East, adjacent to Lebanon including Nineveh, and were using this wood from Lebanon. At one time before it became Armenia, the Kingdom of Colchis, the region where the Golden Fleece was found on the sacred tree, was a huge kingdom, which stretched down the coast of the Black Sea to modern Turkey and into the Anatolia region. The Colchis, known for its yew trees, no doubt also exported its wood.

Eventually, a deluge came to Egypt, a great flood, around 15,000 years ago, as evidenced by the watermarks on the Sphinx and whether for this reason or some other threat or natural or manmade disaster, the sacred tree would have been immediately rescued by priests and moved to higher ground and perhaps out of the country altogether. Mrs J H Philpot in *The Sacred Tree*, 1897, says 'The different cultures brought the tree with them to monastic places'. The need to save the tree, more precious than anything in their world due to its special powers and properties, was so urgent, the last thing on anyone's mind would have been recording what happened at the time, or where the Tree was taken to. Saving it was all anyone would have been thinking about, not recording where it went to or what type of tree it was. Only later after the events are histories written and many details that might seem irrelevant are forgotten and so the pictures in the pyramids show the sacred tree, sacred to Hathor, as the short-lived sycamore, which seems most unlikely, or as a generalized tree showing it as deciduous, not coniferous, as these trees are more likely to produce fruit. There was no clarity or memory about which tree it was. It had almost become a decorative motif and we can imagine the tomb painters embellishing it. While all trees were and are important for the gifts, they give humankind and other creatures, only one tree was godlike. It stands to reason that the Tree of Life has to be a tree capable of immortality itself if it can bestow such a thing on a human and because of its immortality; it was naturally considered a god by the Egyptians. There is no other tree that fits the bill, other than the yew. The Pyramid Texts of around 3000 BCE state that the Egyptians go to seek the Tree of Life where the sun sets in the Western Isles and this may be a reference to the Tree of Life having been brought to Britain. Evidence suggests the Ankerwycke yew at Runnymede may have been an Egyptian planting. The medieval Irish manuscript, known as *The Settling of the Manor of Tara*, also suggests the five sacred trees of Ireland, in particular, that at Fortingall (at that time Scotland was seen as part of Ireland - see *The God Tree*), originated from Egypt too. Later, other cultures such as the Dunmonii, described in a later chapter, also brought the Tree of Life. Of course, seeking the Tree of Life in the West may just be a reference to the land of the dead and the otherworld being in the West with the setting sun but I think not.

There are stories of a sacred tree being rescued from floods which are associated with Uruk where Sumerian legend has it that the god Enki planted the Huluppa tree on the banks of the Euphrates (said in Genesis to originate in Eden), where it was found by the goddess Inanna, who rescued it from being washed away by a flood. Inanna then planted it in her temple garden where the mythical Anzu bird lived in its branches and the 'serpent who could not be charmed' (a wonderful description!), in its roots. It is worth noting that Gilgamesh, originally described as a branch or root or sprouting shoot of the Tree of Life or Mes tree, is known as the 'King of Uruk' on the clay tablets from the library of the 7th century BCE Assyrian King, Ashurbanipal. The same event of rescuing the tree would have taken place at Heliopolis. Cuttings or parts of the Tree of Life with some roots attached would have been quickly gathered up and taken away to a place of safety. They would have been removed as soon as possible by the priests and temple staff, to a place where they could be replanted and guarded, to ensure the life of the sacred tree continued. As detailed in *The God Tree*, when ancient peoples moved, they took their sacred tree with them. Eridu, where the sacred Kiskanu tree (Tree of Life of Anu) grew was the earliest city in Southern Mesopotamia, now known as Teli Abu Shahrain in Iraq. One of the oldest cities in the world, it was founded in 4500 BCE and may have been one of the places that the Egyptian Tree of Life was taken to from Heliopolis. The Tree of Life was recorded in 5000 BCE on Sumerian cuneiform clay tablets as being in Eridu. As a remnant of the Egyptian Tree of Life of Heliopolis, it must therefore have moved north to Eridu, along with the culture and knowledge surrounding it over 5,000 - 7,000 years ago, as documented on cuneiform tablets of that period. We cannot know an exact date. Eridu was seen as the Babylonian Paradise and the tree itself was known as the Tree of Ea, father or mother of the gods and therefore as a source of other Trees of Life. It gave eternal life through the eating of its fruits and is therefore directly connected to the later Biblical story of the Garden of Eden, which must derive from it. In Babylonian mythology, the Tree of Life was a magical tree that grew in the centre of Paradise. The Apsu or primordial waters flowed from its roots, just as the rivers do in Genesis. Eridu was the place where the gods lived.

The description of the Garden at Eridu, translated from the

Sumerian texts and predating Genesis, is quoted here:

In Eridu there is a black kiskanu-tree, growing in a pure place
Its appearance is (lapis lazuli) erected on the Apsu/Abyss
Enki when walking there fills Eridu with abundance,
In the foundation of it, is the place of the underworld
In the resting place is the chamber of Nammu.
In its holy temple, there is a grove, casting its shadow,
Therein no man can enter,
In the midst are Dtu (samas) and Dumuzi (Tammuz),
(the two trees)
In between the river with two mouths.

In 2000 BCE, the Babylonians believed two trees stood guarding the celestial door where Anu, both a god and a tree formed the entrance. These were 'gis-ti', the Tree of Life or 'Bearer of Life' and 'kis-ka-na', 'the tree at the gate of the celestial spheres, or 'Grower of Truth'. These two trees were almost certainly the descendants of Anu, trees grown from layered branches and appear to mark the point where the one tree becomes two, as in Genesis.

As we saw at the beginning of this chapter, the Egyptian name for Heliopolis was Iwni or Innu which are also the names of the yew goddess Anu. Although Anu is associated with Babylonian religion, this indicates the Tree of Life of their mythology came originally from Egypt and may have been a tree grown from a cutting of the tree rescued from floods in Egypt, or it may be the original tree moved to a paradisial place. Offshoots or cuttings of this tree no doubt ended up in the Garden of Eden. The legend of Anu is of two trees that descended from the crown of the tree of Anu and became known much later as the Tree of Knowledge and the Tree of Life, suggesting that the Tree of Anu was the original Tree of Life which gave rise to a tree, which following the flood, was taken to Eridu. The story talks of the sons of Anu, which were trees layered from the mother tree. From Iwni, or Heliopolis, the Tree of Life and its culture moved north into Mesopotamia, through what is now known as Palestine, Israel, Jordan, Lebanon, Syria, Turkey, Armenia and Georgia. In earlier times these places were known as Judah, Persia, Armenia, Lazica, Colchis, Lebanon, Anatolia, Iberia and Gogharena, also known as Gaokarene or Gugark, but boundaries have, of course, changed and no longer correspond. The Kingdom of Colchis, for example, at one time a vast Kingdom is little known today, having been swallowed up by modern states. Cuttings or remnants of roots from the Tree of Life would have been taken north into the Near East, to places such as those mentioned above and in particular to Gogharena, which lay south of the Caucasus Mountains. Dozens of Tree of Life trees seem to have existed in Gogharena, all from the same source with the same DNA. This is a special place for that sacred yew. The Gogharena Tree of Life yew is a source of Haoma, the elixir of life and fits all the descriptions and characteristics of the Tree of Life. The Tree of All Seeds is also this tree, as noted by Andrew Collins in *From the Ashes of Angels,* 1996. It should be mentioned too that Lake Sevan, not too far away on the same continent, near Tbilisi, is the site of another legendary sacred Tree of Life, the Tree of All Seeds which existed with its guardians. The ancient name for Lake Sevan is the Vourukasha Sea where the Tree of All Seeds grew on an island. There are also records of yews of 4,000 years in old Anatolia, although they are not necessarily Tree of Life Yews. One certainly existed in Colchis where Jason and the Argonauts found the sacred tree with the Golden Fleece connected to the yew. It seems this entire continent is full of legends of the Tree of Life.

According to the Bible, this tree, or rather what was by now two trees, originated in Eden. The question is where and when was Eden? Although the story in Genesis is thought to have been written about 3,500 years ago, the actual story is from a culture and civilisation much further back than when it was written. *The American Journal of Semitic Languages* reported that:

there was no place for Eden on the modern map and with the sixteenth century began a flood of speculation as to the location of the lost Eden, which has continued down into our own time... Calvin and others found Eden in Babylonia... Reland and his followers discovered Eden in Armenia, whence flowed the four rivers, Tigris, Euphrates, Phasis and Araxes – a view which long held the field among scholars who tried to understand the Hebrew text of the second chapter of Genesis.

Map placing Eden in Armenia. Other old maps vary but most locate Eden in Armenia or slightly further west towards Lebanon and the coast.

The name Eden is probably derived from the Akkadian word 'edinu', borrowed from the Sumerian 'eden', meaning 'plain'. According to the Genesis story of the creation and fall of mankind out of Eden, this paradisial place lay east of Israel and from here rivers flowed to the four corners of the world. Genesis 2:10-14 lists four rivers in association with the Garden of Eden: Pishon, Gihon, Chidekel (the Tigris), and Phirat (the Euphrates). It also refers to the land of Cush, thought by some to equate to 'Cossaea', a Greek name for the land of the Kassites. These lands lie north of Elam, immediately to the east of ancient Babylon.

The Kassites originated as tribal groups in the Zagros Mountains to the northeast of Babylonia. Their leaders came to power in Babylon following the collapse of the ruling dynasty of the Old Babylonian Period in 1595 BCE and they retained power for about 400 years until 1155 BCE. They gained control of Babylonia after the Hittite sack of the city in 1595 BCE.

Kassite Cylinder Seal. 16th -12th century BCE Mesopotamia

A stone cylinder known as the Kassite Seal, made from milky chalcedony and dated between the 16th and 12th century BCE from Mesopotamia, shows a central male figure connected to two other figures with fish tails by way of what looks like a stream of liquid which flows between them. A two-headed bird is above his head and noticeably he is flanked by two sacred trees. Two streams also flow from the trees and are connected to him. Perhaps the central figure is the god Enki and perhaps this is Eden.

A 1st millennium Mesopotamian seal shows a similar figure, half-human, half-fish before a stylised Tree of Life which in Babylonian mythology grew in the centre of Paradise, with the Absu or primordial waters flowing from its roots. The Biblical Tree of Paradise evolved from this.

In Mesopotamian myth, it is the god Enki who builds a temple at Eridu on the banks of the Euphrates. He lives in the depths of the Abzu (the Abyss or freshwater ocean under the Earth, the source of freshwater streams) and in the myths, Enki is seen as the source of Earth's freshwater rivers. He plants a garden for his temple. In the Biblical Eden, a river rising in the midst of the garden becomes the source of the four rivers, the Pishon, Gihon, Hiddekel and Euphrates. Evidently, Enki's garden has been transformed into Eden and the freshwater Abzu, where Enki lives, becomes the spring in Eden from where the four rivers arise, which encompass the Edenic world. Enki and his consort Shamhat become Adam and Eve. In another parallel in myth, the Sumerian goddess Inanna obtains knowledge by eating from the cedar tree which, as we are beginning to see, is far more likely to mean a yew which unlike the Cedar has fruits you can eat (but not the nut inside the red aril!).

Inanna and her symbols (Kassite).

In the Epic of Gilgamesh, access to trees is forbidden at a place in the Cedar Mountain where Enki has led Gilgamesh and where the monster Huwawa guards and denies access to this protected sanctuary or garden of trees to humans. (Later we shall see how monsters, dragons and serpents always guard the Tree of Life). Are we perhaps looking at the site for Eden or Enki's garden being something of a plateau, high up in a mountainous place, where yew and other conifers naturally grow and where rivers would begin as mountain streams? To add to the potential of this area being Eden, there is a strong likelihood that the most important of the legendary Tree of Life trees, known as the White Tree (more later in the chapter of that name), is likely to have grown in this area of Lebanon and one of the Tree god/desses known as the Lady of the Mountain, is shown dressed in yew branches.

Laurence Gardener, in *Genesis of the Grail Kings*, agrees with this placing of Eden in the land of the Kassites, though he may not call it that and in doing so, also agrees with the Sumerian texts, that Eden lay in the more mountainous northern reaches of Mesopotamia – the Zagros Range of modern Kurdistan near Lake Sevan. This correlates with the Shinto religion and others, who believe the gods are in the mountains and in the case of Shinto that the gods are part of the yew trees. All sources agree Eden was in a mountainous area, perhaps on a grassy plateau but certainly in the mountains.

According to Lars-Ivar Ringbom the 'Paradisus Terrestris, is located in Shiz in northeastern Iran. According to Terje Stordalen, the Eden in Ezekiel appears to be located in Lebanon, a most likely idea:

> It appears that Lebanon is an alternative placement in Phoenician myth (as in Ez. 28,13, III.48), for the Garden of Eden and there are connections between Paradise, the Garden of Eden and the forests of Lebanon within prophetic writings.

It is interesting to read in Ezekiel 31 about Eden which is described as being in Lebanon and about all the cedars and other trees described there and the waters remind us of Enki's garden. Ezekiel also associates this Garden of God with a mountain. Edward Lipinski and Peter Kyle, McCarter have suggested that the Garden of the Gods (Sumerian Paradise), the oldest Sumerian idea of the Garden of Eden, relates to a mountain sanctuary in the Lebanon and Anti-Lebanon ranges.

The Garden of Eden Myth, Walter Mattfield, 2010, locates Eden along the Euphrates near Hit where the Euphrates is one stream that subdivides into four streams near ancient Sippar. However, from the perspective of this book, *The Cult of the Yew,* the Tree of Life and the Tree of Knowledge are the essence of Eden, around which the story of Adam and Eve and their eating of the forbidden fruit of the Tree of Knowledge revolves. As a result, the finding of this legendary place, said to be the very beginnings of humanity, is looked at here from the perspective of the sacred tree. There has been much made recently of Gobekli Tepe, a mysterious Neolithic culture temple, dating back thousands of years before Stonehenge, as to whether it could have been Eden. However, the central issue and interest of Eden is the sacred trees and there is no reference or evidence that such a thing existed there, although the Tree of Life was found depicted on an ancient pot. The Tree of Life was a yew tree, a very special monoecious yew, as discussed in *The God Tree*, which was originally one tree (in the Sumerian texts) but later became the two described in Genesis of the Bible (dated around 1450 BCE), which may have been dioecious (having the sexes separate). As was discussed many years ago with David Bellamy, it seems likely the story of Eve coming from Adam's rib, producing a second being, could have described a singular tree, sharing both male and female attributes which became two. The yew normally has fruits on one tree and male pollen on another. In the case of the Tree of Knowledge and the Tree of Life these could originally have been one tree sharing both male and female attributes. Ancient Babylonian cylinder seals often depict that sacred tree as having two different fruits, or possibly a flower and a fruit (see *The God Tree*) and it seems likely that the yew, known in legend as the Tree of Life, Death and Eternity, in all cultures of the northern hemisphere, was this tree. This is the tree that produced the sacred apples, the only immortal and therefore godlike tree and any suggestion of discovery of the site of Eden must find that place in an area where yew trees grow, or grew thousands of years ago. There is no suggestion of such a tree being of central importance to the site of Gobekli Tepe. On the other hand, Laurence Gardner's view is entirely possible, as the area he pointed to was an area where yews grew and some of these yews still growing in that region are remarkably ancient and over 5,000 years old.

Eden, as we have seen, is associated with the source of four rivers, so my search, like that of other researchers, has involved looking for such a landmark. This turned out to be more difficult than expected! However, around a place called Ophir, for which so far, no modern place name has been found but which seems to have been inland from the coast of the Kingdom of Colchis or Lazica, three rivers have their source. These are the Frat, (which either was the Euphrates or feeds into it), the Cyrus and the Araxes, the latter river rising south of Erzurum in the Bingöl Dağları (mountains) of Turkey. The Araxes flows eastward, forming for approximately 275 miles (440 km) the international boundary between Armenia and Azerbaijan on the north and Turkey and Iran on the south. Maps of the Garden of Eden by scholars from 1838 and 1839 associate Ophir with Eden or Paradise and position it in this general but vague area. The Frat is shown as the source of the Euphrates, running into it. On the 1838 map by Soulier (E Andriveau Goujon *Ancient Empires*), we see a mountain ridge with the three rivers rising around it. In this area, there are scattered individual yews, up in the mountains. Modern-day Rize, in the territory of ancient Lazistan or Colchis on the coast, is as high as 1,500 metres above sea level, and some 100 miles east of it. A 30 ft girth, hollow yew was found in that area recently.

There are several references to Ophir in the Bible, mainly concerning it being a source of gold, but also of precious gems and almug wood. Gold, as we know, was highly valued by the Egyptians, demonstrating their power and wealth and they set up elaborate forts and strongholds along the Nile, to do business in the world for gold. They sourced this precious metal from both south of the Nile and in places north of the country. The location of Eden is described in Genesis 2: 10–14:

And a river departed from Eden to water the garden, and from there it divided and became four tributaries. The name of the first is Pishon, which is the circumnavigator of the land of Havilah where there is gold. And the gold of this land is good; there are bdellium and cornelian stone.

So here is the support that Ophir may be the site of Eden after all, with its gold, precious stones and almug wood!

Map Tabula showing Ophir and the Garden of Eden.

Ophir which had enormous importance for both the Egyptians and King Solomon is a place where almug is sourced and listed in the same breath as gold and precious gems and therefore, with the same importance. Eden may well have been a garden sanctuary within this area. Sourcing the gold, precious stones and almug or yew wood from there may have come later. Eden may even have been plundered at a later date! The temple in

Nineveh may have been being built c. 4000 BCE but Solomon was much later, in around 1000 BCE. The Garden of Eden points to a time well before this.

The Ancient Chaldeans and Assyrians likewise had their World Tree, coeval with Assur, the great First Source. This tree is identified as the Sumerian Tree of Life at Eridu, located in the Forest of Eridhu (Eridu) and means we are looking for a land of forests, which this whole region is. Alexander Porteous in *The Forest in Folklore and Mythology*, 1928, affirms that 'this tree was located in the Forest of Eridhu'. Although we may think of Eden as an isolated place, a garden containing just the all-important Tree of Life, it may have been hidden in plain sight, in a Forest of Yews and other trees, high in the mountains.

In 1 Kings 10: 11-12 we find:

And the navy also of Hiram, that brought gold from Ophir, brought in from Ophir great plenty of almug trees and precious stones. And the King made of the almug trees, pillars for the house of the Lord and for the King's house, harps also and psalteries for singers: there came no such almug trees, nor were seen unto this day

This implies the importing of almug wood stopped. In 2 Chronicles 9: 10-11 we find:

And the servants also of Hiram and the servants of Solomon, which brought gold from Ophir, brought almug trees and precious stones. And the King made of the almug trees, terraces to the house of the Lord and to the king's palace and harps and psalteries for singers and there were none such seen before in the land of Judah.

This implies the almug wood started to be imported at King Solomon's time into Judah but we know there were whole forests of yews in Lebanon, Colchis and Lazica, in fact right along the coast of the Black Sea and yet here we are told of the wood's rarity. The implication is that these yews like those of Egypt were fast being depleted or that it was a rare and special kind of yew wood that was being used particularly for the temple pillars, which may have represented the Trees of Life and Knowledge. I may be reading too much into this and Ophir, which must have been a very busy place with all its gold mining in the times recorded here, sounds like a place of great industry, unlikely to be Eden but we cannot rule out the possibility that it was and that it existed as such, way back before the time of Solomon whose conventional dates are circa 970 to 931 BCE and therefore much later than Heliopolis. The thing is, Eden must have existed in an area conducive to the growth of yews, common or otherwise and this area is just that. We will leave the actual location of Eden to others for now, as in the great scheme of yews, it is something of a red herring but its existence at one time is undoubted as is its location in this area and its importance as the home of the Tree of Life and the Tree of Knowledge.

Where the Tree of Life originated is one we may never find the answer to but its continued existence in our world is something I am utterly convinced of. The Tree of Life is neither fiction nor is it confined to ancient stories or the Otherworld. It is a living tree that still grows in our world and more specifically, it's here in Britain.

Chapter 2

The Tree of Life, the Fruit and the Serpent

The Tree of Life is one of the most pervasive and enduring legends in history. The Tree can bestow death, sickness and poisoning but also life, prosperity and healing.

'The Double Fatal Tree'. Monoprint by Janis Fry.

Belief in its reality extends from deep within the Stone Age to the present. It has always been associated with divinity and immortality. It was the Axis Mundi otherwise known as the World Tree to the cultures of long ago. The Tree of Life is associated with the Earth Goddess and both are extremely potent symbols embedded within the evolving cultures of early man which had their roots in the Andite cultures. The earliest Andite peoples originated more than 25,000 years ago in the regions adjacent to Mesopotamia. (*The Urantia Book,* 1955, pub. in Chicago by The Urantia Foundation, author unknown) Unsurprisingly a third symbol is associated with both the Tree of Life and the Great Goddess and that is the Serpent.

Right across the world, in most cultures, there is a tree that the locals call the Tree of Life. In Seychelles, for instance, it is the coconut that has this title. As virtually the only tree there, the coconut palm keeps islanders from hunger and thirst, gives shelter, firewood, timber, fishing lines, hats, rafts, oil and oxygen. It also provides commodities to trade with. All trees are our most important resource, from the earliest times. Humans simply wouldn't have evolved without them and entire civilisations have been built on them. No wonder so many of us have such love for them.

The yew tree is traceable back 200 million years, to a time when it evolved like other trees, from ferns which evolved into trees to give their leaves a better chance of not being eaten by Dinosaurs. Several other tree species besides the yew have been on earth for just as long. They saw the end of the Dinosaur age, waited while the world changed and became inhospitable for a while and waited for the arrival of humans. It was a very long time indeed before we emerged, just 4 million years ago. The giant redwoods also date back 200 million years and some individual trees are over 1,500 years old, some having been verified by tree rings to be over 3,000 years. The bristlecone pine is another tree that dates back 200 million years and this tree has ages in excess of 5,000 years, with the tree known as 'Methuselah', having been carbon-dated to over 4,700 years. In China, ginkgo trees are reported as being over 3,000 years, while the ginkgo species itself is referred to as the Dinosaur tree. Other trees, like the yew, can be very long-lived: olives can live to 3,000 years and our mighty oak to 1,500 years.

In Chile, a tree referred to as a 'living fossil', the Chilean pine or monkey puzzle tree, reaches an age of 2,000 years. According to *Ancient Trees* by A Lewington and E Parker, 1999, one of South America's indigenous groups takes its name directly from this tree and their lifestyle and culture are intimately connected to it. The Chilean pine or monkey puzzle tree is a Tree of Life to the Pehuenche people, whose name means 'People of the monkey puzzles'. These people live mainly as food gatherers collecting the nutritious monkey puzzle seeds in late summer and early autumn. These seeds are their main staple dietary item throughout the year. Alfredo Melinir expressed his love and connection with the tree when he said:

The monkey puzzle is our tree. It's a symbol for us. It's a tree that God left on earth for us, the Pehuenche. We cannot cut it down, because it gives us our daily bread. In the end, we would rather die than give up defending this tree.

The yew tree, however, the longest-lived of all trees, sometimes known as an immortal giant, is by its very nature, the now undisputed Tree of Life. To us, the people of the Northern hemisphere it was always there in our world, dependably, reliably there, part of our landscape. By the time we emerged, the yew had not changed for aeons. Particular yews were there at a person's birth and still there unchanged at their death. When people travelled, it was one of those things that gave them their bearings, and a place in the world, so the stories of our beginnings were passed on through the generations, with memories of deeds and history and certain trees, which went back generations and which were associated with a certain tribe as their Axis Mundi, a place people gathered to, the centre of their tribal territory. The yew is the only tree capable of not just living for thousands of years but of immortality and continual regeneration and as such is revered as the most sacred of all trees, a tree of great vigour and resilience, known as the Tree of Life by all cultures at one time or another, in the Northern hemisphere, with the earliest known reference to it, being a carving in a cave in Cadiz, dating back to 52,000 BCE, which shows quite clearly the yew as the Tree of Life.

In 2017 I went to the Himalayas. One of the reasons I went, apart from to see where my father was born, was to see if the yew tree was remembered there as the Tree of Life. The knowledge of the yew as the Tree of Life is evident in all cultures across the Northern hemisphere. Ancient yews, although I didn't see them, reputedly grow in the Himalayas but I had only a short time there. One of my aims was to make contact with some of the Brahmins, members of the Priest caste, which I did. When I asked about the Deva Daru, the sacred tree or god tree (Deva means god, Daru or dru meaning truth, is the word from which the word 'druid' came), they said I meant Deodar and pointed to the cedars that covered the foothills of the Himalayas in swathes of forests. Even the name had been given to another tree! Deo as in Deodar like Deva means god. I pointed out that cedars are not immortal. Unlike a god, they die and therefore could not symbolise eternity. They took my point and were immediately interested. It was as if the confusion in calling yew cedar that had gone on since time immemorial, continued despite the record having been put straight. We talked about the red dot, the Bindi that Hindus wear in the middle of their foreheads. Originally this had been made of yew paste, which covered the third eye or pineal gland. Placed here it would have brought visions, wisdom from the yew. One of the priests told me that when people wore this red spot nowadays, it made them feel calm all day. I thought that was probably because the third eye, which is said to be the psychic eye, is covered and not by yew paste these days. Perhaps at one time, the substance in the paste induced trance and enabled people to see into other realms for religious purposes. The Brahmin priest could see that the yew and the Tree of Life must be one and the same. I hope he went back to tell others. Later I discovered that in Nepal there is a yew tree 18 feet in girth whose red bark is used as a dye for staining the foreheads of the Brahmins, so the knowledge is still there in places.

In modern times, the West Himalayan Yew (Taxus contorta) has declined by 50% over its entire habitat but in Victorian times there were hundreds of ancient yews in Sikkim and Bhutan as documented by Professors Huxley and Henslow. Nowadays people have found many different uses for the yew which have contributed to its decline. The wood is used for building and furniture making. In Pakistan, it is often used as fuel. In Afghanistan, 50% of the forest where the Himalayan yew grows have been heavily logged over the last 30 years. The bark, leaves and twigs are used in traditional medicines but like its close relative, Taxus chinensis, it is also used for the commercial production of Taxol, the anti-cancer drug. This is the main reason for its sudden decline of up to 90% in India and Nepal. For some years there was some confusion about the taxonomy of yew trees in the Himalayas and Taxus wallichiana was thought to be the only Taxus species across the entire mountain range. More recently though, yew trees from central Nepal to northern Pakistan and Afghanistan were thought to be Taxus fauna, first recognized in the Tibetan mountains but this species turned out to be the same as Taxus contorta, whose name was given earlier and so these yews that are the same variety are now known by this name.

In *The Lost Language of Symbolism*, 1912, Harold Bailey notes the significance of the different trees. The tree of Osiris was said to be a conifer for instance and the author says the fir was admitted into the Gnostic system because its shape imitates a flame and its cone was taken as the symbol of the element of fire. The sycamore's name links with this, as the word sycamore means the Sun Fire. Bailey says that:

in some parts of Europe the pear tree was regarded as sacred and there is little doubt that the pyramidal form of the trees, in general, was partly responsible for their universal worship.

Although he doesn't say why, no tree is as pyramidal as the yew. Many other trees were sacred to the gods for their different qualities such as the fig, rose, cherry, rhododendron, persea, mountain ash, olive, agave, holly, oleander, lavender, alder, maple and hawthorn. All these trees have special qualities and offer everything that humans needed for survival and therefore trees were worshipped and adored, propagated and protected. The yew tree's quality of immortality, however, is a quality normally associated with the gods.

Something we need to consider at this point is our ideas about 'God'. This is a massive subject and all I want to do here is to touch the surface, concerning the subject of this chapter, as it has a bearing on what the gods of ancient times were all about. Today in our multi-cultural society, we all have different ideas about what God is. Some see God as essentially good, merciful and compassionate, an entity or force that can be prayed to in order to achieve certain results and who has our best interests at heart. This is the God of Love. Others see God as an organising force that mysteriously connects all living things and seems to link up people and events, allowing things to happen. Under this system, the way things work out in life means that somehow you meet exactly the right person at the right time. The synchronicity of life can put you in a certain place on a certain day and you know that if you hadn't been there, then things would be very different and life would unfold in an entirely different way. This is seen too as karma at work, the idea that 'what goes around comes round'. This is the God who has the interests of all living things at heart, striving to keep some balance, a God we might be able to have some meaningful dialogue with. Others, particularly in ancient times, saw God as a vengeful, jealous and controlling force, a lawmaker to be obeyed and feared. As we investigate the dragon/ serpent gods connected to the Tree of Life, we have to consider the idea that maybe such gods, like a dictator, cannot be trusted to work in our interests, are often deceitful, sly and cunning and might be evil, rather than good, or at least both. We have to go beyond ideas of good and evil and realise we are entering the world of pure power, which is used for whatever purpose the god who wields it desires, simply because he/she/it, can. Obviously, we then enter a world where anything can happen, where we are at the mercy of God and rebellion and anarchy are inevitable and society comes apart at the seams. Some would see our world today as being perilously close to this. Everything is unpredictable. At the beginning of the creation of our world, the stories of how it all came about often depict such gods, as natural forces or beings with vested interests who have to be placated or brought on side. This is a very simplistic sketch I have put forward here and there is obviously a great deal more to it but we are essentially talking about power, will and the control of others.

The story of the Tree of Life in the Garden of Eden is the greatest story of all time, the story of who we are and how we came to be here and presents the question of what we are evolving into, where we are going and what might be in charge of our lives and destiny. As for the Tree of Knowledge, (of Good and Evil to give its full title) this sacred tree was/is, exactly that. It embodies these two opposing properties or qualities and confers it on humans, suggesting the gods knew the difference. The explanation in Genesis is that in eating its fruit, we became aware of moral implications, ended our innocence and ended our state of being in pure consciousness, without judgement. Some would say we ended our natural living and being from the heart. It must be noted that the gods the ancient civilisations speak of, who were to do with the sacred tree, did not appear to be acting from either a moral position or from a good heart. This brings me to say that if the dragon/serpent god/dess is the tree and the tree is the god/

dess, then the Tree of Knowledge must also be a serpent. The tail of the serpent can be seen as the root which descends to the ground from a higher branch inside the yew and is swallowed up by the growth of the parent trunk. There are things the tree and the serpent share. Both have the ability to regenerate themselves and in particular to grow new skins. We must not forget that like the viper or serpent, the tree carries deadly poison which can and does kill and has no antidotes. On the other hand, it also provides Taxol that heals cancer. This is a tree of opposites, of contradictions, a tree of good and evil. I would certainly not describe it as benign. It is simply a powerful enigma. We need to approach the yew with respect and caution. In the old days of my grandparents, people were taught to 'fear god'. Something like that applies to the yew. It is not something that lends itself to new age thinking and believing all is well with the world. Frankly, we have no idea what we are dealing with. The yew is a law unto itself, capable of anything and can operate over time and space. This is something the Druids knew and I have personal experience of.

We haven't yet tasted the fruit of the Tree of Life, denied us in the Garden of Eden. It appears we cannot be allowed to do that, to become immortal, in our present state of such duality, deception and self-interest. When and if we ever reach a point when we could taste this fruit, it appears to me it will only be allowed to happen if we reach a state of pure consciousness, of pure heart but then that would seem to imply a state before 'The Fall'. Ending our original state of innocence led to us being thrown out and left to our own devices, but before that we were slaves, living within certain confines and conditions, dictated by powerful gods. There are many theological, philosophical, humanitarian and new age books written about these spiritual matters and the way life works, for anyone who wishes to delve further and so enough said, we return now to the theme of this book, the yew as the Tree of Life and its place in our culture and our world. In early ancient cultures, before Genesis, the two sacred trees of the Bible's version of the Garden of Eden are just one tree and, in this book, will be called simply the Tree of Life. That Tree of Life is a yew, a particular yew with its powers for healing, death and immortality and a certain bloodline. Some believe that this sacred tree is the monitor and the watcher and may hold the fate of the human race.

The Tree of Life is a vast subject of which the purpose of this book is not to give a fully comprehensive account but to look at the ramifications of such an enormous study in terms of the yew tree and the Otherworld Yew and to point the way for contemplation, further reading and an understanding as to what this tree may be. The 'sacred tree' is often said to be the most discussed symbol in the historiography of Assyrian art. Early scholars thought they had secured the theory, that the Tree of Life from the Garden of Eden in Genesis, was to be identified with the tree known from cuneiform sources from the ancient world, as the Kiskanu tree (see *The God Tree*) This was the same tree found in Gudea's temple at Lagash, known as the all-powerful, god/dess Ningishzida, The Tree of Life and Truth. A second interpretation, first proposed in 1888, that became popular, maintained that the Assyrian 'tree' is a symbol of a real tree, that is, it should be understood as a conventionalised or stylised depiction of a date palm! This was because they didn't fully understand at that time, the sacred nature of the eternal tree, the yew and saw it simply as a tree that provided sustenance. It was also at this time that the idea that the Tree was one and the same as the World Tree or Cosmic Tree entered the discussion, though not for long as scholars didn't see the connection. However, the idea that the Assyrian sacred tree represents the cosmic tree was reintroduced in 2000 by S. Parpola in *The ideology of Assyrian Kingship: Sons of God*. As E D van Buren said in *Symbols of the Gods in Mesopotamian Art, 1945,* 'The significance and purpose of the sacred tree has given rise to more discussion than almost any other mythological subject.' Also, in this book, one or two trees other than the Kiskanu tree such as the Mes tree and the Huluppa tree are discussed and you will find more in *The God Tree*. These trees may also be the same tree, because when these sacred trees moved from place to place, they would have been given new names by their new keepers.

The real and actual Tree of Life can be traced back to Heliopolis, Egypt 15,000 years ago as we saw in the first chapter. We don't know where it was before that or where it came from but it may have moved to Eden from there. Eden was just one place where it grew and from the years of research that has gone into this book and my assessment of chronology, it seems the story of the beginnings of our present civilisation in the Garden of Eden, dates back to around 14,000 years ago, after Noah and the flood and after that same flood had driven the sacred tree with those who kept it, north and out of Egypt. Such stories were nurtured and passed down in forms we have difficulty understanding now, so far have we come away from those times when things were seen very differently when life and our preoccupations were different, when consciousness was different, when the gods and wild Nature were all around us on this Earth shaping our lives. We no longer know whether the early legends of the gods and the Tree of Life were truth, partial truth, allegories or myths but even myths come from somewhere and truth prevails.

One of the most important of those ancient gods and goddesses, was the Sumerian goddess who was bound up with the sacred tree and remained a potent figure of power and worship for thousands of years, the god/dess Ningishzida, known also as the Lord of the Tree of Life, Lord of the Good Tree, Lady of the Magic Wand, the Divine Lady of Eden or Edin, Plumed serpent of the deep and Watcher of the Gate.

This god/dess was a serpent with a human head or a double-headed serpent coiled into a double helix and was a power of the netherworld. When depicted in human form, he appears male, he rides a dragon and two serpents' heads grow from his shoulders. If the god/dess was a tree perhaps Ningishzida was a monoecious tree, carrying both sexes but what could a magic wand connected with a tree mean other than a special branch or a sceptre? My mind and intuition goes immediately to a Golden Bough, investigated later in this book, a Golden Bough on a sacred tree. The title 'Lady of the Magic Wand' suggests more than the sceptre and it seems likely that one of the attributes of the Tree of Life was to carry the Golden Bough, a phenomenon that occurs on ancient yews, practically all of historical significance, perhaps descendants of Ningishzida.

Many of the early gods are depicted holding a branch, a sceptre or a wand denoting their authority. If the goddess was a tree, then this would have to be a branch, a particular branch. From the story of Moses and Pharaoh's magicians told in Exodus 7:8 and discussed in *The God Tree*, we know that their wands, rods or staffs were able to perform magic. It may go against the grain today to think that many of these early Mesopotamian or Sumerian god/desses were originally trees and the trees were god/desses, embodying the power of immortality but also of death and healing and the ability to return to life from apparent death but that is how it was and the tree associated with these things is the yew. Joan Eahr in *Asherah*, 2018, says:

Asherah symbolized the sacred tree of the goddess which implies that the tree is regarded not as the abode of the goddess but as the goddess herself along with the regenerative, protective, and nutritive powers that mutually identify her with the tree.

The serpent as a symbol is found again in the Greek Caduceus staff, which has two entwined snakes emerging from its top. This is a later version of the sceptre or magic wand of Ningishzida but the oldest evidence suggests the Caduceus came from ancient Sumer during the late 3rd century BCE. The rod, wand or sceptre so carefully detailed on the Gudea vase is also the trunk of the Tree of Life or the Axis Mundi. It represents Ningishzida and the Gudea Vase of Lagash dates as far back as 4000 BCE and is guarded by two winged dragons.

The Gudea Vase. From Lagash 2200 BCE.

Drawing of the Gudea vase depicting Ningishzida.

The Caduceus with its two snakes is not to be confused with the Rod of Asclepius which has one snake and was used as a symbol of medicine, but the Caduceus was said to return the dead to life and this capacity relates it to the Tree of Life.

What I suspect is that such goddesses as Ningishzida, Inanna and her sister Ereshkigal, who were trees and also serpents, embody something rather sinister and although I don't want to take it on board, it is staring me in the face that the sacred yew was/is also a serpent, along with all that that entails. We have an instinctive fear of snakes and a suspicion of them. They are not to be trusted.

We will come back to the dragon/serpent gods later but first; I want to look at other ancient sacred knowledge of the serpent from other cultures. From the other side of the world and the ancient civilisations this book is concerned with, comes Quetzalcoatl, the Aztec feathered serpent deity, known from several Aztec codices such as the Florentine Codex, as well as from the records of the Spanish conquistadors. Although the yew does not appear in the Southern hemisphere today, I believe Quetzalcoatl; the feathered serpent has a bearing on this sacred tree. Among other things, Quetzalcoatl was known as the bringer of knowledge and the inventor of books, reminding us of the Tree of Knowledge. Another feathered serpent god, Tepeu Q'uq'umatz, was known as the creator of the cosmos, of life (so here may be the other tree of Eden). According to Wikipedia, these weren't the only ones as 'Along with the feathered serpent deity, several other serpent gods existed in the pantheon of Mesoamerican gods with similar traits'. The earliest representations of feathered serpents appear in the Olmec culture of around 1400 - 400 BCE.

The double symbolism used by the Feathered Serpent is considered allegoric to the dual nature of the deity, where being feathered represents its divine nature or ability to fly to reach the skies and being a serpent represents its human nature or ability to creep on the ground among other animals of the Earth; a dualism very common in Mesoamerican deities.

I cannot help thinking of the similarity between feathers and yew tree leaves and the dual nature of this tree. If we then look at the ouroboros, or uroborus, an ancient symbol depicting a serpent or dragon swallowing its tail, this also has a bearing on things.

Ouroborus.

The symbol originated in ancient Egyptian iconography and entered western tradition via Greek magical tradition. The ouroboros is often interpreted as a symbol for eternal cyclic renewal or a cycle of life, death and rebirth. The skin sloughing process of snakes symbolizes the transmigration of souls and this event occurs in the legend of Gilgamesh (The Epic of Gilgamesh was a poem written in Akkadian, during the late second millennium BCE and involves Enkidu and the netherworld) According to Wikipedia:

> The first known appearance of the ouroboros motif is in the Enigmatic Book of the Netherworld, ancient funerary text KV62 from the tomb of Tutankhamun. This may be considerably older than the tomb. The ouroboros appears elsewhere in Egyptian sources, where, like many Egyptian serpent deities, it represents the formless disorder that surrounds the orderly world and is involved in that world's periodic renewal. The symbol persisted in Egypt into Roman times, when it frequently appeared on magical talismans. The image of a snake biting its tail represents the cyclical nature of the year.

The Jungian psychologist Erich Neumann writes of the ouroboros as a representation of the pre-ego 'dawn state'.

The famous ouroboros drawing from the early alchemical text, *The Chrysopoeia of Cleopatra*, originally dating to 3rd century Alexandria, shows the snake in black and white halves, perhaps representing a Gnostic duality of existence as well as the cycle of birth and death. This very much reminds us of the nature of the Yew, while the Seal of the Theosophical Society, founded in1875, has the ouroboros encircling a Star of David enclosing the Egyptian ankh which symbolises the branch of the Tree of Life, the key to immortality. We are touching here on deep and complex mysteries.

Storl, 2004, also refers to the ouroboros image in reference to the cycle of samsara (the cycle of rebirth in Buddhism and Hinduism), as a symbol of immortality, since it is said of the ouroboros that he slays himself and brings himself to life, fertilizes himself and gives birth to himself. All this is exactly what can be said about the yew which was described in ancient times as 'the snake that swallowed itself', referring to the yew's habit of putting down an aerial root inside the old tree to make a new tree inside it.

The winged globe or disc with the eagle was sometimes borne as a standard at the end of the staff and serpent in the manner of the Assyrian ensign, the Roman standard and Hitler's Nazi Germany. The eagle is an important part of this symbol too, representing wisdom, power and spirit. The symbol of the eagle and the serpent are typically reserved for powerful mythic figures, humans of unusual distinction or for royalty considered to be of divine origin as described later. The symbol has very early origins as we see in this *Tree of the Sun* from an Archaemenian seal 6th - 9th century BCE showing symbols of Sun and Yew, obviously predating the later symbols which surely derive from them. You will find more on this in Chapter 23 on Yew mysteries.

'Tree of the Sun' from an Archaemenian seal 6th - 9th century BCE.

Gudea of Lagash laid two ritual foundations, one of heaven and the other of the Apsu and this double foundation has been seen as possibly containing the idea of a temple as a column reaching upwards to heaven and downwards to the underworld. Mlle. N Perrot has shown that two trees at the gate of heaven corresponded to two trees or posts in Gudea's temple at Lagash, one of these being the Kiskanu tree of the Apsu, the god of the freshwater deep of Ea at Eridu. Ningishzida was another watcher at the gate and may have been there as both descendant and protector of Anu who seems to have been a chief tree that gave birth to other Trees of Life. Was this the gate of Heaven and the door or portal between the worlds?

The Axis Mundi, the pole around which the world revolves is the centre of the world. The pole connects heaven and earth. On this vertical column in Sumerian culture, lay the heavenly temple of Anu and the underworld temple of Ea. But the Axis Mundi is also represented by the World Tree or sacred tree said to have been planted by Inanna in her garden. Before Babylon, the Axis Mundi was at Nippur, the abode of the god Enlil and the concept of the World Tree has migrated into other cultures across the world, including South America where it is embedded firmly into the Mayan culture through seafaring nations. The Tree of Life and Axis Mundi is also part of the culture of Siberia on which shamans climb to the upper world and where an eagle sits atop. However, as the earliest source of these legends, the focus here is on the culture of Mesopotamia and Egypt. Aspects of this culture to do with the tree god/desses eventually migrated into Europe where in Norse mythology we find the legends of Yggdrasil, the World Tree, with time and space at the centre of all the worlds. Yggdrasil is a special Otherworld Yew discussed in *The God Tree*. On this tree's highest branch sits an eagle. At its roots there lies a serpent. Under the tree the three Norns or Fates who decide the individual fates of men and women sit. Under the roots lies a spring of water known as Mimir and associated with the World Tree is Odin, the god who received the inspiration of the runes, having hung on the sacred tree for nine days and nine nights.

The Vanites were the ancestors of the Assyrians (*The Urantia Book* p.860) and their main religious symbol was the Tree of Life. The civilisation of Urartu, located in Turkey at Lake Van now in the Armenian highlands, made many images of two genii picking the fruit of the Tree of Life. The Tree of Life, also known as the sacred tree, portrayed thus, made its way into Babylonian and Assyrian culture. To the Babylonians, the Tree of Life was a tree that bore magical fruit, which could only be picked by the gods. Grave misfortune would befall any mortal who dared to pick it, never mind eat it. So, this is most likely what the winged genies with the heads of eagles are doing on the low relief stone panels from the palace of Assurnasirpal, 600 BCE, seen in the British Museum. They are picking the fruit and collecting it in their baskets. However, these images are open to interpretation and for many years I thought they were tending the Tree of Life with pails of water and washing the leaves of the tree with something like sponges and that may still be the case as the baskets or pails are too small to hold much. The fruits, if that is what they are, may simply be symbolic or from an oral tradition of now lost knowledge. Perhaps at the time that the panels were produced, they believed that the cedar was the divine sacred tree, as is still thought in parts of the Himalayas. Just as the two fruits on the tree that looks like a date palm from the Babylonian and Sumerian cylinder seals (illustrated in *The God Tree*), seem to resemble the male flower and female fruit of the yew, the fruits of the Tree of Life are depicted or concluded to be all kinds of fruit. This was perhaps as a result of people forgetting exactly what the fruit was. Pomegranates, for instance, became the fruit of the Underworld triple goddess Persephone, who would have originally been a goddess connected with the yew. The individual pomegranate seeds surrounded by a sweet and juicy red fruit closely resemble the fruits of the yew, although the yew fruits don't appear in clusters. It has been commented that on this particular Assyrian panel, if it is fruits that the genies have in their hands, then the fruits are cedar cones, which is not very convincing as it raises questions as to the purpose of this. The cones are not edible unless the cones are from umbrella pines and contain pine nuts but why would such a fruit (or rather nut) be seen as the food of the gods? Although the fruit of the sacred tree has to be something very unusual, it still leaves me baffled. One of the points I'm trying to make here is that in studying the image of the genies with the baskets or pails and cones or sponges, it is difficult to make sense of it. If I were to be definite about what is being portrayed, although I still think my original interpretation is the right one, then this would become an example of how wrong statements can then become passed down as fact and go unquestioned thereafter and if the process is repeated, then just a few decades later, never mind thousands of years down the line, things can end up miles from the truth. Thank god the stone low relief carving was just that: set in stone!

However, just as the Egyptians forgot which tree the Tree of Life was, depicting it as the short-lived sycamore, the Assyrians may also have forgotten and confused cedar and its cones, with almug or yew and as you will see later in this book, this was the case with other cultures. For what it's worth, fruits depicted on the Sacred Tree (as pointed out in *The Migration of Symbols* by Eugène Goblet d'Alviella), whether they be clusters of dates, oranges, apples, pears, raspberries or bunches of grapes, are naturally adapted to being fruits of a Tree of Life, since they yield some of those fermented liquors which in ordinary language still bear the name of Eau de Vie (water of life!) Like the fruit of the yew, the fruits of the Tree of Life also have incredible sweetness and the Tree is often spoken of as having honey dripping from its branches. A misunderstanding that needs clearing up is that throughout history 'apple' seems to have been a common word for red fruit. The Hittites described the eya tree ('eya' being the earliest word for yew) as a 'mountain apple tree', a goddess. Icelandic sagas talk of an oak, shown in 'The God Tree' to be a yew, that carries apples and across Europe and Asia Minor we come across 'apples of immortality', which we should understand as red fruit. The offence of the seer, the Greek Tantalus, was to steal nectar or ambrosia from the gods and give it to his companions. His fate was to dwell in Tartarus, the deep abyss, a terrible prison beneath Hades, where he was made to stand in water up to his waist beneath the Tree of Life with the fruit forever tantalisingly just out of his reach. If the gods are the ones who are privileged to pick and eat the fruit, then it has to be the fruit of a special otherworld tree, denied to humans, that gives them their immortality. Likewise, it has to be the serpent that ensures no one else shall have it unless it is to serve a treacherous purpose.

Chapter 3

The Dragon Serpent Tree Gods

This is the story of our origins, and the part played by the Tree of Life and the Dragon Serpent gods in creating us.

Dragon Serpent - Kentchurch Yew.

Some readers may find this chapter shocking or unbelievable but it has come out of an authentic search for the truth and you will need to keep an open mind. These things are described as 'mythology' but mythology, though not literal, is a way of describing history, or conveying the truth of how things happened, in a different way. This may not be factual in our scientific sense of the word but it may have been the way people saw energies, powers and forces in ancient times. In Sumeria, the gods who bore the title 'Ushumgal' were a 'Great Dragon Serpent'. The chief of these was Enki, the god responsible for man's creation. Enki's birth mother was Namma, who was also known as Tiamat, the reptilian goddess thought to be 'the monstrous embodiment of primordial chaos', according to Wikipedia. In Sumerian myths, it is Enki (Ea) of Eridu who creates man to relieve the so-called Igigi gods, of the hard labour they bear in his garden in the midst of Edin. In Babylonian myth, it is Marduk, Lord of the Gods of Heaven and Earth to whom all nature, including humanity, owed its existence. Marduk is also called by this title Ushumgal, making him another serpent dragon god. At Nippur, it is the god Enlil who is responsible for the creation of Man for the same reason and who, like the other two gods, carries the name, 'Ushumgal'. So, three gods in Mesopotamian myth, all responsible for creating man for hard work in their garden in Edin, were all-powerful serpent or dragon gods; Enki at Eridu, Enlil at Nippur and Marduk at Babylon. All of them, like Eden's serpent, for better or worse, deny man immortality, which was within their power to bestow. Professor Sayce in the Hibbert Lectures,1887, *Lectures on the Origin and Growth of Religion as Illustrated by the Religion of the Ancient Babylonians*, describes Marduk, the Ushumgal, as the omniscient Lord of heaven and earth, the creator of the universe, who creates man from the blood of the Igigi god, Kingsu, sacrificed for this purpose, mixed with the clay of the earth to create a worker. The Igigi gods were the Sumerian younger or lesser gods of heaven and the servants of the Annunaki. In one myth of the Akkadian garden Paradise, they were put to work to dig a watercourse but rebelled, burning their tools and surrounding Enlil's house and as a result of this rebellion, the Annunaki decided to create man to carry out the work instead. The tendency of these Igigi gods to rebel is something we seem to have inherited from them and is perhaps what made man disobedient when Enki had the toil of the gods imposed on man in place of these gods. In the Akkadian tale of Adapa who dwells on the earth at Eridu in ancient Sumer (now Iraq), we find a similar story. Adapa is created by the culture god Enki or Ea as the 'model of men' and is then given wisdom but not eternal life. In Mesopotamian myths, man is depicted at the beginning, to be without wisdom and knowledge, like the other beasts of Eden.

Zechariah Sitchin in *Earth Chronicles* writes of the colonisation of Earth from another planet called Nibiru and informs us:

> The Sumerian texts stated that Enlil arrived on Earth before the 'Black-Headed People' - the Sumerian nickname for Mankind, were created. During such times before Mankind, Enlil erected Nippur as his centre, or 'command post', at which Heaven and Earth were connected through some 'bond' called 'DUR.AN.KI'... The Sumerians considered the abode of Enlil as the Navel of the Earth...best known by the later Akkadian /Semitic name Nippur, its Sumerian name was NIBIRU.KI – 'The place of the Crossing' representing on Earth the Celestial Place of Crossing, the site of the Celestial Battle, to which the planet Nibiru keeps returning every 3,600 years.

It is interesting to see that in the ancient Mesopotamian legend of Gilgamesh, there is also a place beyond the Forest Gate from which commands are issued. Elsewhere, Sitchin tells us that the gods came to Earth to mine gold in South Africa to mend the atmosphere of their own planet Nibiru, which had suffered from something similar to ozone depletion and that mankind was created to carry out this mining work along with other tasks, such as gardening and canal building, taking over the gold mining from the Igigi gods. The fact that the earliest traces of Mankind are found in the Rift Valley in South Africa from which humans emerged concurs with this and it is generally accepted that humankind came out of Africa and from there populated the rest of the world. Sitchin then talks of the gods called the Annunaki who controlled these space operations but as I am aware I am now on the edge of many readers' credibility, I will leave this subject there and will just finish with this, that in Genesis 6: 4 we read:

There were giants in the earth in those days and also after that, when the sons of God came in unto the daughters of men and they bore children to them, the same became mighty men which were of old, men of renown.

I find it hard to read this in any way other than that humankind is a kind of hybrid breed created from the gods and the early humans or primates they found here and I find it strange that many people will believe what it says in the Bible but cannot take on board texts from a time, not that much earlier.

David Rohl, a British Egyptologist and prolific author writes of a quote from Atrahasis Epic 1:4

They (the gods) summoned the goddess, the midwife of the gods, Wise Mami (meaning the goddess Ninhursag), and asked: 'You are the womb goddess, creator of Mankind! Create a mortal, that he may bear the yoke!'... Enki ('Lord of the Earth') made his voice heard and spoke to the great gods: '... Then one god should be slaughtered... Nintu ('Lady of Birth') shall mix clay with his flesh and blood. The God and Man shall be mixed together in clay.' Thus, in the creation mythology of ancient Mesopotamia, Man was made in the likeness of the gods by combining the clay of the earth with the blood of a sacrificed god.

R A Boulay, in *Flying Serpents and Dragons: The Story of Mankind's Reptilian Past*, 1990, says:

The Adam of the Bible was not the Homo sapiens of today. He was what one might call 'Homo saurus', a hybrid mammal-reptile creature that was to become our ancestor and the first step in the creation of modern man. In just a few years, man had taken a quantum jump in evolution. He had suddenly evolved from ape-man to a hybrid that would become modern man or Cro Magnon Man. Man was created in the image of the Reptile God. The Book of Genesis makes it abundantly clear that man was originally created in the image of his God: 'And God created man in his image. In the Divine image created he him. Male and female created he them.' (Genesis 1.27) Since the Adam of Genesis and the 'lulu' of the Sumerians were created in the image of the serpent god, shouldn't traces of this fact be found in some of the ancient scriptures? Indeed, it is reported in the Gnostic version of the creation of man. One tract describes Eve's reaction in the Garden of Eden: - 'She looked at the tree. And she saw that it was beautiful and magnificent and she desired it. She took some of the fruit and ate, and she gave to her husband also and he ate too. Then their minds opened. For when they ate, the light of knowledge shone for them...They understood very much'. One wonders if this is a description of Eve mating with the serpent tree god.

The idea that we are descended from trees also has parallels in the legend of Yggdrasil where humans are birthed from a hollow tree after Ragnarok, the Norse version of the end of the world. Other cultures also have a similar legend or mythology. Nikolai Tolstoy for instance, in *The Quest for Merlin* writes that the Yakuts believed that the first man was suckled at the foot of the Tree of Life by a woman emerging from its trunk. In Norse/ Teutonic myths the female Ashr (equivalent to Eve) and Embla the male (equivalent to Adam) came from lifeless tree trunks. In Yarech (Hebrew tradition) The Tree Goddess Nin-ti was 'the lady of the rib', the equivalent of Eve who came from the rib of Adam. The idea that men were originally created by a divinity from trees is archaic and is also found in Hesiod's *Theogony* 700 BCE. It is to be noted too that the story of Noah (meaning 'new birth') has people and animals emerging from a boat which can be seen as a hollow tree. In Welsh, ark/arch can mean a hollow tree, boat or coffin. We can also see in Arthur Bernard Cook's

Zeus: a Study in Ancient Religion, 1868, the belief that 'Zeus created men from trees'. Zeus sited his cult in an oak grove. It is also worth mentioning that in modern times Carl Sagan when being interviewed at Kew Gardens made the amazing statement that we share over 90% of our DNA with an oak tree!

The Serpent, who tempts Eve, is inseparable from the story of the Tree of Knowledge. It is even possible the Serpent and the Tree were one and the same, as this Gnostic story seems to suggest, though I don't like to think so. The serpent is always seen as man's enemy, a wily creature to be wary of. It can kill with its venom and is associated with patience, deception, cunning, wisdom, treachery and the ability to hunt and entrap those who are naive and trusting, to kill them or bring about their downfall. In the Mesopotamian story of Marduk and Adapa, this treacherous creature pretends to be man's friend, while robbing him of the gift of immortality which, it had been intended to bestow on him. The serpent has intimate knowledge of the Tree of Life and is closely connected with it. Enki's trees in his garden of Edin are a Mes tree and a Kiskanu tree (both legendary trees discussed in *The God Tree*) It seems the Mes tree became the Tree of Knowledge and the Kiskanu, the Tree of Life.

At the conclusion of one of the Incantations of Eridu (IV. R.15=Cun. Texts, xvi 42 ff.), in which the Fire god prays in Ea for mediation through Marduk, son of Eridu, the tree is spoken of as 'overshadowing the ocean'. The house, 'shady as the wood', would no man dare enter and there dwell Shamash and Tammuz between the mouths of the two streams. Here the gods have planted the kiskanu tree. Shamash or Shammuz was an Assyrian solar deity of justice who exercised the power of light over darkness and evil. He was the equivalent of the Sumerian Utu and was depicted within the solar disk with the wings and tail of an eagle. (See more of this in the Yew Mysteries chapter) Like several other gods, such as Ningishzida, Ninhursag, Anu and sometimes Inanna, he wore a tiered skirt that resembles the overlapping branches of a coniferous tree. Tammuz was a dying and resurrecting vegetation god connected with the tree. These gods are said to live between two streams and by a huge tree which suggests this is the garden of Paradise.

In Sumer, it was the Annunaki goddess, Nin-Khursag or Ninhursag, and her husband Enki who were given the task of creating workers. Enki is known to us as the serpent in Genesis, the one who gave us the ability to think and reason and so was cursed by his brother Enlil who was against mankind having this power. The Hindus have a similar tradition of a serpent creator god. For them, it was the cosmic serpent Ananta who made us. So, at the dawn of man's creation, we have a pair of serpent-like beings to thank for our existence. It doesn't sound too good. Ninhursag is said to be the daughter of King Anu and Nammu. Another of her names being Mammu or Mami provides the name for mother in many languages. Ninhursag is the Sumerian Mother Goddess and one of the oldest and most important in the Mesopotamian Pantheon.

Mesopotamian carving of Ninhursag. Note snakes emerging from shoulders and scarf with yew symbols around neck.

She is known as the Mother of the Gods and Mother of Men for her part in creating both divine and mortal entities. She is many other things too. Apart from being one of the principal creation goddesses, she is Lady of the Mountain, (perhaps meaning she grew on the mountain) and a tree goddess and is shown draped in what appears to be yew branches around her neck and looking like a yew tree in her tiered skirt. It surely begins to look like we are descended from a tree and a serpent. Ninhursag was a goddess of birth and the umbilical cord, known as the wise mother and mother of the gods. She is the triple-headed goddess sometimes shown with what at first appears to be clubs coming from each of her shoulders. Although it is not clear quite what they are, Inanna has something similar described as weapons but these may well be serpents as they are when emerging from the shoulders of Ningishzida. Ninhursag does not have the title 'Ushumgal'. However, as the twin sister of Enki by Anu and Nammu and half-sister to Enlil, she was at least related to the serpent. Enki, her consort, is subordinate to her, the Divine Mother, but Enki is the mastermind and shaper of the world, god of wisdom and all magic and Ninhursag's supreme importance is in the title Ninti which means 'the mother of all things living'. This title is later given to the Hurrian goddess Kheba and also to Eve in Eden, where it is Adam and not Enki who walks in the garden there. Ninhursag was Enki's partner in the creation of Adapa, the model man, equivalent to Adam and thereby also in the replacing of the Annunaki workers. This was achieved through genetic engineering to produce a half breed creation which apparently is us, or at least our ancestor. Ninhursag's symbol is the umbilical cord cutter; the tool used to cut the umbilical cord of gods and modified earthlings. Another of her symbols is the Greek Omega symbol perhaps signifying the end and making her both the beginning and the end.

Sumerian texts, speak of several deformed creatures created by Enki and the Mother Goddess (Ninhursag), in the course of their efforts to fashion a perfect primitive worker.

The very first offspring were trees and were eaten by Enki. One text reports that Ninhursag, whose task it was to 'bind upon the mixture the mould of the gods,' got drunk and 'called over to Enki,' 'How good or how bad is Man's body? As my heart prompts me, I can make its fate good or bad.' Mischievously, then, according to this text but probably unavoidably, as part of a trial and error process, Ninhursag produced a Man who could not hold back his urine, a Woman who could not bear children, and a being who had neither male nor female organs. All in all, six deformed or deficient humans were brought forth by Ninhursag the mother goddess. Enki was held responsible for the imperfect creation of a man with diseased eyes, trembling hands, a sick liver, a failing heart; a second one with sicknesses attendant upon old age; and so on (Sitchin, 1976). It seems mankind was brought about by a process of trial and error before one creation was finally settled on. One wonders if that wasn't flawed as well.

In Sumerian myth, it is the god Enki, King of the Abzu (or Apsu), who plants the Mes tree in Eridu. It is a tree that bears fruits and appears to be the Tree of Life. In the story of Adapa, 'bread' and the 'water of life' are given in the heaven of Anu (in the earthly sanctuary of Eridu), which is to say, the enclosure of the sacred tree. Anu is the high god and judge and is also the tree. It is in this story that we see the depths the serpent's treachery can go to and the lies and deception the creature is capable of. It is as if man never really stood a chance, being trusting and naive. Enki was known as the god of wisdom and Adapa 'knew the heart of heaven and earth and was involved in secret rites and practises and was in charge of the offering table.'

Enki brings Adapa before Anu. Note tiered skirt costumes of the 3 gods and horned serpents coming from shoulders. Anu does not have these. He may have been the Chief Tree God. Anu holds a potted sacred tree and 4 streams (perhaps the 4 rivers from Eden) flow from his hands.

Anu saw Adapa's virtue and was about to give Adapa the food of heaven, which would make him immortal and one of the gods. There are suggestions here of some kind of elixir of everlasting life and it is Anu, who most likely is the Tree of Life itself, the holy of holies of sacred trees, who can give him this, which will grant him the gift of immortality. This suggests the elixir of life, the Soma or Haoma explored later in this book, which comes from the eternal yew. However, Enki, the serpent god, has his own ideas and is determined to thwart this, not seeing it as right that a mortal should become immortal. Enki, the scheming serpent, therefore devised a plot and previously told Adapa not to eat or drink anything offered to him, by Anu, the chief and highest being of all, telling him it will be the food and drink of death! As a result, when the food of immortality is freely offered to Adapa by Anu, his reward for listening to the serpent is that he is fooled into refusing it! Never trust a serpent!

Enki (Ea), the Ushumgal and creator of Humankind became Eden's serpent, persuaded Eve to break the rules and eat the apple, the fruit of the Tree of Knowledge, for which there would be trouble, dire consequences and retribution. We can see that from these ancient cultures, the sacred tree found its way into Hebrew mythology and the creation story of Adam and Eve. However, if we look at this in a different way, Enki, known to us as the serpent in Genesis, can also be seen as the one responsible for giving us the ability to think and reason through eating the fruit of the Tree of Knowledge! He may have been doing us a favour. However, the motives for this trickery were born out of the rivalry and bad blood between Enki and his brother Enlil, another serpent god and if Enki had not tempted Eve with the forbidden fruit, who knows but eventually, the Hebrew god, like Anu or Marduk may have bestowed immortality on them if they were seen to be righteous like Adapa. However, it is always the same story. Immortality is for the gods and the treacherous serpent dragon god, the snake in the grass, is not going to let humans have it and that may actually be a blessing. In the Garden of Eden described in Genesis 2:9 we see that:

> out of the ground God Yahweh caused to grow various trees that were a delight to the eye and good for eating, with the Tree of Life in the middle of the garden and the Tree of Knowledge of good and evil.

The Tree of Life is not mentioned again until Genesis 3:22-24. It is the Tree of Knowledge that is the heart of the Biblical story and stands for the disobedience of woman, the compliance of man and the wickedness of the serpent. Comparing this to other ancient stories and with Sumerian mythology, what have become two trees by the time Genesis was written, started as one and the god changed from Enki to Yahweh. An earlier story of the Tree of Life is written on 5,000-year-old Babylonian and Sumerian clay tablets about an earlier Garden of Eden at Eridu, the Babylonian Paradise where there were two sacred trees known as the Kiskanu tree (Page 51 *The God Tree*) and the Gis-ti tree. It was these two trees that perhaps had split from the one tree, and later became the Tree of Life and the Tree of Knowledge in Genesis. The gishkin tree in the temple of Enki at Eridu may well be the same as the Mes tree and also represent the Tree of Life. In Akkadian texts, there are pictorial representations of the king carrying out certain rites with a stylised tree described in modern literature as the 'Tree of Life', though the term 'the Tree of Life' does not occur in any Akkadian text. Geo Widengren, one of the most famous historians of religions of the twentieth century, wrote in *The King and the Tree of Life in Ancient Near Eastern Religion*, that it is clear that 'this kiskanu-tree', in the Sumerian text 'gis-kin', is identical with the 'Tree of Life' but it is the Mes tree which is Eden's Tree of Life and is described as eternal, which only the yew tree is. However, it was as a result of Marduk's 'discomfiture', and Erra usurping Marduk's throne, that the Mesu or Mes tree, the tree of heaven, became disturbed and was permanently relocated. (All these legendary Trees of Life are discussed in *The God Tree*). Just as there are many versions of the Tree of Life in different cultures, so there are many versions of the story of our creation and the part played by the Serpent god but they are all very similar, which means they must come from the same source in ancient history.

The Serpent Dragon gods were several and we shall look at more of them now. Inanna was, like Ninhursag, one of the most important and bears the epithet 'ama-ushumgal-an-na' meaning 'the mother is a great serpent dragon of heaven'! In fact, Inanna and her husband/lover/son Dumuzi, the Lord of Edin, both bear the Sumerian epithet 'Ushumgal'. The Mesopotamian god, Dumuzi was the dying and resurrecting god, who became Tammuz in Babylonian times and was represented by a cedar pole. Dumuzi, like Inanna, was a tree god as well as a serpent god. There were other tree gods in other cultures, another being, for example, the Egyptian cow goddess Hathor, who had epithets such as 'Lady of the Date Palm' and 'Lady of the Southern Sycamore' but was not an Ushumgal but some of these god/desses were both serpent and tree gods. This may be difficult to take on board but it seems the earliest deities were trees and the yew, the Tree of Immortality, was seen as a god/dess and may also have been a serpent. Its roots often resemble one and at Llanerfyl, the trunks do too.

Serpents Yew. Llanerfyl.

The Sumerian King List said that 'When Kingship was bestowed from heaven, the Kingship was in Eridu'. So, this is where the concept of Divine rule began, with Inanna who was the first to be depicted holding the branch from the Tree of Life. Mesopotamian kings displayed the divine inheritance bestowed on them through such symbols. There is no doubt of Inanna's connection with the Tree of Life and the branch she holds is the origin of the sceptre. In the Sumerian story of Inanna and Enki, Inanna goes to Eridu and she and Enki drink together. Enki then gives her the decrees called 'Mes', which has to include a branch from the legendary sacred Mes tree. The 'Mes' rites include the throne of Kingship and kingship itself. It became a tradition that Inanna was able to pass on this Divine Kingship and the right to rule through a ritual of sacred marriage to her. The concept of Divine Kingship derived from the Tree of Life and from heaven was one of the most powerful concepts to come out of Mesopotamia. The origin of Inanna is unknown but she is a complex and composite deity who evolves into the early goddess cults, finally merging with Eve and Mary Magdalene. Inanna was not a mother goddess. The sceptre, like the Caduceus, is a representation and symbol of the Tree of Life and in the Kingdom of Urartu (centred around Lake Van in the Armenia highlands), we also see this sceptre like shape. It is an enduring symbol and concept. Even today in the 21st century, the sceptre still confers its power on both royalty and the Church. It is down to the power and fascination of the Tree of Life that this symbol, this magical object from a remote time, still holds its original meanings of authority, divinity and kingship. In the symbol for Isis is also the Ankh, meaning eternal life, sometimes combined in Egyptian writing with the Djed, the symbol for Heliopolis and the sacred tree. What is the Ankh but the sceptre of Divine Kingship? It is only in the presence of a Pharaoh that its power of eternal life is activated.

As the perfect likeness of god, the King was god in human form and thus divine himself, that divinity having been conferred upon him through the sacred tree and the sceptre, originally a branch from the Tree of Life, which bestowed and denoted Kingship. This was a tradition that ended in part in Saxon times, for during that time, Kings were inaugurated beneath the yew at Ankerwycke, Runnymede where the sacred yew could confer the divine power on the King. Nowadays the sceptre is still an important object denoting royalty, although Kings and Queens are no longer inaugurated under the sacred tree. The divinity of the King and divine descent was an old theme, as is seen in the Sumerian King List.

The goddess Inanna was worshipped in Sumer at least as early as the Uruk period (c. 4000 BCE - c. 3100 BCE). Her symbols are an eight pointed star and she is associated with Venus. She wears the same horned cap of divinity as Anu, and like Anu, is also both a god and a tree. It is worth noting here that Ningishzida was sometimes depicted as a horned serpent and so it seems the horns, as with Inanna's cap, were connected with the serpent. Inanna goes under various names as she migrated from one culture to another and is called Inanna in the Sumerian pantheon, Ishtar or Aster in the Assyrian and becomes Isis in the Egyptian. Her city was Uruk. Inanna or Ishtar is the highest-ranking goddess in the Babylonian Pantheon, known as the Queen of Heaven as well as Queen of the Sceptre like Ningishzida and although Ningishzida is the main god/dess referred to as 'Lady of the Magic Wand', Inanna was another goddess known by this title, though to a lesser extent, perhaps because her other attributes were considered more important and focussed on but I think it must mean that she as a Tree of Life also carried a Golden Bough. Professor Sayce says that this 'Divine Lady of Eden or Edin (another name shared with Ningishzida) was termed in Northern Babylonia, 'the goddess of the Tree of Life' and that Babylon, before receiving from the Semites the name of Bab-ilu, meaning 'Gate of God', was called in the old language of the country Tin-tir-ki or Dintir-ra translated by most Assyriologists as 'the place of the Tree (or Grove) of Life'. One important story of Inanna connects her with the Huluppa tree, discovered and rescued by her from the banks of the Euphrates following the deluge. Inanna takes it off to her holy garden where it grows for ten years after which time a snake makes a nest in its roots, the

Anzu bird sets its young in its branches and the 'phantom maid', (also a demon) Lilitu, builds her home in the middle of the trunk which makes her one with Inanna/Ishtar, the mediator between the gods and men. Her position in the centre of the trunk of the sacred Assyrian Tree reflects the image of the goddess shown on 3rd century coins, pointed out by Fred Hageneder in *Yew: A History*, although the concept was much earlier.

Eventually, Inanna became the Goddess of Fertility and the opposites Love and War or Hate. She became a woman in order to know sexual love and with her partner tasted the fruit which brought her knowledge, which was the same thing that happened with Enki and Ninhursag. Inanna's consort was Dumuzi. The story of Inanna from an ancient Sumerian text known as *The First Resurrection of Inanna* shows her as the archetypal goddess of love and war, and as such, the forerunner of Ishtar, Ashtoreth, Aphrodite, Venus and numerous other similar deities. In what is a parallel to the Egyptian myths of Osiris and Hathor, Inanna's resurrection occurs in the underworld. The full story appears in the Sumerian and Akkadian versions of Inanna's Descent to the Netherworld', the place Inanna descended to, to seize dominion from her sister Ereshkigal, 'Lady of the Great Place Below'. However, as she approached the palace of Ereshkigal, Inanna had to pass through seven gates and to do that, she had to give up more and more of her divine attributes, finally leaving her naked and powerless. Inanna is uninvited and unwelcome as she is challenging her sister's power and right to rule the Netherworld and as a result is sentenced to hanging. It is the god Enki, 'Lord Earth', who magically resurrects her, but to escape from the Netherworld, Ereshkigal's abode, known as 'a place of no return', she has to find a substitute to be imprisoned there, instead of her. In an act of treachery, reminiscent of a serpent, she chooses her lover Dumuzi, as her unwilling surrogate to be killed by the Ugallu demons in the Underworld but rather than submit to this fate, he negotiates to share his sentence with his sister

Geshtinanna, so that they each spend six months of the year in Netherworld. While there, Dumuzi is known as 'the dying god' but he is permitted to return to heaven for half the year, while his sister Geshtinanna swaps places and stays in this underworld for the other half, resulting in the cycle of the seasons.

Later in Christian painting, Michelangelo was to portray the serpent of Eden with a woman's body and a serpent's tail in the Vatican's Sistine chapel, helping to seal the Church's misogynous attitude and Eve's association with the serpent, laying the blame on her for the downfall of Adam, the man of Eden, paralleling the roles and epithets associated with Inanna and her betrayal of her husband Dumuzi.

Dumuzi's place of death is under the great apple tree lying in the plain of Edin of Kulaba (*Inanna and Dumuzid, The literature of Ancient Sumer* by Jeremy Black, Graham Cunningham, Eleanor Robson and Gabor Zolyomi, 2004, 2006) At least he is promised resurrection and eternal life as his reward, two qualities of the yew tree, known as the apple tree in earlier times. Dumuzi goes under various names; one of them is a Kiskanu tree, a Tree of Life. Ereshkigal's name translates as Great Earth Tree, with 'Eres' meaning yew, while Dumuzi or Tammuz is one of two gate guards, the other being Ningishzida. These gods may be trees who guard the way to Anu, the chief or mother tree in her heavenly abode, the predecessor of Eden.

Other goddesses who share similar stories with Inanna and Dumuzi are Persephone, who is condemned to spending six months of the year in the Underworld, and also Hecate and other triple goddesses associated with Hades. Persephone is the modern equivalent of Ereshkigal, a serpent god, who goes underground. The Tree of Life also took other forms as the god/dess Anu for instance and Ningishzida/Ningizzida, both a dragon/serpent god/dess and a Tree of Life and Truth, who bore the title 'Lord of the Good/God Tree', guarded the gate of Anu, the Sumerian concept of Heaven. Ningishzida's mother is a cedar tree. Andrew Collins in *From the Ashes of Angels* writes:

> Ningizzida was undoubtedly linked to the Hebraic concept of the Serpent of Eden – the good tree, being either the Tree of Knowledge of Good and Evil or the Tree of Life.

Confirmation of this connection is in the fact that the Armenian scholar Moses of Khorenatsi records that an ancient folk song speaks of the descendants of Azhi Dahaka, (Azhi Dahaka, the Avestan Great Snake is a dragon or demonic figure in the texts and mythology of Zoroastrian Persia, being venerated in at least one 'temple of the dragons'). Also, in the Armenia Highlands are a large number of prehistoric megaliths or standing stones, that take the form of serpents which are known as 'vishaps', or dragons, showing the immense antiquity of this Serpent Dragon cult. These vishaps are found over a vast territory and are no later than the Middle Bronze Age and may be as old as 10,000 years. Some of these stones also show the Tree of Life with serpentine roots, which has to mean they are connected. At least one Armenian scholar has associated this archaic worship of the 'vishap' with the Sumero-Babylonian cult of the snake, a cult that spread around the world and is for instance found in Crete at the temple of the snake goddess in Knossos.

The Sumerian god of the Underworld, Ningishzida, the god/dess of the serpent, son of Enki and the Lord of the Tree of Life is represented as the double-headed snake coiled into a double helix (highlighting the duality in nature), flanked by two gryphons (Wikipedia). Ningishzida is also a special tree that has come from Anu, which must mean that she is one of Anu's branches that descended to the ground, i.e. layered. She is known as the White Kiskanu tree, Kin-babbar, the Lady of the Tree of Life connecting her with the White Tree of legend (see later chapter).

Ningishzida is sometimes known as the son of Ereshkigal and

Gugullana and so, like the yew, this god can change sex. His symbol was the serpent Basmu, entwined around a staff, much like the later Caduceus of Hermes. He was also `Lord of the Good Tree' and was also associated with protection and fertility. Sometimes Ningishzida is seen with a tree and sometimes holding branches in his hands as if they were growing from him and in certain icons, he is represented between two upright serpents. Something which we should also bear in mind is that in mystic traditions the snake or serpent represents spiritual kundalini energy, which rises up the spine of the meditator and in Near Eastern parallels Ningishzida iconography fed into Jainism, as well as into the kundalini tradition. The motif of Ningishzida shown with a serpent sprouting from each shoulder implies that their intertwining union is going on inside his body and this also links with the Caduceus, the staff made from two entwined snakes and implies that the trunk of Ningishzida is the trunk of the tree. The logogram 'giz' or 'gis', is the tree sign, while the Sumerian phonetic reading 'gil-ga-mes', means 'the offshoot of the Mes tree'. In his personal name, Gilgamesh is already referred to as the 'Tree' in the Sumerian story *Gilgamesh and the Bull of Heaven*, where he is called 'gis bulug' meaning 'Great grown tree'. The Mesopotamian god Ninhurta, the Rain god and a son of Enlil, is also referred to as the 'king' and as with the human king, likened to a tree, he is the 'cedar rooted in the Abzu' and is described as 'a Mes tree with broad shining canopy'. That the Mes tree refers to the Mesopotamian Cosmic tree is made certain in the Poem of Erra 1 50-53: 'Where is the mes tree, the flesh of the gods, the ornament of the king of the universe, that pure tree, that august hero suited for Supremacy, whose roots reached as deep down as the bottom of the underworld, a hundred leagues through the vast sea waters and whose top reached as high in the heaven of Anu?'. The term 'flesh of the gods' implies that a god occupies the flesh or is clothed in it and perhaps that the god is dressed up as a tree. The Mes tree being described as the flesh of the gods recalls the Japanese creation myth where the gods arrive by sky boat to the sacred mountain and merge with the yew trees that are already growing there. In other words, divinity takes shape or becomes flesh in the form of the sacred tree.

Going back perhaps earlier than even the legends of the serpent dragon gods to the Epic of Gilgamesh, the serpent is there with the Plant of Immortality in the oldest recorded story, where Gilgamesh desires that the magic plant of the place where the Babylonian Noah resides, is brought to Erech for him to eat, in order to renew his youth, 'though old, the man shall become young'. The plant is the gift of the gods and Marduk regarded as the possessor of the 'plant of life'. Assyrian kings were fond of comparing their rule of their people with the health bringing properties of this plant. Ut-napishtim, who is equated with Noah, was warned by the god Ea (Sumerian Enki) of an impending flood that was about to consume the world. He then constructed the Ark and as a reward for having saved the human race and the animal kingdom from extinction, the gods granted Ut-napishtim and his wife, the secret of immortality. It was never, however, to be given to the mortal race, so Ut-napishtim refuses to let Gilgamesh have it when he comes to ask him. Instead, he tells him he might find a plant with the power of immortality at the bottom of the Abzu, the watery abyss beneath the earth, sacred to Ea (Enki) which he does but he is careless in guarding the plant and the snake takes it. The snake/serpent springs from a well or fountain, where the hero has laid down the plant while bathing, eats 'the plant of youth', sheds his skin, emerges shiny and young and then disappears, so the hero of this story like the others, loses the chance of immortality and the serpent becomes immortal.

The only thing left to add to this chapter is a note on Irkalla. The subject of the Tree of Life is vast and complex with threads and connections leading to many places and cultures. Besides being the name of a goddess of the dead, the name of a place like Netherworld from which there is no return, Irkalla is also the name of a sacred tree. In Babylonian mythology, Irkalla, like Netherworld, is ruled by the goddess Ereshkigal, who as stated before, is connected in name ('eres', meaning yew) with that tree. Irkalla was originally another name for Ereshkigal who ruled the underworld alone until the arrival of her consort Nergal, the death god. Both the deity and the place were called Irkalla in much the same way as Hades in Greek mythology is both the name of the underworld and the god who ruled it. The seat of Irkalla is the Netherworld, the house of darkness where Ereshkigal is queen and long before Yggdrasil, the Norse World Tree, Irkalla was known as a vast tree with the same description and prophecies as Yggdrasil. In early cuneiform writing we find 'Irkalla will I shake and the heavens shall tremble.' In the cuneiform text of the Irra myth, Marduk is called Shulpae, the name of Jupiter in the early morning and his Babylonian title is 'the shining one'. He says, 'The root of the tree will I tear up and its sprout will not thrive.' The difference here is that at the end of the world, Yggdrasil is the only thing left standing and as if to repeat history, gives birth to the new human race. This should be compared with the Ark of Noah which gives birth to not just the human race but the animals as well after the destruction of the world through a Great Flood. The Irkalla tree is also an underworld god and it is obvious that the Norse Yggdrasil is derived from Irkalla. Irkalla is a form of Ereshkigal and translates as 'Great Earth Tree', known as a goddess who descends into the earth and sends down aerial roots to birth new trees. This tree also carried the title 'The White One of Eridu' connecting it to the legendary White Tree discussed in a later chapter. The ancient Chaldeans and Assyrians likewise had their World Tree, coeval with Assur, the great First Source, a tree that was located in the Forest of Eridhu. This tree would appear to have been a Cedar tree, the tree that is most often mistaken for a yew.

So, what exactly are we dealing with in the Tree of Life? I

don't believe we can ever really know. The ancients undoubtedly knew the Tree of Life as a god but not in our modern sense of a god of goodness, unconditional love and justice, at least not in the way we interpret and understand these things. The Tree of Life is a god of pure power, and who knows how it regards us or its relationship to us or how it will deal with us.

Chapter 4

The Hittites and the Eya Tree

In the area of Anatolia lay the country of the Hittites. Theirs was the fourth great empire of the ancient world, the others being Egypt, Assyria and Babylon. Their country bordered Egypt, which at that time included present-day Lebanon. Like most ancient cultures, the Hittites had their own sacred tree, a god among trees and the Hittites are the first civilization we can trace to have had a word for 'yew' and to have that tree central and prominent in their culture and belief system. Fred Hageneder points out in *Yew: A History*, that:

> The oldest existing word for 'yew', 'eya' appears in texts of the Old Hittite period c1750 - 1500 BCE, preserved on cuneiform tablets found at Boghazkoy (modern Turkey). It took most of the twentieth century, however, to discover the botanical identity of 'eya'.

Hittite Tree of Life. 900 BCE.

73

The Hittites would have been only too familiar with the yew. Jarabulus at the border of the Cilician Mountains is a place where eastern Taxus survived the Ice Age. To this day, Turkey, the area inhabited by the Hittites, known as Old Anatolia, has some of the oldest yews on earth, some of which are survivors from this period and unlike the yews in Britain's churchyards, which become hollow after 800 years or so, with a more favourable climate, many of these are dateable through their ring counts which give immense ages of over 4,000 years. Yews are known to become dormant at times and so these yew trees could be even older. In 2016 a 4,112-year-old yew tree dating back to the Bronze Age was found in the same area of Turkey at Gumeli, in the northern province of Zonguldak, making it the oldest known yew tree in Anatolia and one of the five oldest trees in the world. It was declared a national monument. The yew was found by Zonguldak Provincial Director of Nature Conservation and National Parks Sezgin Örmeci, who said that local people informed them of the tree, prompting investigations. Ercan Oktan from Karadeniz Technical University's Faculty of Forestry and Murat Yıldız from Anturia Consulting determined the tree to be 4,112 years old after examining its rings in a laboratory. A 2,700-year-old yew tree, again dated by its ring count, located in Andirin town of Kahramanmaras province and found in 2018 is the second oldest living tree in Turkey. These are among the oldest trees in the world.

Ancient Turkish Yew.

Yews grow naturally from low altitude to high mountains and tolerate shade and the company of many other different tree species. From *'A review of the important ancient woods and ancient woodland of Turkey'*, (Researchgate), comes

> Ancient yew symbols on the finds from Troy and some evidence related to Hittite culture, also indicate that Taxus baccata (common yew) was present in that region in ancient times...Ancient documents also reveal that the Amanus Mountains (southeastern Anatolia) were not only a source of cedar, boxwood and cypress (Rowton 1967) but also of yew.... Yew wood has been used by many civilizations for thousands of years. Although today, yew is on the endangered list of species in Turkey, there were once plentiful supplies and it is thought that the Amanus Mountains were where the Egyptians sourced their yew wood... ' Surprisingly some structures

made of yew were found in Central Anatolia, in Gordium, the capital city of ancient Phrygia, whose neighbourhood is almost treeless today.

This just goes to show how the type of trees that commonly grow in places, can change over time. 'Juniper and yew logs were used for the construction of the outer wall of a royal tomb' (Meiggs, 1983), while there was 'a stool whose front and back faces made of boxwood were elaborately inlaid with yew' (Young, 1974; Simpson, 2012). 'Although yew still retains its traditional and trade value in Turkey, as well as many European countries, they have been strongly depleted mainly because of the direct and indirect actions of mankind... Today they occur either as individual trees or groups of trees in a mixed forest stand, or small patches of yew forests' (Mayer and Aksoy, 1986; Svenning and Magdard, 1999; Thomas and Polwart, 2003).

Yew has been used intensively through time in Turkey:

> In Turkey, yew is defined as a species whose existence can be traced back from hundreds of years to neolithic ages in primary or natural/near-natural woodlands. These are not only appreciated as icons of most important wooded landscapes but also as unique components of cultural heritage.

Parker and Levington, 1999, have emphasized that some fine stands of monumental Taxus baccata growing in broadleaf forests still exist in northeastern Turkey outside Europe and the presence of this tree in different parts of Anatolia can be traced far back into history.

'Temple Building among the Hittites' by Gary Beckham makes it clear the Hittites knew the immortal quality of the yew.

They plant a yew and say as follows: 'As the yew is eternally

thriving and does not shed its leaves, may the King and Queen
likewise be thriving and may their words likewise be eternal.

Volkert Haas says that the Eya tree is normally translated as 'the
evergreen tree' or post.

It is obviously not a conifer but is to do with a 'large and
mighty tree', which had a long life span. The wood of the tree
was also important as it was hard and durable enough for use
in making spears and bows.

So once more we are looking at a tree with a dual purpose as
both a sacred tree and as Taxus baccata, common yew, a supreme
utilitarian one, producing hardwood for making religious and
royal objects. The Eya tree is now accepted to have been a yew
and the yew played a significant part in the myths, rites and
spiritual understanding of the Hittites.

The Hittites were highly disciplined warriors, a fierce people,
more or less obsessed with war and defence and weapons
such as these and the swords they forged were an important
part of both their culture and religion. To give an idea of the
extraordinary nature of these people, the Hittites destroyed
Babylon, apparently for the hell of it, almost like an exercise,
as straight afterwards they returned home to their highly
fortified and remote city of Hattusa. The Hatti and the Hurrians
inhabited the Anatolian area at the same time as the Hittites
around 1620 -1325 BCE but they were also there before that time,
the Hittites coming after them. The Hittites are recognised as
one of the great superpowers of the ancient Middle East in the
late Bronze Age (1550 - 1200 BCE), populating the broad lands of
Anatolia (modern-day Turkey) originally occupied by the Hatti
and later expanding their territories into northern Syria and
as far south as Lebanon. The Hittite language written in both
cuneiform and hieroglyphics is thought to be the oldest of the

Indo-European languages and was only deciphered in 1915. The Hittites worshipped so many deities that they referred to them as 'the thousand gods of Hatti'! At the centre of their pantheon, however, were the storm god, Teshub and his wife the Anatolian sun goddess, Hebat, who derived many of her magical powers from her close relationship with the underground forces, one of which was a tree. Their union was sanctified by the power of the sacred tree and their power as rulers was due to the Divine Kingship conferred by the Tree of Life. Telipinu, the son of Teshub, is said to stand before an Eya (yew) tree and in Hittite cuneiform script the glyph for his name is a tree. The female Eyan tree was named the goddess Ninanna.

The Hittite kingdom reached its height during the mid-14th century BCE under Suppiluliuma I and his son Mursili II. The collapse of the Kingdom around 1200 BCE meant the Hittites were driven south where they created a series of neo Hittite city-states in present-day southern Turkey. Some of them lived on into the 8th century BCE before vanishing from history. A tablet found at their capital Hattusa, agreed after the great Battle of Kadesh in 1274 BCE between the victors, the Hittites and Rameses the Great of Egypt who was defeated, is the world's first surviving peace treaty. Hattusa was originally founded by the Hatti in 2500 BCE whose culture would have provided some of the basis for that of the Hittites.

The Hattian and Hurrian culture was part of the Akkadian Empire of 2335 - 2154 BCE and the Hattians are documented to at least as early as the empire of Sargon of Akkad (2300 BCE) until it was gradually absorbed c. 2000 - 17000 BCE by the Indo-European Hittites, who were subsequently associated with the 'land of Hatti'. This is the oldest name for central Anatolia and the resulting expanded Hittite Empire subdued and replaced Hatti, around 1290 BCE and bordered the Egyptian Kingdom, which at this time had also expanded to cover present-day Lebanon. To put this in context, the old Assyrian Empire dates between 2025 and 1750 BCE. The Kingdom of Urartu and the culture, from which Armenia emerged, was at the time of the 9th - 6th centuries BCE. The Hattians were an ancient people who inhabited the land of Hatti in central Anatolia (present-day Turkey) in 2400 BCE. They were invaded by the Hittites in 1700 BCE. The Hittite/Hurrian wars took place between 1620 and 1325 BCE and both Hattian and Hurrian regions of Anatolia came to be dominated by East Semitic Mesopotamian policies in the form of the Akkadian Empire and the succeeding Old Assyrian Empire, both of which set up trading colonies in the region.

The movements of people and the territory they occupied were quite complex at this time with maps, if there had been any, often being redrawn. The Dunmonii for instance lived in the area of Armenia which overlapped Turkey and overlapped with Hittite culture and influence and this they would have brought with them when they came to Devon. They were connected to the Druids and the Persian Mithras which was concerned with the Tree of Life and thereby to the Persian Empire and so as a result they inherited from two sacred tree cultures.

The Hurrians were a people of the Bronze Age Near East. They spoke a Hurro-Irartian language called Hurrian and lived in Anatolia and Northern Mesopotamia. The population of the Indo-European speaking Hittite Empire in Anatolia included a large population of Hurrians and there is a significant Hurrian influence in the Hittite culture. By the early Iron Age, the Hurrians had been assimilated with other peoples and their remnants subdued by related people who formed the state of Urartu. The present-day Armenians are an amalgam of the Indo-European groups with the Hurrians and Urartians and the Hurrian language closely related to the Urartian language, of the ancient Kingdom of Urartu. Thus, it was Urartu from which Armenia emerged and the Kingdom was also known as the Kingdom of Van, centring on Lake Van or Sevan in the historic Armenian Highlands (present-day eastern Anatolia). As we see elsewhere in this book, this lake is the place where the legendary Tree of All Seeds grew on an island. Also of interest is that Urartu is cognate with the Biblical 'Ararat' associated with Noah.

Significant artefacts that give information about the religion and culture of the Hittites were found at a place called Domuztepe. The great importance of the people from this part of the world from the perspective of this book is that the oldest examples we have of objects such as vases and jars carrying Tree of Life motifs, were unearthed in the Domuztepe Mound in the southern province of Kahramanmaras, Turkey.

From Domuztepe. Pot with Tree of Life design.

This place is considered to be the biggest settlement in the region since the term, 'Near East' was first used. Excavations were launched in 2013 and directed by Hacettepe University, Archaeology Department academic, Dr Halil Tekin, under the allocation of the Kahramanmaras Museum Directorate. He stated that the most fascinating find in the Domuztepe Mound is undoubtedly the earliest example of a tree motif, known as the Tree of Life in ancient Near East archaeology, with cumulative motifs. Dr Tekin said, 'The origin of this tree, which has become used as a Christmas tree in the Christian world throughout time, is here, namely in Mesopotamia. The earliest known example of it is in Domuztepe'. He pointed out the cultural significance of the Tree of Life motifs and added very significantly, 'It is not an ordinary tree. It is related to a faith system, a burial tradition'. Dr Tekin stated that the oldest known example of Tree of Life culture came from Domuztepe from where it expanded out to the rest of the world. I'm not sure I agree with this but Dr Tekin, unaware that the eya tree was a yew, affirmed:

We are talking about the period of the 7000s BCE (9,000 years ago) which is certainly a very long time ago and may possibly be connected with the culture and location of the Garden of Eden. The Tree of Life culture travelled south to Basra where it became the most important factor in Sumerian civilisation. There is also a similar tree in the Akkadians, which is known as the eya tree in Hittite documents of the 3000 BCE. And this tree is linked with a description of the Tree of Life motifs at Domuztepe where the writer described a pine tree that never dies.

Coincidental as it may seem, we know, however, that Ea is pronounced as Eya who is the Hittite Yew-God. In the episode of Moses and the 'burning bush' where Moses first hears the voice of God, this god says, 'Eyeh asher Eyeh' or Eyah asher Eyah generally thought to mean 'I am,' 'it is' and 'to be'. Zecharia Sitchin pointed out that 'Eyah asher Eyah could simply mean 'I am called Ea'.

As stated earlier, it transpires that the goddess Ninanna was the Eyan Tree, otherwise known as the Mountain Apple tree suggesting a female yew that grew on high ground. The Eya or Eyan tree was the Guardian of Gateways. The Eya tree was sacred to the Hittites and anyone who had such a tree or even a sketch or outline of it at their gate in the 11th month of the year was exempt from tax! *Hittite Laws Series 1* states that 'The house of him at whose gate an Eyan tree is visible, is likewise exempt' and it is quite striking that this exempt status is reminiscent of the Passover custom and would therefore indicate a class of people, with special status, an elite who were to be spared in some way or another. A Hittite text described yew as a token of being free.

In *The Heroic Age, A journal of early Medieval North-western Europe Issue 15*, October 2012, there is the following:

> During the Hittite new year festival held in March, a ram and a bull were sacrificed to the war god at the Eya tree, which is referred to in the *Edict of the Hittite King Tudhaliya IV* 1265 - 1240 BCE, where the exemption from tax for those with an Eyan tree at the gate is stated.

The Eya tree was the Hittite version of the World Tree, which represents the celestial pole in the context of celestial deities and was also known as the Eya tree of Zippalanda. Wood from the Eya tree was also used by the Hittites to fashion spears, which was quite a pre-occupation and a deity is associated here with a sword rather than a tree. A clue to a possible explanation may lie in the detail, that although wood of the Eya tree was usually placed on the altars of various deities as part of their worship service, the sacrifice of the ram and the bull to the war god took place on an altar above the Eya tree (Puhvel, 1984, 2:253-254). War was a serious concern of the Hittites and one for which they would seek help and support from the gods. The Hittites conducted revolutionary warfare with an innovative style of chariot which ensured their superiority. Herodotus (*Histories Book 4*) reported that among the Scythians in their worship of Ares (the Roman equivalent of Mars), named by Herodotus as their war god, there was a similar set up of an altar above a pile of wood which no doubt became a sacred fire fed by the sacred wood.

The Hittites came to Anatolia from the southern Russian

steppes and established their kingdom around 1650 BCE but had already moved out of the steppes by 2230 BCE. In 2160 BCE the celestial pole shifted from Taurus into Aries, the two signs presided over by the Hittite war god. The Scythian war god, however, was only associated with the sign of Aries. He was the Divine Warrior who took the World Tree, stabbed it across the circle of the zodiac and embedded his weapon in the opposite sign for whatever reason. For the Hittites, the opposite sign would have been a stone throne. So, when the story travelled south from the steppes, the sword that had been planted in an altar became planted in stone. Barber and Barber (2004) have referred to the image of the sword god at Yazilikaya, as 'the divine spirit of this Sword in the Stone'. We are, of course, more familiar with this story in the form passed down to us in the Arthurian tradition where the twelve-year-old Arthur pulls a sword from an anvil atop a stone in a churchyard, whereby he proves his right to become King. Linda A Malcor in *The Hittite Sword in the Stone: The Sword God and his Twelve Companions*, 2012, writes:

> The Hittite version of the Sword in the Stone story, actually has several elements in common with the Arthurian variant. Both feature a sword in a graveyard. Both swords are associated with a king. The Twelve Runners with swords, in the Hittite variant, parallel the Twelve Knights of the Round Table in Arthurian tradition. Also, the anvil of the Arthurian variant preserved the connection between the forging of iron and the story of the god who planted a sword in a stone. The tales are clearly part of the same tradition, yet, by placing the image of the sword god in conjunction with celestial deities at Yazilikaya, the Hittites retained an association that the Arthurian variant has lost which is that the tale of the Sword in the Stone had something to do with the stars.

The other legend with which there are parallels with Hittite narratives and rituals is the legend of Aeneas and the Golden Fleece, a story which I believe concerns the Golden Bough which appears on yew trees and which seems to be the Greek counterpart to the Roman story of the Trojan hero Aeneas and the Golden Bough, which acts as a passport or talisman in his journey through the Underworld. As Malcor also points out:

> The steppe war god himself was not the celestial Ram, but he was represented by the story of the ram, just as Jason can be represented by a reference to the Golden Fleece.

The story of the Golden Fleece is focused on the Colchis and the Grove of Ares, a little north of Anatolia. One wonders how old this legend is. The fleece has a bearing on another Hittite artefact known as the Stag Rhyton.

Hittite Stag Rhyton.

Few Hittite artefacts have survived and as a result, very few remains of religious iconography are left us from the Hittite world. The Stag Rhyton, however, from central Anatolia, made of silver with gold inlay, is of considerable importance in depicting with some clarity, the objects, if not their meaning, that were of central spiritual significance to the Hittites. The Stag Rhyton shows the Eya or sacred tree with a dead stag beneath it and a fleece and quiver above.

The Hittite Eya Tree.

The object may have been dedicated to the Stag god but tells us a great deal about the Eya tree. To the right and with her back to it is a seated goddess. The scholar Maciej Popko stated in his dissertation of 1978, that the fleece, known as a kursa, played an important role in religion and many old Hittite festivals. The kursa was a sacred object and was offered as a representation of a god, made from six rams fleeces and described as 'a godlike fleece'. It was positioned above the tree. It is a cult symbol that stands next to the sacral container with 20 arrows. Popko remarked that the kursa was not a shield as some have suggested as it looks compact, but a skin, a fleece, which protected the arrow container. I would say this was open to question. The fleece may be the prize and the trophy and the arrows in the quiver may be protecting the fleece, rather than the other way round. The drawing is a very accurate, schematic visual statement of a fleece from a sheep. It cannot be anything else. There are very obvious parallels here with the Golden Fleece, the prize sought by Jason and his Argonauts, which hung on the sacred tree, in the sacred grove and was protected by a dragon. It seems to me that this kursa is to do with the original stories of the Golden Fleece that have come from the Hittite and Greek culture of the Colchis. The Hittites used yew bows, indicated by the Eya tree and the arrows of the yew bow are held in the quiver.

Fred Hageneder in *Yew: A History* has another take on it and says:

As the Hittite texts say 'From the Eya tree is hung a sheepskin, hanging in a male yew at the time of the renewal of nature in early spring, the fleece became gold-dusted by the pollen releasing branches. Across the ancient Near East, the ram for all its male vigour was associated with kingship because both king and ram were representatives of the fertilising sky-god. Furthermore, the ram symbolically supplies the very yarn for the goddess of fate, to spin the life threads of individuals and weave them together on her loom of destiny. A ram dusted with a golden pollen cloud by the Tree of Life itself would have been the most sacred animal in ritual'. We may be coming at this from different angles but we seem to be singing from the same song sheet.

Joost Blasweiler in a paper called '*Anatolia in the Bronze Age*' and also Hans Gustav Guterbock, described the pictures on the Stag Rhyton, of which there is a schematic drawing shown here. The rhyton from c. 1400 - 1300 BCE may have been a vessel of the goddess Inara. It illustrates a libation ritual and although strictly speaking not a rhyton, it is a drinking vessel of a type known in Hittite Akkadian as biburu. The main figure on the rhyton is a seated deity, probably a goddess wearing a long dress and holding a drinking cup. She may be Inara, who originates from the Hattian religion, the goddess of fertility and nature, goddess of the hunt, protector of Hattusha (the Hittite capital city) and wild nature and is holding a falcon in front of a Hittite altar. Ton van Bakel, an authority on seals from Babylon and Sumer says that in Sumerian, the bird is the sign for fate and destiny and is also connected with oracles. The Hittite Eya tree stands behind the sitting deity. The Tree of Life which we know to be a yew is also connected with these concepts. The symbols in the tree are the attributes of LAMMA. John Gregory Mc Mahon stated that gods with LAMMA in their title or name have to be understood as tutelary deities of the Hittite state cult. The word can mean 'strong, vigorous'. The deer is a representation of death and imagined to be asserting a message such as 'be my hunter'. All these things are attributes of the sacred yew. Bakel says:

> Animals which are protecting a holy tree or source are mostly depicted as a serpent, crocodile, lizard or turtle, animals that can stay motionless for hours and the collapsed deer lying under the tree is more likely a symbol of death.

The tree, he agrees, might be the evergreen Eya tree. One can see the attributes of the hunt hanging on the tree, the quiver and the kursa (bag of the hunt). Yew was the most powerful of all hunting symbols through many cultures. The spears seem likely to have been a symbol of protection. Elsewhere depicted on the rhyton is a young god standing on the Stag. In Hittite texts, the Hittite God on the stag is a Tutelary Deity. The Tutelary deities were earthly divinities and the combination of stag, bird and hare are a visual metaphor for wild nature. The god of the hunt bestows success on the human (royal) hunter. In other words, the blessing of the Storm god leads to political power and the blessing of the Stag God leads to mastery of the wild creatures in the king's domain. Indeed, the bow and arrows carried by the god are symbols of mastery. However, most important of all from the point of view of this book is that what we have here is a depiction of a sacred tree where a fleece could be hung or be part of the tree.

The Hittites made yew bows and along with the arrows in the quiver, the sacred tree depicted is very likely a yew and the stag, the animal hunted with the arrows. Billie Jean Collins in *Masters of the animals in Old World Iconography,* 2010, says that also on the Rhyton,

> Priests of the Tutelary Deity and the Storm god are present, indicating that the deities and their sacred animals are due special reverence as part of the festival program... The cult of the stag thus centres on the hunt and is the focus of the Tutelary deity and his sacred animal... he fragments which give a testimonial regarding day 10 (of the death ritual) reference a Bronze spear, an arrow and hunting bag (kursa). In sum, symbols of the hunt and sacrifice are scattered through the funerary rites for the Hittite king, reinforcing the supposition that images of animal mastery in the Hittite texts are connected to royal ideology.

It should be noted that the tutelary deity among the Hittites was shown in many different forms such as the tutelary god of the countryside and the tutelary deity of the hunting bag or Kursa so that deities who were not depicted in human form were also represented by objects such as the kursa hanging from the Tree of Life, the Eya tree. However, the purpose of these things, these symbols, must be to say something about some aspect of the tree.

Fred Hageneder sums up the significance of all this on page 100 of *Yew: A History*:

> The killing of animals with a yew spear or bow is likely to have

had a shamanic significance for the Palaeolithic hunter, such as ensuring the rebirth of the animal through the presence of the Tree of Life in the moment of its death. In ancient culture, a symbol of a bow usually represents a yew.

A Hittite spear was also found to be made of yew wood. The presence of the Tree of Life or Eya tree is also of prime importance in the presence of the death ritual, to ask for and to ensure the resurrection of the Stag, so that it might enter into the continuum of life and once more be born, live and be hunted.

The presence of the tree as a sceptre appears in another important Hittite artefact, the Yyszkiewicz cylinder, which comes from Northern Syria or Anatolia. Here a King or deity sits in a chair holding a cup in his right hand and a branch/twig/flower/plant in his left. In Ugarit, Syria, a text was found which witnessed the king's habit of carrying something of this nature like a sceptre. Kings across the world carry this symbol of kingship, such as the Emperor of Japan who carries a sceptre or staff made from yew wood from the sacred mountain and the Egyptian Pharaoh who also had such a sceptre. Geo Widengren's writes in *The King and the Tree of Life in Ancient Near Eastern Religion*, 'In one of the Ba'al Anat cycle passages we read: 'Ba'al's eyes are before his hands, that they wrest the cedar from his right hand'. Widengren says It has already been pointed out that this staff is 'the sceptre from the Tree of Life'. Such sceptres would have been made from yew not cedar, wood from the immortal tree. At Hattusa, a stone carving of the goddess Kybele or Kubaba from 850 - 750 BCE in the museum of Anatolian civilisations in Ankara shows her in late Hittite style under Armenian influence, with what appears to be a sceptre of yew in her right hand depicted by a double chevron pattern, a symbol of yew.

Between 1175 and 1278 BCE, the Mycenae attacked the mighty Hittites forcing them to migrate by boat. Like other cultures, who regarded the sacred tree as a god, these ancient peoples would not have moved without taking the tree with them and the Hittites would have taken it as a branch, root or cutting to be planted once the people settled in new territory. In connection with the male Eya tree and the female tree Eyan tree 5,000 years ago, 'Ea' meant 'life force' or 'eternity' in the Hittite language and as such is more evidence that the Hittites Tree of Life was the yew. Israel Regardie in *The Tree of Life, a Study in Magic*, 1932, says 'Eya, eya, eya', means 'he who is and was and is to come'. In other words, it is the eternal and immortal tree. The statement is, of course, linked to Jesus' claim, 'I am the Alpha and the Omega, who is, and who was, and who is to come, the Almighty.' (Revelation 1:8)

It was from this part of the world then and principally, but not solely, with the Armenian Dunmonii tribe, who inherited the Tree of Life culture of Mesopotamia, that the sacred yew was brought to Britain.

Chapter 5

From Mesopotamia to Britain

At one time, there was a yew culture right across the world but few people today would know that over 2,000 years ago, in pre-Roman times, over half of Britain was dominated by this culture which left its mark on our landscape in the form of ancient yew trees, and places directly connected with them. All tribes of the time, as well as the Romans, were aware of the sacredness of the Yew. The Iberians, Silurians, Ivernii, Cernyw, Eburones and others, occupied large parts of Britain. Most of Ireland was known as Ivernos on maps after the Ivernii tribe. The Yew tribes and their legacy are still with us.

There are still many places that are directly connected with the Yew, a few examples being Eburacon (meaning Yew wood – the old name for York), Iden (Yew tree pasture – Sussex), Uley (Yew wood – Gloucestershire), Ivegill (Valley of the Yew - Cumbria) Iwode (Yew wood - Hampshire), Iford (Yew ford – Sussex) and Ewhurst (yew wood on a hill – Surrey, Sussex and Hampshire). Even rivers were named after the yew such as the River Iwerne in Dorset, the River Yeo in Devon and extraordinarily enough, the Archbishop of York still signs his name 'Ebor', meaning Yew! Dinefwr, meaning the Kingdom of Yews, now a small area where I live in Wales, was once a vast Kingdom which stretched as far as Cornwall and the Isle of Wight. Scratch the surface, and the Yew, once so important in a world of radically different values, is still there, its legacy our forgotten heritage. The ancient yews still stand, living and growing after all this time, so awesome, we can only wonder at them and hope they are adequately and legally protected for the future because they aren't now.

But where did the yew come from? It has been said before that we have to differentiate between the common or indigenous yew that was here in Britain, even before the Ice Age and Taxus Sanctus, the saint's yews and those descended from sacred yews of thousands of years ago. Indigenous yews had already been in Britain for hundreds of thousands of years, as evidenced at Cromer Marshes and the Bristol Channel where fossilised remains of yews have been found. The general opinion is that the yew tree represents the Tree of Life but it's not to say that every yew is that special tree. Many of these yews are hiding in plain sight, mostly in churchyards, where they were planted both before and during the days of Christianity, by ancient tribes and holy people.

Some ancient people of a Celtic tribe called the Dunmonii or Dunmones migrated from Armenia to Britain and inhabited Dunmonia, the area now known as Devon and Cornwall, including Exeter and Plymouth and some areas of present-day Dorset and Somerset, from at least the Iron Age up till the early Saxon period. More than likely, they brought their sacred tree along with them and there are ancient yews which date from the time of the Dunmonii migration in the area of Dorset, the area this tribe, adopted as home. Danmonium is the Latin name for Devon. The Armenians would most likely have brought branches or cuttings of sacred yew to Britain some 3,000 years ago and planted them here. It is not unlikely that some of these trees are still living and growing and that the ancient yews such as those at Mamhead, Kenn and Ashbrittle would have been planted as part of the Yew cult at the time.

Ancient Yew at Kenn.

Ancient Yew at Mamhead.

Ashbrittle Yew.

The Dunmonii erected a temple at Exeter and the ancient, Golden Bough yew of Kenn, a most sacred yew tree lies close by and may have been one of the trees planted by the Dunmonii, being of a similar period. Other yews such as those at Silverton, Shirwell (one of the Dunmonii's tribal areas between 800 BCE and 42 CE), Dartington, Staverton, Stoke Gabriel, Payhembury, Plymstock, Bampton, Stoodleigh, Zeal Monachorum, Broadhembury, Plymtree, Combe Raleigh and Farway, may also have originally come from the East, from Mesopotamia, Iberia, Egypt and the Armenian area but may have been planted later, from cuttings taken from the original plantings. The name 'Mam' as in Mamhead is significant as it is derived from the Mesopotamian/Sumerian and Babylonian language and means 'Mother' and in ancient British would have meant 'Chief Mother'. At a place called Mamhilad in South Wales, there is also an ancient yew. I wonder about its origins.

Ancient Yew at Mamhilad.

In addition to being ancient yew sites, Mamhead, Silverton, Shirwell and Zeal Monachorum were Hundred Court meeting places where people met under a significant tree and there seems to have been a lot of ancient yews planted in this area of Devon from Exeter to Barnstaple 2,000 - 3,000 years ago.

It also cannot be a coincidence that there are many nemeta

(plural of nemeton) or sacred groves in the area that the Armenians occupied. There are no exact dates for these tribal movements but the most likely people to have formed the nemeta and used them, are the Dunmonii. The establishing of protected areas, which are the basis of the nemeta, began back in ancient times where unique territories where a certain tree or animal species were found, were protected as sacred. Some such areas in Armenia were the forests and shrines which contained yew and the prototypes of these protected areas can be traced back to the late 3rd / early 2nd century BCE. Ekwall, in *English River Names,* 1928, suggested that the name 'Iwerne' in Dorset meant 'the Yew river or stream that rises where yew trees grow', which suggests a nemeton. This is based on the Celtic word for the yew tree, with a suffix meaning 'river'. In 1900, General Pitt Rivers excavated a Roman building near Iwerne Minster which he identified as the Ibernio of the 'Ravenna Cosmography' (a list of place names covering the world from India to Ireland, compiled around 700 CE by an anonymous cleric in Ravenna. The River Yeo and the River Mole were once both known as Nymet and Nemet and both run through the area of a sacred grove, known as Druids Grove in Surrey, while names such as Nymet Boghe, Broadnymet and Nemetostatia (meaning 'outpost of the Sacred Grove'), are to be found in the very area settled by the Dunmonii.

In *Historical Views of Devonshire,* 1793, Richard Polwhele writes:

> Let us consider the testimony of one of our chronicles, which speaks to the point of the Armenian emigration. *The Saxon Chronicle* (said to have been written by a monk at Lincoln), positively asserts, that 'the original inhabitants of Britain came from Armenia, and that they seated themselves in the south-west part of the island.

Similar chronicles were kept by the most learned monks in

several monasteries throughout the kingdom. The monk of Lincoln seems to have been well informed: And there is no more reason to dispute the authority of the passage before us, than that of any other part of the book. For it is not a conjecture: It is not hazarded as an opinion: It is a positive assertion and relation of an event, as a thing generally known and understood to be true.

Polwhele also discusses similarities between the early Armenians and Britons living habits including using the caverns which are found in abundance in Devon. He writes:

That these caverns were places of temporary residence in the time of war, whither the Danmonii retired, for the security of their persons, their domestic furniture, and their warlike stores, I should judge not only from the disposition of the Aborigines so congenial with the oriental turn of mind, but from the resemblance, also of our Danmonian excavations, to those in Scotland and Ireland, which are allowed to be military retreats. But whatever was their use, they were very similar to the caves of the eastern nations, and especially of Armenia... 'That the Asiatics, from whose country the Danmonians are supposed to have emigrated, made them the dens which are in the mountains, and caves, and strongholds, is evident, both from sacred and profane history'.

There is a remarkable passage in Xenophon, describing the caves of the Armenians. Xenophon informs us:

that the houses of the Armenians were under-ground - that the mouth or entrance to these subterraneous habitations was like that of a well, but that underneath, they were wide and spreading - that there were ways for the cattle to enter, but that the men went down by stairs. In Armenia, at this day, the people dwell in caverns.

'In a narrow valley' (says Leonhart Rauwolf)

...lying at the bottom of an ascent, we found a great stable, wherein we went. This was quite cut into the hill: And so was that wherein we lodged the night before. So that you could see nothing of it, but only the entrance. For they are commonly so in these hilly countries, under-ground, that the caravans may safely rest there, and defend themselves from the cold in the winter. This stable, twenty-five paces long, and twenty broad, was cut out of a rock... These descriptions of the Armenian caves agree, in several points, with that of the cave near Plymouth, as well as the Cornish caverns. Xenophon's cave is subterraneous: So is that near Plymouth: The apertures of both are narrow: And both caverns are, afterwards, sufficiently capacious.

He goes on to describe place names:

I observe that the caves in Devon, (so like the under-ground habitations of Armenia) are mostly in the Southams, at no great distance from the river Arme, or the town of Armenton, on the banks of the Arme, where the migrators from Armenia are supposed to have first settled.

The *Anglo-Saxon Chronicle* further describes many common characteristics of Britons and Armenians. From the warlike spirit, clothing, social structures, names and living habits. Vallancy, on the authority of Sir George Yonge, adds that 'in S.W. of Devonshire, there is still a river, called 'Armine' and the town and hundred are called 'Armine-ton' to this day.' Finally, Polwhele concludes as follows:

That the settlers in this island were not a colony from Gaul, has been proved, on every view of the subject. And the vulgar theory of the original European plantations would be abandoned, I think, on all hands, after a candid and liberal investigation of it. To such an investigation I should be happy to excite the learned. From the dubiousness of the common theory, I had a right to form a new hypothesis. And I have imagined a rapid emigration to these islands, for the most part by sea, from Armenia... I have not grounded my supposition on the sole authority of the Saxon Chronicle. The evidence of Caesar himself is strong in my favour: And the voice of the Greek historians and geographers is still more decisive. But the character of the Orientals, so strikingly contrasted with that of the Europeans, and yet according with that of the aboriginal Danmonii, seems almost to determine the controversy. The Orientals, at the time of their first emigration into different countries, were impressed with various traits of character; such as we have discovered in their modes of settlement, their civil government, their religion, their commercial communications, their language and learning, their genius and their customs. The wandering spirit and patriarchal policy of Armenia.

Richard Polwhele asserted that he had no doubt that the origin of the Druid religion was to be found in Asia and that there were many parallels and links between the Druids and Persians. He said it was the sublime doctrine of both the primitive Druids of Danmonium and the Magi of Persia that they worshipped the whole expanse of heaven, represented by circular temples under the stars in the open air, (such as the Druid temple of the Silurians at Llanilid). Indeed, Tacitus in *Germania 9* asserted that the Druids:

do not think it is in accordance with the grandeur of the

heavenly beings to confine gods within walls or to represent them in accordance with human features. Groves and woods they consecrate and they call by the name of the gods that remote being that they see through reverence alone.

Michael Tsarion states that the yew was considered sacred by both the Druids and the Egyptian and Persian Magi. During the 2,000 years before Christ, Druidism with its motto 'The Truth against the World' had become established in Britain and King Molmutius had clarified the essence of the Druidic Beliefs into civil laws which were maintained up to the time of William the Conqueror. The wise men or Brahmins of India make several references to Britain as a great centre of religious learning and Jesus would have known of the eminence of Druidic religious wisdom. Extraordinary as it may sound, both Eastern and Western traditions claim that Jesus completed his studies in Britain. At the time, the Druidic universities were the largest in the world, both in size and in attendance with a listing of 60,000 students, (Gildas, *Cottonian MS* and Morgan *History of Britain*) This is affirmed by Greek and Roman testimony which states that the noble and wealthy of Rome and other nations sent their children to study law, science and religion in Britain. Gildas the Wise, (c.500 - c.570 CE) the first historian stated 'In Druid Britain, He (Jesus) would live among the people dominated by the highest and purest ideals, the very ideals He had come to proclaim'.

But where had this knowledge originated and what was it all about? I said at the beginning of this chapter that the Yew tribes such as the Iberians, Silurians, Ivernii, Cernyw, Cornovii, Eburones and others, occupied large parts of Britain. Yews were particularly honoured in Iberia where they were more numerous than oak trees. Dr Myron Evans states that the Celtic languages could have originated in Iberia and that Celtic was a predominant language group around 400 BCE. It seems likely that the migrants brought the veneration of the yew tree with them. Celtic and pre-Celtic societies associated the yew tree with the Triple Goddess - the maiden, the mother and the crone, just as they did the waxing, full and waning moon and the Life, Death and Eternal rebirth associated with the Yew. We can, I think, conclude that the Celtic Yew tribes all came originally from the Mesopotamian area including Iberia to Britain, where they set up their tribal territories.

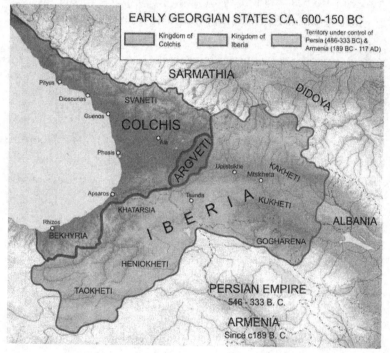

Map of the Yew Kingdoms within Mesopotamia.

The tribes would have had central trees, Axis Mundis, to which they gathered. The Cornovii tribe, for instance, had Wrekin at its centre and at Wrekin, a yew grove is to be found with a 40 ft complete circle of 19 young yews growing around the parent tree, known as the 'secret' or 'hidden' yew, a very old tree in Ercall Wood on Burford Spur. Also, within the Cornovii territory was Uppington near the Roman town of Wroxeter, where a 29 ft yew, was said to be able to accommodate 18 people to dine within its hollow! This seems somewhat far-fetched but of note is that at the foot of the yew tree is a Roman altar and on an outside lintel of a back door to the church, a Celtic carving of a dragon. This was an important spiritual or religious centre. Under Roman rule, Wroxeter became the Cornovii capital. The Cornovii were a Celtic people of Iron Age and Roman Britain, who lived principally in the modern English counties of Cheshire, Shropshire, north Staffordshire, north Herefordshire, Powys and Wrexham. Another significant site of ancient yews within their territory is Wychbury Hill Fort near Birmingham, where seven cairn burials were found directly under yews. This mysterious site seems to have been a burial site before becoming a hill fort and here there are raised circles of yews within other circles. Creeden Hill is an Iron Age hill fort within Cornovii territory, also with old yews growing on it. Their territory was bordered by such tribes as the Brigantes to the north, the Corieltauvi to the east, the Dobunni to the south and the Deceangli and Ordovices to the west. The people who inhabited the very north of the British mainland and modern Cornwall were known by the same name but were quite separate and unrelated peoples.

The small Celtic kingdom of Cernyw was, according to tradition, founded out of a western chunk of the former Silures territory around 437 CE by Eugenius, the son of High King Magnus Maximus. This was the most Romanised area of Wales. It may have been formed of Cernyw and Ewyas but the apparent separation of Ewyas around 440 CE is probably what caused Cernyw to appear as a kingdom in its own right. It was situated west of Gwent and the name Cernyw actually means Yew territory. The British Kingdom of Glywssing was a late 5th century renaming of Cernyw. The customs and traditions of that region's people would have been part Roman and part Silures. There is much confusion when it comes to the Cernyw and there are several genealogies that have Arthur's grandfather as Kusgtenin or Custenin Gornev (and any number of other spelling variations). Custennin Vendigeit (Fendigeid) who appears to be also Custennin Corneu (Gornev) is thought to be of Cornue/Cornow/Cernyw of Dumnonia, (if this Corneu is indeed Cornwall and not Cornue/Cornow/Cernyw of the Midlands - from the Cornovii tribe) before it became Powys/Pengwern and later Powys and Shropshire. Cernyw (Cornwall) doesn't appear until the early 8th century.

Interestingly the hill fort of Dinas Powys lay within Cernyw territory and this was more or less in a direct line with the hill fort of Brent Knoll across the Bristol Channel, Glastonbury Tor and Cadbury Castle and would have formed part of a chain of communications before the Romans. However, what is particularly interesting is that in North Wales within Cernyw territory lies Llangernyw, translated as 'Enclosure of the Yew'. Here there is a 5,000-year-old yew and also pre-Christian standing stones, the only monoliths in the Diocese, at St. Digain's church. This was most likely the tribal centre of the Cernyw. Efernwy was the name of the Gaulish yew goddess and places in North Wales like Lake Vyrnwy no doubt derived their names from her name as does the River Severn, which the River Vyrnwy, flowing from Lake Vyrnwy, feeds. The Cernyw seem more important and influential than is thought at first. Close to Lake Vyrnwy is the ancient Bronze Age yew site of Pennant Melangell as well as other old yew tree sites of Llandderfel, Llandrillo, Llanymawddwy, Llanarmon Dyffryn Ceirog, Meifod, Llanycil and Llangadfan. In Roman times, the whole of Ireland was known as Ivernia or Ivernos. Other ancient yew trees of 3-5,000 years old such as Defynnog, Discoed and Linton, could be centres of territories belonging to Yew tribes. Other younger yews such as that on a raised mound at Cyffylliog, may also be to do with the Yew Cult.

The yew was incredibly important and absolutely central to the culture of Britain at one time. In fact, a whole series of names of people and places contain words meaning 'yew'. 'Eburos', for example, is a word which is at the root of tribal names such as the Eburones between the Maine and the Rhine in present-day Germany, and at other places across Europe such as the Eburovices at Evreux, Eburbriga, Eburomagnus and Eburodunum. Eburacum is, of course, the British name from which the name 'York' derived, although it is within the territory of the Brigantes, where, as previously stated, the Bishop of York still signs himself 'Ebor'. The Brigantes are not known as a Yew tribe but are associated with the wells and with Brigid, who became St. Bride. However, at St. Brides Super Ely in Glamorgan, there is both a well and a yew, the two things being very much connected and in general Britain during Roman, as well as pre-Roman times, was under the influence of the yew. This tree, a one-time common landscape feature, was often used as a landmark as well as being found in a place name. In Brittany we particularly see the word for yew in place names, sadly at many places where the name, based on the yew, still exists but where the yews have gone. In Wales, of note is the 3,000-year-old yew at Llanbedr Ystrad Yw 'St Peter's Church in the Valley of the Yew', in which the vicar used to take tea and chat with a parishioner!

Ancient Yew of Llanbedr Ystrad Yw.

Although just a small area now, a third of England and Wales was at one time known as Dinefwr, the Kingdom of Yews and in Roman times, Wales covered a much larger area and included Devon, Somerset, Herefordshire, Shropshire, Gloucestershire, Yorkshire, Monmouthshire and Cheshire. It is here where many ancient yew names and many ancient yews survive, that the

Yew Cult legacy would have been passed on from generation to generation so that, particularly in rural areas, the Yew is still held in great regard by the people. In early times land was not divided into countries or districts but Kingdoms.

When it comes to the Silures, the Roman writer Cornelius Tacitus gives a racial description of them with:

> the swarthy faces of the Silures, the curly quality, in general, of their hair, and the position of Spain opposite their shores, attest, the passage of Iberians in old days and the occupation by them of these districts... (*Tacitus Annales XL*: translated by M Hutton)

This ancient theory is born out in *Facing the Ocean – The Atlantic and its Peoples* by Barry Cunliffe, 2001, in which the author confirms a shared ethnic origin for the peoples of Northern Spain and the promontories of Brittany, Cornwall, Wales, Ireland and Western Scotland. He states

> The camp in Llanmelin wood may have been the (pre-Roman) centre of the Silures, but the choice of Caerwent for the cantonal capital of Venta Silurum may also have been influenced by its relationship to the Severn ferry.

The Romans, of course, were in a good position to study the Silures, who were known as a powerful and warlike tribe who never gave up fighting them. In the end the Romans had to agree to a power share at their capital of Caerwent. It is very noticeable that many ancient yews are in Silurian territory. Yews such as the extraordinary looking 4,000 year old at Bettws Newydd as well as those at Defynnog (5,000 years), Llangattock Juxta Usk (over 3,000 years), Llanilid (2,000 years), Mamhilad (3,000 years) and Linton (4,000 years) are in their territory and there will doubtless have been others, now long gone. The territory of the

Silures covered the Glamorgans, Gwent and Powys.

No doubt the Celtic tribes co-operated with each other, particularly when it came to fighting the Romans and Caradoc, leader of the Silures at the time, at one point decamped to Anglesey and Snowdonia, where he found support amongst the Ordovices. Later, having escaped after his last battle at Clun, Caradoc found refuge among the Brigantes, although it was here he was betrayed to the Romans by Queen Cartamandua. The Ordovices were not a Yew tribe but within their territory lay Clun, with its important 3,000-year-old yew. The Ordovices in Roman times did not have a yew name unlike many others but they, like most tribes, would have known of the significance of the yew. They rebelled against the Romans and suffered heavy losses, although it is unlikely that the Romans, as they claimed, exterminated the entire tribe and their name is preserved in the place name Dinorwig ('Fort of the Ordovices'). A point of unrelated interest is that the mountains of South-East Wales were the ancient territories of the Silurian tribes and for this reason, outcrops of rocks of the Paleozoic era were named Ordovician after the Ordovices tribe of North Wales and outcrops of rock from the earlier period were known as Silurian, again after the tribe of that name.

Moving on now to the sacred yew trees, which may have come with the yew tribes, the sacred and legendary Gaokarena tree, Tree of Life, Tree of the White Haoma from which came Soma, is perhaps the most important, the holy of holies, as you will discover later and this tree, probably several of them sprung from the same tree, is likely to have been brought here by the Dunmonii the tribe of Armenia. If these trees are here in Britain, it could explain why Britain was known as Albion, the Sacred Isle in the West, the White island by the Celts and people of ancient times. There is more information about the Gaokarena tree in *The God Tree* as well as in this one. Iberia is the yew kingdom and Gaokarena or Gaogharena which lay within it, borders Armenia and Iberia. The Gaokarena tree must have come from the Kingdom of Gaokarena which was located below the Caucasus. If, as is most likely, cuttings from the sacred tree were brought with the Armenians, the ancient yews of Kenn and Mamhead are probably the very trees that grew from these cuttings as their age coincides with the date of the migration some 3,000 years ago. Others such as the yew at Zeal Monachorum may have sprung from cuttings or layered branches taken from the established trees at Mamhead and Kenn. The Persian Gaokarena tree is also known as the Tree of All Seeds (one female and one male tree) and legend has it that it was found on an island in the Vourukasha Sea. It is the Persian Tree of Life and Tree of knowledge.

In the 12th century document called *The Manor of Tara*, Fintan speaks of a sacred tree which came from the Iberian Peninsula. It seems likely that the sacred tree is actually Fintan himself and that it was one of his branches which was 'the many coloured branch from Lebanon'. We can see then that the tree came directly from Iberia wherein Lebanon lies and where the Ivernii tribe who travelled to Ireland originated. I feel for various reasons such as that the Roman writers referred to the branch of the Golden Bough as glittering like metal and its appearance of glinting with many colours, (a phenomena I have been privileged to see in its mature form in Britain), that these things are all connected. Sadly, I am not at liberty to tell where the site of this yew tree with a mature golden bough is, due to the trophy taking that has gone on with the Golden Bough at Defynnog but a 'many coloured branch' is a good description of a mature Golden Bough branch. Omna or Om is Ireland's most sacred tree and this name seems connected or derived from Haoma and the branch from Lebanon, adding weight to the idea that the Gaokarena or White Tree was in fact brought to Ireland.

It seems likely that the sacred yew, the Tree of Life, originally came to Mesopotamia from Egypt. Certainly, it must have been rescued from Egypt at the time of the great flood and taken north up the coast of Iberia and into Turkey and Armenia and planted on high ground where it could not again be threatened by flooding. It was destroyed in Egypt but from there moved to Eden and other places in the area. The Saxons as we have seen called Eden Yewdene. In a 'light bulb' or eureka moment, it became clear to me that the origin of the Holy Wells which sprang up under Sacred Yews in Britain derived from the memory and legend of Eden and the holy river that sprang from beneath the Tree of Life!

As we have seen, the origin of the Yew Cult is Mesopotamia, and although it is probable the sacred tree was also brought to Britain from Egypt (to Ankerwycke for example), it was mainly from Iberia that it was brought to Britain and from Iberia came the culture of the Yews with the Yew tribes who crossed over from Armenia, thus entering into European culture. The Tree of Life, of course, existed before Egypt and came to Egypt from another culture, a previous civilisation but it is not traceable back any further than Heliopolis. Iberia stretched from the Caucasus to Georgia in the 4th century BCE but the only evidence of ancient yews today is in the area from Turkey to the Caucasus. The oldest yews are in the Black Sea area, old Iberia and Gaokarena. There are yews in Anatolia that could have originated from the Tree of Life. People would have come with cuttings from Egypt to Anatolia and other places such as the Colchis and Gaokarena. Anatolia was the land of the Hittites who as we have seen were very much connected to the yew. The Colchis, the place where Jason and the Argonauts, 3,000 years ago, sought the Golden Fleece within the sacred grove of Ares was also within this area and may have been part of Anatolia at one time. As a testament to the importance of this area for ancient yews, the Colchis today is a site of a world prime stand of monumental yew trees, some at least 3,000 years old.

Of the yews that probably came with the Dunmonii, brought

here deliberately as sacred trees are the two ancient yews which rate among our largest yews, those at Mamhead and Mamhilad. Obviously, the names of these places derive from the word 'Mam', which is connected with Ninhursag, the yew goddess and birth goddess known as Mami and the Lady of the Mountain, connected with Lebanon and the important tree of legend, the White Tree. It may well be that these trees are descendants of this great mother tree. Another link is Mamre and in Genesis 19:1-3 divine strangers or gods appear to Abraham beneath a sacred tree at Mamre and there may be a connection between this and the trees at Mamhead and Mamhilad which could be descendants of the sacred tree at Mamre. One of the men in this tale is addressed as 'Lord' while the others are spoken of as 'angels' in the Authorised Version and the Lord is described as being in the tree beneath which Abraham sat. Another tree worth mentioning is that of Heavitree in Devon where there is a very solid looking fragment left of an ancient yew tree. The name Heavitree comes from Heavi which means 'chief'. The etymology of some names is often useful in throwing light on things.

As mentioned elsewhere in this book, the Crowhurst yew has a river Eden running close by which leads one to wonder whether there is a connection here between the Garden of Eden and the ancient Crowhurst yew. It is also worth noting that the Saxons knew Eden as Yoden or Iden and that this meant 'Yew dean' or 'Yew valley', which then looks very much like the Saxons knew that the trees of Eden were yew trees.

Chapter 6

Nemeton, the First Shrine of the Sacred Tree

The Axis of the World brings in touch
Heaven and Earth
The transcendent and the immanent
The circle and the cross

From the Orient comes the image
Of the living creatures,
Guardians of the sanctuary doors.

Certain places, certain natural elements,
Springs, trees, stones,
Repositories of the Sacred,
Open clearings in Forest hollows,
A place of celebration, of the Sacred Tree,
Nemeton,
Delineated by a projection from sky to earth,
Most often in open clearings,
In forest hollows.

Between sky and earth,
Heaven's ladder, the Sacred Tree.
-Anonymous. Discovered at Landevennec in Brittany, said to
be the place where Christianity first arrived from Wales and
Ireland.

On telling of how a thing is born,
We reveal the eruption of the Sacred in the World,
Ultimate cause of all real existence,
All sacred space implies a hierophany,

An eruption of the sacred,
Which has an effect,
the detachment of a territory from the surrounding cosmic
medium
rendering it qualitatively different.
-Mircea Eliade, *The Sacred and the Profane*

A question often asked, is what makes a site sacred? The earliest sacred sites were natural places, discovered by nomadic tribes and early settlers, who felt certain places to be different, singled out by signs in the landscape, by a sensing of the presence of spirit and divine power, a place where communication with this power was possible. Later these places became sacred grove and tree sanctuaries known as nemeta. Centuries later, the Saxons who introduced the idea of hallowed ground were very clear that hallowed or consecrated ground meant there was a sacred tree growing there and it was the tree that made it a sanctuary, a belief also held in Celtic times.

Nemeta (plural of nemeton) were set aside from everyday life. They were places where natural divine powers were concentrated. 'Primitive groves', as Ken Dowden says in *European Paganism*, 'are a special instance of woods and forests, which are themselves...untamed and dangerous places' and which Lucretius points out are places people tend to avoid due to the presence of wild animals. Ken Dowden says such places are where human control runs out and are something of another world that is old and uncorrupted by time. The Roman writer, Seneca said:

If you come upon a grove which is crowded with ancient trees exceeding their normal height and which stop you seeing the sky because of the shade caused by one branch covering another, the loftiness of the wood, the seclusion of the place and your marvelling at such dense and unbroken shade in an open space, provide you with the conviction (fides) that there is a divine power (numen).

I am sure many of us who love the wildwood agree with Seneca. The word for sacred power, 'numen' from which comes the word 'numinous', is related to nemeton and describes what nemeta were: places of sacred power, which emanated from the land, sky and the sacred tree that linked heaven and earth. Nemeta date back thousands of years and were places of tree veneration, which seems to have followed after the cult of the mother goddess and the hunt.

A nemeton, (a Gallo-Brittonic word) was a sacred space in ancient Celtic religion incorporating a grove, which was remarkably thick, enclosing a spacious circular area, situated on an eminence and open at the top, like a clearing in a dense forest. A sacred tree may have stood in the centre. Later as the sites developed, within the area a single or double line of large stones were sometimes erected for persons of different ranks to stand in, sometimes supporting a line of horizontal stones forming a circle above them, as at Stonehenge. Nemeta were similar in construction to round barrows and Cors, which were also, raised mounds in an enclosure surrounded by a ditch and/ or a fence. These places were often hilltop sites, like the hill forts which afforded views of approaching tribes for miles around. At Old Enton there were two massive 26 - 28 foot girthed yews, on the edge of a mound on a huge hilltop site, similar to a hill fort. Nemeta varied in size from very large to very small and unfortunately, of course, they are usually impossible to recognise today, as the terrain has often completely changed with modern development. Only a few still exist. A nemeton could be an entire forest or a single tree on a mound within a small grove. The hedge, fence or wall, was the boundary that demarcated the sacred from the profane or the edge of one world and the beginning of another, so it is not surprising that all these sacred sites had some or all of these boundary marker features around them. Although it is impossible to say exactly what took place within these places, they were religious meeting places, all similarly constructed.

The word 'grove' normally implies yew, as these were the trees that layered their branches to spread and fill a space with younger yew trees and the groves were said to be silent dark places, consistent with the light obscuring dense branches of yew. It is also possible, that other trees were present too but the sacredness of a tree that defied death and was therefore eternal, cannot be understated. Although originating in the Neolithic Age, many nemeta existed in the Iron Age and in some contexts the word implied a variety of ritual spaces, such as shrines and temples within it. In late Iron Age and Roman Europe, there are references to nemeton sites as the chief tribal gathering sites in districts of Gaul and Asia Minor. 'Nemeta were recorded in the 8th century as the name for pagan shrines in forest groves within a list of superstitions objected to by the church' (Watson, 1926). Watson also says:

> Nemeton place names are thought to be closely linked to locations of pre-Christian religious and elite social significance, which were often perceived as being geographically centrally placed. Such locations exemplify the close link between cult practices and the setting of assemblies in early European society.

Nemeta had their beginnings earlier still, following human occupation after the Ice Age, some 10,000 - 12,000 years ago. Sites were appropriated for their topography or atmosphere which made them special and as with Llanfeugan near Usk in South Wales; these places became sanctuaries and meeting places for spiritual purposes. At this special place, there is a confluence of rivers where streams virtually encircle the site built on a mound, itself encircled by 12 enormous yews and there is a deep drop on one side, making it almost an island. The site's natural rise would have been built up and added to, in order to raise the land further.

Llanfeugan nemeton.

Later, Llanfeugan would have become a nemeton whose mysterious energies are still very much present. Nicolaisen (1997) has highlighted the tendency of river confluences, in particular, to be associated with early religious sites in Scotland but this was the case elsewhere too as places where rivers joined were considered to be places of power. In North East Scotland, early churches are often found at confluence locations and sacred Celtic sites, as we see with Celtic churchyards surviving today, were in general situated next to streams or rivers, water being as sacred to early people as trees and stones.

A good example of a nemeton is the famous yew tree site at Fortingall in Perthshire. Less than a kilometre to the north, positioned on a spur on the north flank of the valley, east of Fortingall lies Duneaves, (from the Gaelic, 'tigh-neimh' meaning 'house of the nemed'), which is also associated with a hill fort. Here is situated the Nemorensis Templum and this suggests that the Fortingall ancient yew was an immensely important sacred tree. This tree would have been connected with the nemeton and here a stone with cup and ring marks was found eight feet down beneath the yew. Also found at Fortingall were four beautiful, ceremonial axe heads, dated between 3800 and 3000 BCE. These stone axeheads were made from Alpine Jadeite and were imported from the Piedmont area, around the Swiss-French-Italian border. Jadeite is a very tough stone that is difficult to work and these axe heads were highly polished and unused, clearly status symbols and not utilitarian tools. Such axeheads were symbols of power and prestige and held religious significance as well. They were often used in gift exchanges and may have arrived in Scotland via the Rhineland. Fortingall was clearly an important early religious site with its yew tree dating back at least 5,000 years. Like Llanfeugan, the distinctive topography of the area means it is likely to have been singled out in ancient times for a place of social and religious significance, which later resulted in it becoming a nemeton. Aerial photography has shown it to have been a ditched enclosure.

The Ankerwycke yew at Runnymede was also most likely a nemeton with a ditch around a mound, a ditch enclosure, now the ruins of a Benedictine convent, where the sacred yew tree, possibly linked to Egypt, stands. It was also an island site and islands were considered especially important and sacred sanctuaries. Ankerwycke is dealt with in detail later in this book. The old name Runemed which encompasses the word 'nemeton' is a possible clue to this but other sites without this word in their name were also nemeta, such as Ashbrittle in Somerset where the ancient yew stands on a huge burial mound, south-east of the church. Linton on the borders between England and Wales, site of a 4,000-year-old yew was also likely to have been a nemeton and many very old yews such as the one at Discoed quite likely marked a nemeton. There was also a nymed or nimed at an unusual place, in Devon, remote by modern standards and forgotten by time called by the strange name of Zeal Monachorum, where there stands an ancient and very unusual looking yew tree. Gradually over time, from about 23,000 years ago, nemeta became Cors, which were a further development of the Druid sites.

The surviving evidence for nemeta, other than the sites themselves consists chiefly of inscriptions and place names, which occur all across the Celtic world. Place names related to the word 'nemeton', occur as far west as Galicia, Spain, as far north as Scotland, and as far east as central Turkey. The word, 'nemeton', is related to the name of the Nemetes tribe who lived by the Rhine between the Palatinate and Lake Constance in what is now Germany, and also to their goddess, Nemetona. Nemetona was the Celtic goddess of sacred groves but is recorded on only a few altars throughout Europe. The only existing altar to her in Britain is Aquae Sulis, Bath. In Britain, other goddesses related to nemeton, include Nemesis, the Greek goddess of retribution, who carries the sacred branch and holds the wheel of Fortune on a statue in The Louvre in Paris. The most famous nemus was that of Diana at Aricia, where the priest held the title of Rex Nemorensis, just as she was sometimes called Diana Nemorensis or Diana of the Groves. The grove lay at the margins of the territory of Aricia, on the northeastern side of modern Lake Nemi, south of Rome. As Ken Dowden says, 'Here is a wonderful pagan sense for a sacred place, the nemus and the lake, the so called 'mirror of Diana''.

The Romans, Pliny and Lucan asserted that Druids did not meet in stone temples or other constructions, but in sacred groves of trees. In his *Pharsalia*, the Roman poet Lucan, gave a dramatic description of such a grove near the Greek colony, Massilia, now Marseilles, France, which might be more poetic than actual: 'no bird nested in the nemeton, nor did any animal lurk nearby; the leaves constantly shivered though no breeze stirred. Altars stood in its midst, and the images of the gods. Every tree was stained with sacrificial blood. The very earth groaned, dead yews revived; unconsumed trees were surrounded with flame, and huge serpents twined around the oaks. The people feared to approach the grove, and even the priest would not walk there at midday or midnight lest he should then meet its divine guardian.'

Such sites have been found all across the Celtic world.

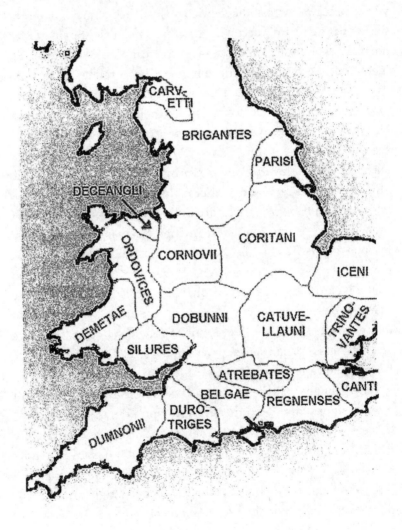

Map of Celtic Tribes of Britain in Roman times.

Attested examples include Nemetobriga near Ourense in North Western Spain, Augustonemeton in the Auvergne, central France, in the ancient lands of the Avernii, Nematacum in the Artois region of northern France, Nemetodurum, at Nanterre north-west of Paris, France, Nemossus south-west of Paris, Noviomagus Nemetum near Heidelberg in West Germany, Drunemeton in Galatia and in Anatolia. Walafried Strabo, the Saxon writer records the name of the meeting-place of the council here, which translates as, 'The Sacred Grove of the Druids', and Medionemeton near the Antonine Wall in Scotland.

At the Romano-British site in Bath, Mars Lucretius (Shining Mars), King of the Sacred Grove and Nemetona appear as a divine couple in Roman-era inscriptions. A nemeton is in the Roman place name, Vernemeton (now Willoughby-on-the-Wolds, Nottinghamshire). In Scotland, nemeton place names are quite frequent as they are in Devon, where they appear in modern names containing Nymet or Nympton and have been identified with the name Nemetostatio in the *Ravenna Cosmography*. Local rivers, in Devon, the Yeo and Mole, were once known as 'Nymet' or 'Nemet' and therefore were themselves named after a nemeton. Coincidentally, Druid's Grove in Surrey is also situated above a River Mole. It is worth noting that the area centred on Bow and North Tawton, have a large number of village names that included the word 'nymet'. The Celtic word 'nimet' translates as 'holy place' and in Ireland 'nemed' meant 'sanctuary', and meant the same thing to the Gauls. This understanding was embraced by the early Church through a process of appropriation. The Latin term, nemus means 'sacred grove'. Iron Age hillforts in some cases are also identified with nemeton, an example of which is Finavon in Angus, Scotland, dated to the 7th and 4th centuries. Finavon was 'Futhynevent' (a name identified with nemeton) in 1370 and was identified by Watson (1926) with old Gaelic 'fidnemed' meaning 'wood sanctuary' and so these sites overlapped in some cases and nemeton may also have overlapped with round barrows.

The evidence for Finavon appears to indicate a pre-Christian sacred-assembly site, perhaps associated with a fortification and judicial assembly. Another hill fort, Merdon Castle, near Winchester which is late Bronze Age/early Iron Age, follows the same pattern being a vast site with deep ditches of at least 50 feet and circular mounds rising above them, which are covered in ancient yews. This site was reused by the Anglo Saxons who established a hall or fort here around 500 CE and then later again by the Normans. Each culture built on the old, developed and remodelled it. Wychbury Hill is a similar place, known as an Iron Age hill fort.

Wychbury Hill Fort. (1)

Wychbury Hill Fort. (2)

A visit to this highly atmospheric, 'weird' place is enough to make your hair stand on end! This site, with its 28-tree ancient yew grove, was not just a hill fort but was probably also a Cor or a religious burial site where ceremony of some kind took place. Seven cairn burials under ancient yews were discovered here by archaeologist Granville Calder. At Corhampton, in Hampshire, a place which was a Cor at one time, there is a yew tree which may have regrown and be much older than first thought. It stands on a pre-Christian mound and it is not always possible to know what a place was in earlier times or how far back it dates. These extraordinary places changed through time and were remodelled to enable different functions. The same places we look at now and label as a hill fort for example may have been something else before, as culture changed but the presence of an ancient sacred yew tree must always indicate a sacred site to do with time, death and eternity.

Nemeta emerged from early gathering sites. Tribal gathering

sites in Europe are thought to have been the main setting for decision making and disputation. Such meetings may also have had a strong cult element and their settings, a religious association. Llangernyw which is one of the most important yew sites in Wales was just such a place. It was the meeting place, the Axis Mundi and the nemeton of the Cernyw, all summed up in the name Llangernyw, 'enclosure of the yew'.

In Saxon times the yew tree was of paramount importance and marked a natural place to meet as it did in Neolithic and Bronze Age times. It also marked such a place for Irish Kings and chiefs. The 'King Yew' in the Forest of Dean, mentioned in the Saxon charters as a meeting place, was called such after the Saxon King Tidenham. Other places such as Braintree and Heavitree were meeting places named after trees and Knowlton Circles, the site of a grove of yews, became a Hundred Court meeting place as many of these places eventually did. Tree meeting places, such as Allestree in Derbyshire, were also known as witangemotes, where council meetings took place. It is important to realise that the sacred tree came first and eventually became a hundred court meeting place, witan or witangemote. A few days before meeting the barons at the yew at Ankerwycke, Runnymede, King John held a meeting under a tree at Merdon Castle near Winchester, where there are many ancient yews. Totteridge and Tandridge, sites of ancient yews, are good examples of places where important decisions to do with the realm took place, witnessed by old and revered yew trees which added solemnity to a meeting and which were originally nemeta. Such meetings and decisions to do with matters of the realm normally only took place at these sacred yew tree sites.

The old Gaelic word 'nemed' is also known to have been used to describe church sanctuaries within an early Christian context, showing something of a continuum. This was a way of aiding a smooth transition from the old religion and in Scotland, nemeton names have been identified in association with several ecclesiastical sites. This strongly suggests the active appropriation of earlier pagan sites that may also have functioned as early meeting places, illustrating the transformation of early cult-assembly sites into centres for Christian worship, community congregation and also burial. (Barrow, 1998).

A well-known nemeton site in Brittany is that in the Nemet Forest near Locronan, Brittany and in the 'Cartulary' of the Abbey at Quimperle in Finistere, reference is made to a wood which is called Nemet (Le Bois de Nemet). Old Celtic beliefs and ideas remain strong in Brittany and the latter is still known as the sacred wood. In modern Breton, the word 'neved', meaning sanctuary, is similar to the one in Welsh – 'nyfed'. Gournay sur Aronde in the Oise department of France also has the remains of a nemeton and echoes of the word 'nemeton', survive in many French place names such as Novionemeton. Nampont for example comes from Nemetodurum meaning door or forum of the temple. In Ireland, there was a chapel Nemed at Armagh and a nemeton has been identified at Matabodes, near Beja, South Portugal. In Britain, nemeton groves are at Lindum in Lincoln, Aquae Arnemetiae, Buxton, Derbyshire, ('The spa town of the sacred groves'), Nemtostatio, North Tawton, Devon, ('The outpost of the sacred groves'), Vernemetum, Willougby, Nottinghamshire, ('The sacred grove of spring') and Medionemeton, ('The central grove), perhaps referring to Barr Hill or Croy Hill on the Antonine Wall in Strathclyde. The Lain word 'nemus' is commonly translated as a grove and was considered to be a sacred enclosure with a sacred tree.

Yews acted as natural shrines. On religious sites, the yew would have been quite ancient during the Roman period and as most old yews are hollow, the space inside would have acted as a shrine where relics and statues of one kind or another were placed as offerings, and the tree itself may have acted as a focus at ceremonies. It was understood that what was brought in to such a place could not be taken out and as time went on, so these objects became precious in a material sense too, as statues were sometimes adorned with gold and silver. Groves were trimmed or cut back only on certain days of the year so that if anyone cut a tree in the grove at any other time, they were known to have violated the grove and a purification offering was then in order. Violation of a grove was also considered to have taken place if the grove was improperly entered or entered outside of certain times and sacred groves were thought to have been polluted if Christians entered them. Dowden says,

> Precisely because groves may not normally be 'violated', it is especially powerful to remove a branch for religious purposes and to use the leaves or trees to form garlands, one of the most important indicators of engagement in a sacred activity.

Divination could be performed with a branch cut from a sacred tree and Dowden says Servius tells us, that in the grove of Nemi, there was a certain tree from which only a newcomer challenging the existing holder of kingship within the grove, could break a branch and that without a sacred branch one may not approach the rites of Persephone. The latter, of course, reminds us of Aeneas who had to present not just a branch but a Golden Bough, torn from a tree in the grove sacred to Juno Inferno, (connected to the 'infernal yew') to Persephone to ensure safe passage through the Underworld. This meant that the grove was especially sacred and the yew here was a special yew tree named after the god Juno. From another point of view, the fact that the grove could not be violated also benefitted those who entered it seeking asylum. Marius found asylum in the grove of Matricia at Minturnae and Gaius

Grechus fled to the grove of Furrina. Feronia was a goddess of groves and was also associated in the 3rd century with slaves and freedom. The idea of asylum or sanctuary to be found between the sacred yew and the church porch was something that carried over into Christian times.

A shrine involving a burial is referred to in *Illustrations of the History of Great Britain Vol. 1* by Richard Thomson, 1828, where he says that as late as 995 CE, during a Danish invasion, 'the brotherhood' were forced to hide their master's bones in the primaeval woods of Durham beneath a shrine made of boughs until they could erect a humble church to hold them. Although such shrines were completely banned by this time, the memory of them lived on and was slow to die out.

Walafried Strabo, who died in 849 CE, writer of *Homily of the Credo*, wrote,

It is therefore clear that the burial mound was yet another focal point for cult practice, not necessarily a substitute for a shrine but possibly a place where some structure would be erected. Any single large tree, growing in proximity to such a site would likewise be held in esteem.

A shrine would not always have involved a construction or anything of a durable nature but it was a place where sacred objects were kept, perhaps in a hollow tree, as stated earlier, where they could be housed, cared for by the priests and ritually displayed to the people who assembled for various seasonal festivals. It is both sad and ironic that nowadays an ancient sacred tree in a churchyard is more likely to be the repository of churchyard rubbish or an oil tank and at Easthope, the irony and connection seem to be completely lost on the congregation, sat in church, facing a rood screen depicting angels guarding the Tree of Life. There are many sacred trees treated in this manner with such disregard and ignorance in Britain and this is a mark of how far we have come from our ancient sacred knowledge and how important it is that we return to it!

Places identified for such sites were later called, 'locus liberatus', a special place felt to be naturally sacred and separated from the profane land, in which a representation of a god might be erected. It is natural for humans to seek their own likeness and see faces in such abstractly patterned things as tree bark, fire and clouds. A tree might appear to have a face or even a whole body, hands and feet. We have all had the experience of seeing a face in a tree. Gradually the divine was personified and became human-looking, being translated into gods and goddesses who were thought to inhabit these sacred places and who were consulted, addressed and prayed to. Sometimes the tree became the residence of a god/dess or such a deity became incarnated as a tree. The Greeks often associated and depicted gods and more often goddesses with trees, something which goes back to Minoan (Bronze Age Cretan) seal stones. The shrine of a god or goddess was described as being located within the grove and so the grove became the grove of a certain god/dess, such as Persephone or Athena. Strabo said Poseidon might be found in his grove and it was in Athena's mysterious grove that Odysseus encountered the goddess just as Aeneas encountered the Sybil in the sacred wood. Groves were sometimes associated with the world of the dead. The grove at Tralleis was, according to Strabo, a grove of Pluto and Persephone where people came for healing and there was a grove of Dis (Hades) and Era (Persephone) at Aquileia. Lucan mentions yew when he depicts the Marseilles grove as a shade inhabited underworld. The grove at Lerna belonged to Demeter and Dionysos where mystery rites concerned with death and the afterlife were offered and where there was said to be an entrance to the underworld. The grove at Kolonos outside Athens housed the shrine of the Semnai, identified as the Furies.

The Divine not only inhabited the grove but could speak. Oracular trees spoke and were understood by listening to and deciphering the rustling of their leaves, which put the spotlight on the tree as a communicating consciousness rather than the god or goddess of the grove. Altis, the grove of Zeus, was such a site where the divinity, whether god or tree, was consulted via the trees. Sometimes pillars made from such talking trees in a grove were said to carry this same oracular power. The Romans told how voices might issue from groves. Cicero said 'Shortly before the capture of the city of Rome by the Gauls (in 390 BCE), a voice was heard from the grove of Vesta ...saying that the walls and gates should be renovated.' Livy reported a 'voice from heaven' announcing the imminent arrival of the Gauls and said that to have a grove was to have heaven nearby. In earlier times before the death of King Tullus, a voice was heard from the grove saying that the Albans should perform their rites according to ancestral ritual.

As the shrine developed, the name given to the area at the shrine entrance was called 'delubrum'. Such an entrance contained a vessel of water for purification. This later developed into the Christian font. It is also possible a delubrum was originally the name for a wooden representation of a god which derived its name from the bark of the tree which was removed before the tree itself was worked into an image of a god. This would all have developed later, centuries after a simple sacred hollow yew without any adornment, stood as the very earliest temple. The process of making a ritual site sacred, whereby it is turned into a deity with a name is well attested to in Hispania where an inscription to Nimmedus Aseddiagus was found in Mieres (Asturias). This name is related to the Celtic word nemeton, the place where communication between the gods or the trees and the humans took place.

In *Technology, Statues, Shrines and Temples*, by Ken Dowden, 2013, the process from the veneration of trees, stones and water to advanced paganism is described and the building of statues and images of gods, 'where the statue becomes the focus and the temple distracts attention from the sacred enclosure', marks the process away from nature. 'In some sense', Dowden explains:

> a paganism with statues and temples was easier to eradicate than a paganism with groves... 'In fact statues develop from and indeed are made from trees and stones, themselves foci of worship.

So, statues personalise religious feeling and take away from a generally diffused, numinal spirit of a natural place. To begin with, statues were little more than a pillar, some just a very roughly carved suggestion of a head but very gradually these things become full-blown ornate, artistic objects, whose origins had begun in the Neolithic and Bronze Age. They were often quite small and portable and were sometimes viewed as offerings and formed the basis of idol worship. Maybe this is what fana idolorum were: a development from a simple unadorned sacred tree to an early shrine with idols, although others think the term simply meant a venerated tree. Shrines in trees and by wells and fountains continued into Celtic Christianity, despite being condemned by the Church and it is not an uncommon thing even today to find such shrines still in parts of Brittany, albeit Christianised but tucked away in the woods sometimes at springs. There is also a most spectacular shrine on view to the public, inside an enormous hollow yew at the Chapelle de Sainte Anne, La Haye de Routot in North West France, providing a direct link between Christianity and Paganism.

Tree Shrine at La Haye de Routot, France.

It would have been at such shrines as the temple of Delphi, that a prophetess or seer would have sat under the yew in an altered state or trance, being aided by the hallucinogenic gas given off on warm nights by the tree and held within the canopy. This would have contributed to a connection between the numinal and the mundane or the personal and the divine, which is what a shrine is all about.

The term 'nemeton' is obviously the basis for ancient place names related to and from, the notion of nemeton, i.e. the concept of the wood as a sacred environment whose mystery conceals and holds the visible presence of the divinity. Eventually, there came a shift to its identification with a temple to a named god that was recorded in text or inscriptions. Eburianus was a deity recorded on a tombstone from Duraton (Segovia), whose name stems from the Celtic Eburos, meaning yew. Other gods and goddesses developed by association with the Yew, or as an expression of it in human terms, were shown carrying yew, or in one case with a tree growing from the god's head, as depicted on a vase from Arcobriga (Monreal de Ariza, Zaragoza).

The groves which formed when a central tree lay down its branches which then grew into other yew trees, went on to inspire the megalithic builders of the Neolithic and Bronze Age to recreate their circles with at first wooden posts and later raised stones. The groves also inspired Gothic architecture, so that to enter many cathedrals and high churches is to feel like entering a forest or grove. For me the epitome of this is at the Abbey of St Gildas de Rhuys on the Rhuys peninsula in Brittany which Gildas founded in the 6th century. There, flat standing stones inscribed with crosses that look more like trees, are raised in a semi-circle in the area behind the altar, in such a way that they are intended to resemble a grove and invoke the feeling of being in one most strongly. Some churches still acknowledge their origins as sacred groves, particularly in Ireland. Irish literature records Cell Iuhbair or Killure, 'Church of the Yew' while at Killeochalle is the 'Church of the yew wood' and in Scotland near the head of Loch Awe in Argyle is Kilneuair, 'The church of the yew tree'. In Wales, there are many Capel Iwans (Yew Chapels) one of which I found was next to the 'Field of the Scholars', an ancient name that suggested it was here that students of the Druids were taught.

The Roman Tacitus who said that Germans did not confine their gods within walls but dedicated trees and groves to them, described the prevalence of grove and tree sanctuaries at the time. After the building of a temple, the sacred tree would have continued to live alongside it and no doubt sanctified the temple itself. The Icelandic and Germanic early round temples are thought to show descent from the tree sanctuary. In Roman times, 'ecclesia eglwys', must have been a barrow whose circular mound still marks the graves of the dead and whereas the tumuli paganorum (an untraceable Latin expression perhaps meaning a particular kind of pagan grave), were repeatedly denounced, no word was said against the stone circle or circus

(Roman for a circular enclosure which became a churchyard.) Neither is there any evidence of a systematic attempt to destroy them. In his book, *The Circle and the Cross,* 1927, Arthur Hadrian Allcroft expands on how the churchyard developed from round or ring barrows which were circular raised grave mounds. In this way, the churchyard's history goes back in an unbroken tradition, to our very beginnings, so that one wonders whether there was simply an instinct in humankind to bury their dead in this way. There was no difference between the barrow and the churchyard, as the word 'barrow' was used on the stone to Padarn's daughter, Rosteece, under the yew at Llanerfyl. From the days of the arrival of the Celtic people in Britain, the dead were buried within the sign of the circle. The circular precincts had held the dead for uncounted centuries before Christianity. Only the consecration was changed. Allcroft says:

> in many cases, one should perhaps rather say that the new consecration was charged upon the old, so that what had been consecrated by the circle, therefore bore also the further symbol of the cross which stood in every Christian burial ground.

Allcroft goes on to say:

> The cross has triumphed and yet abides; the circle has been forgotten, but up and down the country it is still to be found in round barrows of every variety, in stone circles, in Irish killeens and in the graveyards of many hundreds of our village churches... The graves of the Christian and the pagan were precisely the same. Each was a barrow and moreover, each was a round barrow.

He goes on to say:

Anglo Saxons laid their own dead within barrows of every preceding race and every earlier creed, and perhaps most secondary internments are due to this abiding recognition of the sanctity of the ground within the charmed circle.

Even today, barrows and ancient burial sites and mounds are often still found to have ancient yews growing on them.

The height of the churchyard or burial mound was something of a mystery to me as I had always assumed this was to do with the number of bodies piled in there but Allcroft disillusions us of this saying that coffins were not used in ancient times and once the organic matter from a body had decomposed, the bones left of an individual, weighed but 10 pounds. Nevertheless, after centuries of thousands of burials, I would have thought they must have contributed to the height. However, the burial mounds or barrows were deliberately made high by digging out the 'fosse' or ditch, the area around the circle, making a ditch in some cases and using the material dug out to raise the circular site. It is not known why the burial mounds were made so high, often reaching 10 feet but perhaps it was simply to demarcate them and make them stand out in the landscape.

The Germanic term 'harug' and Anglo-Saxon 'hearg', seems to be a comprehensive term for any kind of sanctuary and covers the fanum and frondibus contexta (shrines made from interwoven branches), as well as the groves and assumed the idea of some sort of inviolate enclosure, similar to a nemeton. The Saxon word 'halig', connected with it, means 'holy'. It is worth noting that both Anglo-Saxon heargs and Celtic sacred tree sites, tended to be on higher ground and in Roman literature, a temple simply meant a hollow tree.

At the time of Pope Gregory 1st, (Pope from 590), Paulinus the first Bishop of York, a Roman missionary sent in 601 to Christianise the Anglo-Saxons from their particular form of Paganism, asked the priest (Coitii) who should first profane the altars and fana of the idols together with the fences with which they were surrounded. The priest said he would and according to an early document, didn't delay to immediately approach the fanum (tree shrine) and profane it by throwing the lance he was holding into it. He then set fire to the fanum but this was not entirely Pope Gregory's policy which was that the fanum (also known as templum) should not be destroyed but that people:

> should make themselves huts of the boughs of trees about those churches that have been turned to that use from temples (the fanum or a sacred tree) and celebrate the solemnity with religious feasting.

Although Gregory was most likely thinking of the green booths made from densely interwoven foliage, mentioned in Leviticus, this approach helped provide a smooth and seamless transition from the old religion to the new, which was more likely to be accepted by the people. Pope Gregory, however, seemed to vacillate between a soft approach to the fana and a hard one, imploring the Saxon King Ethelbert in 601 CE to 'attack the cult of idols, demolish the buildings of fana' but it wasn't until 755 CE that it was finally all over, thanks to Wynfrith or as he liked to be known, St. Boniface, who felled the Donar Oak known as Jupiter's Oak.

According to his early biographer, when Boniface started to chop down the oak, a great wind suddenly started up and as if by a miracle blew the ancient oak over and when it was seen that the god had not struck down Boniface and killed him as they all expected, the people were amazed, saw it as a sign and immediately converted to Christianity! Boniface then built a chapel from the wood of the oak, on the site of the great tree, dedicated to Saint Peter. This account from the Vitae, the life of the saint, portrays Boniface as a singular character who acted alone to root out Paganism but in fact it took a great many people to do that and some would say it was never entirely successful. Pagan tree veneration and nature cults proved a hard nut to crack considering it was as early as 350 CE (400 years before) that the Roman emperor had commanded that all Pagan temples be closed and the Goddess Diana, who had ruled supreme for 1,500 years, be finally laid to rest. Today, however, it is impossible to find any trace of the fanum, although some nemeton sites are still recognisable.

John Evelyn gives a good account of booths and temples in his *Sylva*, 1669, in which he quotes from Pliny and other early writers: 'The Feast of Tabernacles had some resemblance to patriarchal devotion under trees in temporary groves and shades in the manner of booths'. From these booths then, some early churches were then developed and constructed from the tree branches that had formed the fana idolorum. Frondibus contexta (interwoven branches), were used to form the first church, as described in *The God Tree*, at Llanarmon Dyffryn Ceiriog and as such formed a bridge between the fanum and the church. The remarkable large yews, one of them monoecious, that enabled this, are still there standing fairly close together. However, the fight to smash the power of the fana was still going on in the late 4th century with Martin of Tours, who was said to have a talent for demolition, destroying large numbers of Gaulish shrines and 150 years later zealots like Caesarius of Arles were almost in a frenzy, to stamp out some of the last vestiges of paganism. The patient words of Pope Gregory were forgotten and instead, violence seemed to be the order of the day. 'Therefore do not allow a fanum to be repaired', Caesarius said, at the end of his tether, but, 'rather, wherever it is, strive to destroy and scatter it. Chop down sacrilegious trees to the roots, pulverise the altars of the devil'! Replacing the old ways with the new didn't happen easily. Caesarius, it seems, had lost all patience, that it all took so long to wash away the lifeblood of the religion of the trees.

In other parts of Europe, similar battles raged. Germans

typically worshipped in groves and archaeologists have found what appear to be specimens of such cult sites in bogs in Thuringis and Northern Germany. Groves were the major centres of religion in the Baltic countries as well as in Denmark. According to the *Chronicles' of Cosmas of Prague* (1045 - 1125), one Christian response to Slav Paganism was to 'burn down with fire, groves of trees which the people worshipped in many places'. The destruction of sacred trees was nothing new. It had gone on for centuries before, usually for one tribe to gain control of another or as part of the Vikings forays to conquer and loot. Only a few centuries later the Christians were doing the same thing as Tacitus says the Romans did in Anglesey, North Wales, where following the defeat of the Druids, their groves on the island were cut down or burnt. However, there is no evidence that there ever were groves in Anglesey. There are very few yews indeed on Anglesey, some around Church Island and some at a small church at Llanidan, named after the 6th - 7th century St Nidan's church on the west side of the island, where there are tumuli nearby. The destruction of groves was more likely to do with false claims and bravado on the part of the Romans who sought to wipe out the Druids and their power bases.

But gradually the fanum (plural for fana), which began as a cell or hollow sacred tree with or without 'idols' kept in them, evolved into early kinds of huts or booths built of twigs, branches and bits of wood built around the sacred tree, in effect a wooden temple with the sacred tree in the centre. Lucus described a fana as a consecrated place, which was often a sacred wood or tree and Jacob Grimm, one of the 19th century German scholars known as the Grimm brothers, famous for their fairy tales, put a Christian twist on this. He wrote, 'It is said of a hollow tree, there are saints in there'. But Christians as we have seen, were not above sometimes axing or setting fire to such venerated trees and in many cases, it is expressly stated, somewhat proudly, that a church was erected on the site of the 'heathen' tree or temple. It was wise for many reasons for the early Christians to appropriate the old sites as the traditional places of assembly, not least because in this way, the people could believe that the old sacredness had not left the place itself, albeit the god to be worshipped there was a new one and the power naturally transferred to him. In this way, the sacred enclosure which had begun with the nemeta became the churchyard. In Welsh, the word 'eglwys' which now means 'church', was a very early name for a burial mound, which later became 'llan' and 'mynwent' but had begun with 'nemus', a sacred enclosure around a sacred tree.

The grove, nemet and nemeton could also refer to a special burial within the enclosure. The Welsh word for a grove of trees was 'llanerch', from which the Welsh/Gaelic word 'llann' or simply 'llan', meaning church or parish is derived. Today at a place in Wales called Llanerchaeron there is a notable old yew in the churchyard. However, this word meaning a wooded enclosure is the modern Welsh form of a word which has fallen out of use, 'nufed', (pronounced 'neev-ed') meaning sacred grove and sounding as if it might have come from the word nemeton was reserved for the most sacred groves. In the Senchus Mor, an ancient code of Irish law, we find the word 'fid-nemed' meaning a sacred grove of trees. Linked with a sacred enclosure and sacred trees are names such as sacrum nemus, de sacris silvatum, Vernemeton (Great fanum). Cultus arborum, frondibus contexta, hearg, harrow, harug and eventually Taxus sanct, Taxus sanctus and Taxus sancti which still exist in Wales, the saints' yews. From all this evolved the words, sanctuary, hallowed, consecrated temple, ecclesia and church. It seems the fana and the nemeta had much in common.

Eventually, as Christianity took hold, crosses were erected at various places, sanctifying a place or marking boundaries much in the same way as boundary marker trees, had once done. Many of the latter were planted in the Saxon era and are still extant in some places as described by Della Hooke FSA in *Trees in Anglo Saxon England,* 2011. It is interesting and significant that the Saxon word for tree and cross was the same, 'Treow', pronounced 'true'. Tree and cross were interchangeable. The word came from 'taru' (Sanskrit, also used in Anatolian) and 'daru' (Latin) and was still being used in early Saxon and late Celtic times. This word also meant 'truth' and 'oath', meaning that a tree didn't lie and also that it was a sentient being that held truth. What is not fully realised is that the modern swearing of an oath takes us back to medieval and ancient times of the Hundred Courts and the witan, where the sacred or holy tree took centre stage at a hallowed site. In modern terms, swearing and laying hands on the Bible is exactly the same as swearing under a sacred tree. The wooden crosses later used for boundary marking or sanctifying, often became part of the name of the place, as in 'Charing Cross'. They were erected in prominent places as reminders of Christianity, or where a tragic accident had occurred, or where spirits or elves were thought to haunt the place but above all, they were set up to consecrate a place of assembly, where there was as yet no church building. Crosses such as these were surrounded by an enclosure and within that enclosure, yew trees would sometimes surround the cross. Such an enclosure with yews was known as a 'lictun', a word related to 'lych gate', or 'corpse gate' and the lictun was a direct descendent of the nemeton. 'Lictun' and 'lych' are words that are involved in the name Lychett Matravers in Dorset, site of a 2,000-year-old magnificent yew tree and we see here that this was the way the tradition and power of the yews were taken into Christianity. Much later, in the 20th century, when the yews had been thoroughly assimilated, the ornithologist William Condry, wrote of a church site called Llanelly, near Usk, where there were originally 18 ancient yews in a circle, 'Nowhere have I felt more strongly that this was the purpose of churchyard yews - as a magic circle, sheltering the dead from the forces of evil'. The circle as well as being for protection would also have been in remembrance of a much older tree.

Llanelly Yew circle.

One by one, the nemeton and sacred tree sites were taken over and Christianised. The people came to the same old sites and ironically in many cases, to the same yew trees they had met at since time immemorial, in just the way Pope Gregory had planned it but now in the centre where there had once been a sacred grove with an open natural space or a sacred tree, a place used for contemplation, prayer, meditation and meeting, there was now a Christian cross with all that it stood for. The hard-won takeover was finally complete but the memory of what once was has never been completely wiped out and still hangs in the atmosphere of the sacred sites, held within the potent silence of the ancient yews who remembered the old times when they were venerated.

Chapter 7

Pre-Christian Yew Sites

The purpose of this chapter is two-fold. First to consider in some depth, some of the places where both the yews and the sites coincide as being undoubtedly pre-Christian and secondly to list others where modern-day archaeological evidence, supports the probable age of the ancient yews found there, as being pre-Christian. Some of these places of ritual and religion were Christianised, others never were. I am aware that many people will say that just because yews that are considered to be over 2,000 years grow on these sites does not prove the age of these trees but taken with other evidence for ageing the yew, it is possible to build a coherent picture as to why these trees were there and why our ancestors sought to share their presence at such places designed for spiritual ceremony. The circumstantial evidence of the co-existence of these prehistoric sites and ancient yews would seem to support the most likely explanation, that these ancient yews were part of the original sites and were planted there in conjunction with the function and purpose of the site. Some yews are obviously not as old as the pre-Christian burial mounds on which they are planted, however, knowledge of the yew tree would have been passed on from generation to generation along with events and history as with the churchwarden at Ashbrittle, in Somerset, whose father, grandfather and great grandfather, passed on such knowledge.

The list of places here is by no means comprehensive, representing the mere tip of the iceberg. Thousands of old and ancient yews have been lost and others lie forgotten under cloaks of ivy and piles of churchyard rubbish or are remembered simply as a good place to store things for the upkeep of the church and graveyard. Until the realisation of the sacredness of the ancient

Llangernyw yew, was restored fairly recently, it was seen simply as somewhere to keep the oil tank.

Ancient Yew of Llangernyw.

As already referred to, at Easthope I came across a fairly common but sad and ironic situation where an ancient yew on the north side of the church, was used to house the lawnmower and various pieces of debris such as stones and planks of wood which were leant against it. The position the yew tree was planted in, on the North side is traditionally where Neolithic plantings are to be found, which could make this ancient-looking tree very old indeed. We must not forget that the eradication of the knowledge of these sacred and ancient trees began with the vehemence with which most early Christian leaders denounced the old religion and ensured that evidence of it, was destroyed. This meant the inscribed stones, idols and altars, along with revered springs, wells, fountains and sacred trees. Even as late as the Victorian era, 'Stonebreaker Robinson', as he was called, prided himself on going around the country with his band of vandals on a Sunday, seeking out and destroying what stones, standing or otherwise were still left by his time. However, it had all started back in 452 CE, where the Edict of Arles had clearly stated 'If any infidel either lighted torches or worshipped trees, fountains or stones or neglected to destroy them, he should be found guilty of sacrilege'.

Pope Gregory's letter specifically stated to Saint Augustine in 597 CE to 'destroy the idols'. Although they may have wanted to, destroying the sacred trees was a step too far. On the whole, the people would not allow the representatives of the new religion to do that and stood in their way but stones and fountains (or Holy Wells) was another matter and meant their wholesale destruction with little left behind today, to witness the fact that there was another religion here before Christianity. Stones were smashed and thrown into rivers, and objects and artefacts systematically removed, buried or destroyed. At least if buried, like the beautiful Tree of Life stone at Broadwell, Gloucestershire, there was the possibility of being retrieved and excavated at a later date and we owe something to those individuals who may have been ordered to break up such beautiful carvings but instead secretly buried them. It is very rare to find any evidence of this previous era. Mass eradication of the old ways was the order of the day across Europe.

The result of this, of course, is that the archaeological evidence for ancient religious sites, where most ancient yews are, is not as easy to find as it might have been if this tide of destruction, the full scale wiping out of a previous culture, had not happened. It means we don't know how many early sites there were but it is undoubtedly far more than has been estimated.

Although sacred yews, some adopted or planted by saints, were left largely untouched in the early days, gradually thousands of these too were destroyed. There would have been yews at all the abbeys. Thirty-nine were cut down at Strata Florida alone. All such places would have had ancient yews from the previous religion. Hill forts and barrows would have been covered in them. There are many yews left at the hill fort known as Merdon Castle near Winchester but there were probably a lot more at one time. Some of these are mentioned by Robert Bevan Jones, in his book

The Ancient Yew, 2002. Sadly, there are many more sites with an ancient yew but no trace of what the site originally was, than there are those which do have such ancient history or archaeological finds. This is very frustrating making it impossible to uncover the reasons why such ancient yews are at these places and leaving us merely to conjecture. One example of this is at Penpont near Brecon, where a double circle of more than 28 yews surround a 27 ft girthed, 3,000-year-old male yew on the east side of the centre. The circle was sadly broken into by the A40 road on the south, shaving off a section of it although it is still an extraordinary site. Many more yews grow in the surrounding woodland, having probably layered from those in the churchyard but there is no information or archaeology to be found to tell us anything of why this remarkable yew site is there.

In North Wales, an ancient yew grows at a chambered cairn near Llangollen called Rhyd-y-glafes. There is a similar place on the hillside above Llanhamlach near Brecon, near a ruined cairn which is close to another more intact across the hill at Manest Court, known as Illtyd's grave, although the site is clearly much earlier than the time of this saint. In all there are three yews in this particular area, on a field boundary which are incalculably ancient indeed, having the appearance of what I would call a white tree, a yew with bleached bark, resembling skeletal remains. There is a noticeable difference in appearance between yews growing in churchyards and those growing on more open or wild sites such as hillsides and fields. The latter seem more compact; often have considerably more roots showing and many adventitious shoots on the trunk, as well as having lower branches, which discourage animals from grazing on them.

It stands to reason that, knowing that the Christian Church took over many of the old religious sites and knowing that yews can live to thousands of years, some yews must have been planted in pre-Christian times. Add to that the evidence of early saints such as Garmon (Germanus) and Augustine who referred to such trees and also our knowledge of the ancient yews at Fortingall and Defynnog and it is clear, that some of the yews surviving today must have been there before the arrival of Christianity. There is also evidence of high ring counts in some of these ancient yews. Richard Mabey in *The Cabaret of Plants*, 2015, points out that Allen Meredith's research led John White, an authority on ancient trees:

> to work out a tentative – though far from definite way - of dating the old trees. It involved a formula relating the density of the rings in the outer wood to their distance from the centre of the tree.

John White said:

> It is not a calculation for amateurs...but it seemed to work quite well when tested on trees whose age was known from documentary records. When it was applied to more ancient specimens, it suggested that Meredith's informed guesses were roughly right. The big trees' ages were more like 2,500 to 3,500 years, rather than 5,000 but it still meant they were older than the churches, sometimes by a huge margin.

The evidence for Pre-Christian yew sites is overwhelming. There are several places in Britain where ancient yews exist on, or alongside, places of ancient historical and archaeological importance. Some of these places such as Knowlton Circles and Fountains Abbey are scheduled monuments. Richard Mabey says:

> Allen Meredith visited almost all the surviving ancient yew trees, measured them and looked deeply into the historical archives. Yew trees were sacred to early people as the tree that didn't die and their evergreen foliage was seen as evidence of this, along with its continued existence, which was witnessed down the generations and knowledge of it passed

on, as at Ashbrittle. The Christian Church appropriating the Yew sites, the centres of spiritual power, also adopted the yews as symbols of eternal life.

We know that some of the early church sites were used in ancient times, whether for ritualistic purposes or community meetings, because of the presence of standing stones, early Saxon, Roman and pre-Roman remains and artefacts. Sarcophagi, Roman altars, Sarsen stones, Ogham stones and human remains, have all been found at these places. It is well known that pre-Christian people revered yew trees, as seen from ancient stone and wood carvings. Yew trees were sacred trees, long connected with the dead and with burial grounds, where yews were the keepers of graveyards and protectors of the dead.

Hadrian Allcroft describes the development of graveyards, in *The Circle and the Cross,* in an important statement that serves to fill the gaps in our understanding of such places:

The word 'Llan' means a clearing, a level space. There is no suggestion of a church originally, or of a building. It was the area where the founder desired to settle and was later consecrated by a burial. To all appearance, the Welsh Llan is a copy of the Irish monastic settlement and cannot have been introduced into Wales much before the year 500 CE. Before that date, the Christian place of meeting was not 'Llan' but 'Eglwys', a barrow (in modern Welsh it now means 'church'). Early Welsh Christianity adopted the circular form of the pagan burial place and many of the churchyards are the actual barrows of the familiar type. In these times a barrow was raised over an important grave, this grave was the 'mynwent', around which the lesser folk were buried. It was to them a sacred place and when a Christian church was built, later on, it became a Christian graveyard. In the early days of Christianity, the church was not built and the circular mound was everything, a place of burial and worship. There is a persistent tradition that the churchyard at Llanfihangel Nant Melan was made within the stone circle, the garth is still circular, though the stones have gone. (At least one is still there.)

Allcroft goes on to say the Romano-British Christians of the third and fourth centuries, as a rule, had no church at all but were:

> meeting places only... the ecclesiae of pre-Constantine Christianity in Britain must have been barrows not buildings and the meaning of eglwys at any time between the second and the fifth centuries... must have been simply this... Some have supposed that such churches had been by accident built over a forgotten grave or graves. Some have hinted at consecration – burials. Others have seen in such cases a deliberate usurpation by Christianity of a site known to be pagan... the early churches were 'barrows' pure and simple!

Allcroft says that all churches within original circular churchyards are barrows:

> We know from excavation and from documentary evidence like the Capitularies, that Christians long continued to lay their dead within barrows of pagan origin so that a pagan barrow might in time come to be hallowed as a Christian churchyard. These were 'ecclesiae' in the sense of places of meeting but they were places of burial only. They were Christian barrows.

It seems to be a natural instinct, for humans to bury their dead in circular mounds, and to gather them all in one marked place and when these places were Christianised, the yew trees that existed there along with the bones of the ancient people were simply passed on to the new custodians of these sacred sites.

Rev. Stedman Davies in *Yew trees in Churchyards*, 1945, describes the meaning of yews growing in churchyards:

A visitor to Llanyre, Cascob and Llansantfraed yn Elwel will notice yews growing on mounds and especially at Llanfihangel Nant Melan, where seven out of ten hollow trees stand on a slight mound. These remind us of the pre-Christian custom of erecting a mound over a grave, and when found in a circular churchyard, as at Llanyre, we have a double reminder of a burial within a circular enclosure which was so sacred to the early Celts and a place of meeting for the community, who, on becoming Christians, built a church of wattle and mortar within its confines, thus handing it down to us through the centuries.

At Llansantffraid yn Elwell, excavation in 1910 found foundations of a rough wall and the site of the original church and the ground itself was found to be a circular ring barrow. It is interesting that modern man, breaking with the tradition of millennia, tends to do things in straight lines, including graveyards. Stedman Davies also says:

The last indicator of early Christian origins and the most widespread and familiar signs are the names of the Celtic saints to whom most of the churches on the most ancient sites are dedicated. Based on this factor, the name of Sant Ffraid (Welsh equivalent of St. Bride) would indicate antiquity because it echoes the pagan goddess Bride or Brigantia. There are numerous dedications to this saint associated with the pre-Christian era as at St. Bride's Super Ely and many churches in Wales dedicated to Sant Ffraid (another of her names in Welsh). Although most early sites are found on hilltops, it is interesting that many of those associated with Brigid or Bride are by water in the form of rivers and Holy Wells which were considered associated with Brigid and ruled by the feminine, as with the reflective moon considered to be feminine, which controlled tides and moved water.

Stedman Davies goes on to say:

> To summarise, factors that indicate age include a circular churchyard, a churchyard older than the church itself, a church high on a hill or by a river, the presence of ancient yew trees and a saint associated with the pre-Christian era.

Sites connected with St. Bride, which are also connected with indications of ancient religious activity such as tumuli, early graves, Holy Wells and yew trees growing on mounds are as follows. These sites have yews that are old (over a thousand years) but not ancient, except for Llansantffraid Juxta Usk and possibly St. Brides Super Ely which are older.

Llansantffraed-yn-Elwel, Powys. An almost complete circle of 10 old yews (largest on a pronounced mound) surrounds the church.

Llansantffraid Glan Conway, Conwy. Holy Well. One old yew.

Llansantffraid Juxta Usk, Powys. One ancient yew.

Llansantfraid ym Mechain, Powys. Two old yews.

St. Brides Super Ely, Glamorgan. Connected with St. Brigid. In 1040 she was still called by her Pagan name Brigid rather than her Christianised name St. Bride. She came to Wales from Kildare in 488 CE and is associated with a crozier or staff. There is an old yew on a mound here. Stedman Davies emphasises that:

> The last indicator of early Christian origins and the most

widespread and familiar sign, are the names of the Celtic saints to whom most of the churches on the most ancient sites are dedicated.

One of the things we know of these early times is that water, standing stones and trees were all held sacred by the Celts and these things were linked together and often found on the same site. Places where there are, or were, dedicated Holy Wells, often had a female yew planted with them. Sadly, few of these are left today. A single yew often stood over a Holy Well as it still does at Hope Bagot, Shropshire, Ffynon Bedr, Conwy and Gwenlais, Carmarthenshire.

Hope Bagot Yew over Holy Well.

The latter also has standing stones but hundreds of sites like these have been lost, many of them lost between the wars. They are an excellent place for archaeological investigation, which can also date how long a site has been used, from found objects. The tradition of offering a bent pin to a well when asking for healing can be traced to Iron Age and Romano British tradition and such pins are often found at Holy Wells. I remember such a thing being found in the Gwenlais well when it was cleaned out. Francis Jones the authority on this subject explains their importance in his book, *The Holy Wells of Wales*, 1954, writing that, 'The wells indicate where the sacred sites of our pagan and Christian forbears were.'

Circles of yews are also part of an early Celtic/Druidic tradition. Bevan Jones says in *The Ancient Yew:*,

There are perhaps 25 examples of yew circles, intact or fragmented, to be found today in isolated sites around Wales... Wales has a unique tradition of yew circles occurring in circular churchyards of great antiquity.

Circles of yews such as those at Llanspiddyd, near Brecon, Llanelly, Llanfeugan, Llanfihangel Nant Melan and Llansantffraid-yn-Elfael in Powys, Overton on Dee, near Wrexham and a remnant of one at Shropshire in Ashford Carbonel, are references back to the ancient yew groves and henges. Yew circles are also to be found at Llanycil and Llanddwywe, Gwynedd and Cwmdu church near Llanbedr Ystrad Yw, as well as at the church of that name in Monmouthshire.

Ancient place names such as Dinefwr (Kingdom of Yews), are an indication of how important yews were. In Brittany, sadly there are innumerable places with a reference to yews in the name, where there are no longer any traces of these trees and in Britain, there are many references to yews and yew place names in the Anglo-Saxon Charters. The Saxons recorded certain trees, normally oak and yew, as boundary markers. These trees were not normally planted as such but would already have been there, like the ancient yew at Bodcott Farm, Moccas in Hereford, poised on a bank over an ancient track.

Bodcott Farm Yew, Herefordshire. Anglo-Saxon boundary marker tree on old track.

An Anglo-Saxon Charter mentions a yew at Barnhorne. The place is on a boundary called 'Iwedise' - 'iw', meaning yew (iw) and cultivation - perhaps a field. At Coldwaltham, in West Sussex, the exceptional yew there is recorded as a large tree in Saxon times.

Coldwaltham Yew.

At Tidenham in Gloucester, a yew valley is referred to, At Stoke Bishop, a Yew combe, in Havant, Hampshire, there is 'Yew dwellers' hedge', at Hannington, Hampshire we find 'ywyrstac stigel', meaning Yewhurst stile or gate and at Michelmersh, Hants, another yew feature is mentioned. At Upton on Severn in Worcester, a yew ridge is referred to and at Martyr Worthy, Hampshire, Itchen Abbas, 'iwigath' may mean Yew Farm. A very old boundary yew is recorded here. The 3rd Charter of 939 CE refers to what is probably the same yew, still standing at Itchen Abbas. These are just a few examples. Apart from the Saxon Charters, which did not name all boundary yews, evidence of yews is found in old Saxon Chronicles. In particular, many Sussex place names contain evidence of there having been yews.

The Churchill Yew in Worcester was recorded in *King's Roll* in 1086 and the ancient yew at Hoo St. Werburgh in Kent was recorded in 738 under a document called *Sancta Werburgh de Hou*. The yew was known in Saxon as 'Derewolds Treow'. 'Treow' as stated earlier is the word for both tree and truth. This tree was burnt out but has resurrected and is alive again.

At some places such as Uppington and Gresford, Roman altar stones found

Uppington. Roman altar stone near ancient Yew.

151

with or close to the ancient yews, are, of course, suggestive of these trees being considered important and sacred in earlier times.

Robert Bevan Jones, points out there are five known churchyard sites with Roman altars and yews of 25 feet and more in girth, including two in Hampshire and two in Shropshire. As Richard Morris says in *Churches in the Landscape*, 1989:

> Roman altars and chunks of religious sculpture have been found in and around a considerable number of churches... together with churches like Silchester, Lullingstone and Kirby Underdale, which stand upon or close to the sites of Roman(o-Celtic) temples.

Prehistoric stones with inscribed rings or spirals are sometimes found in Britain. Two such inscribed stones of the spiral and the yew are in the porch at Llanafan Fawr in Powys. This site is very ancient and known to have been a barrow with the yew tree there, planted 3,000 - 4,000 years ago. Artefacts such as these are rare survivors of the mass destruction and sweeping away of evidence, of an earlier religious period.

The following is a list of ancient yew sites which have been established by archaeologists to be Saxon, Roman, Iron and Bronze Age. There are a great many archaeological finds made at other churchyards and religious sites where ancient yews once stood but are now lost, but there are still those where ancient yews survive as living evidence. Of these Knowlton Circles, is an important example of a site where scientific examination has proved the yews of Knowlton Henge to be undoubtedly ancient. Sadly, there are countless lost ancient yews on pre-Christian sites, such as that at Argoes Fawr in Tregaron, where a large megalith still stands but the large ancient yew that 'cast its shadow', has gone as have those on the Bronze Age elevated site at Meidrim's church of St. David in Carmarthenshire. Unless the law is changed, those ancient yews that are left on these ancient sites are in grave danger of not surviving too. Detailed chapters will be found later in this book on Ankerwycke and Fortingall. Defynnog was dealt with in *The God Tree*, and you will find a detailed description of some other important sites at the end of this chapter. What follows here is a general list of sites.

Pre-Christian sites with ancient yews and archaeological evidence of antiquity.

Wales

Caerhun, St. Mary's Church, Conwy. Ancient yews on Roman fortress complex.

Defynnog, St. Cynog's Church, Brecon. Celtic/Roman incised tombstone from c.5th century with Ogham letters, in porch. Another stone known as the Defynnog or Llwyel stone with Celtic sculpturing, Roman writing and cup and ring mark, now in British Museum known as the Defynnog or Llwyel stone, was found in the area. Viking font with a runic inscription. Nearby Iron Age hillfort. Roman doorway in the back wall of the church. Neolithic implement found near Defynog Farm, now in National Museum Cardiff. Exceptional 5,000-year-old ancient yew, north, in two parts, a female with a male branch.

Discoed, St. Michael's Church, Powys. Old stone set in the churchyard wall. Well near the yew tree. Nearby is 8th century Offa's dyke. Adjacent round barrow. 5.000-year-old 27 ft girth yew, on a raised hilltop mound.

Gwytherin, St. Winifred's Church, Clwyd. Bronze Age site. Four standing stones in a line on the north side between two ancient yew trees. Celtic cross-slab. Burial mound adjacent. Two ancient yews one east, one west.

Llanarmon Dyffryn Ceiriog, St. Garmon's Church, Denbighshire.
Churchyard was originally more curvilinear. Large Bronze Age
mound or tumulus at the west end of the churchyard, known as,
'Tomen Garmon' with an unmarked stone slab on top. Site of the
first church, known as Frondibus Contexta (woven together yew
branches). (see *The God Tree*) Two ancient yews one male, one
female, grow close together on the south side.

Llanafan Fawr, St. Afan's Church, Powys. Iron Age site, church
on a mound. 3 pre-Christian carved sacred stones, cemented in
porch. Left of the altar is a single pillar stone incised with a Latin
ring cross dating from the 7th century. The ancient yew is on the
east of the churchyard suggesting a Celtic planting and marking
the end of the long mound on which the church is built.

Llanbedr Ystradyw, St. Peter's Church, Breconshire. Said by
archaeologists to be an authentic example of a raised churchyard.
An ancient settlement known in Roman times, the name meaning
'St. Peter's church in the Valley of the Yew'. Two standing stones,
Cup and ring marks on foundation stones of the Celtic church
remains on the east side of the church. Ancient, massive hollow
yew on the north side. Two others on the south-east.

Llandre, St, Michael's Church, Ceredigion. Holy Well. Iron Age
hillfort nearby. Ancient yew on north-east grows on a mound in
three separated fragments.

Llandysilio, St Tysilio Church, Powys. Circular enclosure.
Standing stone incorporated into the altar of St. Tysilio.
Elsewhere barrows are enclosed in the precinct of the church.
Ancient yew north-west.

Llanfaredd, St. Mary's Church, Powys. Circular churchyard. Tumuli and spring nearby. Ancient yews west and east.

Llanfeugan, St Meugan's Church near Usk, Powys. Possible nemeton, natural landscape features likely to have lent themselves to a raised barrow, Ancient yew grove.

Llanfihangel Nant Melan, St. Michael's Church, Powys. Prehistoric site. The site is a raised mound or tumulus. Stone circle. Several ancient yews.

Llangeitho, (Pant y Beudy), Ceredigion. Roman camp. Prehistoric cist. Ancient yew on the boundary between the ruin of Pant y Beudy and the field to the South named Caer Ywen (Field of the Yew).

Llangernyw, St. Digain's Church, Conwy. Standing stones. 5,000-year-old yew north.

Llanilid, St. Ilid's Church, Mid Glamorgan. Roman stone. Lead coffins found and reburied. The pre-Christian Cor site is still extant. Ancient yew, south-south-east.

Llansantffraid yn elvel, St. Bride's Church, Radnorshire. An almost complete circle of 14 yews arranged concentrically within a larger curvilinear enclosure.

Llantrithyd, St. Illtyd's Church, Glamorgan. Close to Prehistoric enclosure and Iron Age hill fort. Ancient yew.

Llanwrthwl, St. Gwrthwl's Church, Powys. Pre-Christian massive standing stone. Circular churchyard. Old yew north and another west on a mound.

Llanwrthwl standing stone.

Llanyre, St. Llyr's Church, Powys. Circular raised burial mound known to have been a barrow. Spring or well some 200 yds away. Nine old yews, on edge of the mound, largest north-north-east.

Maesymynis, Old Church near Builth, Powys. Celtic cross once stood here, now in National Museum of Wales, Cardiff. One of the oldest churches in the county. Ancient yew north.

Manest Court, Llanhamlach, Powys. Remains of a kistvaen or cromlech under an aged yew tree and surrounded with stones from a dispersed cairn consisting of three upright stones, two forming the sides, about five feet in length and one at the end, about three feet wide, the whole height not exceeding three feet from the ground. The site normally designated Ty Illtyd. Two other ancient yews within a mile on this hillside, all impossible to measure due to fencing and low branches, appear to be part of a complex ancient site with many large stones resembling those from a cist, strewn along an old track leading to a dismantled cairn.

Pennant Melangell, St. Melangell's Church, Llangynog, Powys.
Roman stone. Middle Bronze Age site. Excavations in the late
1980s discovered prehistoric remains and Bronze Age burials,
Bronze Age pottery. Evidence of early cremations going back
over 3,000 years. Archaeologists also examined small stones
used by Celts in burial rituals. The site was a cemetery from 1500
BCE. Roman stone with markings found near one of the yews.
Holy Well nearby. Prehistoric charcoal filled pits. Prehistoric pit,
hearth and copper-alloy slag found. Ancient yews.

Rhulen, St David's Church, Powys. Bronze Age burial mound.
Circular churchyard. five large yews on the edge of the mound.
Ancient yew with three stems on a mound, north-east. Ancient
yew south-south-east.

Rhydyglafes near Llandrillo, Denbighshire. Chambered cairn
also Roman camp close by (250 metres away). Old yew grows in
a field next to a stone-built ruin.

Silian, St. Sulien's Church near Tregaron, Ceredigion. Possible
three pre-Christian stones. One ancient yew, with three stems,
on a mound.

St. Brides Super Ely. Holy Well. Old yew on a mound.

England

Alderley, St. Nether's Church, Cheshire. Altar stone/standing
stone incorporated into the altar of St. Nether. Ancient yew.

Alton Priors, Wiltshire. Church surrounded by barrows. Well,
Sarsen stones. Ancient split yew south.

Ankerwycke, Runnymede, near Staines. Raised Bronze Age

burial mound. Site of Magna Carta. Ancient yew.

Ashbrittle, Church of St. John the Baptist, Somerset. Pre-Christian mound. Yew growing on top of a Bronze Age Bowl barrow. Exceptional ancient yew south-east.

Ashtead, Surrey. Double trunked old yew west-south-west on earthworks.

Broadwell, St Peter and St Paul's Church, Gloucestershire. Pre-Christian Tree of Life stone found. Holy Well. Old yew.

Chepstow, Gloucester. Roman remains. Ancient yew north-east.

Claverley, All Saints Church, Shropshire. Roman finds. Two fonts, one Saxon or Pre Norman. Ancient yew.

Clun, St. George's Church, Shropshire. The settlement of Clun dates from the Early Neolithic period. Numbers of flint weapons found. Raised churchyard/ burial mound. Ancient yew.

Broadwell Tree of Life stone.

Coldwaltham, St Giles' Church, West Sussex. Saxon font. Exceptional ancient yew.

Compton Dando, St. Mary's Church, Somerset. Private woodland. Historic site. Roman altar. Ancient yew.

Corhampton, Saxon Church, Hampshire. Roman sarcophagus under the yew tree. Church built on a mound with a ditch. Old yew south-east.

Corhampton Yew.

Cradley, St. James the Great's Church, Herefordshire. Saxon stone in the tower. Ancient yew on the east.

Darley Dale, St Helen's Church, Derbyshire. Roman burial urn. Decorated Saxon grave slabs. Exceptional ancient yew south-south-west.

Duck's Nest Tump, Dorset. Long barrow. Ancient shattered yew with six stems on the long barrow, strange shape.

Kennington, St, Mary's Church, Kent. Burial mound opposite the church. 35 ft exceptional ancient female yew south-west. Another fragment of yew next to it may be split away from this same tree. Three other old yews.

King Yew, Eastwood, Forest of Dean. Boundary marker ancient yew mentioned in Saxon Charter.

Kingley Vale, Chichester, West Sussex. National Nature Reserve and SSSI site. Remains of a Romano-Celtic temple at Bow Hill. Iron Age settlement site known as Goosehill Camp, the Devil's Humps. Bronze Age round barrows and flint mines. There are also several unidentified archaeological remains in the form of linear earthworks, a rectangular enclosure known as Bow Hill Camp and evidence of settlement at the base of the hill. Ancient prehistoric yews.

Knowlton Circles, Dorset. Church in a Henge monument (circular earthwork of religious significance dating to around 2500 BCE) Part of a complex of henges in this area. Seven ancient yews still standing around henge perimeter.

Linton, St. Mary's Church, Herefordshire. Neolithic settlement. Yew stands on a Neolithic burial mound. Ancient remarkable 30 ft yew.

Long Sutton, All Saints Church, Hampshire. Sarsen stone. Site adjacent to 5000-year-old Harrow Way. Ancient yew.

Loughton churchyard, Shropshire. At old church, area of a Roman settlement. Site of Roman occupation. Ware found. Archaeologists say this is a pre-Christian site. Exceptional 3,000-year-old 33 ft ancient yew east.

Middleton Scriven, opposite St. John's Church, Shropshire.

Roman and Anglo-Saxon settlement. Two ancient yews known as 'The Twins' one male, one female in field opposite church. Roman artefacts found in a field near yews.

Old Enton, Godalming, Surrey. Possible Iron Age hill fort. Two ancient yews on edge of hill fort mound.

Peterchurch, St Peter's Church, Herefordshire. A tall standing stone behind the church. Church houses a Saxon stone altar. Originally two yews here ('of immense girth' - Samuel Bagshaw 1851) one exceptional yew remaining 30 ft girth north.

Peterchurch standing stone.

Sandhurst, St Michael and All Angels Church, Oxford. Sarsen stone. Ancient yew in three fragments west.

Snoddington Manor, Hampshire. Burial mounds in area of ancient hollow yew in a field with an internal stem. Exceptional.

South Moreton, St John's Church, Oxford. Ancient burial mound nearby. Ancient yew east.

Stanford Bishop, St James' Church, Herefordshire. Menhir stone in the church wall. Ancient yew north-west.

Tangley, St Thomas of Canterbury's Church, Hampshire. Three small Sarsen stones in the churchyard. Old yew.

Totteridge, St Andrews Church, St. Albans, Hertfordshire. Fort site, Hundred Court meeting place. Ancient yew west.

Tredunnoch, Monmouthshire. Roman stone on the north wall in the nave of the church is a tombstone memorial found three feet down in the churchyard to a Second Augustan Legion soldier. Ancient yew.

Uppington, Holy Trinity Church, Shropshire. Roman altar found by sexton digging a grave near roots of the yew tree. Two Corinthian capitals. Site of Romano British enclosure. Saxon tympanum in church. Exceptional female ancient yew with a male branch.

Wychbury Hill Fort, Hagley, Stourbridge. Ring barrow/hill fort/ ancient burial ground. Seven cairn burials under ancient yews.

West Tisted, Hampshire. Archaeological remains on the estate. Round barrow cemetery of probable Bronze Age date (2000 - 700 BCE) nearby. Ancient yew recorded by Saxon charter.

Winchester, Merdon Castle, Hursley, Hampshire. Iron Age hill fort. Norman castle. Hundred Court meeting place. Several ancient yews. Oldest by the entrance.

Winchester Stubbs Copse, Michaelchurch, Hampshire. Boundary yew recorded in the Saxon charter as 'olde yew'.

Zeal Monachorum, Church of St, Peter, Devon. Possible nemeton. Anciently named Sele Monachorum. The latter part of its name due to its being long held by the monastery of Buckfast, to which it was given by King Canute. Ancient yew south.

Zeal Monachorum Yew.

Scotland

Fortingall, Coeddi, Bishop of Iona's Church, near Aberfeldy, Glen Lyon, Perthshire. Important, well documented, ancient site. 5,000-year-old ancient yew, male with female branch north.

Ceremonial axe head, cup and ring marked stone. Exceptional. See later detailed chapter.

Ancient yews were also a feature of barrows, often planted on them as at Wychbury Hill Fort, near Hagley, Kidderminster. Barrows have often been recorded as having large old yews on them and often these yews are old rather than ancient, begging the question as to where they may have come from and who planted them. But this is often down to the process of layering. Sometimes an ancient yew (or yews) still stands on these sites as at Merdon Castle, while others around it are younger.

Merdon Castle was an Iron Age hill fort that had continuing use as a Norman castle and Hundred Court meeting place. The oldest yew is by the entrance at 24 ft 6". At 'Manaur Trumur' near the Wye, in Monmouthshire, there is 'cumuleu iriuenn' - 'yew barrow'. It claims the date of 625.

It is worth quoting Robert Bevan Jones at this point, on barrows and hill forts from his book called *The Ancient Yew:*,

> Situated close to the River Wey, 200 yards south of Bramshort Court, is a mound 46 ft (14 m) in diameter, five and a half feet (1.7 m) high with no ditch, that is known locally as 'Druid's mound' and is surmounted by old yew trees.

Danebury Hillfort still has some large yews, which were referred to by Freeman-Williams as 'old yews on banks at Danebury'. Also, in Hampshire in the New Forest, is Denny Lodge, by the River Beaulieu, is Yew Tree Heath, with six bowl barrows and a bell barrow. One barrow, 85 ft (26m) by eight feet high is mutilated by a giant central crater. Large craters are often the places where large trees have been removed, by early antiquaries or looters who opened the barrows. The site may bear comparison to barrows found at Yew Down in Oxfordshire. Hampshire's largest yews are of great interest, as their longevity means that some of the five Hampshire Anglo Saxon charter yews may still exist.

Some of the most convincing evidence of all, of the importance of the yew to early people, making it obvious they would have planted them on the barrows, are the graves themselves. In 1930, A S Newall excavated a round barrow in Amesbury, Wiltshire and found a grave lined with yew wood and leaves. This was the primary burial within the barrow and was thought to be probably that of a chieftain and dated as Bronze Age at 1700 - 1300 BCE. It evidenced the importance of yew in pre-Christian burial ritual in Britain. We also have evidence of the importance of yew in ritual and belief systems from well-documented artefacts from the Bronze Age period through to Roman times with such objects as the five late Bronze Age figures from Roos Carr in Humberside, the Ralaghan figure and the Llanio head, all made of yew wood. Handling such objects would put the person into direct contact with immortality. With the understanding of the yew's connection with eternity, it would be strange if yew trees were *not* to be found planted on early graves and barrows! Such places are also likely to have been connected with sacred groves and would altogether be part and parcel of the belief system held by the yew tribes to be discussed shortly. We also need to bear in mind the continuity of early burial sites becoming churchyards as at Meidrim, St. David's church, Carmarthenshire, a Bronze Age burial mound whose ancient yews have only fairly recently been cut down. Breaking that long tradition with the deep and distant past is a sad process born of ignorance.

Reverend Elias Owen in *Old Stone Crosses* says 'That Christians appropriated sites and objects venerated by pagans, is indisputable. In many countries, this was the case'. He quotes a passage from *Ogham inscribed monuments of the Gaedael* by Richard Rolt Brash:

That stones inscribed with Ogham characters should have been found on sites hallowed by Christianity is only reasonable to expect and it is well known that many of our early churches were erected on sites professedly pagan; and that these inscribed memorials found on the spot should have been used as headstones to the graves of Christians sanctified by the addition of the cross, is consistent with probability and the practice of primitive Christianity.

Taliesin Williams in his pre-1923 book *The Doom of Colyn Dolphyn*, largely a poem, writes:

> The Christian Churches in this kingdom were founded either on the sites of Druidic Temples... Llanilid and Llangewydd in Glamorganshire among many others are corroborative instances. At Llanilid the old Druidic oratory (Gwyddfa) still remains, nearly perfect... at Llangewydd... two large stones, apparently the remains of a cromlech, before Christianity, yet stand there. (The Gwyddfa is the Cor).

The following is a more detailed look at some of these places which have ancient yews.

Fountains Abbey, North Yorkshire.

Fountains Abbey, previously a religious site is a World Heritage Site and Grade 1 listed building, owned by the National Trust and maintained by English Heritage. One of the best-preserved Cistercian monasteries, it was founded in 1132. The yews here were mentioned by Lowe as being of 'incredible size'. In 1758 there were seven of them on the South side of the Abbey. Now there are only two set in an enclosure on the West of the Abbey, one female of 22 feet. The Abbey building itself would have been built near the existing yews which were probably saved from demolition by the monks living under them until the Abbey was built. Remnants of yews sit on an earthwork called Kitchen Bank, south of the Abbey along with younger yews. A large piece of an ornamental Anglo-Saxon cross was found at the site but any other evidence of its history was swept away.

Sadly, of 500 or so Abbey sites in Britain, only a few still have yews. At one time they all would have had yews but such is the extent of the destruction of these trees that we must take action before any more are lost.

Gwytherin, Conwy.

Gwytherin Yew and standing stones.

Gwytherin is an ancient site dating back to as early as the Bronze Age and was the home of the Welsh St Winifred. It is debatable whether the churchyard is circular or rectilinear, but it is built on a barrow which may also be a spur and the ground drops sharply away to the north and east above the valley of the Cledwen, the church occupying the highest point in the enclosure. On the south side of the church, the ground drops down into a natural hollow before rising to another knoll. This hollow lies within the churchyard but it is not clear whether this is a later intake - the scarp slope may represent an earlier boundary and could be natural. Nearby there are other significant mounds. Gwytherin has a sense of being a special location with the mound being the highest part of the village and the ground behind the stones dropping down dramatically into an adjoining stream.

In the churchyard of this ancient site stand a row of four small stones aligned east-west. They stand about three metres apart from each other and one bears a Latin inscription of a style dated to the 5th or 6th century CE. Some authors believe the stones to have been erected in this early Christian period but they are much more likely to be ancient in origin with the inscription being the re-use of a Bronze Age row of stones as a personal Roman memorial. This is, of course, a process that commonly happened as different cultures took over older sites and made them their own. The stones, however, must have held a great deal of power and were probably a meeting place and a place of ritual for the local population. As such they would have been a source of concern for the early Christian missionaries who occasionally, though rarely, found it more prudent to keep them and Christianise them to diffuse some of this power without alienating the locals. The site was 'Christianised' by the founding of a church - St. Eleni. There is some debate as to whether this inscription could mark the grave of St. Winifred who lived here and was connected with this site but the inscription is Roman, dated to the 5th or 6th century and is inscribed with: 'VINNEMAGLI FILI / SENEMAGLI' meaning 'of Vinnemaglus, son of Senemaglus'. The lettering can be read as 'Winne' giving rise to the idea that it meant St. Winifred! (originally Gwenfrewi) who was the Abbess of a convent here in the 7th century and some thought this the site of her original tomb. It is also possible that the Latin carving was placed over an earlier Ogham inscription to obliterate it.

There is a one metre high scarp around the south side of the church which curves slightly as it runs around the east side. This may indicate a former boundary though it could be largely natural. At the east end of the site, the church occupies a levelled platform.

There are two ancient yews here both female of similar girth. One with a 29 ft girth on the west and the other with a 28 ft 8" girth on the east.

Knowlton Circles, Dorset.

One of the oldest sites of ancient yews is Knowlton Henge or Knowlton Circles in Dorset where barrows and ring ditches survive within a one-mile radius, the most important being the Great Barrow, the largest barrow in the county. Henges were ceremonial sites. There are nearly a hundred in Britain dating from around 2,000 - 3,000 BCE. The main earthwork at Knowlton is a henge dating from this period. There are three other main earthworks nearby: the northern circle, the old churchyard and the southern circle. Associated with this group of henges is one of the greatest concentrations of round barrows or burial mounds in Dorset, numbering at least 35. There is a high number and diversity of prehistoric and later archaeological remains in this area. Two large stones were ploughed out of the southern henge. One bears a design of four concentric circles. A standing stone was also found on site. There were at least eight ancient yews in a line here leading to the henge. Six yews remain. One male yew, in particular, is 25 feet in girth and dated to over 3,000 years. Two female yews next to each other are on the enclosure bank near the Norman church, which sits in the middle of one of the henges, while the others are outside the henge and could have been part of a processional way to the north henge where they end in the middle of it. To the east of Church Henge, also known as the central circle, is an Anglo-Saxon cemetery

To put Knowlton Circles in context, just a mile and a half south another ancient pre-Christian yew site exists at All Hallows where in a semi-circle of yews, the largest yew is 29 feet. There is also a line of yews beginning with a large 27 ft girth tree proceeding along an old trackway, leading up the hill towards these yews.

Llanafan Fawr, Powys.

Llanafan Fawr. Inscribed stone. (1)

Llanafan Fawr. Inscribed stone. (2)

Llanafan Fawr, a huge parish, now rather deserted, was once an important monastic centre and a well-populated area, with much evidence of hut circles and stock enclosures witnessing busy times in the Bronze and Iron Age periods. The Romans were also here and had a hard time subduing the population of this area, while the pub, the Red Lion has stood here for a thousand years!

The church stands concentrically on a barrow, a raised oval platform that is more marked at the back of the church. In the outer part of the yard, there are faint traces of what appears to be radial ridging but its origin and significance remain unclear.

The yew itself, although very large, may have been even bigger in previous times. It has four main stems that appear to come from one rootstock and give the yew a girth of 32 feet. The yew is female and on the east of the churchyard, suggesting a Celtic planting and marking the end of the mound on which the church is built. The churchyard is exceptionally large and although now reduced, was clearly once a sub-circular enclosure in excess of 130 metres across. On the south, a minor road has cut through the churchyard but the line of the original enclosing bank and ditch with an outer circular wall or rampart is visible as an earthwork, in the field to the south. Leading archaeologist Graham George, reports it to be linked to the churchyard and date back to the Iron Age. He believes it was a stone or wood henge with a defensive moat and wall built around it. Most interesting of all, however, is the fact that the church mound and the circular mound next to the pub are in alignment with the rising of the midsummer sun which must be intentional and means the two mounds are obviously connected and the area altogether a well-preserved prehistoric landscape.

St Afan or Avanus was a Welsh saint, most likely the 10th century Bishop Ieuan who was murdered by the Danes or Vikings on one of their incursions into Wales. His tomb, which was moved from a previous resting place, stands in front of the church. Inside the church and to the left of the altar is a single pillar stone incised with a Latin ring cross believed to date from the 7th century. Ancient stones found on site and now cemented into the porch are extremely interesting. One is a cross with a leaf or yew pattern, another is a leaf and the third is either a spiral or concentric rings. It is hard to tell which as the fragment is not quite large enough to be able to see properly. There are several impressive standing stones in the immediate area.

Llanfihangel Nant Melan, Powys.

Llanfihangel Nant Melan. Fallen standing stone.

Rev. Stedman Davies, MA, in 1945 wrote of this site in his book *Yew Trees in Churchyards*:

In the early days of Christianity, the church was not built, the circular mound was everything, a place of burial and worship. There is a persistent tradition that the churchyard of

Llanfihangel Nant Melan was made within the ring of a stone circle, the garth is still circular, though the stones have gone.

However, he is wrong about this as two of the stones are still there within the hollow of the yews. Seven out of ten hollow yews stand on a slight mound, one encasing a standing stone on its side and eight of its original 12 ancient yews still encircle the site. Church literature states the yews pre-date the church. A stream runs adjacent to the site. Pre-Christian remains were found west of the church.

From GN Rees, *The Rectory* (Nov. 1982):

The church was built within the circle of yew trees of which only 6 remain of the original 12. They may be pre-Christian in origin, for there are pre-Christian remains to the west of the church and the site is very probably a pre-Christian centre

The following yews were noted by Allen Meredith on Boxing Day 1982:

1) Yew south from church 13 ft 4" at 4 ft from the ground, obviously hollow at some stage, new growth on inside and out.

2) Yew south-west 30'2" girth. This tree consists of three stems, one of which appears to be dead, the other two quite healthy, though partially decayed. This tree grows on a mound. Although separated, the yew appears to have been a single trunk at some stage.

3) Yew west 16' 4". Only half of the trunk left but vigorous in growth, half that is left is hollow. A large stone about 2 ft across and 4 feet in length lies half-buried at the base of the tree.

4) Yew north-west, about 22 ft in girth, consisting of two large stems. Here there is also a stone but smaller than

the previous one.

5) Yew north-north-west, the dead stump of what was a very large tree, hollow and burnt out.

6) Yew north, another dead stump of what must have been a yew of some considerable size, judging from the remains. A small yew sprout comes from it.

7) Yew east, about 18 ft in girth, most of the inner growth is dead, new growth on the outside.

8) Yew south-east, on a mound, decayed and hollow, had a much larger girth at some stage.

Llangernyw, Conwy.

Llangernyw is an ancient place with standing stones and an ancient male yew dated to 5,000 years on the north of the burial mound or churchyard. The male yew consists of five stems, three living and two dead. Reg Wheeler of the Forestry Commission measured around the root system at eight inches above the ground and found it to be 34 feet in circumference. The name means 'the sacred enclosure of the Cernyw' (a Celtic yew tribe). The two undressed standing stones, incised with early Christian crosses, probably from Roman

Llangernyw standing stones.

times, are close to each other at the back of the church, close to the church walls. One is 52"/ 132 cm tall and the other 51"/ 129.5 cm.

These are the only monoliths in churchyards in the Diocese of St. Asaph with incised crosses on them and would have originally been unmarked 'meini hirion'. The close proximity to each other suggests they were a cromlech at one time and supported a flat stone between them. 20 yards away are another set of stones with an altar tomb between them. Together with the others, they point to a series of prehistoric remains which once stood in Llangernyw churchyard. It is very likely that the church was deliberately erected near these stones and that the church of Llangernyw is built on a spot dedicated to religious rites in pre-Christian days.

Pennant Melangell, Llangynog, Powys

Male Yew at Pennant Melangell.

Female Yew at Pennant Melangell.

This is one of the most sacred sites in Britain and is a place of pilgrimage, well established since the 15th century and without a parish. It is found at the end of a two mile single-track road in a remote mountain area near Bala in North Wales, which gives the site a sense of otherworldly peace and beauty outside of normal life. It is known as a healing place and many who come here attribute this healing to the two ancient yews, a female and a male on the right on entering through the gate. The female with a girth of 24 ft 9" is on a mound and the largest yew, a male next to it on the east end of the church is 29 feet. Of the six yews, four are ancient and maybe the remains of an ancient yew grove. A Roman stone with markings was found near one of them while there is a Holy Well nearby.

The site is Middle Bronze Age and excavations in the late 1980s discovered prehistoric remains, Bronze Age burials and pottery. There was evidence of early cremations going back over 3,000 years. The archaeologist also examined small stones used by the Celts in burial rituals. Prehistoric, charcoal filled pits were found as well as a prehistoric pit, a hearth and copper-alloy slag.

Pennant Melangell was a cemetery from 1500 BCE. It sits at the foot of a breast shaped hill which one cannot but think lent significance to this site. It links with the female saint and may have been linked to a goddess figure before this. This is very much a Celtic churchyard, having all the attributes of one, being circular, with ancient yews, a drop on the east side to the river and being surrounded by mountains. It is in an ideal location for a hermitage site, which legend has it, was the case. The church is dedicated to an early saint, Melangell, given the land in the valley as a place of sanctuary by Prince Brochwel of Powys. The 15th century rood screen tells the story and the church itself is full of carvings of hares which also appear on the rood screen. The church boasts the oldest Romanesque shrine in Britain which lends an awesome and ancient atmosphere to the church. The shrine was demolished during the Reformation and reconstructed in the 17th century.

Rhydyglafes, Denbighshire.

Rhyd-y-glafes Yew.

Rhydyglafes is the name of an area also known as Frongoch. This site is a chambered cairn, and is not easy to find, although it is visible from the B4401 between Llandrillo and Cynwyd, Denbighshire but only if you keep your eyes peeled! The cairn capstone is massive, around three metres long and propped up on small boulders at one end whilst the west end disappears under the grass into a 30 ft long burial mound or long barrow. This is a prehistoric burial site of the Neolithic Age. As we know, churches were often built on ancient religious sites and it appears Rhydyglafes is no exception. Right up next to the old church wall, is an ancient yew which has seen better days. This yew is female and of no great girth but is clearly ancient with the outer trunk much decayed but sustained by internal stems and fresh growth. Near the yew is a field called Tir Ywen, which is an ancient name referring to the yew. In the same area, there are several other ancient sites.

Darley Dale, Derbyshire,

Darley Dale Yew.

179

Darley Dale Tree Cross.

Although not one of the most ancient yews I have included here, it is nevertheless a female ancient yew of over 2,000 years and a tree of remarkable size (33 feet in girth) and appearance. I admit it may seem I have included this yew at random but it is one that really captures my imagination. This massive and imposing yew of strong red-brown colour grows on the south-west and was considered particularly important by the Saxons who adopted it. It grows in a position in the graveyard or burial mound, which was the place for Saxon planted yews. However, it is earlier than that and would have been there before them. It is particularly impressive to see the Saxon grave slabs in the porch with a very good example of Saxon Christian crosses which are modified sprouting trees. There are several incised slabs and early worked stones here. Celtic carvings have been built into some Christian churches which show the progression of beliefs and at this Darley Dale church of St. Helen's, small carvings or statues of Sheela-Na-Gig, the goddess of creation and fertility, can be seen.

At Gresford, All Saints church, Wrexham, Clwyd

Gresford Yew.

Included here for similar reasons to Darley Dale, although strictly speaking it should not be in this chapter as it is not ancient, although verging on it but the Roman altar to the yew found near the tree is quite, quite remarkable! The 29 ft male yew is also very impressive, has the same colour as the Darley Dale yew and is interesting from the perspective of being younger than you might think for such a sizeable tree! It grows on the south-east and is around 1,800 years. It may be a Roman planting, an idea which is supported by the Roman altar found in the churchyard, a short distance away which has direct reference and relevance to it and the site itself is thought to be Romano-Saxon.

At Gresford in North Wales, a sculptured altar stone was

excavated from near the east wall of All Saints Parish Church. It is to be found now inside the church and may have originally been kept under the ancient yew close by, as were other Roman altars. The stone has a depression on the top suggesting something like a bowl may have been placed there. This stone, considered to be Romano-Celtic, was known as the Atropos Altar stone or the Nemesis stone.

The Atropos stone, Gresford.

Atropos was a Greek deity who cut the fate or thread of life like the Greek goddess of divine retribution: Nemesis. The god depicted carries a large pair of shears and is connected with the fate of a human being and the length of their life, issues connected with the yew tree. In Greek mythology, Atropos was the oldest of the three Fates, the

Moirae, female associated with the yew, deities who supervised Fate rather than determining it.

Triple goddesses are associated with the yew tree and represent, like the yew tree itself, life, death and eternity. Atropos was the Fate who cut the thread or web of life. She was known as the 'inflexible' or 'inevitable' and she cut this thread with the 'abhorred shears'. She worked along with Clotho, who spun the thread and Lachesis who measured the length of it. They were the daughters of Zeus and Themis (the mother of order). The Roman names for the three Fates were Nona, Decuma and Morta. However, this being a Roman stone, it may be that the goddess depicted here is Morta, the Roman equivalent of Atropos, but it is Atropos who is typically depicted with a large pair of shears and this is why this altar stone is called the Atropos Stone.

This stone holds a great deal of meaning for me. Following the side of the stone that depicts Atropos, the next face shows a chevron pattern, known to be a yew tree symbol. This is followed on the next face by an arch and then finally, on the last face, another arch, this time with a cosmic disk. To me, it is very clear that what this stone is saying through these symbols, is that the yew governs our going out (retreat to the otherworld with no sun) and our coming in (returning to our world, a place where the sun shines). It stands at the gate of life. The stone also suggests reincarnation, which many cultures such as the Celts believed in. To me, it speaks of the way through back to this world, shown by the presence of the sun, after travelling in the other direction to the Otherworld, back to Atropos who measures the length of the next life.

To end this chapter, I would like to draw attention to a few other ancient stone carvings which have stood the test of time to tell us how early cultures viewed the eternal mysteries of life, death and rebirth. At Broadwell in Gloucestershire, there is the most magnificent ancient carving of the Tree of Life, depicted on a stone found in the churchyard which is now in the porch.

An old female yew grows here on the south side but with the Tree of Life carved stone present and the extraordinary large and complicated spring or well system below and opposite the church, it would be very odd if there had not at one time been an important and older yew at this site that has long gone. At Uppington in Shropshire there is a Roman altar under the ancient yew on the south side and a lintel outside at the back of the church with a Celtic dragon carving. It is similar to the one at Acton Beauchamp in Herefordshire.

There are other places, mainly church sites which have ancient stones but insignificant yews and these include the pre-Christian circular churchyard at Old Radnor which has old stones both standing and forming part of the churchyard wall and also a font said to have been made from a large standing stone. Another place is the churchyard up on the mountain at Ysbyty Cynfyn, near Aberystwyth, dedicated to St. John the Baptist,

Ysbyty Cynfyn standing stones.

It is obvious that knowing what we do of pre-Christian religious sites, that these places would have had yews at one time.

Of the stones that are left in churches and churchyards, most of these are undecorated standing stones, mostly ones it was deemed too difficult to move. Many of the remaining ancient inscribed stones were removed to museums for safety and preservation but such interesting stones are still to be found occasionally at places such as Nevern in Ceredigion and Munsley in Herefordshire. At Acton Beauchamp a Celtic stone is used as a lintel as is another at Uppington and yet another in the bell tower at Defynnog. The one at Acton Beauchamp makes me wonder whether the decrepit tree there is older than might be guessed.

Acton Beauchamp Yew.

Acton Beauchamp Celtic stone.

Many of the Welsh stones are depicted and well documented, in both Nash Williams' book, *The Early Christian Monuments of Wales* and J O Westwood's *Lapidarium Walliae: The Early Inscribed and Sculptured Stones of Wales, Delineated and Described*. But there are still unexpected discoveries to be made.

Chapter 8

Nevern, the Bleeding Yews
and the Holy Wood

It should have come as no surprise when a Golden Bough appeared on one of the bleeding yews at Nevern but it is always a surprise and a moment of great delight and magic to see it. (Golden boughs are investigated in later chapters.) The Welsh name for Nevern is Nanhyfer which contains the word for heaven - 'nef' and the word for brook - 'nant' and the heavenly brook passes next to the churchyard giving it the mark of a Celtic place. Nevern always was a special place and a place of great mystery with its inscribed stones and dates back to the Irish St. Brynach who founded it in the 6th century and with three of the stones commemorating three Kings; it is a place of national importance to Wales. The yews themselves are a mystery and the place has always pulled me like a magnet. I so love being there. There is a feeling of deep peace at Nevern, of being taken out of our world and back to ancient times, as if nothing has ever changed here. It shares this same feeling with Llanilid as if a great deal happened here a long time ago but now no longer does anything change as time stands still.

Bleeding yews are very rare, rarer even than a Golden Bough. Such trees also exist at Brecon Cathedral, Druid's grove, Newlands Corner and Chillingham. Like the younger avenue of bleeding yews at Brecon, I have seen all the Nevern yews bleed at different times. Allen Meredith always wondered what happened to the original yew tree here. There is no sign of an old stump but he thought there should have been one, as there often is at very old church sites without a very old yew. The yew trees here are small and thought to be fairly young in terms of yews. Yews that grow in an avenue are always smaller and younger-looking than their years would suggest because they compete for light and nutrients, appearing to be half the age or more than they actually are. Even so, 800 years was the most Allen would give them. In November 2017 I took another look. The tree on the left as you enter the churchyard is made up of two stems, one with a girth of nearly nine feet, the other just over seven. Like all the other yews here, it is monoecious, another rare phenomenon, although this one is predominantly male. So here, there are yews with all the possible attributes. They are monoecious, bleeding yews, one of which carries a Golden Bough and since all the yews in the avenue here appear to be from the same original tree, the others could also sprout a Golden Bough. Nowhere else to my knowledge, do all these things come together although this could change and yews can suddenly develop one or more of these attributes. For example, the incredible serpent like yew at Llanerfyl which is monoecious recently started bleeding. The yew in question here though at the entrance to Nevern churchyard seems small and unimpressive but it grows on a mound indicating it was planted over an old burial and I was able to collect some specimens of old wood from inside it which inexplicably had a ring count of 55 per inch. I did not expect anything as high as this and there is no evidence to suggest it may, at one time, have been larger. The yew tree simply doesn't look old enough to have this many rings but far more samples would be needed to come to any conclusions and these were simply not forthcoming. It is therefore a mystery as to how anything like this number of rings could be found in what seems to be a fairly young tree. Having recently seen a yew on the mountain near Llanhamlach of a similar girth to those at Nevern, an ancient White Tree of great age (at least 2,000 years and likely more), it's obvious a small yew tree isn't necessarily a young tree. However, those on the mountain, particularly this bleached skeletal yew, are clearly considerably older than the Nevern yews.

At the time when Dyfed was said to have had seven Bishops, Nevern was probably the seat of one of them as the parish of

Nevern was the largest in Pembrokeshire. Appearances are often deceptive and it is hard to believe this was once an important and busy place and that only 200 years ago, there were twice the number of people as now but on the high point above Nevern is a Norman castle, destroyed in 1136, once home to Norman lords and Welsh princes. Due to its topography, it is likely it was occupied since early times, certainly since the Iron Age, although to date, no prehistoric remains have been found here. However, Gilbert, Blackett and Wilson in *The Holy Kingdom* describe Nevern as the most celebrated holy place in Dyfed and this would seem to be the case. It was certainly considered to be a very special sacred place, long before the coming of Christianity. Nearby is Pentre Ifan, known as the finest dolmen in Wales. Also nearby, the bluestones were taken from the Preseli Mountains to Stonehenge, so there was something of ancient importance, well known in prehistoric times, about this area, which led to Nevern continuing to be on the map down the centuries.

The church itself is dedicated to St. Brynach, who is said to have conversed with angels on nearby Carn Ingli, the 'Mountain of Angels' and Brynach was led to Nevern by a dream in which a white sow indicated where he should build his church on land given him by King Clether, who lived in the hill fort nearby. The present church dates from the 12th or 13th century but would have been built over an earlier site. Within the churchyard, several early Christian inscribed stones are to be found, many of them burial monuments. They may have moved location several times and may also have marked routes or crossing places at one time. There is confusion as to who the Vitaliani Emerito stone, as it is called, belongs, whether it is to Vortigern, or his son or grandfather. The stone originally stood, on the north side of the church. It was first mentioned in 1695 by Gibson, of *Camden's Brittanica*, as being there but it later disappeared and had apparently been stolen by a farmer and used as a gatepost. It has holes in its side which were probably put in at this time. It was later restored to the church and now stands on the south side of the church, east of the porch. The stone has Ogham writing (an early Irish script) along its edge and the Latin reads 'Vitaliani Emerito', meaning 'to the honour of Vitalianus'. This stone is dated to the early 6th or late 5th century. Circumstantial evidence would therefore suggest that Vortigern who lived in the 5th century, was buried at Nevern. He represented the Pelagian party, which was in conflict with Ambrosius who was probably Roman. As an adherent of Pelagius, which was considered a heresy, Vortigern was also in conflict with St. Germanus, who persecuted him for having received the Saxons but doubtless also because of the Pelagian heresy which Germanus was tasked with putting down while secretly being intrigued by it (detailed in *The God Tree*). Germanus who was probably Romano British besieged Vortigern in a castle which eventually burnt to the ground. The mythological story of Vortigern is that his castle kept falling down until Merlin told him about two dragons, a red and a white one, who were fighting under the foundations. Vortigern's was a ruling house in Powys and Constantine's eldest son Constans is said to have been murdered by him. Nennius' writes in *Historia Brittonnum* that Ambrosius fought a battle against a certain Vitalianus (mentioned on the stone at Nevern) who was thought to be the grandfather of Vortigern. This would mean then, that Ambrosius has been wrongly placed in the time of Vortigern and belongs to the time of Vitalianus, probably in the 4th century.

The Maglocunus stone is another early stone also inscribed in Latin and Ogham. Both inscriptions mean it is the monument of Maglocunus, son of Clutorius and is probably of a similar date to the Vitaliani Emerito stone. This stone and a beautifully carved and interlaced Celtic stone are cemented into the window sills of the south transept inside the church. Both were found in the wall of the priest's chamber, the low door of which is by the window. Maglocunus is thought to have been King Maelgwyn of Gwynedd. He was elected Pendragon of Britain in 580 and is mentioned in the Life of Cadoc. It is odd that he is buried in

Dyfed rather than Gwynedd and this fact alone rather suggests that Nevern was considered to be a place for Kings.

In case we had any doubts of this, in the front of the church and to the right is the Nevern High Cross, a large stone, decorated on all sides in the Celtic style, known as Brynach's Cross but dedicated to Hwyel Dda, a famous 10th century king. This stone is thought to be the best example of its kind. It is thirteen feet high with the top headstone separate and fixed on with a mortice and tenon joint. The stone goes down seven feet into the ground making it absolutely massive. Hywel Dda lived from 880-950. His name means Hywel the Good. He was a highly esteemed man who established traditional Welsh law and marked a turning point in Welsh history by bringing it into modern times. He eventually came to rule most of Wales from Powys to Gwynedd. He was recorded as King of the Britons in the Annales Cambriae and the Annals of Ulster and although his was a violent reign, Hywel Dda wisely came to an understanding and a balance of power with the first Anglo Saxon King Athelstan of England, establishing peace and stability between the two countries. It is an assertion of the importance of Nevern, that Hywel Dda was buried and commemorated here.

Last but not least of the inscribed stones, is The Pilgrim's Cross which is carved into the rock face along the Pilgrim's route, a short distance uphill from the church. Beneath it is a very smooth, worn and dipped kneeling stone and above it is Nevern Castle. Nevern was on the important pilgrims' route to St. David's and pilgrims would have stopped to pray here. It was a popular route, two pilgrimages to St. David's being equal to one to Rome. However, John Starkey in *Pilgrims Ways, the Grand Pilgrimage to St. Davids*, says it is more likely that the 'kneeling stone' was hollowed out by falling water and Francis Jones in *Holy Wells of Wales*, 1954 lists Gavil Pistill Brynach as a healing well associated with the local saint and as far as can be made out, this may be its location. Dowsers pick up water behind the area of the Pilgrim's Cross which is on the cliff face. All this is uncertain and there is mystery surrounding this cross. The cliff face into which the cross is carved is partly natural and partly man-made from small, slate-like, local stone, which is interwoven with the natural rock face, as an infill, to make the cliff face a complete wall. The cross itself is in two parts. The substantial part of it is an equal-armed cross, which is a pre-Christian symbol and may have been carved by St Brynach, who could have used the cave said to be behind the wall as a cell. This cross has in recent years, been turned into a Christian cross by lengthening the lower part of the upright, building it out of the same small stones used in the man-made part of the wall.

Nevern. Cross on cliff.

We know this to be the case because both J O Westwood's *Lapidarium Walliae: The Early Inscribed and Sculptured Stones of Wales, Delineated and Described*, 1923 and *The Royal Commission on The Ancient and Historical Monuments and Constructions in Wales and Monmouthshire - An inventory of the Ancient Monuments in Wales and Monmouthshire*, 1917, show it without the lengthened upright.

Nevern Pilgrims Cliff Cross. Illustration from J.O. Westwood 1923, 'Lapidarium Walliae: The early inscribed and sculptured stones of Wales, Delineated and Described'.

This may also help date the man-made part of the wall as the lengthened part of the upright seems to be part of it and made at the same time. However, no one knows why the wall was built. Adrian Gilbert, Alan Wilson and Baram Blackett report in their intriguing book *The Holy Kingdom,* 1998, that behind this wall is another wall, made from more substantial stones with a gap through which a cave can be seen. Unfortunately, CADW, the historic environment service of the Welsh Government has blocked all further investigation into what might lie behind this wall, sparking all kinds of speculation. Gilbert, Blackett and Wilson say the Pilgrims cross suggests this is the last resting place of the True Cross brought here by Empress Helen, a British Queen and mother of Constantine the Great, who became ruler of the Roman Empire from 324 CE. Extraordinary as it sounds, these two well-known figures lived in this remote part of Britain for at least 10 years in the 4th century!

In *The Holy Kingdom* you can read the whole amazing story of how Empress Helen of Constantinople, Constantine's mother, travelled with an army to Jerusalem to demand the True Cross which she brought to this area of Wales, where she paraded it around, renaming places around Nevern with such Biblical names as Constantinople, Gethsemane, Jericho etc. Many of the places in this area had names that included 'cross', such as 'Dinas Cross' (City of the cross). The collection of medieval stories which formed *The Golden Legend* (1260) includes the story of how the Holy Wood was verified and this was also the subject of a painting by Piera Della Francesca commissioned by the Roman Church in 1452 and painted as a fresco in the Cathedral of Arezzo in Italy where it forms part of a whole series of paintings by this Renaissance artist, of the Legend of the Holy Wood, in a tower constructed for them. This particular painting depicts the part of the Golden Legend where Helen is presented with three crosses and in order to discover which one is the True Cross all three are passed over a corpse. When the True Cross was passed over the corpse, the corpse returned to life. Returning with the Holy Wood to Wales, Empress Helen triumphantly carried it along a route in West Wales which was then marked by names to do with the Cross.

In the *Black Book of Carmarthen*, thought to be the earliest surviving Welsh manuscript, dating to the mid-13th century, it was recorded that the Cross was in Dyfed (the old name for that part of the world) in 920. Gilbert, Blackett and Wilson in *The Holy Kingdom* write that 'it was said of Hywel Dda, that it was his king lists that gave Dyfed as the Cross' hiding place'. There is no record of what ultimately became of the Cross, although there is a later tradition of King Arthur sending to Dinas Cross, five miles from Nevern for the Cross which is depicted on his shield at the Battle of Badon. Legends such as this are no real evidence but are often a remnant of a lost tradition and should not be discounted. The other related story is found in The Mabinogion, the book of the earliest prose stories of the literature of Britain, compiled in Middle Welsh in the 12th - 13th centuries. It tells of Peredur, one of the Keepers of the Grail secret investigated in *The God Tree*, who may have been Perceval of the Arthurian quest for the Grail. In the story, Perceval comes across a beautiful valley with pavilions, water and windmills where the chief miller tells him that the Empress of Constantinople lives there and the mills provide food for her people. Felindre Farchog, a mile from Nevern means the mill of the Knight. In *The God Tree* we showed that the Grail, the Holy Wood and the Tree of Life were one and the same thing and the Keepers of the Grail Secret, three warrior saints Illtyd, Cadog and Peredur were also Arthurian Knights. What eventually happened to Constantine and Helen is unclear but it is said Empress Helen's cremation ashes are interred at Redstone Cross, north of Narberth where she had her main court.

Gilbert, Blackett and Wilson speculate that the True Cross was hidden inside the cave, leaving the crucifix as a sign that it is there. However, it was pointed out to me by a friend of mine, Ron Cooper, and stated earlier that in J O Westwood's book, *Lapidarium Walliae: The early inscribed stones of Wales, delineated and described*, that the lengthened upright is not there on the drawing or description, although the man-made part of the wall seems to be suggested. The bottom part of the present cross was added sometime after the drawing was made for the book. In Westwood's book of 1923, it clearly states the cross is an equal-armed cross and so the addition of other stones was an attempt to turn the pre-Christian cross into a Christian one. Although the lengthened upright looks like part of the original man-made wall, there is nothing to say that it could not have been added at a date later to the building of it. Whatever may or may not be hidden behind this cliff-face, (and the way the cliff face is built up suggests that something is or why go to the trouble?) I believe there is another explanation as to what happened to the True Cross and the importance of the stoned-up cave may simply be as the grave of Brynach.

Returning to Constantine, the inventor of Christianity in its present form, like all Romans of the time, he was a devotee of the popular cult of Mithras, before becoming a Christian. It may seem that it was his mother Empress Helen, who of the two, was the most concerned with the Cross or Holy Wood. However, this is not the case. Constantine was originally involved with the worship of Mithra, or Mitra, the Iranian/Persian god of the sun, who was known as Mithras in the Roman Empire, during the 2nd and 3rd centuries CE. There is a Vedic Mitra and an Iranian Mithra and some evidence that Mithra was a Yew God, who was connected with carrying a sacred branch. It should be noted that Mitra is an anagram of amrita, another name for haoma or soma, the elixir of immortality described in a later chapter and that amrita was in the possession of certain gods known as the Assures who were made immortal by it. Like Haoma, the drinking of the blood of Christ, known as the Eucharist is, as Ignatius of Antioch said in his letter to the Ephesians, 'the true medicine of immortality'. Yew blood is a potent magical substance and was no doubt an ingredient of the Elixir of Life, of Haoma and Soma.

As documented at great length in *The God Tree*, there was a tradition of planting staffs, pieces of Holy Wood and branches from sacred trees brought from the Holy Lands. The most likely thing to my mind is that Constantine, a follower of Mithras, which was originally a Yew Cult involving the drinking or tasting of yew sap, planted the wood brought from the Holy Lands by his mother. If so, and the wood grew into a tree, which such wood often did when planted by many holy people as detailed in *The God Tree*, the resulting tree, now gone, could have become the parent tree of those in the avenue. The eight trees could all have sprouted as cuttings taken from the same wood. It is, of course, always possible that a bleeding yew was already there, and was nothing to do with the True Cross, in which case this would have greatly interested Constantine and drawn him to this place. Certainly, considering the history as well as the ancient sacred nature of Nevern, sacred before the time of Brynach in the 6th century, it would be unlikely if a yew of some importance had not been there.

In ancient times, the properties of certain sacred trees and pieces of yew wood were well known and the sacred Tree of Life, the one Jesus hung on, was no doubt a bleeding monoecious yew. What do we have here but a whole avenue of bleeding monoecious yews? It is thought that only one of these yews bleeds, but at different times I have seen them all do so. It is quite a horrifying and unforgettable sight to behold the tree bleeding. At the time of writing one of the yews, second on the right in the avenue at Nevern, clearly labelled, bleeds from what looks like a severed artery.

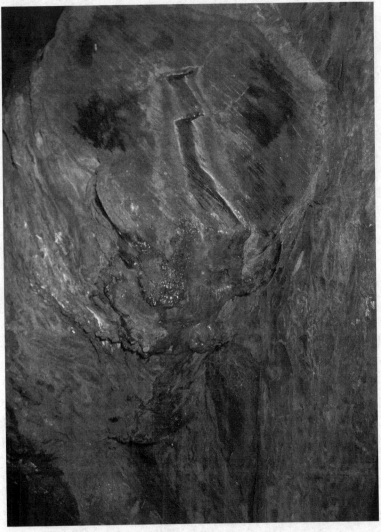

Bleeding Yew at Nevern.

It is shocking to see and nothing can prepare you for the sight of it, as it looks exactly like congealed human blood! I also discovered all the yews are monoecious (each tree, bearing both sexes) and clearly of the same variety or subspecies of Taxus baccata. The yew blood has never been scientifically investigated and to this day we do not know what causes this phenomenon or what the 'blood' consists of. Whether it is caused by a fungus, a bacterium or by rain getting in or something else entirely, we have no idea. However, on a historical, spiritual and mythological level, it is another matter and blood of any kind is highly significant in many religions. Tammuz, for example, the Mesopotamian Vegetation god was a yew god, a bleeding god who was also connected with Dumuzi, a Mesu or Kiskanu tree. This dying and resurrecting god was a tree that bled when a spear pierced him and this piercing and bleeding became a yearly ritual. Ovid in *The Metamorphoses* 737-759 Table VIII describes a sacrilegious act in the Grove of Ceres, where the son of Triopas cut a sacred oak, with green leaves and many acorns.

As soon as his impious hand had made an incision in its trunk, the blood flowed from the severed bark, nor otherwise than as at the time when the bull, a large victim, falls before the altars, the blood pours forth from its neck.

(Interesting too that the yew and the bull are linked here as in Mithraism.) The Grove of Ceres was a yew grove, not an oak grove and the tree was worshipped as a goddess. As Fred Hageneder says, referring to the yew, 'No other European tree can react like this.' The theme from the Yew Cult of the blood and the tree was a strong thread, an undeniable and obvious connection which continued into Christianity with Jesus becoming the bleeding god. The bleeding and the tree is an important combination and Jesus can be seen as being in the tradition of the sacred tree gods.

If Nevern has become a Christian pilgrimage site due to the bleeding of the yews being seen as a symbol of Christ's wounds, bleeding as he hung on the tree, it is no wonder that such a tree as this was every bit as important in the old religion as in the new, denoting a sacred tree of the goddess with her menstrual blood and as we saw in the earlier chapters, such trees were not symbols but actual gods and goddesses. Yews that bleed are extremely rare. Apart from those at Nevern, the ones I know of include the yews that make up the young Brecon Cathedral avenue, the yew at Chillingham in Northumberland, the one at Bishopstree in Hampshire and the 13 foot girth tree at Bishopstrow in Wiltshire. One at Llanerfyl has recently begun to bleed. These are just a mere handful of yews, which makes them even rarer than the Golden Bough yews. There is surprisingly little known, concerning ancient spiritual practise around bleeding yews. Science has yet to explain the phenomena and what the red blood-like fluid that oozes from wounds to the yew is. Considering how awesome a sight it is, you would expect there to have been some celebration, sacred knowledge or entire sites built around this phenomena in the ancient world and this must have been the case although you will have to dig deep to find any evidence or records. At the tree of the goddess, Deoia Quercus (indicating an oak, often confused in ancient texts with yew), in the sacred grove of Ceres, when the tree was struck by an axe, blood streamed forth from the wound. It is also notable that in discussions about the Hittite tree called 'Eya' which we know is the yew, the Czech archaeologist and language scholar, Bedrich Hrozny, in 1915, came across a Hittite ritual text, which describes a sacred tree, 'an apple tree' (actually a reference to yew with its fruits, known as sacred apples) as standing over a spring and bleeding. At first, he thought this must refer to an animal sacrifice left at the tree but could not ignore the fact that what was really being said was that the actual tree was bleeding. It's one of those things that make the yew unique and extraordinary and our ancient ancestors would have seen a bleeding yew as being alive in the human and animal sense. It is almost as if such a tree has crossed species.

Some years ago, the churchwarden at Nevern told me that a tree surgeon had cut off a branch of one of the yews in the avenue and had changed from an extrovert, happy-go-lucky personality to a psychically disturbed and depressed introvert who committed suicide six months later. There are several modern legends as you might expect, to explain the bleeding of the yews, one telling of a monk who was executed in the churchyard and swearing his innocence declared that the tree would bleed for him in proof of this. The yew blood is a shocking sight being the same colour as human blood. It pools at the foot of the tree and congeals just like ours would.

After the acceptance of Christianity by Emperor Constantine in the early 4th century, Mithraism rapidly declined. Constantine put these two great religions together to form a remodelled version of Christianity for various reasons, mainly political. Both Mithraism and Christianity centred around a bleeding god (Mithras and Jesus). It was Constantine who put Christianity together in the way it was to officially be, divorcing it from the Tree of Life by changing the circumstances of Jesus' death from a hanging on a living tree, to a crucifixion on a post of dead wood in the shape of a cross. This was a new symbol developed from an old. It wasn't that different from pre Christian crosses but it made Christianity different from earlier spiritual understandings, divorcing Christianity from the pagan truth of resurrection within the natural world and separating us from the natural world. It did not escape the notice of people like the Celts and the Saxons who represented their Crosses as trees with leaves and roots which connected us to Nature. Until Constantine humans were part of Nature. The Sacred Tree is central to most religions as with the Buddhist Bodhi Tree of Wisdom and the Muslim Lote tree. Finally, as Simon Schama says in *The Verdant Cross*:- 'Christianity was reunited with the Tree of Life through the scriptural and apocryphal traditions of the Tree of Life being grafted back on to the Cult of the Cross.' The old saying: 'You can drive Mother Nature out but she'll always come back' used to be true, but for how much longer if we refuse to work with her. We now have a lot of work to do to persuade her to return. We need to accept the supremacy and ultimate cosmic laws of the Yew and Nature and stop trying to subdue, exploit and control things more powerful than us. If we bring Nature down, she will take us with her.

Under Constantine, Christianity was brought into being as a world religion through a synthesis of Mithraic thought on eternal life gained from the blood of the sacrificed saviour (like a bull) and Jewish rituals of animal sacrifice, with the blood of the sacrificed saviour, Jesus Christ. It is also thought that the cannibalistic elements of the Christian Communion, (drinking and eating the blood and body of Jesus represented through the 'host' and the wine), the Eucharist and the imagery of the blood of Jesus granting eternal life (like Mithras), are all derived from the merging of Roman Judaism with Mithraism. Bipin Shah says that the Indo - Iranian cult of Mithra (Old Persian) preceded the Roman Cult of Mithra by at least 4,500 years and the origination of the sacrament ceremony of Christianity is deeply rooted within the Indo-Iranian religion of Mitra-Mithraism.

What is less known is that in its earliest form, Mithraism was a Yew Cult and the tasting of blood was the imbibing of yew blood, the blood of an immortal tree god which was thought to bestow immortality, as only that particular tree might. So, the origin of the blood of immortality was the yew blood, the blood of the God Tree. In fact, Zoroaster denounced the sacrifice of the bull, so it seems likely that this ceremony was a part of old Iranian paganism and different to the actual Cult of Mithras. This is corroborated by an Indian text in which Mitra reluctantly participates in the sacrifice of a god named Soma, (the drink of immortality which like Haoma derived from the Yew), who often appears in the shape of a white bull which is then transformed into the moon.

In 313 CE Emperor Constantine who may have already been living in Wales in the Nevern area, declared December 25th to be the birthday of Jesus (December 25th had been prescribed earlier as the birthday of Mithra by Emperor Aurelian) Much of the New Testament was tampered with and parts of it radically altered by people like Constantine, who destroyed things that did not fit with his political thinking and aspirations. He suppressed much of the early material and in 333 CE ordered the destruction of all pagan works about Jesus. Earlier in 326 CE he had ordered that all books written by Christians holding differing views from the official teachings should be destroyed, making it very difficult to get a true picture of what really happened in the life of Jesus, including his use of a wand. Under Constantine, the Sabbath day became Sunday, as it was the day of the Sun (another element from the Mithra worship). Mithraism and Judaism merged and became Christianity. Jesus, son of the Hebrew sky God and Mithras, son of Ormond, are the same myth, the same story. The rituals of Christianity coincide with the earlier rituals of Mithraism, including the Eucharist and the Communion, matching each other in their detail, so that the language used by Mithraism was a significant part of the language used by Christianity. St. Paul, who came from Tarsus, a major Mithraic centre also helped with this merging and as we shall see, became involved with the Silurian Druids of Llanilid who venerated the Yew. Constantine died in 337 CE.

The big question is, did Constantine plant a bleeding yew at Nevern or was it already there? The likelihood is there was a sacred yew tree at this place before those of the yew avenue. Constantine's associations with the Cult of Mithras, that cult's connections with yew blood, and his mother's obsession with the Holy Cross must add up to something, and that legacy was left behind at Nevern. We have seen how rare a bleeding yew is. Perhaps it was Constantine who brought the tradition of the sacred tree here. I think it very likely that the Holy Wood, the Wood of the Cross is still here, hidden in plain sight.

PS. WARNING!! All parts of the Yew tree are known to be poisonous except for the fleshy fruit of the aril and it is not recommended that you taste the yew blood.

Chapter 9

The Three Cors of Britain, Avalon and Bernera

Cors were sacred circles, eternal circles where Druids met each other face to face, across an enclosed space, open to the sky and the cosmos. With their feet planted firmly on the earth, they were in touch with both the elements of Nature and with the heavens.

Although there were several Cors in Britain, perhaps as many as 40 or 50, such as Caer Broc in the Isle of Wight, and Corhampton, there were only three major, central ones. One of these Cors was Cor Eurgain at Llanilid, subject of the next chapter, which then moved to Llantwit Major where it is said to have become one of the Perpetual Choirs. This Cor equates with the one known as Caer Caradoc in the Welsh Triads.

The early Christian settlements, holy places and churchyards were circular too, as they followed on from the Cors in a seamless transition from the earlier religion. The three main Cors of Britain became the Perpetual Choirs of Britain which were Christian monasteries of which it was said that choirs, as in the musical kind, were a central feature, The early Christian choirs were also circular, and the real meaning of 'Cor' was forgotten and used then for the holy places associated with particular saints. These places were sometimes known as Bangors, as in Bangor-is-y-Coed (the name Bangor contains the Welsh mutation of the word Cor). Bangor was the name for several early religious foundations, monasteries and colleges, which were places of learning. The perpetual choirs, which had their roots in the Cors, seemed to have been instigated by the monastic movements to give praise to God continually day and night. This was according to Iolo Morganwg, whose authority is unfortunately always in question, as he was known, to embroider history and invent things but nevertheless, it is possible. In 1801 he wrote that:

> in each of these choirs there were 2,400 saints; that is there were a hundred for every hour of the day and night in rotation, perpetuating the praise and service of God without rest or intermission.

Learning from Susan Elizabeth Hale about the way sound and music is a vibration that can change the atmosphere of places, has put a different complexion on choirs, drumming and music for me. I now wonder if this singing was to perpetually praise God or to create a certain vibration for a particular purpose as Susan did at Llanilid, creating an atmosphere of joy in the church, the Cor and the churchyard.

The Welsh Triads give the location of the three Perpetual Choirs of Britain, instigated by the monasteries, which evolved from the Cors. These were said to be the Isle of Avalon, Caer Caradoc and Bangor-is-y-Coed. RW Morgan in *St. Paul in Britain*, 1861, says the three Cors were Cor Sarlog (Old Sarum), Cor Ilid (Llanilid) in Siluria and Cor Avalon (Glastonbury) so at least we have some agreement here with our conclusion that Caer Caradog was Cor Ilid (Llanilid).

It was assumed that Caer Caradoc, of which there are several such named places, was Old Sarum on Salisbury Plain. This place, which is still surrounded by old yew trees, although many have been cut down, may well have been a Cor. However, I believe Caer Caradoc is actually Cor Eurgain and that Cor Eurgain, named after Eurgain, daughter of Caradoc and granddaughter of Bran, is the Cor at Llanilid. This also concurs with the statement by Iestyn ab Gwrgant who said Eurgain was married to Sarlog, who coincidentally was Lord of Caer Sarlog, Old Sarum, Salisbury! This all adds up to a mystery solved. It is also likely that, through a long-standing association with Joseph of Arimathea, Llantwit Major was elevated by some to be ranked as one of the Perpetual Choirs in some of the later versions of the Triads.

Spending some time at Bangor-is-y-Coed, (translated as 'monastery by the Woods'), otherwise known as Bangor on Dee near Wrexham, looking for evidence of it having been a Cor, led to disappointment, for like Llanelltyd Fawr (modern-day Llantwit Major), where there were said to be some of the oldest and largest yews, no evidence of this was found. Furthermore, no evidence was left either of a large community of the size needed for such a choir. William of Malmesbury, however, described the ruins at Bangor-is-y-Coed in his day as the most extensive he had seen in the kingdom and so it seems all evidence of something of extraordinary importance at one time, has completely vanished along with any earthwork and this all seems rather strange to me, making little sense. Certainly, the Venerable Bede stated that the number of monks at Bangor was 2,100 and the scholars were considerably more but in 615, the large monastery was said to have been destroyed by the Saxons. Allen Meredith concluded that the Cor referred to as Bangor-is-y-coed or Bangor Iscoed is actually Discoed, whose name is a corruption of is-y-Coed. Here there is a massive male yew of 4,000 - 5,000 years on a mound on the north side of the church with a girth of 37 feet. It is obvious that as Druidic sites, the Cors would have centred around an ancient yew tree, being also an Axis Mundi or nemeton and on today's evidence, Discoed is the only place that fits the bill and it seems likely that it was a Cor.

However, the earliest monastic site, the earliest monastery in Wales, was said to be that at Bangor-is-y-Coed, where the Yews of Bangor on Dee were once known, along with those at Henllan, as the most wonderful in the whole of Wales but sadly they have long gone and 2,000 - 300 years ago, nothing more than a stump of a yew was recorded there at the place where the yews were famous. Allen believes that Bangor on Dee was Bangor Esgob, the place connected with Henllan, as these two places are generally mentioned together. The coed as in Bangor-is-y-coed or Discoed was, in this context, a Yew grove, spoken of by the bard Gwynfardd. In a book called *Arboretum Fructicetum Brittanicum* (The tree and shrubs of Britain), by John Claudius Loudon, 1838, we read the following: 'In the words of a very ancient Welsh bard, we are told of two churches renowned for their yew trees':

Bangor Esgob, a Bageibyr Henllan
Ysaid er clodvan er clyd Ywyz

Dr Owen Pugh translates this as 'The Minister of Esgob, and that of Henllan, of celebrity for sheltering yews'. Henllan, meaning old parish or burial ground, also signifies an old grove, showing that its church stood where Druid worship had been performed.

The third Cor is the Isle of Avalon, the renowned place of legends, an Otherworldly place, visited by boat across a strip of water, approached with trepidation, existing behind a veil, a mist that separated the sacred sanctuary from ordinary life, a place ruled by the old gods where divine kings were buried or left in an enchanted sleep awaiting the right time to return to save a nation. Avalon has for some time been assumed to be Glastonbury but for many reasons, in line with most scholars, I dispute that Glastonbury ever was Avalon and after decades of searching and researching the location of this legendary place, have finally found the trail to lead to the anciently known and sacred Isle of Bernera, off the coast of Lismore, off the West Coast of Scotland, an island known significantly by the Irish as Emain Avallach.

Bernera Island.

This was the place St. Columba was drawn to and where he is said to have set up his church under a yew tree that grew on the cliff. Lismore's early name 'Lios mor', meant 'the great monastery' (and not 'the great garden', as some have translated the name), for Lismore too, had a significant history. Here St. Moluag set up the monastery which would have been fortified and as Niall, Coarb of St Moluag, Abbot of Lismore, Baron of Bachuil says in his book *St. Moluag*, 'The monks lived in bee hive cells, worshipped together in an oratory and ate in a communal refectory'. The two saints Moluag and Columba who lived within the same time frame, were as opposite as opposite can be. Moluag was a Bishop known for his blessings and miracles of healing, while Columba, a penitent, was known for his curses and acts of cruelty, at one point in his career, burying a man alive beneath a wall on Iona and at another making a father throw his son off a cliff. One story told of the two saints was of Columba cursing Moluag with such things as 'May you have alder for your firewood' (a wood not known for being the best choice for burning), to which Moluag replied 'And may it burn exceedingly well', which apparently it does to this day on Lismore!

Columba, or to give him his Irish name, Columcille, was from all accounts, a violent man and a decidedly controversial figure. Born in 521 in Donegal, Ireland, Columba, according to the Abbot of Lismore, was 'dispatched to the monastic school at Maghbile (Morville Abbey) where he studied under the famous St Finnian. He had a feisty temperament and was given the rather ironic nickname of the 'Dove of the Church''. As a novice, he coveted Finnian's psalter and asked permission to copy it. This request being refused, he did it anyway and when St, Finnian told him to give the copy up, he refused his Abbot's order, which was seen as a serious crime but Columba went further, going over the Abbot's head to appeal to Diarmatt, the High King. When his petition was unsuccessful, as stated in *St. Moluag:*,

> Columba's fury knew no bounds. He persuaded his relatives, the northern O'Neills, to rise up in rebellion. This led to the Battle of Cul Dreimhne in 561 during which 3,000 men were killed... Columba was exiled for the 'shedding of Christian blood'... As a result of his many crimes Columba was excommunicated... This was a severe but just sentence as it meant that no Christian could converse with him or even offer him a glass of water.

The Battle of Cul Dreimhne was seen in some circles as a battle between Druids and Christians. So here is the reason as to why Columba left Ireland. St Brendan of Bitt, however, defended him as a result of a 'heavenly vision' and the elders dropped their charge:

Legend suggests that it was St. Molaise who imposed this penance of two parts. The first was that he was to be exiled from Ireland, never to set eyes on it again and the second that he should work as a missionary to bring as many souls to Christ as had been killed in the battle... he was simply made a priest so that he could serve the sacraments and baptise converts... There is no evidence that Columba ever succeeded in bringing 3,000 souls to Christ (and even Columba's supporters can find no evidence that he carried out any missionary work). Columba could not or did not deign to speak the same language as the Picts and could only converse with the Gaelic speaking Scots.

This then contradicts the story of Columba developing a large congregation on Bernera, as he would have been unable to preach to the people there. The story of his leaving Ireland as 'there was one thing he feared more than death itself and that was the sound of the axe in Derry' (said to have been the cutting down of the five sacred trees of Ireland), is equally untrue as it was the Norse men, the Danes or Vikings who did this at a much later date. 'Bradley', however:

> whose book was published by the Iona Community and so must be considered sympathetic to Columba, has some interesting conclusions. Columba had two very different sides to his personality... an intensely human figure with faults and weaknesses as well as extraordinary depths of gentleness and humility.

Much has been written of the Isle of Bernera in *The God Tree* but I will recap some of it here as Bernera cannot be underestimated as a place of considerable spiritual importance in early times, the hidden holy of holies, central to the Druids and early Christians alike and eventually, perhaps deliberately confused with Iona, in an attempt to draw and divert people away from it to protect the yew and the sanctity of the place. Thus, after some time spent there, St. Columba eventually decamped to Iona, often called 'Yew Island' but which before he came, was called Inis Druderrach, 'the Island of the Druids'. There is no evidence that there ever were or ever have been any yews on Iona. It was Columba himself who called Iona, Iuna, another name for yew, which could only have been to mislead people to think this was 'Yew Island'. When Columba left Bernera, just as he intended, the mists of forgetting fell on that island like an invisible cloak and it became, once more, a secret otherworldly island remaining unchanged and existing outside of time. When the Vikings eventually arrived on Iona, a few hundred years later, they didn't even notice Bernera but focused on Iona which must have disappointed them, describing it as completely barren with no tree cover, let alone sacred yews. An essential to being a Cor, or Avalon itself, is the presence of ancient yews and Iona had none. Columba went on to establish Iona, some 40 miles away from Bernera as the crow flies, as a Christian place, and the Culdees monks who were there before him left. He set about building the Christian community and settlement Iona is known for, ensuring Bernera disappeared from everyone's memory.

The small deserted island of Bernera, next to Mull in the Firth of Lorne in the Western Isles of Scotland, is easy to cross to at low tide from the larger island of Lismore, across a narrow channel, although the causeway between the two islands is only open for three or four hours at a time.

'Yew Island' Painting by Janis Fry.

There are several ways to approach it: by sea from along the coast or another island, being careful to navigate the rocks and shallow waters on approaching the beach, or on foot by way of the narrow causeway. A visit to Bernera can never be casual but involves planning a deliberate pilgrimage in the knowledge of there being a certain amount of time, a brief window of a few hours, before the sea once again closes the causeway, demanding a return to the world of the mundane. Bernera is a place on the edge of the world, existing in the numinous, and like a riddle, joined to the land but not joined, opening its 'door' only with the tide. The visitor must watch and wait, watch and wait. Bernera demands to be approached with a pure mind and heart. Never have I felt so alone, like the last person left on earth, as I did on Bernera, looking out from its summit in all directions into the far distance at island behind island, with not a person in sight. In Bede's day, Bernera was known as a monastery or monastic cell, linked with a holy man but it had originally been a nemeton or sanctuary.

St. Columba was a lover of yew trees and a member of the O'Neill clan, a Druid tribe, who were being persecuted. Although Columba was with the Church, the time in which he lived was that interesting period of history where the old religion and the new overlapped and elements of the two were certainly held within his spirituality. One version of events leading to Columba leaving Ireland for Bernera is that, at the instigation of the Vikings, the inauguration tree of the O'Neill clan in Ireland was cut down by a local tribe. However, it is unlikely to have been the Vikings, who didn't arrive till later but apparently for this reason and as well as others already mentioned, Columba found himself on Bernera, where he would have known of the enormous yew growing out of the cliff, a sacred tree which had most likely been there for thousands of years. Bernera was doubtless a holy place known to the ancients for some long time before Columba who is said to have sheltered his congregation under the great yew there but as the Abbot of Lismore pointed out, Columba could not have had a congregation as he was unable to speak the language of the local people. However, the two places, Bernera and Iona have become muddled and Iona is certainly not the island they were talking about in the 6th century as it was not called that until much later, when around the 14th century or later, scholars confused the name Ioua and wrote an 'n' instead of a 'u' turning it into Iona. Iona was never Yew Island but the name is a corruption or deliberate play on the word Ioua meaning yew, from Bernera's early name 'Ioua insula'. The name 'Iona' actually means 'dove', one of Columba's names.

The earliest form of the name 'Iona' enabled place-name scholar William J. Watson to show that the name originally meant something like 'Yew place' but it seems likely this was more in honour of Bernera than the island that carries the name nowadays. Columba, who was apparently in fear of the yew tree at Bernera being cut down as he predicted it would be one day, may have taken the name from Bernera and set up Iona as a decoy, drawing people away from that holy sanctuary. This second island was then established by Columcille (St. Columba) in 563 as the first foundation in Celtic Christian practices. As Allen Meredith says in his paper called *Iona: Origins of a Druid Island*, 'The name Iona or Hii is a puzzle, for the 7th century Abbot Adamnan referred to it as being Ioua Insula, meaning 'an island of yew trees', when there were none'. In *The Sea Kingdoms*, Alistair Moffat writes, 'It appears that Iona is a mis-rendering of 'Ioua', which comes from 'iogh', the Gaelic word for 'yew tree', so that 'Ioua Insula' translates as a Yew Isle.' However, Bernera is the only place for miles around which is home to yew and it rather looks like the name Iona, was a corruption of Ioua, a name which migrated from Bernera with Columba. Bernera, an Old Norse name, was also not that island's original name. It was called by several names such as Eo or Hii or Hy, which are all Yew names, to be translated as Yew Island.

Walafried Strabo, the travel writer, described Bernera, in 831, as 'the island of the Picts, 'insula pictorium''. He also called it 'Eo insula' meaning 'yew island' and said that 'on the coast of the Picts is pointed out an isle poised in the rolling sea whose name is Eo' but Bernera in various other sources is frequently called 'I-una', another name for yew used in such documents as 'Gallic Antiquities' translated by John Smith in 1780.

By the 13th to 15th century, all scholars were adamant that Bernera was the sacred island, the yew island and the island was identified as such in *Scoticarum Historia,* written in 1506-1582, by George Buchanan, a Latin scholar, who gives important evidence about Bernera, calling it by an old name for it, 'Berneray' and stating in Latin:

> Bernera olim sacrosanctum asylum dicta, silva taxi nobilis, Molochasgir, Drunacha spinis, sambuco et magnarum aedium ruinis operta. This translates as 'Bernera, once the inviolate holy sanctuary of the noble yew, covered in Molchasgir (which is untranslatable and thus unidentifiable), blackthorn, elder and large ruined buildings.'

It is highly significant that Buchanan describes Bernera in such terms as the most holy sanctuary and neglects to say any such thing of Iona. There is no sign today of any large ruined buildings on Bernera but elder, the yew's companion, is still there, along with an abundance of vicious blackthorn bushes which appear to see their job as protecting the regenerated yew, that grows in Bonsai form along the cliff, by drawing blood from any would-be visitors.

George Broderick, quoted in the *Journal of Scottish Name Studies 7* of 2013, describes the origin of the name Iona 'as seemingly a scribal misreading of Ioua in a text ultimately derived from Adomnan', (the ninth Abbot of Iona who wrote the life of Columba 100 years after Columba's death). Adomnan's 'Ioua' he says:

> is an adjective formed from the name of the island...Ioua seems to go back to a derivative 'Iuoua' which might mean Yew Place...though yew trees are seemingly unknown in Iona.

Another Gaelic form of the name 'IlhI', may derive from the Proto-Semitic word for 'island, isolated place with the foregoing meaning or the sense 'island of a special sort, a holy place'. Broderick mentions the name place scholar William J Watson, who shows that the name Iona originally meant something like 'yew place'. The element 'Ivo' denoting 'yew' occurs in Ogham inscriptions and Gaulish names and may form the basis of early Gaelic names for yew like 'Eogan'. Mac an Tailleir in 2003 lists the more recent Gaelic name for Iona, 'Eilean Idhe', meaning the Isle of Iona, stating that:

> the modern English name Iona, comes from an 18th century misreading of 'Ioua'... which was either just Adomnan's attempt to make the Gaelic name fit Latin grammar or else a genuine derivative from 'Ivova' meaning 'yew place'. Ioua's change to Iona may have resulted from a transcription mistake resulting from the similarity of 'n' and 'u' in Insula Miniscule.

Whatever the reason for the confusion of names, it is important to realise there is no doubt that Columba's original sacred island was Bernera, the yew island, and that the name changed and followed him to Iona, the better known and second holy island, causing much possibly deliberate, confusion, which disguised and hid Bernera, the great secret, the true Avalon, one of the three sacred Cors of Britain. The fact that we are seeking here the most important holy place, central to the most closely guarded secret in the spiritual history of Britain, is the reason it is so important to identify the place beyond doubt.

The essential identifying factor to Bernera being Avalon, the third Cor, is its Irish name, Emain Afallach. This Gaelic name came originally from Emain Aballach. Later the name Avallach changed again with different cultures and eventually became Avalon. This highly significant name means 'Island of the Immortal Fruits', which can only mean the fruit of the yew. It is a name that implies a place in the Otherworld, an elusive isle, a spiritual place existing in another dimension rather than a completely real place. It is said to lie at the centre of the world, like the World Tree and other places such as Eden and the Hesperides. The Egyptians, as we saw in *The God Tree*, sought the Tree of Life in the Isles of Britain, in the west to be precise. One wonders if this could have been Bernera. The Egyptians were known to have been in Britain and very likely planted the sacred tree, the yew at Ankerwycke near Runnymede, the site of the inauguration of Kings. How the yew came to be on Bernera no one knows, for yews are not native to this area but it could have been there, growing on the island's cliff since ancient times and considering how unusual a yew is in this part of the world, it is not beyond the realms of possibility, that the Bernera Yew was brought here and planted by ancient people such as the Egyptians.

There are in fact connections with Egypt in Ireland and Scotland. Some of this was discussed in *The God Tree* where what is most likely a 13th century document called *The Settling of the Manor of Tara* was investigated. This document describes an important journey made from Egypt to Ireland and Scotland. The document also tells of the giant Trefuilngid Tre-eochair who brings seeds or a yew branch described as Lebanon wood on this voyage, from which the sacred trees of Ireland are thought to have grown. Lebanon is where the Egyptians sourced yew wood. Also discussed in *The God Tree* is the burial found on the Hill of Tara of an Egyptian from the time of Tutankhamun. Further evidence of the Egyptian connection is found in *St Moluag*. Most authors now accept that the church in Ireland grew out of the monastic traditions of the East. This is what St Moluag believed as can be seen in this seventh-century Antiphonary of the Irish monastery of Bangor, which was founded by him and St. Congal, 'This house, full of delight is built on the rock and indeed is the true vine transplanted out of Egypt.' Earlier in his book the Abbot of Lismore writes:

In Ireland, the monastic system flourished as it fitted closely with the tribal culture of the people. Monasticism had spread from Palestine to neighbouring Syria and Egypt... The Eastern influence was very strong in the Celtic Church. There seemed to be a peculiar affinity between the tribal or clan system of the Celts and the monasticism of Egypt... Elements of eastern orthodoxy were merged into Irish Christianity... It was common to name monasteries in Ireland 'deserts' since they wanted to emulate the desert fathers of Syria and Egypt... In spite of its remoteness the Celtic Church of Ireland retained direct contact with the monasteries of Egypt.

This evidence supports the idea that Bernera was indeed the western isle spoken of in the Pyramid Texts (the oldest ancient Egyptian funerary texts dating to the late Old Kingdom). The oldest of the Pyramid Texts are dated to c 2400 - 2300 BCE and were reserved for the Pharaoh. According to Wikipedia, these are the oldest known corpus of ancient Egyptian religious texts and were carved into the subterranean walls and Sarcophagi of pyramids at Saqqara from the end of the Fifth Dynasty into the Eighth of the First Intermediate Period around 2500 BCE. If the Bernera yew was planted at this time, at the time of Columba it could have been around 3,000 years old. Bernera is the Western Isle off the Western Isle of Lismore, an island considered holy in itself.

To add to the evidence for the early connection between Egypt and Scotland, Rev. John Stirton in *The Celtic Church and the Influence of the East*, 1923, stated:

The earliest type of monumental cross in Scotland is an Egyptian or Coptic wheel cross. It appears on several Christian carved stones at Kirkmadrine in Wigtonshire (from at least as far back as the 6th century), along with the Alpha and Omega. The Crux Ansata, the emblem of life in Egyptian hieroglyphs, is found on a stone at Nigg in Ross-shire and another at Ardbue in Ireland.

Furthermore, according to Barry Dunsfold in *Sacred Connections Scotland - Scotland's past links with Ancient Egypt:*

> The old Scots Chronicles also record that during the 2nd century BCE certain 'Egyptian philosophers' (probably from the Egyptian mystery temples) came to Scotland to advise the Scots King of the period...During the early centuries CE the Celtic monks in the British Isles, much of whose texts were rooted in a pre-Christian Druid tradition, saw Egypt as the true holy land rather than Palestine due to the ascetic Desert Father tradition established there which they sought to follow and emulate. Hence, we find in Scotland and Ireland, a number of dysarts (desert) place names which record monastic settlements and retreats founded on the Egyptian anchorite model.

The knowledge that Avalon was in this area of the Scottish islands goes back thousands of years and by medieval times the Isle of Arran was also thought to be Emain Avallach. The position of the World Tree is actually marked on old maps! Although there is no evidence of such a sacred tree growing on Arran, the idea may have migrated from Bernera as things do. On Mull is an anciently named crag, Crag Ure, a Gaelic name meaning Yew Crag. From there, Bernera could be seen and so the name may not have meant that the Crag was home to yew which it isn't but that the yew on Bernera could be seen from it.

The yew tree on Bernera stood on the cliff on the edge of the small island, with wide branches which spread half over the land and half over the sea, so far in fact that it was said to be capable of sheltering a thousand people beneath its canopy. From *The Barons of Bachuil* by Alexander Carmichael LL.D. in *The Celtic Review*, 1909, we read the following:

> The people of Mull and Morvern came in their skin coracles

wherein they sat out the service, while the people of Lismore came on foot and sat, on the ground, the island being accessible by foot at half-tide. From the circumstance of Colum-cille preaching there, the island of Bearnery was looked upon as holy ground and the tree under which he preached as sacred. (Bearnery was Bernera from the Gaelic Bearnaraigh) The remains of a small oratory and an oblation cairn are close by where the yew stood.

Columba had his cell in a cave at the bottom of the cliff, beneath the yew tree and it is still possible to see, if not a cave, certainly, a sheltered space receding into the cliff beneath the yew. As already said, it is hard to see how Columba could have preached as he did not speak the Pictish language of the people but perhaps people simply came to see the wild holy man and the rare yew tree.

Columba prophesied that the tree would eventually be cut down and destroyed and that when that happened fire would ensue, blood would be spilt and people would drown. It may have taken a long time for Columba's prophecy to come true but eventually it did in the eighteenth century (full story. in *The God Tree*). Modern people are dissociated from the knowledge of the spirituality of trees, stones and wells to such an extent that most consider it madness to think of a tree as having consciousness. However, the Campbells of Loch Nell who took the yew for a staircase for Loch Nell castle were left in no doubt that this was the case and that it was their action that caused serious repercussions to the family resulting in bad luck in the form of fires, accidents and deaths which plagued them for centuries. Recompense was eventually made for the destruction of the sacred tree by Dr Livingstone (Abbot of Lismore) and Mr Campbell on behalf of his ancestors. Dr Livingstone is a modern-day descendant of the original Dr Livingstone, a native of Lismore, who travelled in Africa, and who was famous for being presumed to be Dr Livingstone. They obtained a cutting from the regenerating Bernera yew, grew it into a small tree and planted it on Lismore, thereby lifting a curse that had dogged the Campbell family for 300 years.

When I visited Bernera some 30 years ago in search of where the original tree had been, it was noticeable that the girth of a yew stump I saw some 15 feet above the beach and the 'cave', was not that big, less than a metre in diameter which is somewhat at variance with Robert Hutchinson FRSA, author of *The Old and Remarkable Yew Trees of Scotland,*1890, who describes the yew as being of a 'huge size'. It's possible I had the wrong stump or perhaps the branches were particularly long and large and the trunk not so large but strong and dense. The terrain here is almost impossible to navigate. I couldn't help thinking of the limestone cliff-top yews, known to be the oldest and densest yews in Britain, predating the Ice Age, as their roots, often dragged by glaciers, survived under the ice. Even if this yew was not as old as that, the adverse conditions for a yew growing on a limestone cliff would mean it would be much smaller than might be expected for its actual age, as cliff-top yews are. It is not unlikely that this rare yew tree growing on the limestone cliff of Bernera and of a considerable size at the time of St. Columba, 1400 years ago, was known and revered since ancient times.

Allen Meredith's research paper, *Iona: Origins of a Druid Island,* goes into much detail about the confusion between these two islands, Bernera and Iona. The extraordinary thing is that such is its vigour, that today the Bernera yew has regenerated as yews do but with a completely different habit. Although two small yew trees appear on the cliff, which must be part of the original, most of the body of the tree now appears as a bonsai version of its former self, travelling for quite a distance at low height, clinging to the cliff and emerging from every crevice in the rock. Never have I seen a yew growing like this.

Cliff yew regenerating on Bernera. Photo by Maggie Wallis.

The following verses are attributed to Saint Columba, and are purported to be about the Bernera yew:

> This is the Yew of the Saints
> Where they used to come with me together
> Ten hundred angels were there
> Above our heads, side close to side.
>
> Dear to me is that Yew tree
> Would that I were set in its place there!

The Island of Bernera has the remains of an oratory and cairn and the site of a church is indicated on the map as being on the beach, all suggesting that the island was used at different times for religious purposes. There is an old staff known as the Bachuil Mor, which is also called the Great Crozier of St. Moluag and is linked with Lismore and Bernera. From *St. Moluag:*

> The Bachuil Mor of St. Moluag was treated with veneration akin to awe by the people...Like the staff of St. Patrick of Armagh, the famous Bachuil Isu or 'Staff of Jesus', (burned by the Englishman George Browne, Archbishop of Dublin in 1536), the staff of Moluag possessed, the simple faith of the times, miraculous powers. It ensured safety at sea, truth on land, secured man from plague, woman from death and cattle from murrain.

The staff still survives in the keeping of the Coarb, the Abbot of Lismore. It is a walking stick of blackthorn, raising the question as to whether there was an earlier staff made of yew. Its origins are unknown. Nigel Tranter in *Columba* says that according to tradition, Moluag may have been related to Columba and gave Bernera to him for a spiritual retreat, for prayer and meditation away from the world. The fact that he gave it implies he had some claim to it. In early times payments were made in kind and those to the custodian of the staff of the Bishop of Lismore were made in lands. A small estate was given to him near the cathedral and he was created a baron. The Cathedral Church of Lismore is dedicated to Saint Moluag and it was the staff of Moluag which was the pastoral staff of the Bishop, so it seems likely that Moluag did own land in the vicinity and possibly Bernera itself. In the latter part of the 6th century, Bernera was settled by monks of the Irish Culdee church under the leadership of St. Moluag. A separate tradition concerning Iona says that Conall gave the island of Iona to Columba and this was mentioned in the Ulster Chronicle (AU s.a. 573).

Simon Andrew Stirling, the author of *The King Arthur*

Conspiracy, is the only other author who in his well-researched book, comes anywhere close to identifying the last resting place of King Arthur but as the saying goes, a miss is as good as a mile and his book is all about Iona being that legendary place. Stirling's account of Arthur's life is entirely believable but time and again I have found that mistakes in history are compounded when one mistaken fact or assumption goes unquestioned and from there on, others just repeat the error, rather than going to the heart of the matter to establish whether or not it is true. Stirling has done just this, taking for granted that the highly publicised Iona must also be the site of Arthur's burial when in fact it is Bernera, not Iona which is the sacred Isle of Avalon, the place of the everlasting apples, the fruits of the yew, the tree of eternity and immortality. Stirling's book is well worth reading to understand what Arthur was doing in Scotland. The author gives a detailed account of Arthur's battles there, his involvement with the Welsh warrior saints Cadoc and Illtyd, the role played by St. Columba who was a contemporary of theirs and pinpoints the site of the final battle on the plain of Camno, close to the River Isla. Here Stirling says Arthur was mortally wounded and taken on his final journey down that river to the sea and on to the Sacred Isle.

Stirling says that Arthur's last stand was 40 miles from where Cadoc had established a monastery near Doune and where he harboured some of Arthur's enemies. St. Columba, he says, predicted that Arthur's death would be brought about by a companion of whom he suspected nothing (possibly Illtyd - see *The God Tree*) and that he died on the 23rd July 594 and Columba on 9th June 597. Arthur's head, Stirling says, was buried where the World Tree stood at the Navel of the sea just as Christ was nailed to the World Tree at Golgotha. Stirling has to be given full marks for identifying Columba as the missing link in the mystery of King Arthur's final resting place, the Isle of Avalon. This place Avalon was an incredibly important place well before

Arthur. Stirling may well be correct in all he says up to that point but when it comes to the location of Avalon, he narrowly misses the target and doesn't appear to know of the existence of Bernera, unless he is deliberately shielding it. However, his book has a great deal, mostly deprecatory, to say about Columba who he believes, along with Cadoc, betrayed Arthur, whose queen Gwenhwyfar he raised in his own household. Perhaps Stirling too was trying to hide the existence of Bernera and for many reasons, the mission to disguise and hide the holy isle has been highly successful but be warned, this sacred place, this holy of holies, has its own way of protecting itself from those who are not of a pure heart and a raised consciousness. You should be prepared and very aware if you wish to make such a pilgrimage.

What is sad is that so many vested interests, not of Stirling who simply got the wrong place in the right area but of others, who wishing to make revenue from Avalon and Arthur, have deliberately lied, colluded and distorted the facts for so many years, leading people to wrongly believe that Arthur belonged to Glastonbury. It is time to put the record straight. Bernera is Avalon. Avalon is Bernera, the Isle of the Immortal Apples. As Stirling says, (getting the location wrong but the description right), 'The greatest hero Britain has ever known was laid to rest in a 'hidden retreat' under the Cairn of the Yews, on the apple bearing isle'. St. Columba, who spoke of yews and angels in the same breath and who kept the secret of Bernera and Avalon, whatever the truth of his deeds, his morality and character, will be remembered as a holy man whose life and spiritual beliefs spanned the time of magic and the divinity of the trees and the Church and the advent of the Age of Reason.

Chapter 10

Llanilid, Joseph of Arimathea and the Tree of Life

The day I went to Llanilid with Susan Elizabeth Hale of Earth Day Sing for the Trees (an annual global event), was a perfect day, made even more perfect by Susan, who seemed to break a spell that held the place in something like a dream. When I'd visited this place before, Llanilid had always seemed to be sleeping, frozen in time, dreaming of long ago, a rather musty place where great things, now buried and forgotten had once happened. But Susan woke it up through her singing and now it feels as if it's ready for 'the next phase', ready to be put on the map in its rightful place as the site of the very earliest Christian church. The yew tree and the place, whose history has been sidelined, will eventually go through a renaissance the way Defynnog has.

One of the most noticeable things about Llanilid is the Cor, the only one of the three Cors of Britain still extant as an earthwork. The Commission for Ancient Monuments describes the Cor at Llanilid as prehistoric and as a prime site in that part of Wales.

Llanilid - The Cor.

It is circular, a doughnut-shaped arena some 70 metres across and 25 feet high, with an internal measurement east to west of 30 metres, slightly more north to south, with an opening to the south, facing the present church. It has a well-marked moat that is missing on the east, said to be the only real moat in the County of Glamorgan. To the west of the site, there is a counter scarp. This ringwork was situated on the highest part of the glacial hillock with the church to the south, slightly lower down and at the time of King Arthur and Arimathea, this place would have been an island, the sea coming in from the south and flooding the plain in front of the site. For some time (see details on page 203 of *The God Tree*) I thought this place was Avalon and although it now seems most likely Bernera was Avalon, there is still a possibility that Llanilid was the place. In Nennius' *History of the Britons*, 822 CE, there is an account of a secret and extremely important burial of a holy man with an altar above his face, whose body was brought by ship along the sea coast of Glamorgan. The arrival of the body was awaited by St. Illtyd, King Arthmael of Gwent's cousin, whose other name was Galahad. Arthur as we know sleeps in Avalon on the Isle of Apples (apples of immortality - yew apples), a description which would fit Llanilid at the time, as well as Bernera. It was a Druidic temple and meeting place and central to the Silurians. We have no idea what took place at these meetings. It seems unlikely, being open to the elements that they were for meetings to do with practical or political matters but were for spiritual or ceremonial purposes, which were conducted outside beneath the stars and in direct contact with Nature.

Llanilid, meaning 'enclosure/parish of the Israelite', was named after Joseph of Arimathea. It was originally the capital of the Silures, the Celtic Yew tribe. Ilid is mentioned in the Genealogy of Saints as 'a man of Israel'. Bran the Blessed, otherwise known as Bran Fendigaidd (translated as Blessed Crow), King of the Silures, had his seat here, at a place known as Trevran, where his son Caradoc or Caradog was born. In 36 CE Bran abdicated his throne in favour of his son, to assume his office as Arch Druid of the Silures but his family was shortly to become the Royal Christian Dynasty of Ancient Britain. Caradog, known by the Romans as Caractacus, and renowned as a fierce warrior, fought against the Romans and led his tribe, the Silurians, the greatest fighters of the Celtic tribes, into many a battle against the Romans. They never gave up but Caradog, after some 40 pitched battles against the Romans, was eventually betrayed and captured at Clun where he fought his last battle and was taken to Rome for trial. The Romans, however, in recognition of the bravery and persistence of the Silures, who were never beaten, finally agreed to share power with them at Caerleon, which had become their capital.

The royal boundaries of the Silurians were divided into two sections. Arviragus ruled over the southern part of England and Caradog, his cousin, over Cambria (Wales). Arvirargus was aware of the coming of Joseph of Arimathea who settled at Llanilid by the invitation of Eurgain, Linus and Claudia, Caradog's children and under the protection of Arvirargus (Rev. William Morgan *St Paul in Britain: or the Origin of British as Opposed to Papal Christianity*). Arvirargus and Caradog were both chiefs of their own domain but in times of war, they united as Pendragon or Commander in Chief. At that time, they represented the most powerful warrior clan in the whole of Britain. Arvirargus who commanded a fleet of ships to hold back the Romans, ruled as Pendragon while his cousin was held captive in Rome and he continued to conduct the war against the Roman Empire in a manner that gained him immortal fame. Edmund Spencer wrote 'Was never king more highly magnifyde nor dread of Romans than was Arvirargus'. He was the great enemy of Rome. The Romans were repeatedly conquered and put to the rout by this one tribe, the Silurians. Even after the treaty which incorporated Britain with Rome (118 CE), two-thirds of the whole military force of the island continued to be stationed on the frontiers of Wales at Chester and Caerleon.

Caradog, was taken with the rest of his household to Rome where he delivered his legendary speech in Latin, which was so eloquent that it was recorded by Emperor Tacitus and earned him his pardon, or rather his reduced sentence of seven years confinement in that city instead of execution. After this time, Caradog returned to Wales in the company of his father Bran and other members of his household, including Eurgain, his daughter, on condition he took an oath that he would never again take up arms against the Romans. It must have been a strange homecoming. Several other notable people came with him and according to *The Beginning of Christianity* by Harvey Gardner, Caradog kept his oath to Emperor Claudius and the famous ex Pendragon of the British Silurian armies ended his days quietly and was laid to rest next to his wife and other relatives in Llanilid of Siluria.

Also, as part of the company returning to Britain, were Joseph of Arimathea (who came directly from Jerusalem), Barnabas the apostle, a Jewish Cypriot and Aristobulus. These were the first preachers of Christianity in Britain. In addition to being known as Joseph of Arimathea and St. James the Just, Joseph was called Ilid by the Chronicles of Wales. He became the patron of Llanilid in Gwent, having founded a mission at Cor Eurgain, the Cor at Llanilid where Eurgain, daughter of Caradog, was born and where she returned as a converted Christian, with twelve early Christians, her own disciples. Eurgain is recorded as the patroness of the Pauline Mission at Llanilid and for that reason it became more commonly known as the Cor Eurgain Mission. Cor Eurgain as an institution later moved and resettled at what is now Llantwit Major or Llanelltyd Fawr, marking the change to a Christian institution from a Druidic one.

The 'Cywydd to St. Mary Magdalene' in the *Gestyn Ceriog*, refers to Joseph as Ilid, as does the manuscript of *The Sayings of the*

Wise; *The Achan Saint Prydain* (Genealogy of the Saints of Britain) which states that 'there came with Bran the Blessed from Rome to Britain, Arwstli Hen, (Aristobulus), Gyndaf - men of Israel' The Welsh Triads also mention Cyndaw being in the company from Rome. (The Triads are a group of related medieval manuscripts containing Welsh folklore, mythology and historical fact in groups of three. They relate much of British history and also tell of the Welsh King Arthur and contain memorials of remarkable events in ancient Britain but without dates and they range from extremely ancient to the 12th century.) Llanilid became the first Christian site in Britain, established by Aristobulus, a disciple of Jesus and friend of Joseph of Arimathea and Caradog's family, who was ordained as first Bishop of Britain by St. Paul and was therefore also, the very first Christian Bishop. In his 2nd letter to Timothy, 4: 21, St Paul says, 'Do thy diligence to come before winter. Eubelus, greeteth thee, and Pudens and Linus and Claudia and all the brethren'. Eubelus was a variation of the name Aristobulus, Pudens was a loyal friend of St Paul, who became a saint and martyr and may also have been Claudia's husband. Linus and Claudia were Caradog's son and daughter. The fact that St. Paul directed Timothy to come must mean that he, St Paul, was already there at Llanilid.

Aristobulus became the supervisor of the Church at Llanilid with Bran whose father Llyr Llediaeth, (Shakespeare's King Lear) was converted and baptised by Joseph before founding the church at Llandaff near Cardiff. Bran continued to be the apostle to Siluria at Llandaff. These were extraordinary and revolutionary times with the Christianising of Britain. Aristobulus also had a Welsh name, Arwystl Hen. He was sadly martyred and probably buried at Llanilid. At the time there was understandably, a hatred in Britain for the Roman invaders and suspicion of anyone associated with Rome, such as Aristobulus who came to Britain from there, although he was of the Church of Jerusalem, along with his brother, Barnabas, and Joseph of Arimathea. It was only the people's love of Bran and their loyalty to his son, their national hero, Caradog, which led them to accept, perhaps reservedly, his companions from that city and it is likely it was this suspicion and hatred, which led to Aristobulus becoming the first Christian martyr and the only one of this period to be martyred by the British. It happened when he travelled beyond the territory and protection of the Silures to preach in the lands of another Celtic tribe, the Ordovices.

Aristobulus was the elder brother of Barnabas, who was also there at Llanilid. It was Barnabas who wrote about Jesus being hung from a tree and not crucified (Epistle of Barnabas 8 'the reign of Jesus is on the tree') and so Aristobulus was also fully cognisant of the true nature of Jesus' death. He was one of the seventy elected by Jesus and it was his wife who was healed by a miracle of Jesus, recorded in St. Matthew's gospel. He was the father in law of St Peter and father of James and John. There is a considerable body of evidence to show that Aristobulus travelled to Britain and died there, including from Hippolytus, born around 160 CE, the most learned member of the Roman Church of that period, who was probably Bishop of the Greeks in Rome during the episcopates of Zephyrinus and Callixtus. Hippolytus mentions Aristobulus as 'Bishop of the Britons'. Aristobulus was one of the 70 disciples and a follower of St Paul the Apostle, with whom he preached the Gospel. He was chosen by Paul to be the missionary Bishop to the land of Britain and St Paul also appointed Linus, son of Caradog, and as such a Royal Prince of Siluria and Llanilid, as the first Bishop of Rome. Dorotheus, Bishop of Tyre in 303 CE also testifies to Aristobulus being in Britain as does Haleca, Bishop of Augusta and in *Genealogies of the Saints of Britain* we find written:

There came with Bran the Blessed from Rome to Britain, Arwstli Hen (Aristobulus the Aged), Ilid (Joseph of Arimathea), Cyndaf (chief or head man of Israel), Maw or

Mawan, son of Cyndaf (Josephes – Joseph of Arimathea's son).

Within a year of his return to Britain with Bran, Ilid, 'a man of Israel', otherwise known as Joseph of Arimathea, whose family loved Aristobulus, took charge until Paul arrived. Theodoretus in 435 CE testifies: 'Paul liberated from his first captivity at Rome, preached the Gospel to the Britons and others in the West'. The loss of Aristobulus was a terrible blow to Paul who was devastated by his loss and sent his salutations and commiserations to his friends and family in Rome. Jowett also states that Aristobulus was in Britain before St. Paul wrote his epistle to the Romans. Thus, Aristobulus with Joseph of Arimathea and the family of Caradog with whom he was closely connected, made the first mission to Britain, the mission to Wales.

The antiquity of Llanilid is asserted by Martin of Louvain in his *Disputoilis Anglis it Gallioe in Councilio Constantiano* of 1517 where he says:

Three times, the antiquity of the British Church was affirmed in Ecclesiastical Councilia. Firstly, The Council of Pisa, in 1417 CE. Then, the Council of Constance, 1419 CE and finally, The Council of Siena, 1423 CE, which stated that the British Church took precedence over all other churches, being founded by Joseph of Arimathea, 'immediately after the Passion of Christ.' This was then acquiesced in. In fact it was the only time the matter was questioned and that for political reasons. The Churches of France and Spain were bound to give way to the points of antiquity and precedency to the Church of Britain founded by Joseph of Arimathea.

Gildas, the Wise, the British historian, (500 - 570 CE) expressly stated that Christianity was introduced in the last year of Tiberius, by Joseph of Arimathea (38 CE). This was also asserted by Gregory of Tours (538 - 594 CE) in *History of the Franks*, that this happened five years after Jesus' death. Robert Parsons, the Jesuit, in his *Three Conversions of England* admits, in common with the great majority of Roman Catholic writers that Christianity came into Britain direct from Jerusalem.

The 7th century monk known as the Venerable Bede, contesting Rome and refusing to acknowledge Augustine, also wrote as fact that the church of Llanilid was the very first Christian church built in Britain and said, 'The Britons are contrary to the whole Roman world and enemies to the Roman customs, not only in their Mass but in their tonsure'. He asserted, 'Our obedience is to the Bishop of Caerleon or St. David'.

The year 35 or 36 CE is the year in which Joseph of Arimathea and his party left Palestine and arrived in Britain. An extract from *Ecclesiastical Annals* referring to that year reads:

> In that year, the party mentioned were exposed to the sea in a vessel without sails or oars. The vessel drifted finally to Marseilles and they were saved. From Marseilles, Joseph and his company passed into Britain.

Why such hostility was shown to the Holy family is a matter of conjecture. There is also an ancient manuscript in the Vatican which states that St. Joseph, Lazarus, Mary and Martha and others were put into a boat off the Levant and landed at Marseilles in 35 CE and there is a tradition in Marseilles of Mary Magdalene and her daughter Sarah, reputedly Jesus' daughter. They are said to have founded the Merovingian dynasty. This was just a couple of years after Jesus' death in 33 CE. Other traditions say Joseph of Arimathea arrived in Marseilles in 37 CE, the last year of Tiberius, with the Holy family and from there made his way to Britain from Bordeaux arriving in South Wales in the same year but dates for events in these times can be contradictory and unreliable. At St. Maximin in Southern France,

Mary Magdalene's skeleton is said to lie behind a gold mask and St. Marie de la Mer claims to be the place where she landed. A 9th century document says she came with Joseph of Arimathea.

The Roman invasion of Britain commenced in 42 CE and Arvirargus, cousin of Caradog, carried on waging war against them in Caradog's absence. Sometime after 42 CE when the Romans invaded, it would have become untenable to remain in Llanilid, the home of Caradog, the famous opponent of Rome, particularly for those converts to the outlawed religion, Christianity and it was this, probably more than anything else that would have precipitated the move to Llantwit Major or Llanelltyd Fawr as it was called after Saint Illtyd. It is easy to see why the names Ilid and Illtyd have always been confused being so similar. Caer Worgorn, the name for Llantwit at the time, later became Llanelltyd with the arrival of Illtyd who set up a college monastery there in the 6th century. Cor Tewdws was founded there around 395 CE after Cor Eurgain, in honour of the Roman Emperor Theodosius and refounded once more in around 508 by St Illtyd who gave his name to Llanelltyd. So Llanelltyd Fawr was not called that till nearly 500 years after Cor Eurgain was likely to have been settled there having been removed from Llanilid.

Llanilid, was at one time a port, with its road, Heol Porth Mawr (Great Port Road), possibly Roman in its straightness. This was navigational, a causeway from the port to the church and implies there was a community here big enough to warrant such an important road and was due first and foremost to King Bran the Blessed. It implies a shoreline, no longer there and thus access to the sea. Other Roman sites in the area are mapped. A site called Gadlys below the church may have been Roman originally. It was certainly built as a garrison or military camp and thought of as Roman up until the 1950s.

Simon Zelotes or Simon the Zealot who arrived in Britain in 44 CE according to Cardinal Baronius and Hippolytus was also brought by Joseph of Arimathea. George Jowett states that every time Joseph of Arimathea went to Gaul he came back with more missionary helpers, Simon Zelotes among them. Simon is said to have been martyred and buried in Britain in 61 CE. As stated in *The lives and the Deaths of the Holy Apostles* by Dorman Newman, 1685, he was arrested under the orders of Catus Decianus and was tried, condemned to death and crucified.

Jestyn ap Gwrgant, Prince of Glamorgan, wrote in the 11th century that in the days of Cyllinus ab Caradoc, a wise and just King (son of Caradog), many of the Cymry (the Welsh), embraced the faith in Christ through the teachings of the saints of Cor Eurgain and many godly men from the countries of Greece and Rome were in Cambria. Joseph of Arimathea converted King Arvirargus, cousin of Caradog to Christianity as referred to in the *British Chronicles*. It is said Arvirargus gave Joseph land in Glastonbury but it is clear that most of his work was carried out at Llanilid, his first point of arrival with the other Christians. It was after 42 CE, at some point in the history of the early church that everything moved from Llanilid, where it had all begun and resettled at Llantwit Major. This would have included the removal of Cor Eurgain which must originally have been the institution based at the Cor next to Llanilid church as it is now. Eurgain, daughter of Caradog, became the first female saint. She is said to have been converted by Paul in Rome and was a committed and fervent Christian. The Cor at Llanilid was abandoned, no doubt along with many of the old Druid ways as this is the cross over point to the new religion. It is very noticeable if you look at the map, that Llantwit is a mere seven miles or so away by a straight track south, along which would have been carried anything that could have been removed from the site, such as inscribed stones and probably a cutting from the yew tree, to be planted at Llantwit Major, though there is no sign of such a tree there now or the artefacts that would have been moved there.

The famous Llwyel stone, reputed to show Joseph of Arimathea's coming to Britain from the East, may have originally been at Llanilid.

It shows Joseph with a pyramid, indicating Egypt. It was

discovered being used as a gate post in the Trecastle area near the Brecon Beacons and bought from the farmer for £10 before ending up in the British Museum where the less important side with the Roman inscription is displayed and no record seems available of the Celtic sculpturing on the other side! (at least not when I went to investigate). It was found near another much less important Ilid site known as Capel Ilud, which is along the Roman road from Trecastle. The stone seems to have been in the wrong place for such an impressive artefact but may have been taken there for safekeeping by followers of Ilid. It is dated to the 5th

The Llwyel Stone.

century but is probably much older. Anything Celtic seems to be dated by the church to a later date, even as late as the 7th century, for political reasons to do with the Roman Church, pushing the date of the arrival of Christianity to a later one. Today at Llantwit Major, the place where an old yew tree may have stood is taken up by a new extension to the church. It was the custom, as we have seen, for migrating ancient people when they moved, to take their sacred trees with them as rootstock or cuttings for replanting at the new settlement. Many of us can relate to this, taking our special plants with us when we move house and I cannot imagine something of Ilid's tree not being taken to Llantwit. Cor Eurgain was apparently moved and set up as a college there. However, today there is no sign of the monastic buildings that would have been needed to house the 2,400 that supposedly formed the Perpetual Choir. Local lore has it that the college lay to the north of the present town but its precise location is unknown. The names Ilid and Illtyd have always been confused but it was Illtyd's monastery at Llanelltyd Fawr (Llantwit Major), set up much later in the 5th century which gave the name to the place and although the Welsh Triads and the Llandaff Charters refer to this being the arrival point for Joseph of Arimathea and his disciples in 37 CE, there is no record of this place existing as any form of religious site at this time. However, it must be assumed to have been the site of Cor Eurgain *after* the removal of the Cor institution from Llanilid. Archaeological evidence does show occupation from the Neolithic period to Roman times at Llantwit, probably due to its favourable position geographically and it is quite possible that it was once a collection and export point for copper ingots from the Great Orme mine in North Wales. Being such a short distance across the Bristol channel from where lead was exported, it would have saved foreign traders having to travel further north for these metals and this could well have been one of the reasons for the tradition of Joseph of Arimathea here, the other, of course, being to meet with the Druids and Christians, a short distance away at Llanilid. Joseph was familiar with the tin mining areas of Britain such as Cornwall and South Wales and as a merchant was considered to be one of them by the Britons, enabling him to move around freely.

Joseph of Arimathea, our central character, was a member

of the family of Jesus and according to Talmud was the younger brother of Jesus' mother, Mary and therefore Jesus' uncle. With the death of Mary's husband, in accordance with Jewish law, the guardianship of Jesus would have fallen to Arimathea and this is why Pontius Pilate granted Joseph's claim to the body of Jesus. He was known to be a wealthy man, owner of a fleet of ships trading regularly with the Cornish tin mines and the lead mines of the Mendips in Somerset and probably also dealing in metals such as gold and copper from Wales. It is not unlikely that Jesus would have accompanied Joseph on some of his trips and may even have studied here with the Druids as authors such as Tricia Mc Cannon in her book called simply *Jesus* and Dennis Price in *The Missing Years of Jesus*, point out in exploring the 'lost' or unaccounted for years of his life. Joseph of Arimathea's title of Nobilis Decurio indicates he had sole right to import lead and tin. His ships would sail up the Bristol Channel and Llantwit was just twelve miles north of the Somerset coast.

I agree with other authors such as Gilbert, Blackett and Wilson in the *Holy Kingdom*, that more or less everything to do with the history of King Arthur and the church of Joseph of Arimathea being in Glastonbury is a complete fiction, now largely discredited by historians, where monks like William of Malmesbury forged documents to fake history. In fact, there is far more documentary evidence for Joseph being in Llanilid than there ever was for Glastonbury. The history of the early Church having its roots at Llanilid was suppressed, as a result of the Roman Church wishing to be seen as the first to introduce Christianity to these islands with St. Augustine but probably also as a result of the monks of Glastonbury making a fictional case for Glastonbury to bring funds to their monastery and drawing attention away from Llanilid. That Joseph spent time in Glastonbury is not in dispute but the importance of Llanilid as the place of the first church in Britain cannot be overstated.

The significant thing, as far as this book is concerned, is that Joseph brought to Britain a branch from the Tree of Life, the tree that Jesus was hung on. The evidence for the subsequent planting of a branch or cutting from this at Glastonbury Chalice Well is well documented in *The God Tree*. The branch planted by Joseph grew into a tree which was later cut down. A piece of wood from this yew tree with root attached was found by Dr Rahtz in an archaeological dig carried out in 1964. With it, at a depth of 11 feet were found some Roman coins. There were also signs of cuts from a Roman axe found on the branch and tests at Leeds University showed the living tree, planted in the first century to have been cut down in the third. All this is documented in Dr Rahtz' book, *Glastonbury, Myth and Archaeology* by Dr Rahtz and Lorna Watts 2009.

Like all good gardeners it would seem most likely that Joseph would have made the most of the greenwood he brought from the sacred tree and split it up to maximise the number of potential pieces or 'cuttings' that would be likely to sprout, take root and grow into a tree. A Yew tribe such as the Silures who were known to have planted many yews, some of which still survive in Wales, would have known and recognised the sacred tree that Joseph was bringing in the form of a staff and it would have been received and planted at Llanilid with much awe and ceremony. News of his special cargo, the Holy Wood, from the Sacred Tree Jesus had hung on would doubtless have preceded him. It is important to understand how important the yew was to the Silurians, a Celtic yew tribe, how much knowledge they had of it and that Joseph's main mission was to preserve the Tree of Life, to propagate it and ensure it grew on for future generations. In Joseph's tradition, the Tree of Life was central and Jesus' role in hanging from it was to demonstrate its resurrective and healing properties. At the time of its planting at Llanilid, no one would have dreamt the company would soon be needing to move and that the thousands of years of it being a central Druidic meeting place and Silurian capital of the ancient world was about to come to an end. Jesus' resurrection from the most important Sacred Tree, the Tree of Life, the same one which grew from a seed given by the Angel Gabriel to be planted on Adam's grave was the central mystery in a tradition which demonstrated the life-giving properties, the mysteries of eternity, and the continuity of life after death. In *The God Tree*, the fact that Jesus was never crucified but hung on the Tree of Life is explained in depth. The Tree was at Golgotha, the Place of the Skulls, and the site of Adam's grave; hence it was here that the atonement for the sin of Adam's son Cain who murdered his brother Abel took place. The truth is that Jesus was hung on the Tree of Life, despite the later myth-making which turned Jesus' death into a crucifixion with the Romans in charge rather than the Jews, whose tradition it was and who planned it all. The events leading up to Jesus' death led to a ritualistic death for which he would have been prepared all his life and which would have been managed by Nicodemus and Arimathea. At the time of the early church founded by Joseph of Arimathea, there was no tradition of the crucifixion which was invented later for political reasons to distance Jesus from the Tree. Early Christian Celtic symbols as well as Saxon crosses are based on a tree, not a wooden cross.

And so, Joseph split the branch which he brought in the form of the staff he carried, into at least two pieces. It was likely it was Joseph who planted both the tree at Chalice Well, Glastonbury where he was said to be in 63 CE and the one at Llanilid. It is known that yew wood can survive for many years in a dry state and still grow if planted. On the mound on the south side of the present church of Llanilid is a tree dated by Allen Meredith, from wood samples and other evidence, as being between 1,800 and 2,200 years old, with an average of 55 rings per inch counted on the old wood.

Llanilid Yew.

A smaller and younger clone of this tree exists to the south-east. The first tree is rather decrepit, its health compromised by ivy and brambles which I cleared with friends. The tree is extraordinary, in that like its companion, it allows certain other trees to live with it and is said at one time to have sprouted seven trees of different kinds. Today there are the remains of an oak, which grew in its centre until it fell and took part of the old yew with it. Over the many years that I have looked at yews, I have never seen a yew share space with another tree in this way, though I have noticed that elder is a constant companion of the yew. The yew allows elder to come close, right up against its trunk. You can be in a place where no elder is growing around and yet there it is with the yew. The other traditional 'magical tree' is the rowan and until recently a rowan grew inside the large yew on the south side at Llanilid, along with the oak, a prunus and honeysuckle which now grows up into the canopy. It is also remarkable that the same trees, apart from the oak, also grew, until recently, in the cloned yew, showing there is something about this particular yew that encourages these other trees to grow with it. This is not the usual way with yew.

One thing that puzzled me about the large yew is that it is

male. I would have expected the Tree of Life to be monoecious. However, we do know that a yew tree can change sex and perhaps this has happened here or perhaps a female branch has been removed, as the tree has been chopped about over the years. The important thing is that the yew on the south side of the Llanilid site, in the position normally favoured by the Saints for their plantings, is of an age that overlaps with the time of Joseph of Arimathea and the most likely thing is that it was he who planted it. Sitting under the yew I was convinced that Joseph himself was buried beneath it. It would have been the obvious place although Allen Meredith is equally convinced that he is buried much higher up near the Cor. If he's right, it would fit with Melkin's prophecy that Joseph of Arimathea was buried 'on the bifurcated line'. Such a line would be formed by the connection of the two circles, one which formed the Cor and the other the churchyard. 6th century Maelgwyn of Llandaff described the grave of Joseph of Arimathea as being in a place surrounded by water, which is how Llanilid was in those times with something of a moat surrounding the Cor and other waters (shoreline and river) close by. In Roman times a giant causeway was built to stop the sea from coming in and flooding the place. One of the stiles into the churchyard gave access onto this causeway which is no longer there. Joseph was also said to have been buried with the Grail. In *The God Tree*, it was established that the Grail was the Tree of Life. A statement of what the 'Grail' or Graal was, was furnished by the 12th century Wolfram von Eschenbach, who disclosing the secret of the Grail at great personal risk, revealed it to be 'The perfection of Paradise, root and branch'.

It is of considerable frustration that the whereabouts and documentation of two empty lead coffins found and reburied in the churchyard along with the records of an archaeological dig at the Cor in the 1950s, as reported by Church Warden, Kevin Murphy, have been so far untraceable, as they suggest the presence of Roman artefacts. There is confusion too with another

Ilid site near Brecon where Roman remains were found. It is also very frustrating that those in charge of Glastonbury Chalice Well will not allow the DNA of the branch found in the well to be tested. If this could happen, then the DNA could be tested against the DNA of the yew tree at Llanilid to see if there was a match and, although it is doubtful an accurate reading could be made as the wood was waterlogged, a laboratory in Germany is willing to try.

Although something of an aside, one of the things that interest me about the Cors is that it may have been them to which the 5th century prophet and seer Melkin, a monk of Glastonbury referred when he chose to give the location of Joseph of Arimathea's tomb in the form of a riddle. In this, it is suggested that 'circles of portentous prophecy', in connection with a choir, geometrically expressed the whereabouts of Joseph's resting place, on a 'bifurcated' (or double forked line). Two circles that touch each other would form just such a line and it strikes me that that is exactly what we have at Llanilid, a line formed by the touching of two circles formed by the Cor and the churchyard. Furthermore, these two circles could well be described as 'circles of portentous prophecy' marking as they did the passing of the time of the Druids while auguring the time of Christianity. It is here at Llanilid on the threshold between these two momentous ages of our history that Joseph sleeps with the Tree of Life, having fulfilled his mission, held within the time when everything changed.

Chapter 11

Ancient Yews in Britain aged between 2,000 and 5,000 years

In Britain and in particular, Wales, there are the largest number of ancient yews in the world (A total of at least 174 at the most recent count). Yews are the oldest living trees. Although there are still undiscovered yews, we now believe that in Wales, there are at least 44 yews aged at 2,000 years plus, 11 of 3,000 years plus, 1 at 4,000 years plus and 3 at 5,000 years plus, totalling 59 yews aged at over 2,000 years, in Wales, therefore proportionally more than in the rest of Britain.

In the rest of Britain, we have recorded 115 yews aged at over 2,000 years. This total is made up of 79 yews aged at 2,000 years plus, 32 at 3,000 years plus, 3 at 4,000 years plus and 1 at 5,000 years plus. These figures are based on current information and may expand further. In addition to ancient yews, Wales has a larger number of 1,000 years plus yews and a special feature are circles of these old yews typically made up of 7 or 8 trees.

WALES

Churchyard yews aged 5,000 years plus (3 yews)

Defynnog Yew.

Defynnog, Brecon
Discoed, Powys
Llangernwy, Clwyd

Churchyard Yews aged 4,000 years (1 yew)

Bettws Newydd Yew. New tree inside old.

Bettws Newydd, Monmouthshire

Churchyard Yews aged 3,000 years (11 yews)

Llanafan Fawr Yew.

Alltmawr, near Builth Wells, Powys
Llanafan Fawr, Powys
Llanbedr Ystradyw, Breconshire
Llandeiniolen, Gwynedd
Llandre, Cerdigion
Llanfaredd, near Builth Wells, Powys
Llanfeugan, Breconshire (2 yews)
Llangynyw, Powys
LLanymawddwy, Gwynedd
Llantrithyd, Glamorgan

Churchyard Yews aged 2,000 years (30 yews)

Llanarmon Dyffryn Ceiriog. 2 yews.

North Yew, Llangathen.

Aberedw, Powys
Cyffylliog, Denbighshire
Discoed, Powys
Gwytherin, Conwy (2 yews)
Llanbedr Ystradyw, Breconshire
Llanarmon Dyffryn Ceiriog, Clwyd (2 yews)
Llanarth, Gwent
Llanelly, Monmouthshire
Llandrillo, Denbighshire
Llanddewi Rhydderch, Monmouthshire
Llandeiniolen, Gwynedd
Llanfeugan, Breconshire
Llanfihangel Nant Melan, Powys
Llangathen, Carmarthenshire
Llangattock Juxta Usk, Monmouthshire
Llanilid, Glamorgan
Llanspiddyd, Powys
Llanwenarth, Monmouthshire
Maesmynis, Powys
Mamhilad, Gwent
Meidrim, Carmarthenshire
Mynydd Islwyn, Gwent
Nantmel, Powys
Pennant Melangell, Powys (2 yews)
Penpont, Powys
Rhulen, Near Builth Wells, Powys
Ystradgynlais, Powys

Non Churchyard Yews aged 2,000 years plus (14 yews)

Llangeitho Yew.

Abergwesyn, Builth Wells, Powys (2 yews)
Caer Alyn, Llay, near Wrexham, Clwyd
Edge of field Dolfor, Newtown, Powys. (2 yews on the hillside)

Dolforwyn Castle, Yew tree cottage, Welshpool, Powys. Yew next to well

Ffynon Bedr, Conwy

Pantllidw, Machynlleth, Powys

Pant y Beudy

Llangeitho, Ceredigion

Rhyd-y-Glafes, near Llandrillo

Ty Illtyd, Llanhamlach, near Brecon, Powys (3 yews on the hillside)

Yew Tree Farm, Discoed

Offa's Dyke, Powys/Herefordshire border

IN THE REST OF BRITAIN

Churchyard Yews aged 5,000 years plus (1 yew)

Fortingall Yew. Photo by Pauline Elliot.

Fortingall, Scotland

Aged 4,000 years plus (3 yews)

Crowhurst Yew, Surrey. Photo by Andrew Maclean.

Crowhurst, Surrey
Linton, Herefordshire
Tisbury, Wiltshire

Churchyard Yews aged 3,000 years plus (16 yews)

Peterchurch Yew.

All Hallows, Dorset
Ashbrittle, Somerset
Clun, Shropshire
Claverley, Shropshire
Coldwaltham, Sussex
Farringdon, Hampshire
Kenn, Devon
Kennington, Kent
Long Sutton, Hampshire
Lytchett Matravers, Dorset
Payhembury, Devon
Peterchurch, Herefordshire
Stansted, Kent
Woodcott, Hampshire
Woolland, Dorset
Yazor, Herefordshire

Non-churchyard Yews, aged 3,000 years plus (16 yews)

The Borrowdale Yews. Photo by Andrew Maclean.

All Hallows, Dorset (One 30 ft yew outside the churchyard)
Boulsbury Farm, near Martin's Wood, Hampshire
Bulbarrow, Dorset
Bodcott Farm, near Moccas Park, Herefordshire
Borrowdale, Lake District. National Trust
Bulbarrow Hill, Woolland, Dorset. On ancient barrow
Druids Grove, Surrey
Garnons Wood, nr. Mansell Gamage, Herefordshire
Keffold's Farm, Haslemere, Sussex. Possible monastery site
Kentchurch, Herefordshire. Private estate (3 yews)
Knowlton Circles, Dorset. Henge monument
Norbury, Shropshire
Old Colwall, Herefordshire
Whitbury Hillfort, Dorset

Churchyard Yews aged 2,000 years plus (45 yews)

Crowhurst Yew, Sussex.

Cradley Celtic Yew.　　　　　　*Buxted Yew.*

Acton Scott, Shropshire
Aldworth, Berkshire
Ankerwycke, near Runnymede, Buckinghamshire
Astbury, Cheshire
Awre, Gloucestershire
Boarhunt, Hampshire
Buckland in Dover, Kent
Buxted, Sussex
Challock, Kent
Cradley, Worcestershire
Crowhurst, Sussex
Darley Dale, Derbyshire
Dunster, Somerset
Eastling, Kent
Elworthy, Somerset
Hambledon, Surrey
Harrietsham, Kent
Hope Bagot, Shropshire
Huntley, Gloucestershire
Kemble. Gloucestershire
Leeds, Kent
Loose, Kent
Loughton, Shropshire
Mamhead, Devon
Martindale, Cumbria
Mid Lavant, Sussex
Molash, Kent
Old Enton, Surrey
Overton on Dee, Shropshire
Prior's Dean, Hampshire
Ulcombe, Kent
Uppington, Shropshire
West Tisted, Hampshire
Wilmington, Sussex

Rycote Manor, Oxfordshire
Sidbury, Shropshire
South Hayling, Hampshire
Staunton, Worcestershire
Stedham, Sussex
Stockbury, Kent
Tandridge, Surrey
Tangley, Hampshire
Tettenhall, West Midlands
Totteridge, Hertfordshire
Zeal Monachorum, Devon

Non Churchyard Yews aged 2,000 years plus (34 yews)

Merdon Castle Yews.

Fallen yew re-rooting at Craswall Priory.

Askerswell, Dorset

Barlavington Farm, Sussex

Bernera, Lismore, Argyl

Bruce's Yew, Loch Lomond, Scotland

Coldred, Kent (On burial mound opposite the church)

Churchill, Worcester

Kidderminster area. Old Church site

Compton Dando, Wandsdyke, Somerset (On dyke)

Craswall, Herefordshire

Ducks Nest Longbarrow, Dorset. Private land

Eardisley, (Holy Well Dingle) Herefordshire

Fountains Abbey, Ripon, Yorkshire. National Trust

Great Frazer Yew, above Loch Ness

Great Yews, Odstock, Wiltshire (Yew grove)

Hanchurch, Staffordshire (Near a house called 'The Yew Trees')

Holywell, Eardisley, Herefordshire (SSSI)

Jays Copse, Haslemere. Surrey (Boundary marker tree)
King Yew, Eastwood, Tiddenham Chase, Gloucestershire
Kingley Vale Kyre Park, Worcestershire
Lydney Park, Gloucestershire
Lorton, Kendal, Cumbria (Wordsworth's Tree. By stream in field)
Marston Bigot, Somerset (Private land)
Merdon Castle, Winchester, Hampshire
Middleton Scriven, Shropshire (2 yews in field opposite church)
Newlands Corner, Surrey
Old Enton, near Godalming, Surrey (Possible hillfort)
Old Church, Ullswater, Cumbria (Hotel grounds)
Rye Hill, near Knowlton Circles, Dorset (On farmland)
Snoddington Manor Farm, Tidworth, Hampshire
Temple Farm, Longleat, Wiltshire
Yew tree knob, Wintershall private estate, Bramley, Guildford
Surrey White house Copse, Cranbourne, Dorset
Yew Tree Field, Damerham Dorset

Chapter 12

Britain's Lost Yews

Dead yew at Cantref with Rowan tree growing inside.
Photo by Heather Hornung.

The almost dead south west yew at Cantref, rescued and restored to life with the help of Heather Hornung.

The dead yew at Cantref died for no discernible reason although normally yews only die if deliberately destroyed or left to their fate from neglect, and being swamped by ivy or brambles. The second yew shown here, also at Cantref, shows it is sometimes possible to return these ancient yews to life. This one was saved from near death by Heather Hornung who painstakingly cut away vegetation which had actually penetrated the tree trunk, as well as swamping it and preventing light from reaching it. Other yews, even if cut down with no greenery left, like the one at the Holy Well of Gwenlais, can also return to life but sadly many magnificent yews have been lost for various reasons.

The following list, taken from many sources, is not a comprehensive one but an estimate of the number of yews lost in Britain, mainly since World War II. There were also losses in Victorian times with the loss of the knowledge of the sacredness of the yew trees. There is no way of knowing the true figure as records were not made and collected at the time. This list may be just the tip of the iceberg, as it is not always obvious when a yew has disappeared forever. For instance, I am certain there must have been a much earlier, older yew at Nevern in Pembrokeshire and at Llanelltyd Fawr but no old stumps or evidence can be found. Between the Victorian era and World War II, thousands of yews, of which just a few examples are included here have gone and since then somewhere in the region of 500 have been destroyed. This list has been researched from old records and books such as Arthur Mee's *King's England* 1930s, Vaughan Cornish's *The Churchyard Yew and Immortality* 1946, E.W. Swanton's *The Yew trees of England* 1958 and old illustrations and engravings of churches with old yews, where the yews are no longer there. This list is mainly about churchyards known to have lost yews. Many of those places would typically have lost several yews like Myddfai in Carmarthenshire, where only one yew remains on the north side, out of a circle of at least five or six originally there.

In the process of putting this list together it has become clear just how many places originally had a circle of yews planted as part of pre-Christian religious practices. Yew circles, commonplace in ancient times, were there to protect the dead. Circles typically consisting of a dozen yews or more, are now reduced to just a few trees which indicate (if the stumps are left) how great these magnificent circles were. These circles were prolific, particularly in the Brecon and Powys area. On this basis, it is easy to see that many churches have lost three-quarters of their old yews. The face of Britain has changed in more ways than one! Counties that seem to have lost the most are in Gwent and also Glamorgan, although Gwent and Powys still have what is perhaps the greatest density of the largest and oldest yews. Yews were very important at one time and some place-names indicate this as previously explored.

Sometimes when a yew is destroyed all evidence of its ever having been there is removed, as at Ashford Carbonel in Shropshire a few years ago. At other places the stumps survive to tell the tale, which is useful for gaining more information as to the girth, ring counts and age of the yew, as at Llanspyddid. Yews, particularly during the time of Edward 1st, were often destroyed altogether, due to a fashion for 'lawned' churchyards (no trees). This matter was discussed in Parliament in 1307 when the law prohibiting the cutting down of churchyard trees (almost entirely yews) was reviewed and restated, as there was concern for the damage happening to church buildings as a result of the lack of protection from the weather once offered by the yews. This marked a particularly dark era in our yew history, where any concept of sacred yews was largely forgotten and yews in the main were seen as being there purely for the utilitarian purpose of protecting the fabric of the building from high storms and for sheltering the congregation waiting to enter the building. The law was re-instated for this reason rather than for any reverence for yews.

However, since World War II, perhaps as a result of modern machinery making it easier to demolish trees, Britain has lost at least 500 yews, which were over a thousand years of age. Some of these were enormous, spectacular and truly ancient. We may well have already lost the best of them. Several were of a 30 ft girth indicating a 2,000 - 3,000-year-old yew. All were important, once celebrated trees.

A recent report in the Royal Forestry Society Quarterly Journal contains the concern that 223 notable yews have been lost from churchyards and highlights the need for better safeguarding for the unique habitat of what is the world's finest collection of yew trees. The report also shows rather startlingly 'that 10% of large yew trees, previously recorded in churchyards have disappeared, the majority over the last one hundred years, for example at Sullington, Sussex where only one of six yews now remain. Whilst churchyard yews, like other trees, fall victim to storms, they also fall foul of health and safety fears, poor management and development.' I would add that becoming cloaked in ivy, which is, unfortunately, the norm nowadays, is likely to cause a yew to be more vulnerable to being broken by storms and also indicates a lack of interest in the tree.

Records are patchy and incomplete and gathered from many sources. One writer, Rev. Daryl Evans recorded not just yews in *The Churchyard Yews of Gwent*, 1988, but also stumps. Where specific details about these lost yews are known they are included here. Describing a yew as 'north' for example is significant as, if the yew growing there is also very old, it could be Neolithic.

It is worth remembering that the destruction of yews is almost always unnecessary. Yews are unlike other trees that have a certain life span before falling into decay at the end of their life. In most cases, yews, capable of continuous regeneration, do not need to be destroyed and removed without a trace. Careful management, removal of ivy, rubbish, oil tanks and old Victorian ornamental walls around the base of the tree (gradually over several years to avoid shocking the tree) is normally all that is needed to keep yews alive, growing and thriving.

Known Lost Yews of over a Thousand Years

Site	Girth (feet), date and details
Aber, Gwynedd	Originally a circle of 10 old yews recorded in 1983, now just 1 left.
Asthall Leigh, Oxfordshire	19 ft yew cut down in 1985.
Ashford, Carbonel	21ft yew cut down in 2011.
Bignor, Sussex	20 ft yew cut down in 1985.
Bishop Stoke, Eastleigh Hampshire	1 yew cut down.

Bishopston, Gower	20 ft yew removed in early 1990s.
Blaina Aberystruth, Gwent	At least 1 substantial yew lost.
Bolton Abbey, Yorkshire	Yew removed in 19th century.
Bowden, Cheshire	1 very old yew. Yew still there in the 1980s.
Brabourne, Kent	57 ft yew gone.
Bridwell, Pembs	1 large yew gone. Stump left.
Buckleberry, Berkshire	27 ft yew removed around 1954. 1 other yew lost.
Cantref, Brecon	1 dead yew on west with Rowan tree growing inside.
Capel y fin, Powys	1 lost yew.
Cascob, Powys	1 yew gone; stump left.
Cefnllys, Powys	Out of an original circle recorded in 1953, only 2 are left. 1 yew was set fire to in 2006.
Cenneys Commander, Gwent	1 yew gone.
Chipstead, Surrey	24 ft Remains burnt down.
Christchurch, Newport, Gwent	Substantial yews now vanished.
Congresbury, Somerset	St Congar's yew (staff planting)

	lost in 1900s.
Cholsey, Oxfordshire	Blown down in 1989.
Chilham, Kent	30 ft yew cut down pre 1790.
Chirk, Denbighshire	3 yews gone.
Cilmery, Powys	15 ft yew felled in 2009.
Coldred, Kent	1 old yew gone.
Colemore, Hampshire	1 old yew gone.
Condover, Shropshire	1 lost yew.
Craswall Priory, near Hay on Wye	1 massive old fallen yew, still lives on. Other stumps.
Dibden, Hampshire	30 ft yew cut down in 19th century following storm damage.
Durfield, Derbyshire	1 yew cut down after storm damage.
East Lavant, East Sussex	28 ft yew cut down in 1982.
Eastrey, Kent	1 lost yew.
Fountains Abbey, Yorkshire	26 ft yew lost. 7 cut down in 1975.
Garth Brengy, Powys	10 lost since1862. Originally a double circle of 33 yews.

Gartheli, Carmarthenshire	1 yew cut down in 1985.
Glyncorrwg, Glamorgan	4 Killed by neglect and poisoning by cement and stone wall built around them.
Goudhurst, Kent	27 ft yew lost.
Goetre, Gwent	1 very large yew cut down.
Gwenlais Holy Well, Carmarthenshire	14 ft yew cut down but regrown.
Gwytherin, Conway	1 yew lost.
Gyffin, Gwynedd	Yews felled in 19th century.
Hampstead Marshall, Berkshire	1 yew lost from the woodland, reported to have been 59 ft in 1830s.
Hardham, Sussex	Hollow yew destroyed in storm.
Kenardington, Kent	1 old yew gone.
Little Chart, Kent	1 yew lost prior to 1936.
Llanafan, Carmarthenshire	4 yews cut down in1980s.
Llanddewi Rhydderch, Monmouthshire	4 yews gone.
Llandderfyl, Gwynedd	1 yew cut down in 1991.

Llanddewi Ystradnni, Powys	1 large old yew used to store a coal house inside its hollow trunk, destroyed in 60s or 70s.
Llanddewi Fach, Gwent	30ft Cut down and burnt in 1975.
Llandyfaelog Fach, Brecon	10 yews gone from original circle of 13 yews.
Llanelen, Gower	Hollow yew set fire to.
Llanelly, Gwent	6 yews gone from original circle of 18.
Llanfihangel Abercywyn, Carmarthenshire	Cut down in 1980.
Llanfihangel Nant Melan	8 or 9 yews lost from a circle.
Llangovan, Gwent	1 yew.
Llangua, Monmouthshire	8 yews.
Llanhamlach, Brecon	6 or more yews cut down in 1985.
Llanhilleth, Gwent	9 yews, stumps left.
Llanlleonfel, Powys	18 ft yew destroyed by 2002 'tidied and made safe'.
Llanfoist, Monmouthshire	27 ft yew. Blown down in 2012.
Llansantfraed yn Elvel, Powys	At least 5 yews gone from a circle of 14.

Llanspyddid, Brecon	Around 7 yews cut down in what was once described as a 'noble yew grove'.
Llantarnam, Monmouthshire	North yew, large stump left.
Llantwit Major, Glamorgan	1 large old yew.
Llanddewi Rhydderch, Monmouthshire	4 large yews. Stumps left on north
Llanwrin, Powys	28 ft yew cut down in 1984. Resurrected.
Llanwrda, Carmarthenshire	2 yews, 1 very large, 1 cut down in the 90s, other previously.
Llanrhidian, Gower	17 ft yew deliberately burnt down.
Llanyre, Powys	2 yews lost from circle.
Lydney, Gloucestershire	1 large yew gone 1980.
Mathern, Gwent	22 ft north yew gone.
Meidrim, Carmarthenshire	At least 2 yews gone.
Meopham, Kent	1 old yew gone.
Mobberley, Derbyshire	1 yew gone.
Myddfai, Carmarthenshire	6 or 7 yews cut down in the early 90s.

Old Colwyn, Clwyd	1 yew cut down.
Orcop, Herefordshire	30 ft yew.
Overton on Dee, Clwyd	4 yews cut down.
Patterdale, Lake District	26 ft yew gone.
Penpont, Brecon	24 ft yew cut down in 1970.
Pontardulais, old church of St. Teilo	Yew cut down when building removed to St Fagan's.
Rhulen, Powys	Yew partially blown down, cut up in 1987.
Sanderstead, Croydon, London	2 old yews felled in 1962 and early 2000s.
Sandhurst, Berkshire	Large yew stump - yew cut down.
Sandford Orcas, Dorset	1 yew.
Sedburgh, Yorkshire	2 very large yews gone.
Shute, Devon	1 yew gone in 1954. Came down in gales and removed.
Stanford Bishop, Worcestershire	Over 30 ft yew. Cut down in the 1880s.
Stoneaston, Somerset	1 old stump.
Stone, Kent	28 ft yew removed in 1980.

Strata Florida, Cardiganshire	39 yews originally. Only 2 survive.
Sullington, Sussex	5 yews gone.
Tankersley Park, Yorkshire	Yew gone which was so big and hollow it was said a horse with rider could ride around inside.
Taplow Court, Buckinghamshire	21 ft yew removed in 1889.
Trevethin, Monmouthshire	Largest yew cut down in the 80s.
Trostrey, Gwent	Tree felled years ago but still lives.
Uffculme, near Birmingham	1 large old yew cut down in 2016.
Uppington, Shropshire	1 yew gone.
Vowchurch, Herefordshire	1 large stump.
Walmer, Kent	1 old yew gone.
Wilcrick, Gwent	Outside churchyard 18 ft north yew stump far larger than other living yews.
Windlesham, Berkshire	Hollow yew gone.
Woodford, Essex	17 ft yew destroyed in 1987 Damaged by building works and gales and also set fire to.
Wormelow Tump, Herefordshire	Yew on tump disappeared.

In addition to this list, some 65 more lost yew sites are described in an article by Tim Hills of the Ancient Yew group

- https://www.ancient-yew.org/userfiles/file/Lost%20Welsh%20Churchyard%20Yews.pdf

Tim Hills also lists another 10 in the Diocese of Bath and Wells

- https://www.ancient-yew.org/userfiles/file/Bath%20and%20Wells%20lost%20yews.pdf

Chapter 13

The History of Legal Protection
of Britain's Yews

The Ankerwycke Yew, Ankerwycke

Record ID: 123107 / MNA147320
Record type: Landscape
Protected Status: Scheduled Monument
NT Property: Ankerwycke; London and South East
Civil Parish: Wraysbury; Windsor and Maidenhead
Grid Reference: TQ 00410 72710

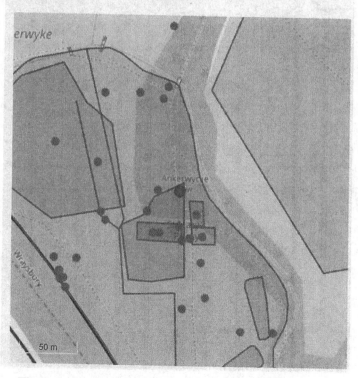

The Ankerwycke Yew: Designated Scheduled Monument.

Most people assume that ancient trees are protected but this is not the case unless someone has gone out of their way to have a Tree Protection Order placed on a particular tree and even if a tree has a TPO, the level of protection offered is not much of a deterrent to a developer who will often simply include the cost of the fine in the cost of the development. However, there were old laws concerning the protection of yews and there is now an urgent need to bring these up to date. They should be reinvoked as they have gone into abeyance and with every year that passes, Britain is the poorer for the loss of more of these heritage trees. It would need a test case and a lawyer interested in pursuing it or, of course, a change in the law. There are thousands of ancient yews in Britain and it seems unlikely we will ever get protection for them all and therefore I felt it more prudent to concentrate on getting the most ancient and historical yews protected when I set up the Campaign for Legal Protection of Ancient Yews in Britain in September 2018.

To begin with, we need to look at the historical context and establish the fact that the sanctity of the yew in Britain and therefore the idea that it should be protected against harm, most likely originated with the Silures, the Welsh Celtic yew tribe, conquered by the Second Augustan Legion from Caerleon, in the first century. The yew as we know was sacred in Bronze Age Britain and in earlier times. Saints planted them in churchyards and adopted those already there in an environment separated from the mundane and considered to be a safe, protected sanctuary.

The earliest law for the protection of trees on sacred sites is the letter from Pope Gregory dated to 597 - 601 CE instructing Abbot Mellitus to tell Augustine not to destroy the fana, (meaning the sacred trees), only the 'idols' placed in them so that people would still come to these sites. Another similar term to 'fana' was 'frondibus contexta', meaning 'interwoven branches'. These terms were translated as 'temples' because the first church was just that: a temple made from interwoven branches of trees found on site, most likely yew branches, part of the sacred grove or nemeton. The very earliest shrines or temples were simply hollow trees with an image of the presiding deity in them. Before Christianity, the first temple of Artemis was an aged cedar tree containing an image of this goddess. William Smith's Dictionary of 1875 defines an early temple as a hollow tree in which there was an image or statue but in fact, it was the tree itself that was the deity.

Jacob Grimm in *Teutonic Mythology* 1880, says, 'It is said of a hollow tree... there are saints in there, that hear all people's prayers'. His information came from the early Saxon period, when he stated:

> The hut ('bower' is more accurate) in which we are to picture ourselves under the term 'fanum' or Anglo-Saxon bower, was most likely constructed of logs and twigs around the sacred tree.

'Sacrosanct' means sacred sanctuary, holy of holies, something not to be touched for fear of reprisals. The Saxon word was 'hallowed', as in hallowed ground. This was consecrated ground. 'Hallowed' means Temple. Hallowed or consecrated ground expressly meant land that had a sacred tree growing on it. At Pepper Harrow, in Surrey ('harrow', also an agricultural term, is from the same source as 'hallow') a sacred site of the Saxons, there is a yew of around 1,400 years old, which was probably planted by Saxons. All Hallows in Dorset is also Saxon and has a 30 ft girth tree. The Saxons usually planted their yews on the south and south-west of the burial mound. Although Saxon law may never have been written down, it was accepted as old tribal law and was just as binding.

In Latin writings about the 'booths' (another word used for these early green temples), the word 'fanum' or 'fana' seems to mean hollow trees, used as shrines or cells. Homer in *The Iliad* (8th century BCE) implies that the earliest temple was a booth of branches, which would have been an extension of the monk's cell. The Roman Pliny describes the first temples as hollow trees or trees with interwoven branches (Nemorensis Templum) and the first church in Britain, raised by St. Garmon at Llanarmon Dyffryn Ceiriog, North Wales, would have been of this kind, made from branches, still attached to the tree (in this case from two yew trees), woven together to give some shelter to the congregation. The term 'Frondibus contexta', is something also referred to by Constance de Lyon circa 470 CE in *Germain* as a shelter put together to celebrate the Christian Day of Resurrection, because as the yew symbolises resurrection, it was fitting to use the yew branches for the purpose.

Pope Gregory affirmed that 'At festivals, the people shall be allowed to build their booths of green leaves' and from Leviticus 23: 33-43, we see that the custom of building green booths was widespread in many parts of the world, 'that the wood for the booths be selected from leafy trees, trees of interwoven foliage'.

According to *The Antiquities of the Cymru* (Bede) (book 1, chap. 20), Vol. 1 Williams, about the year 565, 'the practise of constructing churches of stone was unusual amongst the Britons'. The natural progression through time of the construction of a church, would have been from live leafy branches still attached to the tree, to cut leafy branches as a temporary construction, to cut and dried timber and eventually timber and stone, a similar process to the evolution of the henges from the nemeton, the central living tree and surrounding circular grove, to wooden posts and finally standing stone pillars. Both nemeton and fanum refer to the sacred tree and the circle. The circular grove and the sacred tree is one and the same thing. An example of this is found at Llangernwy, which means enclosure of the sacred yew.

Later on, in 10th century Wales, the laws of Hywel Dda protected yews and referred to the 6th century Saints Dubricious and Teilo and their sacred trees. *The Laws of Hywel Dda* (a Welsh King 915 - 48 CE), records a difference between saint's or consecrated yews ('Ywen sant'), yews either adopted or planted by a saint, worth one pound and secular yews ('ywen goat') worth fifteen pence. These were the fines for cutting them down. In Latin, it is said:

> Leges Walliae 262 (Sancti) sancto nempe alicui didcata, Dubritio v. gr. vel Teliao, quales apud wallos in Cemerteriis etiam-num ('frequenter visisntur, translated as reading the yew trees in the churchyards dedicated to Teilo and Dubricious were sacred (Taxus sancti)).

Sacred Yews (Taxus sancti) or saints yews, (ywen sant) were considered to be of higher value than all other trees and here it stated that the sacred yews of Saint Dubricius (also known as Dyfryg – spiritual father of 5th and 6th century saints) and Saint Teilo, which stood in the Welsh cemeteries, were protected by law. Elsewhere it is said that the Welsh King Hywel Dda endorsed a huge fine of 60 sheep on those who cut down yews 'dedicated to saints'. It should be noted that this proves these yews were substantial trees over a thousand years ago. Several of them are still alive today, another thousand years on.

The 12th century book of Llandaff records from earlier records that the space between the yew tree and the church was a sanctuary in the 5th century and earlier, as inviolable a space as the interior of the church itself.

One of the early laws which protected yews, was that noted in the *Book of Llandaff* otherwise properly known as *Liber Landavensis, Llyfr Teilo: Ancient register of the Cathedral of Llan-daff*, under the heading 'The Village of Miluc'. All scholars believe this was a church and yew tree by the River Ely but 'Miluc' does not exist today. The site, whose exact location is unknown, is on the route to Llandaff and is most likely to be St. Brides Super Ely, which has a large old yew tree. The text tells us that

Iestyn sent his 'household' containing the wicked Twrwerd and Iestyn's grandson Eineon, 'filled with an evil spirit', to Llandaff. Ignoring the protection of the holy cross and the asylum given by the Llandaff saints of Saint Dubricius, Saint Teilo and St. Oudoceus, the sinners 'took away a virgin who had fled under the protection of the church and from between the yew tree and the church'. The girl, Eurddilad, daughter of Cynwal was 'violated' and the perpetrator became deranged. The bishop cursed Iestyn and his criminals for such an outrage but it must be noted that the punishment was for the violation of the protected 'refuge' and not for the rape of the girl! Apparently, the criminal came to his senses when restitution was made to the church (not the girl). Although not actually stating that the yew was acting as a 'protector' in its own right, there would appear to be an inference that the area between the church and the yew tree was a sacred space or 'special refuge' and known as hallowed ground. This refuge or asylum was begun by Teilo and Dubricious. What also seems apparent is the acceptance of the yew as an integral part of the site or 'llan'.

At the time of Edward 1st in 1272 - 1307 we find attitudes to Yews becoming utilitarian and it being promoted that the reason yew trees were planted in churchyards was to protect the fabric of the building from high storms and also to shelter the congregation before entering the building! Thus, in 1307 CE, we have the notable statute 35 'Ne rector prosternat arbores in cemiterio' (i.e. the rector must not cut down trees in the churchyard, save as the act proceeds to specify, for the repair of the chancel). This Statute was a reiteration of the Synod of Exeter 1287, which forbade the felling of churchyard trees and expressly stated that they are often planted to prevent injury to the building during storms! The whole of the Latin reads as follows:

Ne Rector prosternet arbores in Cemeteris, Arbores ipse proper ventorum impetus ne Ecclesiis noceant seps plantatur.

Prohibernus, ne Ecclesiatum Rectores ipsas presumant prosper nere indistiicte, nisi cum Cancellos Ecclesiae necessaria indigent reflecdtione. Nec in alios usus aliqualiter convertantur (from: *Sir R. Phillimore, Eccles, Law 2nd edition* 1895 p.1407. Brand, Pop. Antiq., 11.p.3256. G. White, Selbourne, p. 421. Statutes of the realm 1810, 1 Antiq., 11. p.221. The date of the Act is said to be uncertain).

It is pertinent to remark that the law is still binding as stated by Walter Johnson in *Byways of British Archaeology* 1912. It is also worth noting that the yew, as the only European tree associated with death, would be the principal, if not the only kind of tree, which grew in the churchyard and needed preservation.

Further to this, in 1781 it is interesting to note that there was a Parliamentary debate on the Edward 1st Statute 'Ne rector...' which as we have seen was a reiteration of the law made by the Synod of Exeter in 1287. This was in response to yews at Gyffin in North Wales being cut down to a stump. Following the destruction of these yews, which were remarkable for the fact that their 14 feet girths had hardly changed in size in 100 years, they had storms that did damage to the tower, so they then thought that the trees were there to protect the buildings and were already by this time it seems, unconcerned about the sacredness of the yews. The fact that the old law was being brought up in Parliament means that, although it was still known, it was not generally understood or considered important by the clergy, or at least not by some of them.

In *The Parliamentary Register: Or, History of the Proceedings and Debates of ...By Great Britain, House of Commons, Parliamentary Debates* 1781 (2), we find the following:

Mr. Courtenay then said, that on reading a very ingenious book, which threw great light on the spirit, manners and characters of our ancestors, in the book he alluded to,

(Observations on the Statutes, chiefly the more ancient ones), there was an act of the 35th of Ed, 1, A 1307, entitled, 'Ne Rector arbores in Cemeretis prosernet.' But as the season of the prohibitory state was not well understood, several of the country clergies, carried away by the modern taste for improvement, chose to lawn their churchyards and cut away the noxious yew trees: but after the supposed improvement was made, the wisdom of the act and the utility of the trees were uncovered, as several churches, especially the church of Gyffin, near Conway, in Wales, (for this spirit of improvement had travelled far), were materially injured, by being exposed to the storm, deprived of all shelter and protection. Let us improve on the hint and not let rash and sacrilegious hands, prune away, the thick and sheltering foliage of prerogative, lest we thereby injure the temple of Liberty.

It is surely clear from this history of the protection of the yew, that in the interests of gaining legal protection for our ancient yews, these old laws should be updated and made legally binding within present-day British law. In these times of the demise of the Church in Britain where lands and buildings are being sold off, the consequences of leaving our ancient yews vulnerable to 'development' of their environment are too dreadful to not prepare against the possibility of losing heritage trees.

In September 2018 I began an online petition on change.org for the Legal Protection of Ancient Yews in Britain. The petition reached 266,000 signatures. Our Barrister Paul Powlesland arranged for a hearing in the House of Lords in June 2019 at which representatives from most of the National Tree organisations such as the Tree Council and the Woodlands Trust were in attendance.

Campaign for Legal Protection of Britain's Ancient Yew Trees at the House of Lords. Left to right: Julian Hight (Tree author and hotographer), Janis Fry (Campaign leader), Andy Egan (former CEO International Tree Foundation), Rob Mc Bride (Tree Hunter), Paul Powlesland (Campaign Barrister), Jerry Ross (Arborist).

However, Paul knew that the Campaign could not win as two-thirds of the ancient yews were on Church property and the Church saw no need for legislation, has its own law (known as Canon Law), saw no potential threat to the yew trees and had no intention of altering their position. As a result, the House of Lords meeting was more a PR exercise than anything else. It has to be said that many of the fellings of yews we have seen in churchyards have been as a direct result of action taken by the Church and ignorance as to the importance of these trees as well as a failure to look after yews and prevent them being engulfed by ivy which can block light and nutrients and cause branches to break in strong winds and storms.

However, although English Heritage initially said they were

not going to give Scheduled Monument status to trees but only to buildings, they have given this status to the Ankerwycke Yew at Runnymede! Along with the Tree Council I feel this has now set a precedent for other heritage yews of similar national historic or cultural status to be given that same degree of protection and recognition. Although the process of protecting our ancient yews in modern times has only just begun, the status given to the Tree of the Magna Carta is the crack in the wall that was needed, although several years later, the Yew at Runnymede is still the only mature or ancient tree in Britain to be given this status. People find it hard to believe that something so important should be so difficult to achieve. Unfortunately, it says a lot about our values in a country that has the largest collection of ancient yews (the oldest of trees) on earth but doesn't value them even as much as a building of far less age.

Chapter 14

The Ankerwycke Yew - Living Witness to the Magna Carta

The Ankerwycke Yew. Photo by Sean Walters.

On the banks of the River Thames at Ankerwycke, opposite Runnymede, stands an extraordinary ancient, male yew. No one knows exactly how old this enormous tree is but it is generally believed by many authorities to be more than 2,000 years old and there is therefore little doubt that this tree is of pre-Christian origin. Yew historian Allen Meredith, some 30 years ago, proved beyond a reasonable doubt that the tree was the site of the oath swearing and agreement to the Magna Carta.

The Ankerwycke Yew, however, has been a tree of immense historical importance for many centuries and for this reason English Heritage, in 2019, made an unprecedented case for a tree becoming a Scheduled Monument. If only this status and level of protection could be given to other ancient and heritage trees! The Ankerwycke Yew may have been an Axis Mundi, the sacred central focus of an ancient tribe in the area and the rediscovery of this awe-inspiring tree has ignited the imagination of all who visit it. Described by Meredith as a 'deva daru', meaning an ancient guardian of wisdom, recognised and venerated by the Druids, a holy of holies, most sacred of all trees, it commands enormous respect as both a living monument and a sentient being. This tree has witnessed thousands of years of human events; the Magna Carta oath swearing itself would have used the name of God and a holy relic, such as a priest's staff. The King would have been likely also to have honoured an ancient custom of the 'laying on of hands, or 'touch wood', upon a yew staff, uttering words such as, 'Be this tree, my witness.' The custom of honouring the sacred wood continued at least until medieval times.

Yews are slow-growing trees that can live for thousands of years and thus they became sacred for their longevity, being seen as eternal in a changing landscape, through generations of the same tribe. More often than not a yew tree becomes hollow after a thousand years or so (at least churchyard yews do). The Ankerwycke Yew is no exception and its first recorded girth measurement by Dr Samuel Lysons in 1806, of 30 feet, has increased by little more than a foot since that time. A measurement of this size can indicate a 3,000-year-old tree. John Lowe, in his book of a century ago, *Yew trees of Great Britain and Ireland* 1897, describes the Yew thus:

The base was a good deal broken away and hollow up to five feet. The trunk above this point which at one time was hollow is now filled with a mass of large trunk-like roots, to a degree more remarkable than any I have seen.

Lowe was a little ahead of his time when he said that ancient historical trees, such as the one at Ankerwycke, should be treated as a national monument by such auspicious bodies as the National Trust. In fact, it took over a hundred years for this to happen and it wasn't until 1990 that a Tree Preservation Order was finally granted! Shortly after the Preservation Order, 'Friends of the Ankerwycke Yew' was formed by Dr Patrick Curry who wrote the foreword to this book and battled long and hard, along with residents, to ensure the tree was saved from being cut down to make way for a golf course and housing development. This eventually led to the National Trust taking over the site.

Nearly 800 years ago in 1215, the agreement of the bill of rights, known as the Magna Carta, became one of the most important historic events of Britain. Even at that time the Ankerwycke Yew would have stood strong, proud and immense. At Runnymede on the 19th June, the barons of England, finding themselves in conflict with King John, after nine days of talks, obliged the King to swear to the Magna Carta.

The Magna Carta itself merely states that the event took place 'in the meadow that is called Runnymede, between Windsor and Staines.'

In the area of Wraysbury and Runnymede there is archaeological evidence, which includes Bronze Age and Saxon artefacts, of early settlements. From the 3rd century BCE Runnymede was a special meeting place long before the Magna Carta or the Norman Conquest. As Gordon Gyll describes it in *History of Wraysbury*, 1861: 'Runnymede, said to be called the Meadow of the Runes, or magical charms, the field of mystery and the field of council.' In Saxon times it was known as Rune-mede, implying a place of council where, originally, the runes would have been consulted. Originally from the Vikings, runes, made from yew sticks and used for divination and consultation, were connected with yew trees which inspired them. The name 'Runnymede' may also be derived from the Anglo Saxon 'runieg' meaning 'regular meeting' and it is worth noticing that with a slight difference in emphasis, 'runemed' would also point to the place having been a nemeton. Even just the word 'mede' can mean the same thing. The Ankerwycke Yew is in the centre of Saxon territory and the Witan, Witangemote or Council of the Anglo-Saxon Kings of the 7th to 11th centuries was held from time to time at Runnymede, in the open air, particularly during the reign of Alfred the Great. Inaugurations of early Saxon Kings are likely to have happened at this sacred yew which connected the king or tribal leader with the heavens and made the hierophany of sovereignty possible.

On what was a small island in the Thames known as Ankerwycke, across the river from Runnymede, are the ruins of a Benedictine convent, just south of the Ankerwycke Yew, which was founded in about 1160. This yew must already have been there for some considerable time. It is likely, as is the case with so many Christian buildings, that Ankerwycke was chosen for the site of a religious house, precisely because it was already a sacred site, thanks to the yew. The convent was built in a way that the nuns would have been able to see it from their window. The word 'Ankerwycke' actually suggests two possible derivations or origins. First of all, it can indicate an early hermitage ('ankerage', meaning a place of retreat) and the word 'anchorite', meaning 'one set apart', may derive from the Egyptian language. Perhaps in the days before the arrival of the Saxons, a hermit or holy man would have used the tree, (which was quite likely hollow even then) as his shelter and cell. This was a practise known of in other places. A Saxon-Norman manuscript called the Ancren Riwle, dated to around the 13th century, gives evidence of a hermitage tree at Ankerwycke.

Secondly, the place name Ankerwycke may reveal earlier connections with Egypt where the Ankh was a symbol of the Tree of Life and a branch of the tree was held to the nostrils of Pharaohs to give them immortality. The word 'Ankerwycke' is made up of two parts and the second part is likely to be from the name 'Hwicca', which was the name of a Saxon tribe who practised magic. 'Wicca' is a word still used by modern witches.

Far-fetched as it may seem to suppose the Egyptians ever came here, there is certain evidence that the Egyptians did indeed come to Britain. It is possible then, that they may have planted the Ankerwycke Yew next to an important river, the Thames, which reminded them of their own sacred river, the Nile. Rivers were of extreme importance to the Egyptians. If we look for evidence of the Egyptians being in Britain in ancient times there is plenty to be found in the place names which derive from the Egyptian. The Thames area in Berkshire, Buckinghamshire and Oxfordshire are the main areas for Egyptian names. For example, the name of the village of Bray is the Egyptian name for barley, while Isis, a stretch of water at Iffley near Oxford, is named after the goddess. Ipsden is another Egyptian name and Monkey Island is a corruption of mo-nk or mu-ankh, i.e. the water of life. This place is not far from Ankerwycke and there is a good possibility that Ankerwykce may have a connection with the Ankh or sacred branch from the Tree of Life.

The famous Ankerwycke yew may originally have come from a tree in Egypt and been brought to Britain in a tradition of branch or staff carrying, where cuttings, taken to propagate the bloodlines of certain sacred trees, were moved from continent to continent by migrating people. We cannot rule out an Egyptian connection where the Ankerwycke yew is concerned.

Going into this further there are many other examples of Egyptian names across Britain. Rendell Harris in *Egypt in Britain* 1927 states that it was 'superstitious fancy that the Egyptians were a non sea-going people' and states 'there was an Egyptian migration into the British Isles in the long distant past'. He believes they approached Britain via Kent, whose name is derived from the Egyptian 'Khent' and that the name of the Isle of Thanet came from the Field of Tchanet in the Egyptian Delta. The14th century document called *The Settling of the Manor of Tara* precisely details the journey of ten of Pharaoh's ships under the direction of the daughter of Pharaoh Arkenaten, from Egypt to Ireland, where she and her people took up residence.

It is something of a mystery and a coincidence that at Laleham church just a few miles away, there is some strange graffiti to be found on one of the pillars inside the church. The pillars are said to be 12th century and made from clunch, which is a form of chalky limestone found in the east of England and in Normandy, where some believe the pillars may have come from. However, although believed to be 12th century, architectural objects such as pillars are often recycled and as a result, it is possible these pillars could be older. The graffiti found on them, much of which is cryptic, also features such things as a tree with berries and an eye in the middle of a tree. The drawings are not large, just a few inches high and are scratched on in a similar way to the Templar graffiti found at Domme, which was put there by prisoners. The drawings are reminiscent of Egyptian or Mesopotamian imagery and the eye in the tree is particularly interesting and evocative of such cultures.

Whatever the exact history of this tree, it is almost unique to find a yew of this age, planted on low lying ground, as it was not the custom in these islands. Yews are normally found, planted by pre-Christian people as well as those of Christian times, on hilltops and high places. Evidence that this yew is ancient, rather than simply old, lies in the high number of rings per inch (60 - 70), found in some of the decayed wood. There is no possibility of this being a random planting, natural growth from a seed or the tree being part of a vanished yew forest. Ankerwycke is a raised Bronze Age burial mound and the yew was very definitely planted on what would have been in many ways, a well-calculated site. The Egyptians, whose River Nile flooded each year, were experts in flooding rivers. How important and well-considered the site was, is perhaps indicated by the extreme floods in early 2014, which did not reach the yew or the priory, although the river was bursting its banks all around Wraysbury and Staines.

The origins of the site and the yew tree are certainly ancient and predate the 12th century ruins of St. Mary's Priory, the Benedictine nunnery dissolved in 1536, which stands south of the yew. It seems most likely, as stated earlier, that this place may once have been a nemeton, i.e. an ancient Druidic site or centre with a sacred tree. If so, Ankerwycke, a raised Bronze Age burial mound, would have been a nemeton, a sacred shrine of ancient Celtic religion before it was a Saxon site. At one time too, there were carved, inscribed stones here which were reported as having been on the site and which may still be somewhere in the vicinity. There are some long stones that were probably originally standing stones lying in the ditch, which were seemingly made into a bridge and may have formed the nuns' way to and from the island until the bridge collapsed.

Ankerwycke - Old stone in ditch.

The Ankerwycke Yew has likely been the centre of the evolving spirituality of several different cultures. Tree veneration is a cult traceable back to megalithic times.

As an important Axis Mundi, a tree made sacred by tribes that formerly lived there, the Ankerwycke Yew is likely to have been the spot where many English Kings were inaugurated. This was a historic practice, where the yew tree lent divine powers of authority and protection to the King, a practice which continues today in some parts of the world, such as Japan. In ancient times, the Axis Mundi or sacred tree, at the centre of tribal territory, became the place of ceremony, the place of Kingship and Sovereignty. Huge trees were seen as being, like the hub of a wheel, the centre of a tribe's world, a place where great decisions were made. Such a tree was considered to be a divinity, at the centre of kingdoms and tribal lands, whether Celtic or Saxon and formed a natural meeting place. It is no coincidence that the Ankerwycke Yew is not only at the centre of Old Saxon territory but also at the meeting place of four counties: Middlesex, Buckinghamshire, Surrey and Berkshire. The Runnymede area has been linked with the inauguration of early kings and Ankerwycke would therefore have been the ideal place for the agreement to such an important deed of rights as the Magna Carta.

Both the barons and King John would have wanted to meet on territory which afforded them protection, as each side distrusted the other. Ankerwycke would have provided such protection and concealment from a surprise attack with the Yew hiding the company, beneath a great canopy of branches, on an island surrounded by water. Ankerwycke would also have been regarded as neutral ground, as neither side would have wanted the reputation of having desecrated a convent by acts of violence. More importantly still, the tradition of the Axis Mundi may well have lingered and King John could have derived authority from the tree as chieftains and kings had done in the past, giving the occasion authenticity and solemnity. To the nobles the site may have appealed as the natural and traditional spot where weighty matters of state were adjudicated. However, if Ankerwycke is the most likely place in the area for the swearing of the great charter, how is it that it was Runnymede that was stated as being the place where it all took place?

At the time of the agreement to the Magna Carta, Ankerwycke covered a large area that included Ankerwycke Purnish and Little Ankerwycke. At the time of King John Runnymede was a small island meadow in the area known as Ankerwycke. The Thames has changed course several times since the 13th century. Runnymede and Ankerwycke are now on opposite sides of the Thames but at the time of the Magna Carta, experts believe it was all one area on a flood plain.

These ideas are supported by Dr Andrew Brookes, a geomorphologist from the National Rivers Authority: 'Ten thousand years ago the Thames flowed around a series of islands. It had a braided pattern and only in the last 400 years or so has its main channel been centralised, widened and deepened for the needs of navigation'. Indeed, the old course of the Thames can be seen at the base of Cooper's Hill and local historians point out that Langham Ponds were once part of the old river course. The shifting of the course of the Thames may have been caused, at least in part, by the causeway built in around 1250, during the reign of Henry III, on the Egham side of the river. As Professor Sir James Clarke Holt, the leading expert on the Magna Carta stated, 'Everything depends on establishing the line of the river at the time.' The river is known to have changed course and it seems Ankerwycke was once part of Runnymede.

More supporting evidence for the site of the agreement being Ankerwycke comes from the Benedictine monk Matthew Paris who wrote in Latin, 'propre villam de stanes, juxta flumen Thamasiac, in quadam insula' – indicating that the final agreement of the Magna Carta took place on a small four cornered island in the river Thames near Staines. It also turns out, that Sir Gilbert de Montfichet, one of the signatories of the Magna Carta, was both benefactor of the convent that stood next to the Yew and owner of the Manor of Ankerwycke and naturally he may have suggested the site as a safe and discreet meeting place. Richard de Montfichet was also one of the twenty five barons present at the agreement to the Charter.

Since the meadows around Runnymede were open the only safe place in the area would have been the island of Ankerwycke, not only physically protected by the river but offering the very sanctuary that neither King John nor the barons would violate. King John is likely to have known of the Yew's ancient history and significance, especially since his chief aide, Gerald de Barri, had written a book called *Topographia Hybernica*, which details the importance of sacred yews!

It was J J Sheahen, however, who, writing in 1862, plainly stated:

Here the confederate Barons met king John and having forced him to yield to the demands of his subjects, they, under the pretext of securing the person of the King from the fury of the multitude, conveyed him to a small island belonging to the nuns of Ankerwycke, where he signed the Magna Carta.

An anonymous poem, written in the 19th century, also suggests Ankerwycke:

What scenes have pass'd since first this ancient Yew,
In all the strength of youthful beauty grew!
Here patriot Britons might have musing stood, And plann'd the Charta for their Country's good.
And here, perhaps from Runnymede retired,
The haughty John with secret vengeance fired,
Might curse the day which saw his weakness yield
Extorted rights in yonder tented field.

And in 1840 the historian S C Hall wrote about Ankerwycke:

> It is probable therefore that Edward the Confessor occasionally held his witan or council there during his residence at Old Windsor and that the barons chose the site as well on account of its previous association with those very rights they met to assert, as it was a convenient distance from Windsor, sufficiently near for the King but far enough removed to prevent any treacherous surprises by his forces.

John Richard Green in his '*Short History of the English People*' 1874, states:

> An island in the Thames between Staines and Windsor had been chosen as the place of conference, the King encamped on one bank, while the Barons covered the marshy flat, still known by the name of Runnymede, on the other. Their delegates met in the island between them but the negotiations were a mere cloak to cover John's purpose of unconditional submission. The Great Charter was discussed, agreed to and signed in a single day.

As points of information, the Magna Carta was never in fact signed, the final agreement was reached on the 19th June after oaths were sworn by both parties and 'Magna Carta Island', shown on maps, is a misnomer as it is the wrong island. Apart from the ancient yew, there is also a mysterious avenue of around 30 old yews at Ankerwycke. Today nothing is known about these but it is a local tradition that they were planted in 1215 to commemorate the agreement of the Magna Carta, as their likely age suggests.

The original place where King John and the barons met for early discussions concerning the Magna Carta was on the north bank of the River Thames, somewhere between Staines and

Winsor. We know that just a couple of days before that meeting, King John was at Merdon Castle near Winchester swearing oaths to the effect that anyone travelling to Runnymede would have the King's protection. The north bank of the Thames was on the Middlesex side. This is supported by letters written at the time and later confirmed by Matthew Parys' statement:

> In the meeting of 1217 between Henry III and the barons, the Forest Charter and the new version of the Magna Carta was ratified on an island meadow near Staines Middlesex, where they had met before for the original Charter.

There are other stories of the yew's history, such as a legend that a dove conveyed a bough of the Ankerwycke yew in its bill to Germany, where a convent was built to protect the relic. It was later allegedly transplanted to Spain. Another story links royalty with the tree. Henry VIII is said to have occasionally met the unfortunate Anne Boleyn there when she was staying in Staines to be near Windsor. As Jacob George Strutt said in *Sylva Brittanica* in 1882:

> Ill-omened as was the place of meeting under such circumstances, it afforded but too appropriate an emblem of the result of that arbitrary and ungovernable passion, which, overlooking every obstacle in its progress, was destined finally to hurry its victim to an untimely grave.

Within a short time, King John had reneged on the Magna Carta and it had to be restated. Within a year of that King John was dead.

In time-honoured tradition, on June 15th 1992, 777 years after the signing of the original Magna Carta, a group of people again assembled under the Ankerwycke Yew to make an oath. This pledge was as relevant to its time as the first had been. It was a 'green' Magna Carta, drawn up by David Bellamy and setting out to protect the world's wild spaces and wildlife, it reads:

> We the free people of the islands of Great Britain on the 777th anniversary of the signing of Magna Carta do: Look back and give thanks for the benefits that the signings, sealings and swearings of oaths on that document handed down to us. Look forward to a new age of freedom through sustainability by granting the following rights to all the sorts of plants and animals with which we share our islands and our planet.

Ten pledges then follow for protecting all forms of life and allowing them to 'live and complete their cycles of life as ordained by nature.' And so the place of grave political events, serious vows and profound and auspicious matters, continues to lend itself to the hopes and intentions of its people for a better future.

In the light of the dire statements from the scientists of the United Nations Climate Change Conference in November 2018, warning of imminent and irreversible climate change threatening all life within ten years, unless we implement immediate change, this, like the Magna Carta, needs to be restated and adhered to.

Chapter 15

Runnymede and its Yew Tree rediscovered
Research by Allen Meredith

'Sealing the Magna Carta beneath the Yew at Runnymede'.
Painting by Janis Fry.

The exact spot of Runnymede has long baffled historians, but after many years of research one field, or to be correct I should say 'island field' in particular seems to stand out as the spot. In bygone centuries, there appears to be overwhelming evidence pointing to the north bank in Middlesex, near the ruined priory and the ancient yew, as the place of Runnymede.

Runnymede is variously translated as 'meadow of the runes', 'pratum consilii/ field of council'. Matthew Paris, a chronicler of that period, seems to indicate Runnymede as both a field and an island. Even today it is clear to see why it was mentioned as both island and meadow. He indicates the site as juxta, or near, Staines. In the actual charter of 1215, it states the meeting took place at 'runemed' between Staines and Windsor, but Matthew Paris and others give a little more detail and place 'runemed' in a field/island near Staines.

One of the most eminent scholars concerning the Magna Carta was Sir James Holt of Cambridge University, establishing the site of Runnymede. He says, 'everything depends on establishing the line of the river at the time.' This is a crucial point, as the course of the Thames has changed since 1215. We know that in the reign of Henry III around 1250, a huge causeway was built making the river more navigable, thus altering its course for some distance from below Cooper's Hill.

Being at Runnymede today it becomes quite clear that the area immediately below Cooper's Hill would have been part of the River Thames. Part of the river still exists here, known as Langham Pond. Such an important meeting of the King and barons would have been very foolhardy, not only because of the river but because of a likely attack from nearby Cooper's Hill.

Perhaps one of the most convincing events of the suitability of the site in Saxon times for special meetings in the open and the one with King John and the Barons, in particular, was when Runnymede was completely underwater in 2014. Between Windsor and Staines there were floods everywhere and one of the few sites not underwater was the small island/meadow of the priory site at Ankerwycke. I would suggest this was a man-made mound from several thousand years ago that was periodically built up over later centuries. Chertsey Abbey from Benedictine times records 'no flooding at the Ankerwic priory'. There would have had to have been a very good reason for building a priory on a flood plain apart from it being untouched by floods and that is that it was already a sacred site marked by the sacred tree.

In a document of 1236 Matthew Paris states that the Kingston Treaty, that is the Peace Treaty or Forest de Charter of 1217, took place on a small island near Staines. He goes on to indicate that it was the place of council known from older times. In earlier Saxon times it was a Witangemote, a place of the meeting of the Witan or council, to make important decisions concerning the peace of the realm. Such councils would have been held in the open air and quite frequently under a sacred tree.

The location of this yew may have been the reason why the priory was built. It is pretty well established that Runnymede was a small meadow unlike the present-day Runnymede, which covers a very large area. Ankerwik where the priory and yew stand, was recorded in Chertsey Abbey documents and included Little Ankerwik, Greater Ankerwik and Ankerwik Purnish, which covered a great deal of land. It was Hugh of Chertsey who gave many acres of land over to the nuns in Ankerwik and Runnymede was just a small field or island meadow within the area of the ruined priory of Ankerwycke with its ancient yew.

Evidence suggests that the swearing of oaths took place on the 19th June 1215 in the vicinity of the Priory and would have been witnessed by a select group. What is generally agreed is that this took place between Windsor and Staines and that the barons and the King met on the north bank of the Thames in the county of Middlesex. Matthew Paris is more precise and says that the meeting of June 1215 and the later meeting of the Peace Treaty (Charter of the Forest 1217) took place at the same site, 'where they had been accustomed to meet in more ancient times, where great decisions of the realm took place in a meadow near Staines'. *The Articles Of The Barons* constituted the schedule of terms agreed on 10th June 1215 by King John and a group of barons mostly though by no means all of northern origin, who had been provoked into resistance by years of what they regarded as unjust and extortionate government. As for the choice of meeting place, we have seen that Staines, on the north bank of the Thames, was being touted as a suitable place for negotiations between Langton and the barons as early as 27th May 1215.

Matthew Paris referring to 1215 and 1217 writes, 'Sancitum antiques, quadam insulam in Thames quadam pratum sancti', which indicates an island/meadow near the Thames long used as a sanctuary in ancient times. We know in Saxon times that oaths of fealty could only take place using sacred objects at a sacred site.

Although it is generally stated that there was no record of Runnymede before 1215, this is not entirely true, as Matthew Paris indicated, and various extracts from the following documents need further investigation. Norman documents such as the charter called *Monasticon Anglicorum and Chertsey Records*, 1188: Grant to Martin de Coue of place of meadow called Le Runemed Curia Regis Rolls, support the priory island as being Runnymede (runemed prioratus). Although *Le Runemed* is from a Norman document, I have yet to confirm the date, as it may be a Norman document number. There is another document called *Chertsey Records Runemed Prioratus*, 1208, 'Bury Chronicler' where 'Runemed' is stated as being a meadow near Staines Middlesex 1215 ('in prato de stanes'). ('Prato consilli in prato de stanes') is also used, meaning 'Field of council in a field near Staines' and would have been the way the place was referred to before 1215. The name 'Runemed' was probably only used in official documents. However, various Court Rolls prior to 1215 record Runemed and other documents not only record Runnymede before 1215 but use the term 'pratum consilli' as well. 'Runemed/renimed' was a field within the Ankerwic estate.

The fact that King John was taking solemn oaths at Merdon Castle near Winchester for the safe conduct concerning the barons or anyone else to the meeting at runemed is of some interest, as Merdon Castle was an early Saxon meeting place or witan, where great decisions of the realm took place. By order of King John, letters were issued at Merdon on 8th June, offering safe conduct to all who should come from the baronial side to Staines. The raised area around the priory site is quite extensive and would have been surrounded by a series of dug out ditches, evidence of which is seen today. Part of this, which is close to the priory site is shown on older maps as linear earthwork and may have offered further protection.

In Leland's *Itinerary of 1635*, he records 'Prior de Ankerwik infula' and 'Ankerwik nunnery a little above stanes, Middlefex Side' and John Selden, in 1726, writes 'Renimed, alias Runingmede', (near Stanes, Middlesex).

William Camden's *Britannia* also appears to confirm a place near Staines in Middlesex as 'renimed', place of the agreement of the Great Charter. In the 1610 edition of *Britannia*, a map clearly shows Running Mead near Stanes Middlesex. Camden records; 'Near the aforementioned stone, there is a famous meadow call'd Running-mead, and commonly 'Renimed', wherein was a great Meeting of the Nobility in the year 1215'.

Apart from the mention in Camden's *Britannia*, the River Colne is recorded as 'Colne Ditch', and there stands by what is called 'London Mark Stone' 1793. In 1845 there is another mention of the stone, 'A little way above the bridge, near Colne Ditch, on the margin of the Thames, is the boundary stone.' Now this stone would have been moved several times over the centuries before ending up in its current position. For instance, in about 1750 the stone was moved about 500 metres upstream near the present site of Lammas between Wraysbury and Staines. This just happens to be the present Middlesex/Buckinghamshire boundary but, of course, over the centuries boundaries change and rivers were often used as boundaries. Camden's Runnymede must have been the priory site at Ankerwycke only some 700 yards from the confluence of the Colne and Thames.

One of the most interesting items of note comes from A. Morley Davies D. Sc, F.G.S. in the *Cambridge County Geographie's*

Cambridge University Press, 1912 page 102 where it states under BUCKINGHAMSHIRE:

> On that Monday in June, seven hundred years ago, when King John coming from Windsor and the Barons marching from London met at the Thames, it was in Buckinghamshire 'in the meadow which is called Runemed' near the Benedictine Priory of Ankerwyke where the Barons were encamped, and it was on an island within this county that John sealed the Great Charter.

Brief Summary

The raised area around the religious site may have covered several fields and the original meeting and encampment of the barons was most likely opposite the Priory and closer to the Thames. I have no doubt that at the conclusion of the charter on the 19th June 1215; the swearing of oaths would have taken place under the ancient yew now known as the Ankerwycke Yew, near the Priory. Sir Frank Stenton and his colleagues indicate that the name 'runemed' had been the scene of earlier unrecorded assemblies, as is significant in the description of the name. We should take into account the numbers of people present during the period leading up to the final agreement. This can be assessed at the site.

The Facts

(1)   The old course of the river Thames would have occupied what is now called Runnymede in Surrey.

(2)   It is known that King John and the Barons arranged to meet on the north bank of the Thames, the Middlesex side, now part of Buckinghamshire.

(3)   The *Curia Regis* documents (royal council or king's court) record 'runemed' before 1215 and duly note it as a witangemot, (a meeting of council).

(4)   Runnymede (runemed) signified 'field of council'. This

referred to a specific meadow on the north bank of the Thames within the area of Ankerwick.

Matthew Paris (chronicler) stated that the name 'runemed' was received from a more ancient council.

(5) June 15th - 19th was 'sanctae trinitatis' (holy trinity week), which would almost certainly have meant the meeting taking place on a sacred site.

(6) Because of the auspicious nature of the occasion, oaths of fealty would have taken place, which would have included swearing and laying of hands on sacred objects such as a bishop's staff, or simply under the 'gemot treow' (meeting tree) or witena-treow (tree of the councillors). (Occasionally old English writes this as 'witen' or 'witena'.

(7) Chertsey records record 'runemed' before 1215 under 'runemed benedict' and runemed prioratus. A separate record records Runemed Prioratus in 1208.

(8) The documents *Magna Carta* and *Carta de Runemed/ Charta de Foresta* of 1215 and 1217 took place at the same site. Matthew Paris mentions that both events took place in a meadow on an island near Staines (this is a good description of the priory site at Ankerwycke).

(9) Pratum confilii, Pratum et Stanes, Prato de Stanes 'villam de Stanes, juxta flumen Thamisae inquadam insula. Runemed Middelsex. (Field of council on an island near Staines.)

(10) Matthew Paris is quite clear that Magna Carta was agreed at a site known by early Saxon Kings. He writes: 'runemed, partum confilii, eo quod ab antiquis temporibus id est ibi de pace regni faepius confilii tre-ita a bantur'. (Runemed, field of council, a place known of since ancient times for meetings for the peace of the kingdom). He also wrote the Magna Carta took place on 'Thamisiae in quadam insula' (an island in the

Thames).

(11) In *Monasticon Chronichorum*, (a medieval document probably copied from early chronicles such as that of Matthew Paris) we find,'quadum partum insulum in Thamis' (In a certain field on the Thames) (Ankerwycke)

(12) Lelands' *Itinerary* 1535 records Prior de Ankerwik infula - Ankerwik Nunnery a little above Stanes on the Tamife Bank on Middlesex Side.

(13) Professor Holt of Cambridge University writes, 'Concerning the actual site of Runnymede, 'everything depends on the course of the river'.

(14) It is known that during the reign of Henry III, a giant causeway was built altering the course of the Thames. The present-day Langham Pond was once part of the old river course.

(15) The name 'Runemed/Runnemed' may simply mean 'field of council' but in much earlier times, it may have referred to a sacred meeting place, a 'nemed' (nemeton) or 'meadow of the runes', both of which indicate a 'gemot treow' (meeting tree).

(16) The site of a possible Saxon palace or fortification was found at Old Windsor, which was once known as Kingsbury, the king's manor or farmstead, similar to Kingston/Kingstun on Thames. This was similar in several ways, being both next to the Thames and linked with the inauguration of Saxon Kings. The Saxon Kings Alfred and Edward the Confessor were at Kingsbury and within five minutes boat ride from the island sanctuary 'runemed'.

(17) There have been many recordings of a 'charter island' near Wraysbury between the 16th and 18th century. This has been confused by Lord Harcourt of Ankerwycke House's invention of the Victorian Magna Carta Island introduced in the early Victorian period; some distance

away from the priory site at Ankerwycke which I believe is the original charta island.

To sum up, the name 'runemed' was said by many authorities to be first recorded in 1215. This is not true as it was mentioned in earlier documents.

'Field of Council' or 'meadow of runes' is the accepted translation of 'runemed'. This indicates a site used in more ancient times. Even further back in time, runemed or run-nemed could have referred to 'rune' and 'nemed,' (a ditch enclosure with a sacred grove or tree) The swearing of the oaths probably only involved some 30 or 40 people including Stephen Langton and Bishops, Almeric master of the Templars, Earl of Pembroke William Marshall, King John's entourage and selected barons.

It becomes obvious when you look at the raised area around the priory that this land had been purposely built up over the years to avoid flooding from the river Thames. The original meeting of the barons and King John, as stated by early documents, took place on the 'north bank' of the river Thames, the raised area in the field between the ruined priory and the river. The 'swearing of the oaths' would almost certainly have taken place in the vicinity of the priory and the yew.

Curia regis is a Latin term meaning 'royal council' or 'king's court', a form of 'witan', a special meeting place, which was active between 1066 to1215.

Several early documents refer to 'runemed' and 'ankerwik'.

In 1288, 'Ankerwick ait' (Ankerwycke island) was referred to and also in 1268, which mentioned 'the nuns of Ankerwik' (near stans).

In addition, there are descriptions of Ankerwycke priory from *Monasticon Anglicanum*.

'Ankerwikensis prioratus in agro' (Ankerwik in the field of the prior).

'Quadam insulam in thamis qua vocatur' (which is an island

in the Thames).

These Latin words 'Quadam insulam' (a certain island) and Qadam pratum (a certain field), sum up the crux of the whole matter of Runnymede and its location.

In *Records of Buckinghamshire* vol 4. 1870 pages 380 - 391 'Notes on the Ancient Nunnery of ANKERWYKE in Buckinghamshire' by Walter De Birch there is on page 387:

I may here remark that Leland, the antiquary, gives the same derivation, and seems to favour the opinion of John of Beverly, 'pratum consilii quod antiquis temporibus, ibi de pace regni saepius concilia tractabant' - 'In ancient times the councils concerning the peace of the Kingdom was frequently assembled here.

Some crucial notes from *Sir John Denham (1614 - 1659) Reassessed: The States Poet*, Philip Major 2016. *Concerning Peace Treaty Forest Charter, reaffirming the Magna Carta*, states that the Treaty of Kingston after John's death omits to mention the initial negotiations which, according to Matthew Paris, took place on an island near Staines, a place of likely symbolic importance for the Barons who had encamped there in 1215. In centuries gone by the Priory site was frequently referred to as Ankerwyk meadow and Ankerwyk by Staines.

There is a strange legend of an oak tree associated with Runnymede, Saxon kings and the Magna Charta, and it appears that this was confused with the ancient yew on the island. An ancient tree has long been associated with Runnymede and the yew was always (in older times) referred to as an oak in older times even though those writing about it had never seen it. In *From Runnymede and Lincoln Fair*, by J.G. Edgar, 1866, a work of historical fiction we read,

In earlier days, when the Saxon Kings had a palace at Old

Windsor, Runnymede had been celebrated as a place where the people assembled to discuss public questions of great moment; and where now cattle graze and wild flowers spring, grew a gigantic oak, under the shade of which Alfred or Athelstan perhaps had occupied a throne of stone, and sat in royal state, when rallying subjects to the standard to resist the inroads of Danes. It was around this oak, which the English regarded with a superstitious veneration, the origin of which might have been traced back to the times when the Druids performed their mysterious rites, and sacrificed and feasted under the shelter of its spreading branches that the King and the barons met.

The published work of J G Edgar has been described as English historical fiction, but it is known that Edgar closely followed the chronicles of Roger of Wendover and his editor and continuator, Matthew Paris, who was the greatest of the 13th century chroniclers. He also drew upon other sources of that period.

It seems that in early times the Priory yew was referred to by many as an oak, by legend or by those who had not seen it. In the publication by Nicholas Murray Butler, *Magna Carta,* 1915, he writes 'Assembley of wise men, the witenagemot, had gathered at Runnymede under its spreading oak.'

Pedigrees of the barons, John S Wurts, 1942.

Page 266 THE MAGNA CHARTA OAK; 'At Runnymede, a great oak stands.'

Modern Chivalry: Containing the Adventures of a Captain Teague Hugh Henry Brackenridge, 1815.

The various legends and stories of how the Magna Carta came about would have been passed on from generation to generation and the only surviving witness to the great event is the ancient yew.

Chapter 16

The Fortingall Yew
(Written in collaboration with Allen Meredith)

Fortingall Yew. Photo by Pauline Elliot.

The Fortingall Yew is one of the oldest trees in the world, on a par with the Defynnog Yew, investigated in *The God Tree*, with which it shares some similarities. Unlike the latter tree which has also spilt into two halves, this tree is much further advanced in decrepitude and is now protected by a wall and railings. Another difference is that there is far more documentation and recorded historical information about the Fortingall Yew than there is about Defynnog, which seems to be obscured in the mists of time, due to a lack of interest in recording its history.

From the evidence of Jacob George Strutt's engraving of 1825, showing a funeral procession about to walk through the separated portions of the yew, it is clear that when Pennant and Barrington measured the yew over 200 years ago, it was not only already completely hollow but had already separated in two. The measurement around the whole tree they found to be 52 feet, which was an assumption as most of the tree was missing. When this tree was fairly intact, perhaps a thousand years or more ago, Allen thinks a measurement of about 40 feet would have been more accurate and it is worth noting that this is the same measurement as the larger of the two portions of the Defynnog Yew. In Robert Craig Maclagan's *The Perth Incident of 1396 from a folklore point of view* 1905, an unknown poet is quoted as saying:

> The yew Mugna, great was the tree,
> Thirty cubits was its girth,
> Hidden for a time was it,
> Three hundred cubits in height

This can only be describing the Fortingall yew, there being no other similar tree in the vicinity and 30 cubits is 13.71600 metres or 45 feet, which is quite possible for its girth, though the height given, equivalent to 450 feet, is obviously not. It is important just to note here in this verse that the yew is described as 'Mugna', an ancient name for a sacred yew.

Robert Craig Maclagan goes on to say that, since then, the tree had undergone a considerable change:

> partly through the influence of time and partly through the injury suffered from the boys of the village being unhappily allowed to kindle their Beltane fires at the root of it. At that date (meaning 1769 when Pennant was writing)

> it showed no sign of the decay of age...The two stems composing its trunk were so close to one another that a schoolboy could hardly press himself through between them. Now they are so far apart that 'a coach and four might pass between them.

'Still', he goes on to say, 'the larger stem is over thirty-two feet in circumference'.

When Allen Meredith saw the Fortingall Yew in 1986, he said that part of the original bole could be seen still poking a few inches from the earth. From one portion of the trunk to the other, the separation or gap was about eight feet, so there was very slow movement in separation since 1825 for the gap was quite substantial at that time although more of the tree existed. In some instances, Allen says, large portions must have been taken away.

According to records in the last 200 years, fires had been lit inside the hollow cavity and souvenir hunters had taken samples of the yew, so that much of it had disappeared. The larger of the two fragments is now approximately 20 feet 6 inches in girth, which means that twelve feet has been lost from its girth in a little over a century. 'This fragment', Allen said in September 1986,

> has taken on a great deal of new growth, so much so, that it has the look of a separate tree to the other fragment. The smaller fragment of old trunk is quite impossible to measure

as it grows right up against the enclosure wall; however, a rough measure around both trunks was about 48 feet.

In 1890, Hutchison noted, 'The earliest notice of this remarkable relic of many generations is by Pennant, the famed traveller, and by the Honourable Daines Barrington, a Barrister, later a Judge on the English Bench, who seem to have stumbled on it about the same year (1769). Daines Barrington, by his own testimony in *Philosophical Transactions,* 1769 said 'I measured the circumference of the yew twice and therefore cannot be mistaken when I inform you that it amounted to fifty-two feet. Nothing scarcely now remains but the outward bark, which hath been separated by the centre of the tree's decaying, within these twenty years. What still appears, however, is 34 feet in circumference.'

Thomas Pennant's *A Tour in Scotland,* published in 1771, states that in the churchyard of Fortingall:

there is the remains of a prodigious yew 56 and a half feet in circumference... the middle part is now decayed to the ground but within memory was united to the height of three feet; Captain Campbell of Glen Lyon having assured me, that when a boy he had often climbed over, or rode over the connecting part. It is now however decayed to the ground and completely divided into two distinct stems, between which the funeral processions were formerly accustomed to pass. It is impossible to ascertain its age but judging from its present state and appearance, it is not too much to suppose that its date is contemporary with that of Fingal himself, whose descendants the highlanders in its vicinity are fond of styling themselves.

(Fingal was a legendary hero or God/King who gave his name

to Fortingall and was the original name of the ancient yew tree there.)

Dr Patrick Neil in *Edinburgh Philosophical Transactions Journal,* 1833 said:

Considerable spoliations have evidently been committed on the tree since 1769. Large arms have been removed and masses of the trunk carried off by the country people with a view to making quechs or drinking cups and other relics. What still exists of the trunk now presents the appearance of a semicircular wall. Great quantities of new spray have issued from the firmer parts of the bark and a few young branches spring upwards to the height perhaps of 30 feet. The side of the trunk now existing gives a diameter of more than 15 feet so that it is easy to conceive that the circumference of the bole when entire should have exceeded 50 feet.

Reverend Robert Macdonald wrote in *The topographical Statistical and Historical Gazetteer of Scotland* 1841:

At the commencement of my incumbency, 32 years ago, in 1806, there lived in the village of Kirkton of Fortingall, an old man of the name of Donald Robertson, upwards of eighty years of age, who declared that when a boy going to school, he could hardly enter between the two parts of the trunk. Now several yards separate them. The Rev. Robert Macdonald, parish minister of Fortingall in 1838, wrote that the dilapidation was caused by the boys of the village kindling fires at its root or kindling their fires at Baeltainn, within the hollow trunk. Sir Robert Christison had this information verified by Dr Irvine of Pitlochry, who was a grandson of a former owner of the Fortingall burying ground, Stewart of Garth. His mother often told him, when she was a girl about the year 1785, she could with difficulty squeeze through the gap and that her father at the time built the wall to protect the tree from dilapidation.

Dr De Candolle had information about this yew dating from 1831. His method for measuring and computing its growth led him to state its age as between 2,500 and 2,600 years in 1770. He called it a veteran of European vegetation.

G and P Anderson in *Guide to the highlands and islands of Scotland, including Orkney and Zetland* 1842. Wrote:

> The churchyard is remarkable for the remains of an enormous yew-tree, which furnished many a goodly bow when the weapon formed a part of a Scotsman's armoury.... About a century ago, the trunk was single and measured 56 feet, now it presents the appearance of two stems, about twelve feet high; of these the largest, which is quite hollow, is 26 feet in girth. Though so much decayed in the core, it is completely sprouted over with young branches.

Sir Robert Christison in *Trans Botanical Society Edinburgh*, 1870, wrote:

> Little information as to its rate of growth is to be got from sections of the Yew itself. On many parts of the shell and the branch, the rates varied from one inch in 48 to one inch in 60, 68, 70 and 90 years. None of these rates could be reasonably taken as denoting the growth of the trunk for more than its last hundred years of life. It is better to use the general rules arrived at, according to which the tree in the first place is assumed to have attained a girth of 22 feet in a thousand years, after that age no information yet warrants a rate of more than one inch (circumference) in thirty-five years.

Christison estimated the Fortingall Yew to be over 4,000 years.

The *Journal of Forestry* in 1882, stated in *Curious and historic Trees:*

The great tree in Fortingall churchyard spanned the pathway with its gaping trunk and the funerals of highlanders borne to the grave passed through the opening under an archway of overshadowing foliage. It was a common practice for mourners in funeral processions to gather yew boughs at the gate of the graveyard and these were borne along and finally held over the coffin and then placed upon it in the grave.

The placing of yew sprigs in the grave is a solemn burial rite and enables passage and protection of the soul/spirit to the otherworld. This dates back to prehistoric times and evidence of yew has been found in Neolithic burials.

Robert Hutchison in *A few notes from Old and Remarkable Yew Trees in Scotland* 1890 wrote:

The well-known and frequently quoted Fortingall Yew has naturally been visited and examined...This aged and now sadly dilapidated patriarch has formed the subject of much controversy amongst botanists and scientists as to its age and it has, by eminent authorities, been credited with an antiquity far beyond that of any other tree in Britain, and has been thought indeed by no less an authority than De Candolle, as possibly 'the most venerable specimen of vegetation in Europe... One of the portions of the trunk bears now a vigorous head clad with healthy foliage and 16 feet in height and the other a fine crop of branchlets and larger arms, very healthy, and upwards of 24 feet in height. Outside the enclosing wall is a vigorous young yew which may be either a seedling of the veteran or the product of some surface root from the old trunk, with a cylindrical trunk, somewhat grooved, 53 inches in girth at five feet from the ground.

Berries from this young female yew of perhaps a hundred years or so, that is still there on the other side of the wall outside the enclosure, could well drop on to the old yew making one think the Fortingall Yew to be monoecious (both male and female). This would be an easy mistake to make, and so, in 1995, I climbed onto the wall to examine a branch that carried berries and discovered it came from the large yew and not the small female outside the enclosure. This made the Fortingall yew a rare monoecious tree, just like the Defynnog yew only the other way round! While the male Fortingall Yew carried a female branch, the female Defynnog yew, carries a male branch! A few years ago, it was probably in 2015, Max Coleman of the Edinburgh Botanic Gardens confirmed my observation. It would be interesting to carry out a DNA test on the small female yew just outside the enclosure, as it is not unlikely it will be found to be part of the old tree and share its DNA.

The Fortingall yew grows in a north-westerly direction in the churchyard which connects it to Neolithic culture, as it was people of this period who planted yews on the north side of the burial mound, making the tree a great age, in excess of 5,000 years. To reinforce this evaluation, a cup and ring marked stone, known to be of the Neolithic culture, was found a short distance away from the tree, at 8 feet below the surface. It is now to be found above ground, a short distance from the tree. In *Fortingall Churchyard Perthshire, the northern Antiquarian*, 1910, it says it was found 'at a point not many feet distant' from the yew and so may have been closer at one time. As we see with the Defynnog Yew, trees that separate will 'walk', or move away, to give more space to the separate portions and it is entirely possible that this stone was at one time directly underneath the Fortingall Yew, to mark it out as special. The yew is unique in Scotland indicating a very special sacred site and the tree may have been planted to mark the grave of a most important person.

Today the Yew stands in an enclosure, which makes it difficult to see and even more difficult to photograph but it is much visited and celebrated. 2 parts of the shell remain - one on the south side, a mere rim of old bark, 3 feet in length and the same in height, from which one large limb about 9 feet grows westwards and the other on the north, much more solid and imposing with 2, what might now be called main trunks but which must have originally been secondary growths, forming quite an imposing tree with an excellent canopy of green above. The circumference of the larger mass at the ground is about 20 feet, and the widest line between the two remaining parts is slightly over 18 feet, which more than bears out the original measurement of over 50 feet in girth. These measurements have been kindly confirmed by the Rev. William Campbell of Fortingall.

There are many place names in the Fortingall area that would seem to link the yew to a long-standing sacred site. One is a farmhouse called Duneaves, described as opposite the church of Fortingall. Professor W J Watson, an expert on Celtic literature, observes that the name Duneaves means 'house of the nemed'. This word derives from the same root as 'nemeton', meaning a sacred enclosure and 'nemus', translated in Sylva as indicating a wood or tree. So we might surmise that in ancient times this was not only a sacred site but more importantly that a sacred tree existed on that site.

In correspondence with Mike Strachan, who works in the area for the Forestry Commission, Mike said he was aware of 'an old turf wall that is still visible from aerial photographs. This covers an area of about three acres around the site and might be the nemeton you refer to'.

Other place names in and around Fortingall most certainly appear to indicate not only a sacred site but a most sacred tree. The etymology of nearby Coshieville, confirms that 'cos a bhile', comes from the Gaelic, meaning, 'at the foot of the sacred tree'. The 'bile', like Mugna, referred to earlier, indicates a sacred tree, not just any tree, but almost certainly a tribal tree in the centre of tribal territory. Local place names such as Coshieville and Tullochville, indicate that a 'bile' or sacred tree was, or is, in the vicinity. (*Walking in Scotland* by Sandra Bardwell, 2001) Mike Strachan adds the following:

> Coshieville, or more correctly, 'cas a bhile', means at the foot of a sacred tree and probably more noteworthy is a place name in Fortingall of Magh or 'achadh a bhile' – 'the field of the sacred tree'. In *Chronicum Scottorum*, 825 CE, we find that at a place called Magh-Bhile or 'Field of the Ancient Tree', an ancient yew existed. This site was regarded as 'Fidh-nemedh' or 'sacred tree'.

Mike Strachan further observes that:

> Fortingall is probably derived from Fother-cill, meaning the cell beside the forther, fort or dun. Immediately to the north of the village is An Dun geal – the white fort. Therefore, the suggestion that a monks cell existed at this location is probably correct.

Other place names which may be of significance in the vicinity of Fortingall are Dun-Fother, Fother-dun, Fionn-lairig-Tir, Artair-Sithchaifionn and Dail Chiarain.

When it comes to traditions, there are similarities between Ireland and Scotland with an intermingling of ideas. According to Brian Taylor, in *Exploring the Supernatural*, Nov. 1986:

legend has it that on the festival of Samhain (the Celtic festival at the end of October, marking the start of the dark part of the year), a fire was built on the Bronze age Barrow, situated at the head of Glen Lyon... A ceremony which was still being held at Fortingall in Perthshire into the early part of this century, offers us a glimpse of this much earlier Celtic culture. Held somewhat unusually on November 11th, the bonfire was a communal effort, built on a low hill known locally as 'The Mound of the Dead', in reference to a local legend, which claimed that it marked the site of a plague pit, though the truth was more interesting than this. This mound is a Bronze Age tumulus and Samhain, (which celebrated the dead and the ancestors), was always closely associated with such burial mounds, for it was believed that they were entrances to the 'otherworld'.

It appears that bits of the yew wood from Fortingall may have been used to light fires during the festivals of Samhain and Beltan (biletain). Apparently, on Samhain (Old Hallows Eve - 11th November), a huge bonfire was built on a huge mound, made of furze and sticks, the people held hands and danced around the blazing fire and boys ran into the fields with burning faggots. The story seems to indicate that in recent centuries bits of the yew may have been used by boys as firebrands, not realising or perhaps not caring, about the sacredness of the occasion and that the yew sticks, brands and wands were meant for a ceremonial purpose and would have been used sparingly in Druidic times in a tradition of sacred fires found in various places in the world. (As we have seen, this practice, for example, was observed by the Hittites) Only on great occasion would these yew sticks have been used in a similar manner to runes, as it was the casting of these sticks and the making of yew wands and talismans that gave rise to the tradition of the runes. A verse from 610 CE illustrates an early connection between the yew and Samhain: 'At Samhain, beneath my Yew tree, he said to me a saying grievous to hear'. There is also the following from Silva Gadelica, translated by S H O'Grady, 1892, 'Patriarch of long-lasting woods is the yew, sacred to feasts as is well known'.

An interesting but unsubstantiated tradition is that when Pilate's father was a Roman officer of high standing his camp was in the area of the Fortingall Yew and his son Pontius Pilate was born and brought up in the Fortingall area. According to legend Pilate was supposed to have carved his initials on the tree and returned to Fortingall to die and be buried there. In a few notes taken from E H M Cox's *New Flora and Sylva* – Volume 3 (c.1930) we read:

> The village of Fortingall lies at the entrance to Glenlyon, one of the most lovely and picturesque of all Scottish glens, a few miles to the west of Aberfeldy, in Perthshire, and just north of Loch Tay. Apart from beauty of situation, Fortingall is of some historic importance. It is possible, though extraordinary, that it was the birth place of Pontius Pilate. The story goes that his father was one of those sent by Caesar Augustus to the Scots. Perhaps peace treaties took as long to arrange in those days as they do now; at any rate, while the meeting was taking place between the ambassadors and King Metellanus, Pontus Pilate was said to have been born at Fortingall.

While this is the stuff of legend, there is no smoke without fire and there was certainly a Roman legion in that area, which was written about by F. Hunter in *Guide to Perthshire; Evidence of Roman intrusions in the Fortingall area*, 2000:

> Here at Fortingall are the most northern known works of the country and the Roman Camp said to have been formed by Agricola, who fought a battle with the Caledonians in the neighbourhood, can still be traced. Many interesting Roman

remains have been found from time to time in and about the site of the camp. Of these may be mentioned a Roman standard, the shaft of which encloses a five fluted spear and which is preserved at Troup House. In the praetorium of the camp was found a vase of curiously mixed metal, and in a shape resembling a coffee pot. This was found about 1733 and is preserved in Taymouth Castle. Of late years, a number of urns and flint arrows have been picked up, in and around the camp.

Something I find very interesting and also amusing from *Gaelic Kingdom in Scotland, its Origin and Church with Sketches of Notable Breadalbane and Glenlyon Saints*, by Charles Stewart, 1880 is:

It is a remarkable fact... that the traces of the Druidic worship should be found to such an extent in the glen, whilst the peculiarities of Roman Catholic worship should have almost if not entirely vanished.

Fortingall is an ancient place whose past throws long shadows. Something that has mystified archaeologists for decades is the aerial photos showing a faint line in fields around the village but, in 2011, as reported by The Scotsman newspaper, an archaeological dig led by Dr O'Grady and a band of local volunteers opened up two exploratory trenches and revealed a wide bank with large upright stones that may have once stood as high as two metres. The bank is believed to be the remains of a Pictish monastic enclosure, also known as a vallum monastery dating from the time when the Picts were converting to Christianity more than 1,300 years ago. This is only the second Pictish monastery to be excavated to any great extent in Scotland and its discovery supports existing evidence of an early Christian monastery at Fortingall. This can only be because there was already religious history at this place. Also found were the remains of a substantial Pictish road passing through one of the enclosure's main entrances. A geophysical survey carried out within the enclosed area indicates the remains of a major settlement with many internal divisions and possible dwellings. Neil Hooper, chairman of the heritage society said 'It just shows how important the ancient monastery at Fortingall must have been.' O'Grady, who previously led excavations at Scone Palace, thinks that Fortingall could have once been a major cultural and religious centre in the Celtic world. He said

> I am beginning to see this more on the scale of a royal monastery, a venue where links between dynasties were forged through marriage or even where inaugurations were held to affirm royal power.

As we have seen there was a history of such inauguration ceremonies being held under ancient sacred yew trees. Very unusually, an Anglo-Saxon bead was found embedded in the surface of the Pictish road. Christian missionaries may have built on a prehistoric monument centred around the famous Fortingall yew.

It is crucial to know as much as possible of the importance of Fortingall if we are to understand the presence and significance of the Fortingall Yew. The location of the great battle during the early period of the Roman occupation of Mons Graupius, (the Grampian Mountain) has never been positively identified and has been the source of endless debate among archaeologists and historians. However, at this battle led by Agricola, 10,000 Caledonian tribesmen, under the leadership of Galgacus, died at a cost of just 360 Roman dead. The battle was fought around 84 CE at Grampius Badon which is near Tay, near Fortingall, the traditional and geographical centre of Scotland where the yew tree represented the centre of tribal territory. Historically, trade routes travelled east/west and Fortingall would have been at the crossroads of trade. Some four miles due east is the ancient stone circle of Croftmoraig (circa 3,500 years old) and to the north of it is a burial chamber that predates the circle. This occupies a prime site, where key hills are perfectly framed from its centre. Crannogs have existed on Loch Tay for at least 2,500 years, which may have been related to the burial chamber. There is therefore significant historical information pointing to people living and trading in the area for at least 3,500 years and it would seem likely that the Fortingall Yew was a focus of pilgrimage and due to its presence spanning thousands of years, may have been regarded as a god or supernatural being, displaying immortality. In the chapter called 'Nemeton', in this book, you will see that an important nemeton also existed in this area and that a ceremonial agate axe head from the Neolithic period was also found buried under the yew as well as the cup and ring marked stone. The evidence is clear that the historic importance of Fortingall and its yew dates back thousands of years.

Fortingall. Ceremonial axe head, like one of these, found beneath the Yew.

A point of some interest in yew affairs is that some important customs link the Pan-Celtic deity, Finn along with his Otherworldly connections and shamanic character, with the Fortingall yew tree. Finn is the archetypal seer and poet sometimes known as Fionn or Fintan. 'Fionn' means white or tree and 'tan' means red. These are both words connected with sacred yew trees. Fintan is the Salmon of Knowledge, who swims in the waters of the Holy Well beneath the yew tree, his pink colour due to the yew berries which drop into the well. The name 'Salmon of knowledge' is a translation of 'eo feassa', where 'eo' is yew and would seem to indicate that the salmon and yew are one and the same thing with the salmon's knowledge coming from the Tree of Knowledge, or yew. In the story related in the 13th or 14th century Irish document known as *The Settling of the Manor of Tara*, Fintan, known as 'The White Ancient', tells of how he came to Ireland with the first invaders, who as we saw in *The God Tree*, came from Egypt. He says he has lived for a very long time and seems to be implying thousands of years. It becomes obvious in the telling of the story that Fintan, 'son of Noah', is actually the yew tree itself and his name may mean 'red tree'. This is investigated in depth in both *The Sacred Yew* and *The God Tree* and it could well be that the Fortingall yew is one of the sacred trees of Ireland. Ireland is just a short distance away from Scotland by boat and the ship that brought the 'invaders' to Ireland, may have travelled on to Scotland from there.

One of the mysteries of the Yew is to be found in *The Settling of the Manor of Tara*. Here we find an extraordinary visual description of Trefuilngid Tre-eochair, the giant who makes an appearance at a great assembly of Irish nobles with 'a shining crystal veil about him like unto a raiment of precious linen'. In his right hand, he carries the branch with the three fruits – nuts, apples and acorns (fruit of the tree of the thrice-blessed fruit – the yew). As already pointed out, the branch was described as a 'golden, many-coloured branch of Lebanon wood', which sounds somewhat like a Golden Bough. As Fred Hageneder agrees, this was yew wood. From the giant's appearance, as well as from his mission to ensure the rising and setting of the sun, he would seem to be a sun god but Fintan describes the giant as either an angel of God or God himself. He may also have been an ancient yew tree. When the giant leaves, he gives Fintan some berries from the branch he carries which Fintan plants and which then sprout and grow into the famous five sacred trees of Ireland, so it is from this mysterious branch which the five sacred trees of Ireland were descended.

As it says in *The Sacred Yew*, 'It then becomes clear that Fintan's role is coming to an end and in the new Christianised Ireland, his fate is linked to the sacred trees', (which were cut down by the Danes and by warring factions of Irish tribes). 'The passing of Fintan and the passing of the sacred trees are linked', but Fintan was not destroyed and it is intriguing to see the Egyptian connection here. Fintan is said in *The Settling of the Manor of Tara*, to have arrived in Ireland, 'with the first invaders'. These were from Egypt and as described in *The God Tree*, were descendants of Akhenaten, or Moses, who were exiled after the death of the Pharaoh. Akhenaten's daughter Scota, is said to have founded Scotland and an Egyptian burial site, containing beads and artefacts from the era of Tutankhamun, was discovered at Tara in Ireland, although faience beads have also been found in Scotland In a book called *Scota, Egyptian Queen of the Scots* by Ralph Ellis, evidence is given that:

> Queen Scota and King Gaythelos were actually Queen Ankhesenamun and Pharaoh Aye, who appear to have been thrown out of Egypt in 1320 BCE, and went on an exodus to Spain and then Ireland. Their son was said to have been Hiber, from which we apparently derive the names for Iberia (Spain) and Hibernia (Scotland). This would fit in very nicely with the story of Queen Scota, a story gleaned from ancient Irish and Scottish chronicles.

Ralph Ellis says there is lots of evidence pointing in this direction, indicating that the ancient chronicles are correct. There is also other evidence of the Egyptians having been in Scotland. Rev. John Stirton in his essay called *The Celtic Church and the influence of the East*, 1923 states that:

> The earliest type of monumental cross in Scotland is an Egyptian or Coptic wheel cross. It appears on several stones at Kirkmadrine in Wigtonshire, along with the Alpha and Omega. The Crux Ansata, (the Ankh symbol), the emblem of life in Egyptian hieroglyphs, is found on a stone at Nigg in Ross-shire and on another at Ardbue in Ireland.

According to Barry Dunford in his website *Sacred connections Scotland - Scotland's past links with ancient Egypt:*

> The old Scots Chronicles also record that during the 2nd century BCE certain 'Egyptian philosophers' (probably from the Egyptian mystery temples) came to Scotland to advise the Scots King of the period...During the early centuries CE the Celtic monks in the British Isles, much of whose texts were rooted in a pre-Christian Druid tradition, saw Egypt as the true Holy Land rather than Palestine due to the ascetic Desert Father tradition established there which they sought to follow and emulate. Hence, we find in Scotland and Ireland, a number of dysarts (desert) place names which record monastic settlements and retreats founded on the Egyptian anchorite model, so ancient historical links between Scotland and Egypt seem fairly likely.

The point of pursuing this line of thought is to establish the possibility or even, the likelihood that the Fortingall yew is an Egyptian planting; not as impossible as it may sound.

This Egyptian connection occurs again at Ankerwycke, where

it would seem that the yew tree was also likely to be an Egyptian planting. Fintan's full name is Fintan mac Bochra, meaning 'The White Ancient', undoubtedly a name for an ancient yew of supreme importance. This Fintan was said to still be alive after 5,000 years which he would be if he was a yew tree. As was said in *The God Tree*, a yew tree can continually regenerate 'itself from itself', (an ancient mythological phrase used for a tree god)'. In *The Settling of the Manor of Tara*, Fintan relates stories as far back as Noah and the Great Flood, he being the only one to have survived it, lending further credence to his identity as a tree as does the fact that in other versions of this story, Fintan himself, rather than the giant, carries the branch with the three fruits. All this underlines the fact that we are dealing with stories passed on through oral tradition which became muddled over many years. However, the motifs remain the same. The golden branch would single this tree out as a very special, sacred yew since the property of bearing such a branch is found in just a small handful, some eighteen ancient yews to date, of historical importance and the fact that the giant, Trefuilngid Tre-eochair, is also said to bear this branch underlines the number three as in 'Tre', the three fruits, the triple goddess/god of life, death and eternity, connected with the immortal and eternal Tree of Life. (Tre is from Proto-Albanian (trei), from Proto-Indo-European (treyes) and cognate to Latin (tres – three) and Sanskrit (tri – three). At present, the Fortingall yew does not bear such a Golden Bough, although I would expect it to but it may have done in the past and may do again. It is simply not possible to unravel all stories and mythology but at the same time, it is not difficult to read between the lines. In conclusion, it all points to Fintan, the White Ancient, the Fortingall Yew being one of the five sacred trees of Ireland, yew trees that originated in Egypt. *The God Tree* goes into much depth to identify the Fortingall yew as being, more than likely, one of these trees, despite it being in Scotland.

In *The Perth Incident of 1396 from a folk-lore point of view*, 1905,

Robert Maclagan suggests that Fortingall was the place of one of the legendary trees of Ireland and that 'the plain in the north' meant Scotland and the 'navel or centre', the place where the yew stood. 'Erin' was a name for Ireland but it was not always used exclusively for that country and 'Ierne', a name used by the Romans for Ireland, seems also to have included Perthshire, the Western highlands and islands, as well as the area to the north of the Forth, which included Fortingall. Our modern perception is that Scotland and Ireland are separate and different countries but this may not have been the case in ancient times. It is also highly likely that the legendary tree of Tara which grew on the hill of Tara, was the original tree planted by the Egyptians when they first arrived and that the Fortingall yew came from the same stock. Both these trees would have been planted over 3,000 years ago if we follow the story that they came with Arkenaten's family from Egypt and if we take account of Fintan's description of himself having survived the Great Flood, it would make the stock from which they came, older again. It's possible both stories are true and the Egyptians saved and preserved the original tree by one means or another, as a cutting or seedling or from rootstock taken from a sacred tree from the time of Noah, for which there is no definite date. Two books, *The Jahwist*, composed in the 10th century BCE, and *The Priestly Source*, from the late 7th century BCE, make up the chapters of Genesis which concern Noah but when dealing with antiquity and legend we cannot really know of such dates. Some scientists date the Great Flood or Deluge to 2348 BCE, which would put the age of a yew tree rescued from it, at around 5,000 years which is, of course, within the realms of possibility for the Fortingall Yew but we do not know for sure. Other scholars date the Flood to 15,000 years back due to evidence of watermarks found on the Egyptian Sphinx.

On another matter, concerning the yew, the toxicology and psychotropic properties of this tree investigated elsewhere in this book, with Soma and Haoma, are likely to give some insight into the possible activities of the Cult of Finn or Fintan, which are likely to be much the same as the practises and preoccupations of the Yew Cult wherever it was found. A friend of mine, Tom Beels, who lives in Glenlyon, gave me some interesting information about the Yew Cult in this area. St. Adomnan/Adamnan who was also known as Eonan in Glenlyon, a name which could translate as 'Little Yew', was both a disciple and a relative of St. Columba and like him was an Abbot of Iona. He had a yew staff and when the Great yellow plague came to that area in 664, it left no one alive in Fortingall and continued to advance 12 miles from there up to Glenlyon where the people implored Eonan to save them. Eonan responded by placing his staff into a hole in a stone and ordered the plague into the hole. This stopped (or stayed) the plague. Apparently, the Plague Stone where he placed his Yew staff is still there and has a hole that goes right through the stone. A standing stone by the side of the road marks the spot where Eonan stayed the plague. Tom believes Eonan came to Glenlyon precisely because Glen Lyon and Fortingall were areas with an active Yew Cult.

In Simon Taylor and W J Watson's *Celtic Place names of Scotland* 1926, we find concerning the Fortingall Yew at the entrance to Glen Lyon, 'This place name is understood as 'fort', from Gaelic 'Fartairchill', in old record Forterkill. The fort stands on a commanding bluff near the church and is known as the 'White Fort', traditionally the residence of the legendary figure 'Fionn mac Cumhaill', a hero god king, also known as Fingal, as we read in *Twilight of the Celtic Gods*, 1996, by David Clark and Andy Roberts, another form of the Celtic Lugh. According to legend Glen Lyon was his home and the ruins were manned by his 9,000 warriors. A large standing stone in a field at Killin (Cill-Fhinn - 'cell of Fingal') is supposed to mark Fionn's final resting place and his name may be another name for Fintan. The River Lyon takes its name from an old god/dess, known also as Lug, Leu (similar to Lleu - Welsh for lion), or Og/Ug etc. In a strange coincidence, one of the oldest yews in Wales at Discoed overlooks another River Lug in Powys, while in the village of Fortingall, pairs of strangely shaped stones resembling lions, guard the gateposts at Glen Lyon House and the parish church itself. It is perhaps strange but true that ancient long-lived trees were sometimes looked upon as gods and in saying that, the Fortingall yew is likely to have been just such a one. It is also possible that a king or chief may have referred to a sacred tree rather than a person, and that the Fortingall Yew in ancient times is likely to have been looked upon as a tribal chief. In Gaelic, the Fortingall Yew, according to Prof. W J Watson in a book on place names in Scotland called *Scotland North of Forth*, 1927, was known as the North King. Certainly, such chiefs and leaders would have been buried under sacred trees which then became Axis Mundis, around which the life of the tribe centred. The idea of the tree and the King may have become inseparable. The Fortingall Yew is part of the mythology of ancient Britain and has lived through an age when certain trees would have been looked upon as gods or goddesses, particularly an immortal tree connected with stories of the tribe's history passed from generation to generation. In an uncertain world, the tree, like a deity, was always there.

As a final note to this chapter, there is another legendary figure connected with the Tay besides Fintan and that is King Arthur! (always one to pop up!) In *The Inverness Trans Gaelic volume*, 1887 - 8, we find, 'After the Glenn Turret battle, Arthur struck Loch Tay and went round it by the west or Killin end. He has there, on the north side of the loch the place name of Tir Artair, 'Arthur's Land' and this land embraces the promontory of Fionn-Lairvig. The next place name trace of him which we find in this Grampian region is at Fortingall'. In the chapter in this book on Bernera, you will also find compelling evidence of Arthur's presence in this area, when Arthur was taken down the River Tay, on his way to his last resting place thus adding more flesh to the bones of this story.

Chapter 17

Jesus' Wand - Magic and Miracles

As we saw in *The God Tree*, saints and holy people such as Joseph of Arimathea carried a staff, many of which were yew staffs taken from a particular sacred tree or trees. They were sometimes carried across continents from Egypt and the Holy lands to Britain where they were planted and grew into trees. Some still grow where they were planted today. It seems some may have been cuttings from the Tree of Life or other sacred yews with special properties, such as that given to St. Padarn; a very special and highly prized staff, the greatest of gifts, from the Archbishop of Jerusalem which was said to bring peace in any dispute and was so revered that praise poetry was written to it and the staff bore the name Cyrwen, meaning 'holy white power'. Staffs like this were planted here in Britain for safety and protection, to grow on for thousands of years into the future.

Probably the earliest mention of a staff or rod of power is in connection with the Exodus of Israel from Egypt where the words 'rod' and 'staff' seem to be interchangeable. The rods referred to here are known as the rod of Moses, the rod of Aaron, and the rod of Levi and are also referred to as the rod of God. The rod played an important role in the deliverance of the Israelites from slavery in Egypt and Moses and Aaron used their rods or staffs to compete with Pharaoh's magicians in Exodus 7, Aaron's rod also magically blossoming, to show him to be the High Priest. Perhaps then it should come as no surprise that Jesus should also have had such a rod or wand, although this is not generally known now. Jesus used his staff for his own purposes and neither Moses nor any other figure from the Old Testament is portrayed as Jesus is, as possessing the power to raise the dead with his staff or wand.

Jesus raising Lazarus with the use of a wand -
on a sarcophagus in the Lateran c.340.

Lee M Jefferson writes in *Christ the miracle worker in Early Christian Art* 2014:

Staffs have a long history as a symbol in literature and in art.

There are various terms in Greek and Latin that refer to some type of staff or wand that projects otherworldly power in the minds of a Late Antique audience.

It would seem that it is specifically the yew staffs which have these powers and these staffs were real objects.

Jesus is shown in early Christian art with a staff of power which acted as a wand able to direct magical or miraculous happenings. It is not known for sure what became of Jesus' staff. St Peter is also shown in the catacomb paintings with such a thing which some thought to be the staff which had belonged to Jesus, and had been passed on to him but there are also legends that Jesus' staff was passed on to St. Patrick by a hermit who waited for him on an island in the Etruscan sea. In this convincing version of what became of Jesus' staff, it was brought back to Armagh Cathedral in Ulster and then was taken to Ballyboughal around 1113 where land was set aside for its preservation and protection in 1173 and there it was recognised as the staff of Jesus. Unfortunately, in 1538, it was burnt as a 'superstitious relic'! Such was the importance of St. Patrick's crozier, known as the Bachall Isu, the staff of Jesus, that during legal disputes, people would swear on this staff, considering it more seriously binding than swearing on the 'Holy Evangelist'. If this was the true version of what happened to Jesus' staff then it is likely that Patrick was the first Guardian of the Grail Secret investigated in *The God Tree*.

If you Google 'Jesus' wand in early Christian Art', you will see a series of paintings, many from the catacombs of the 3rd and 4th centuries, of Jesus using such a magic wand or staff to bring about magical events. Jesus healing the sick and raising the dead were very apt funereal themes on sarcophagi, seen as declarations of the reality of the resurrection of the body proclaimed and demonstrated by Jesus. As such, they were popular images of comfort for the relatives of the dead who would visit the deceased in their tombs and were confirmed in Jesus' message depicted in the paintings which were also a not insubstantial means of spreading the news of the wonders of Jesus, the belief in salvation and the superiority of the new religion. When Jesus was seen ordering the paralysed man to arise, the visual imagery spoke louder than words, with well-nigh the same impact as it had on those who witnessed it and the visual story had parallels with and hints of the resurrection, in the paralytic's return to full use of his body. At a time when most people were unable to read this early Christian art was a powerful and effective means of telling the story of Jesus and inspiring a new faith. Apart from the most popular and frequently used image of the raising of Lazarus, other dominant images of resurrecting the dead showed Jesus raising Jairus' daughter, and the widow's son at Nain. Jesus was also depicted as Ezekiel in the Valley of the Dry Bones, where he points his staff downwards to a figure lying on the ground, to indicate his power to resurrect. In the original story it is the hand of God that does this, so here the parallels are clear. Jesus is a divinity who wields a god-like power through the staff. Typically these paintings show Jesus pointing towards or touching the figure, with his wand or staff, in a dramatic gesture, which commands the power of life over death, restoring and returning the person to their living relatives. Jesus with his staff had the monopoly on this. This was not the kind of magic performed by other magicians and his miracles demonstrate the life-giving properties of his staff. With his staff he conquers death.

To give further emphasis to Jesus' power through the staff and to place him in line with the patriarchs in the catacomb of Peter and Marcellinus, a picture of Jesus raising Lazarus is positioned next to an image of Moses touching the desert rock with his staff to produce water by miraculous means. It is remarkably similar to the images of Jesus using his wand. This same scene of Moses using his magic staff also appears with that of Jesus raising Lazarus at the Vigna Massimo catacomb and the juxtapositioning of these two images appears quite frequently in the catacombs. This had the effect of stressing the importance of the staff and also of linking Jesus with Moses, and on one occasion with St. Peter, who is depicted doing the same thing and in the same pose as Moses touching the rock with his staff to obtain water. Clearly one of the purposes of the catacomb paintings is to show Jesus and Peter in the same category as Moses.

The sarcophagi in the catacombs are not the only place where Jesus is shown healing and performing miracles with a wand. We see him depicted thus on the doors of Santa Sabrina in Rome and while he uses the wand to change water to wine, multiply the loaves and fishes and raise Lazarus, often when pictured healing, he is shown laying on hands, rather than using a wand, which seems to show the dilemma between Christian healing and Pagan magic. Some scholars suggest that only the Gospel of Mark, the Secret Gospel of Mark and the Gospel of John (the so-called 'Signs Gospel'), portray Jesus as a wonder-worker, user of magic, a magician or a Divine man but the other synoptic gospels also give prominence to this. As Lee M. Jefferson writes:

> There are over 35 references to the healing power of Christ in the four gospels, the most belonging to Matthew. In early Christian texts, Jesus' superior healing ability was so emphasised that the statements reveal that Jesus' status as the greatest healer was disputed.

In other words, in the first centuries before Christianity was properly established, Jesus was competing for supremacy with other gods and magicians.

Other miracles where Jesus uses his staff or wand are not to do with healing or raising the dead but show the power Jesus had over the physical world, over nature, like Moses. In a 5th century portrayal, Jesus is turning water into wine with a magic wand at the wedding at Cana. A woman, possibly Mary Magdalene, stands beside him. It was Hebrew custom in Jesus' time that the groom provided the wine at wedding feasts. Many believe this was Jesus' wedding to Mary Magdalene and early Christian art suggests he produced the wine by magical means.

In the version of this story shown in the *Vigna Massimo* Jesus is also shown performing the miracle of multiplying the loaves by touching the baskets with his staff. Here the Magi are also portrayed, emphasising and giving credence to this aspect of Jesus as a magician. Elsewhere in the catacombs Moses is shown using the magical staff of power to command Nature and cross the Red Sea. Thomas F. Mathews writes in *Clash of the Gods* 1993:

> In Exodus 14:16-27, Moses used his wand on the Red Sea twice, once to part it and again to close it. Interestingly, the moment chosen in the early Christian art is not the parting but the closing of the Red Sea over the pursuing enemy after the Israelites had safely emerged on the other side. Pharaoh raises his hand in despair as Moses' wand draws the waves over him and his horses.

You can't help wonder, considering the similarities with Jesus' nature-commanding miracles, whether we are to surmise that this was the same staff passed from Moses to Jesus and then to Peter, although significantly it is only in the hands of Jesus that we see the staff's resurrective properties. Such was the strength of this artwork that Jesus' fame and the success of Christianity were largely made by the image-makers of the catacombs. It is interesting that here the stories from the life of Jesus that were emphasised were those of the miracles. Thomas F Mathews writes, 'The miracles make up the bulk of the narrative while the infancy and passion stories are reduced to one or two subjects'. He goes on to say of the Christians, who wore clothes emblazoned with pictures of Jesus' miracles, 'To such Christians, the life of Christ consisted simply of a series of miracles.' The new images were tools that actively competed with the old and Thomas F. Mathews states,

> The decline of the gods, had much to do with the bankruptcy of their images and the appearance of a more forceful set of divine images...The images of Christ determined what people were to think of him, not only in the early centuries of the current era but ever after.

The paintings from the catacombs of Rome are the main, though not the only reference, for Jesus using a wand and offer some of the most vital forms of evidence of the connection between Paganism and Christianity.

Eventually, the paintings ceased to be made and were forgotten after Christians came into jurisdiction and it was not till 1578 that they were rediscovered. The catacombs are vast, extending six miles deep underground. Rome has some 600 miles of them and they are considered to contain the single most precious collection of early Pagan and Christian art in the entire world. It comes as another surprise revelation that the paintings made here show Jesus as a young and beardless man with short hair, quite different from how he was later portrayed. Jesus is also shown using his wand to heal the blind man and the woman with the issue of blood. It was at some point, before the end of the 5th century, that the Church decided to censor the wand and about the time where he ceases to be portrayed with it, he instead gains a halo! This was all to do with the image-making of Jesus and when the Church council met in the 5th century, they also decided to depict Jesus with a beard and long hair, perhaps to distance him from the early paintings of him as a magician. Up until this point it had served Christianity to emphasise Jesus' abilities as a magician as a means of competing with other religions to gain converts, by portraying Jesus as a magic or miracle worker par excellence, superior to any rival deity.

Lee M Jefferson says in *Christ the miracle worker in early Christian art:*

In Late Antiquity, the line separating the category of healing and miracle-working from that of religion was often quite fine. Figures such as the healing god, Asclepius or the magician Apollonius of Tyana, were parallels as well as potent adversaries of the emerging Christian religion and its chosen deity of Jesus Christ...but Christ was greater than Asclepius in every way... In fact, after Constantine and his conversion to the new religion in 312, Jesus had finally won the battle or competition with Asclepius and his other rivals. Jesus was promoted as the supreme physician who heals the soul as well as the body. The belief in divine healing maintained a powerful place in ancient medicine. Methods of healing in antiquity encompassed medicine, miracle and magic and religion seeps through all three areas. Miracles of Paganism and Christianity were a direct appeal to the gods and were acts of divine benevolence bestowed upon believers in response to their faith...Christ is credited with several resurrections in the four gospels though most notably the raising of Lazarus in John 11:1-10. Although resurrection stories can be described as miracles, it is still debatable whether healings should be considered as such. In John, the Lazarus story is not necessarily a healing but it is restorative. Lazarus is not resurrected to eternal life just yet. He is restored to a human condition...A resurrection may not appear to be a typical healing. However, in the Bible and art, resurrections and healings appear to operate similarly.

There were obvious differences between the healings and miracles of Jesus and those of other magicians. Essentially Jesus was not doing these things for effect, to build his reputation or for money but to create a change of consciousness in those involved, as a kind of call to moral reformation, transformation and recognition of the power of the Divine. The miracles were to prove to people that there was a superior power that operated outside of their ordinary lives, a power held by the staff and commanded by Jesus. Those involved and those who witnessed the miracles would hopefully henceforth live their lives differently, with the awareness of God. Other practitioners of magic often had critics who were afraid of the influence of magic or saw it as a threat to religion and Plato for one, thought magicians threatened the relationship between humans and the gods, making people believe they had the power to change the will of the gods, rather than submit to their power.

A book called *Portraits of the Incarnate God* by Robin Margaret Jensen, 2013' says 'Representations of Jesus holding a wand gradually disappear after the beginning of the 5th century, when the wand is sometimes transformed to a cross or dropped altogether.' Thomas F Mathews says

The wand is not incidental but a standard and necessary feature in Early Christian art. Sometimes an effort is made to 'Christianise' the wand by putting a little cross on the top of it, but it is still used as a wand to convey magic power by touch.

Back to the book in the V&A and:

Interestingly in the later scriptural narrative scenes, that appear, especially in ivory carvings such as the mid-5th century Andrews diptych, or on domestic bowls, fabrics and in mosaics, when Jesus is shown with a halo, his wand is often omitted. Conversely in cases when Jesus is shown with a wand, his halo is then omitted. This is very clear on two 5th century ivories that show both halo and wand but not in the same scenes. The significance of an apparently deliberate choice to give Jesus one or the other attribute is difficult to explain, unless the wand somehow makes the halo inappropriate, a theory that would be challenged by the image on a 5th century silver relief that shows both a halo and a wand. The simplest answer is that the wand was an attribute that was gradually phased out, perhaps because viewers were more and more removed from a time when competing with the other gods or wonderworking was necessary. By the end of the 5th century, the contest was over and the wand appeared no more.

Sadly, in his treatise entitled *Of True Religion*, the important and influential St. Augustine of the late 4th and early 5th centuries, in order to accommodate rationally minded philosophers, said that miracles were relevant for the early Christians and happened then but were not needed today! Miracles had no place or purpose in the world of his time, he said, and had taken place at that earlier time simply because people had to be made to believe before they were able to reason about divine and invisible things! He said that images of Jesus demonstrating miracles and healings were promoted to instil faith and bring together a large body of believers. This is a very cynical approach but for Augustine anyone who carried on believing in miracles taking place after that time was foolish and irrational!

Later, however, Augustine's views backfired on him when he found himself in an untenable position concerning miracles while promoting the importance of saints' relics and he was forced by his congregation to acknowledge the present-day reality of miracles, saying, 'God grants us these favours from the dust of the dead'! So magical events resulting from a dead saint's finger were one thing but Augustine drew the line at miracles being the result of the staff of holy wood. The difference may have been to do with the possible loss of the income brought to the Church by saint's relics.

Since Jesus commonly appears on ancient Christian sarcophagi in the role of a magician wielding a wand it may be that the catacombs were closed off to suppress these ideas. Although Jesus is depicted in the Bible as a miracle worker, somehow miracles are seen as Christian and magic as Pagan but there is a fine line, a mere sliver of difference between them. Catholic tradition holds that the diversity in early Christian belief stems from heresies that branched out from an original kernel of orthodoxy rather than the other way round. Their view of the roots of the early diversity in Christian belief is difficult to reconcile with the books of the New Testament which are presumed to represent the earliest Christian writings as well as the so-called heretical works, such as those by Justin Martyr and Tertullian. Christian history also holds that, while Gnostic sects like the Valentinians existed in the city of Rome, they had either died off there or had ended up conforming by the third century and that Christian belief by that time was very similar to that of today. This is too simplistic a view and the imagery from ancient Roman sarcophagi, carved in stone, is evidence of Christianity being incompletely formed in Rome well into the late 4th century. The funerary imagery clearly shows a problem and huge inconsistencies when attempting to form ideas of the ancient Christian community from the texts of the clergy.

The fact that magic in the first century was extremely important is introduced early on in the New Testament at the very beginning of Jesus' life story, with the appearance of the Magi at the Nativity. It could be said that their appearance to worship and bestow rich gifts upon Jesus was to recognise and announce him as the supreme magus. Some believe that Jesus was taught magic during his time spent in Egypt, which is quite possible, although there is no actual evidence for this. The magic wand was important to the ancient Egyptians and part of their magical practice and historically the wand as the sign of a wizard originated in Egypt in the Middle kingdom. In the ancient world Memphis was seen as the capital of magic. The catacomb paintings may be trying to show that Jesus inherited the magic of Egypt through Moses who according to Exodus was taught how to use his magic wand (his magic staff (rabdos) by Yahweh himself. In the light of understanding the miraculous holy wood it becomes obvious that it is not the saint, patriarch or holy man who performed the miracles but the staff that caused things to happen and we see in the Old Testament, with Moses and Aaron's rods, that the staff can act independently and later in the age of the Celtic saints these staffs, as described in *The God Tree*, were able to cause all sorts of events by their presence. In the catacombs we are obviously supposed to see a connection between Moses, Jesus and Peter with all three using wands. It may be that Jesus is also meant to be seen as inheriting the magic of the Chaldeans with the depiction of Daniel and his friends in the lion's den with a fourth person, 'like a son of the gods' (Daniel 3:25) who protects them with a magic wand or staff.

A document known as the *PGM* (*The Greek Magical Papyri*) contains a collection of spells and formulae from Egypt from the second century to the fifth, as well as hundreds of magical incantations used for oracles, divinations and encounters with the gods through dreams. However, this is not the kind of magic practised by Jesus, although he also used a wand. Never is his wand used for his own ends, to prove himself or change his destiny, as true magic was. His magic is spontaneous in answer to an immediate situation, to help and to heal and Christians believed his powers were divine. Unlike other magicians he did not seem to need to prepare himself for these acts, use words or chants and did not call upon gods or any other powers before making his magic.

The wand is a symbol of power, the staff a symbol of authority and there is a connection to be found in the pyramids with the Ankh, which is no doubt a branch from the Tree of Life, held to the face of the Pharaoh with the intention of offering eternal life. This is a privilege that doesn't seem to be given to ordinary people in the Egyptian tradition. There is also a painting of Thoth resurrecting Osiris with the Ankh while holding two staffs entwined with serpents like the Caduceus. It was believed by some early Christians that Jesus acquired the Ankh and used it to perform his miracles. This has more than a ring of truth about it, for after all what is the Ankh but a branch from the Tree of Life with which Jesus was strongly connected? Taking this further, perhaps that branch was a Golden Bough which we will come to in the next chapter. It also suggests that Jesus perpetuated the Egyptian teaching of not only Moses but also Thoth as well as Akhenaton (for whom there is much evidence to show that he most likely was Moses). His healing with the wand or staff was therefore in the same tradition as the Egyptian gods, who used the Ankh to bestow eternal life.

The Gnostics frequently called Jesus, 'the Tree of Life' or a 'branch' and at Domme, in the Dordogne in central France, rough carvings of Jesus are to be found in the chateau there, where Knights Templar were imprisoned during the surprise attack in 1307 by the Catholic Church. These carvings, sometimes known as graffiti, are a mass of sketches, showing Jesus with his wand, crosses, a fish and the Tree of Life. The wand here may in fact be a branch from the Tree of Life. There is also a depiction of Jesus' execution that is slightly different from the official Church version. (The Templars denied the Crucifixion and the Cross as a symbol of Christianity although they carved crosses on the walls of their prison at Domme.) Here on Jesus' left, a pregnant woman holds a wand or a rod. This is perhaps Mary Magdalene, who in some traditions was said to have carried Jesus' child. The chateau carvings may also be trying to say that she took guardianship of his wand. (From *Jesus' magic wand and the Templar engravings at Domme*, by William Henry.)

Knights Templar graffiti at Domme.

In another sense it could be said that Jesus didn't just have a staff or use a wand but that he embodied those things. He was the staff, the magic wand of eternal life and the resurrection. He was referred to as the Tree of Life, the root and branch of Jesse or, as is said in the Book of Isaiah, Christ would come forth as a rod from the root of Jesse. He symbolised these things, as did some gods and goddesses before him. In this mysterious graffiti, left behind by the Templars, there are clues and messages to something of the mysteries and esoteric knowledge they had discovered, probably during their time spent guarding the Temple of Jerusalem. They could never have put these things into words as the Catholic Church, who was pursuing them as heretics, seeing them as a major threat to their control of the creeds, stories and beliefs about Jesus, would simply have destroyed the words. Secret societies have of old conveyed their knowledge in symbols which were left as signposts, messages and statements for those who were able to decipher them and realise the truths and knowledge they were trying to preserve and pass on. What better way than to put these things into what appear to be the insignificant drawings and meaningless scratchings of those passing time in a condemned cell. The imprisoned Templars, it seems to me, found this way to preserve esoteric knowledge and truths surrounding the death of Jesus, and it is up to us to translate their language and read their symbols. It is a mark of Jesus' utter belief in the Tree of Life that he willingly offered himself up as a sacrifice and went to his death with his total faith in the life giving and resurrecting properties of the Tree of Life on which he hung, confident that this was not the end. Mary Magdalene, more than likely Jesus' wife, may have been left with his wand or staff, to pass on to his successor and she, according to some traditions in the south of France, gave birth to his daughter who was named Sarah. According to these versions of events, she was put into a boat with Joseph of Arimathea and landed in France after Jesus' death, where the holy family founded the dynasty of the Merovingian Kings. Having accompanied Mary this far to safety, Joseph left as soon as possible, with a staff from the Tree of Life, to travel direct to Britain. Whether this staff was the same one as Jesus' or a branch from the tree on which he hung, we don't know, but he lost no time in reaching Britain where arrangements were doubtless already being made by the Druids of Siluria, to plant the staff at Llanilid.

Chapter 18

The Golden Bough and the Golden Fleece

The Defynnog Yew, 'Stairway to Heaven' Painting by Janis Fry.

It was at the turn of the millennium, on Christmas Day 2002, that the author and researcher for *The God Tree* first discovered a Golden Bough, growing on the ancient yew at Defynnog near Brecon. This was the very yew which is the contender for the title of Oldest Tree in Britain and possibly in the whole of Europe. Some years later in 2020, it still grows on the same tree, though sadly picked apart by visitors. Higher up, however, in the tree, some out of the reach of people, new golden sprigs are sprouting upon the branches, Next to the main tree, part of the original trunk which split away to form a separate tree, a nest of golden twigs gleams, like a Golden Fleece. The yew tree drew royal interest when Prince Charles visited it on July 8th 2017 and was fascinated by the Golden Bough, returning later with just his driver for another look.

In the 40 years that we had studied yew trees, a Golden Bough was never seen growing on a yew before that fateful year, 2002. The mythology and legends associated with the *Golden Bough* are well known and the phenomena was written about in a book of that name in 1915 by J G Frazer, who famously considered many trees in Britain, to discover which tree could carry it, many trees that is, except the obvious one, the yew! This has led to much speculation as to why that was, from a man who belonged to a clan who had their own famous, Frazer Yew. Before our time, the Golden Bough was last seen and heard of 3,000 years ago, written about and immortalised by many of the Roman writers such as Virgil, in connection with the Trojan hero Aeneas, who appeared in both Virgil's *Aeneid* and the Greek writer, Homer's *Iliad*. Such was the subject's fascination that these writers were writing about events that had occurred a thousand years before them.

Aeneas was said to be the son of the Prince Anchises and the goddess Venus (Aphrodite) and the second cousin of King Priam of Troy. Aeneas features in both Greek and Roman mythology. In the Roman, he is celebrated as their first true hero. Aeneas was a warrior and in Virgil's *Aeneid* we learn that he was one of the few Trojans who was not killed or enslaved when Troy fell but fled the scene shortly before the end. Troy was on the northwest corner of what was Anatolia, Hittite country, now modern Turkey. When, in the Greek Homer's *Iliad*, he fell under the assault of Achilles, the central character of the Trojan War in the Greek version, the god Poseidon notes that Aeneas, though from a junior branch of the royal family, is destined to become King of the Trojan people.

The legend of the Golden Bough is of Roman origin, whereas

the better-known legend of the Golden Fleece and Jason and the Argonauts, who steal it from where it hangs on a sacred tree in Colchis, is Greek, but the story concerns a similar quest and also a yew forest. Both the Golden Bough and the Golden Fleece have to be found and taken by a royal hero. In the Roman story this is Aeneas and, in the Greek, Jason. The ancient kingdom of Colchis where the Golden Fleece is found is one of the most important areas of ancient yew forests in the world, known as a world prime stand for monumental yew trees, with some of the oldest trees in the world. Hecate, the triple goddess of the underworld and yew groves, was worshipped in Colchis' ancient city. In the story of the Golden Fleece, Medea, associated with serpents, uses her powers to soothe the immortal dragon who is the guardian of the sacred tree where the Golden Fleece hangs. In reading the stories it becomes obvious that these two legends from different cultures are from the same source.

In 2017 I was sent photographs by Andrew MacLean which showed a tree in Sussex at St. Margaret's Church, Buxted with what looks like a fabulous Golden Fleece hung over a high up branch!

Buxted Yew Golden Fleece. Photo by Andrew Maclean.

It is formed of adventitious shoots, a mass of little shoots, growing close together, sprouts of leaves like the tufts of wool on a lamb, which cover a section of the main trunk of the yew tree. I had recently seen something very similar at Llanelltyd in North Wales.

The Hittite texts say, 'From the Eya tree hangs the sheepskin'. Eya is the name for Yew and one wonders if they were talking about the same thing as these extraordinary phenomena that are now appearing in Britain. The Colchis lie at the far end of the Black Sea, where the Golden Fleece, said to be a ram's fleece, hangs from the sacred tree. Pindar, the Greek mythical poet 518 - 438 BCE, describes the Golden Fleece as an 'immortal coverlet, the fleece glowing with matted skeins of gold'. The word 'immortal' may mean 'imperishable'. Pindar, in propria persona, anticipates the immortality conferring quality of the Fleece and the gold of the Fleece is seen as a sign of the brilliance of immortal fame that success confers on heroes. As often in Pindar, gold attends the mortal encounter with divinity. The Golden Fleece is a magical artefact with powerful healing. It restores Thalia, who had been transformed into a pine tree but more than that, the Golden Fleece restores the kingdom's prosperity. In the legend of Jason, Medea and the Argonauts, Jason is sent on a quest to find and gain the Fleece by King Pelias who has usurped the throne, the success of the mission being the condition necessary to place Jason rightfully on the throne of Iolcus in Thessaly. The Fleece represents kingship and prosperity and discoveries about the Hittite Empire in Bronze Age Anatolia show celebrations where fleeces were hung to renew royal power. The story was current in the time of Homer (8th century BCE) who got it from Hesiod of the same time period, but it was set around 1300 BCE, a generation before the Trojan war and is essentially about immortality and the restoring of life. The tale came out of the region of Thessaly in Greece where early epic poetry developed. In the 2nd century BCE, the Greeks held the yew sacred to Hecate, a triple goddess who represented the crone, the waning moon and the death aspect of the Great Goddess in their pantheon. Triple goddesses associated with the yew tree were generally triple in two aspects: the maiden, mother and crone along with life, death and eternity which is associated with the yew tree as these goddesses are too.

Hecate and Athena were both known as 'triple goddesses', as were others, such as Hera, Demeter and Proserpina or Persephone. These goddesses are all linked with the Underworld and in the Roman story of the Golden Bough, described in detail in *The God Tree*, the passage is known as Tartarus by the gloomy banks of the River Styx or Cocytus. This is the lifeless stream where the yew tree, sacred to the triple goddess, grows. Like Persephone, Hecate has a direct association with the yew tree and both she and Athena have been associated with yew groves. Anciently depicted with a yew branch, she was celebrated at festivals with yew garlands. The Norse Valla, similar to the Sybil, is also depicted holding a yew branch.

The Golden Fleece hangs from a tree in the Grove of Ares, where it is closely guarded by the immortal dragon of a thousand coils, rather like the serpent who guards the Tree of Life. It is interesting that Ares, the Greek counterpart to the Roman Mars, is sometimes depicted as holding a snake or with a serpent emblazoned on his shield. Several of the mystical shrines of Ares were endowed with monstrous guardians and the sacred Amazon island of Ares was also protected by birds that shot arrow-like, or dagger-like feathers, reminding us of the Gandharvas that protected the Tree of Life where the soma was found. As we have seen several times before, the oak, as this particular sacred tree is described to be, is often confused with a yew. It is true that Jason's quest to claim the Fleece, in order to secure the vitality of his homeland, is a different quest to the Golden Bough but Aeneas' quest to enter the Underworld to speak to his dead father may have been for similar reasons, of matters of state and homeland, as he comes from his fallen city of Troy. It may not be relevant but it is something of a coincidence that Ares was a Trojan ally, eager to help the warrior sons of Troy. To put Troy in context with the rest of the world at the time, to the west of it lay Greece and to the east, the Hittites who dominated Anatolia. Troy was wedged between two war-like peoples. The Trojan War, according to Homer, took place in the Late Bronze Age and lasted for 10 years.

In the Greek story of the Golden Fleece, Jason is helped by Medea who has the skills to soothe the dragon, which was born from the blood of Typhon, the arch serpent from the Corycian Cave, which points to the Anatolian origins of the story. Anatolia is the ancient name for the area in northern Turkey where Troy was. It is also where a yew tree was recently found to have 4,012 rings. It can hardly be a coincidence that the Colchis in the Caucasus, the home of the Golden Fleece, one of the most important regions of yew forests in the world, is renowned for its monumental ancient yew trees. Herakles also travelled to the Colchis with Jason. It was he who wielded a yew club and like the triple goddess Hera, was connected with both the yew and the entrance to the Underworld.

Returning to the Roman story of the Golden Bough, at the end of the Trojan War, there were few survivors. Aeneas escaped from Troy to Italy and decided he must see his dead father, Anchises. Protected by the Golden Bough, his talisman, he journeys into the Underworld where he meets with not only Anchises but also his dead wife Dido and at this meeting in the Underworld, his father reassures him by showing him the future of his descendants and thus the history of Rome.

This was the last that was heard of the Golden Bough and the Golden Fleece until the present time, 3,000 years later. Make no mistake, their reappearance and rediscovery is one of the most unexpected and extraordinary, mystical events of our time. Since the Golden Bough and Fleece were found, at Defynnog, one or other has been seen on at least 20 ancient yews in Britain. One by one they have appeared. Remarkably, the yews that bear them are practically all trees of some historical importance, and one wonders if these trees were possibly originally planted by those who knew they were special and different from other yews, knew they had the ability to produce this special bough. Perhaps in fact they all came from the same stock originally. The question is, were the Golden Bough/Fleece trees of Britain brought here originally as cuttings or staffs taken from these legendary trees in ancient times and did the ancients know they were capable of producing a Golden Bough? Did they know these particular yews would start to produce Golden Boughs or Golden Fleeces at a particular time in history, almost as if they were programmed to do so? Their reappearance since the beginning of the new millennium on ancient yews of historical importance after an absence of 3,000 years feels highly significant and raises questions as to the purpose and meaning of this event. Some have suggested they are here to mark the coming of a Golden Age. If so, a cleansing preceding what's known as The Great Turning by some indigenous people, who have never entered our modern age, has to happen first. We are now in a time where we are realising the errors of our attitudes and the way we live. It is almost too late to change the fate we have been unconsciously cultivating but at least we do know now that we must change radically or become extinct. A new era where humanity lives once more in harmony with Nature, as predicted by certain Native American tribes, will come only after we pass through the darkness and fear of our days of reckoning as we are brought up against the power of Nature unleased upon us. The Golden Bough is here as a talisman to light the way, as it was for Aeneas travelling through the Underworld.

Although the Golden Bough was investigated in depth in *The God Tree*, I feel it necessary to repeat some of that chapter here to keep abreast readers who may not yet have read it. According to Virgil, the Golden Bough was always a rare sight:

Showing the bough enfolded in her robes –
'you know it well'
The Sybil says no more.
The Ferryman, marvelling at the awesome gift,
The fateful brand, unseen for many years.

The Sybil, the Valla and the Furies were the 'go betweens' the humans and the goddess. They were priestesses and prophetesses, concerned with ensuring that the Golden Bough was found, taken and eventually presented to Persephone, Goddess of the Underworld.

In the Golden Bough chapter of *The God Tree* is all the evidence needed as to why any claims of the Golden Bough being either the mistletoe or the Holme oak can be dismissed. The tree described by the ancient writers is a special tree, a most sacred tree. Virgil called it a 'fatal tree', a 'fatal branch', the 'double fatal tree in a gloomy vale'. A tree referred to in this way could only be a yew, as the yew is the tree connected from ancient times with Fate. Virgil describes 'The lurking gold upon the fatal tree' and says, 'Conduct my steps to find the fatal tree' (In ancient terms the 'fatal tree' could only refer to the yew tree. Virgil's reference to 'double fatal', or 'double tree', concerned the death-dealing poison of the yew and the tree's life-giving properties.) He describes the tree as 'The double tree that bears the golden bough' The yew on which this fatal golden branch grows is not just any old yew tree but a most special yew, for it is only on one tree in the sacred grove at the entrance to Avernus, the Underworld, that this Golden Bough could be found. Later Aeneas visits the forest of Avernus next to the yew grove. As in medieval texts, the forest is the place between the worlds of the mundane and the spirit and is something of a no man's land, which has to be crossed to reach the underworld. (*Trees* by Richard Hayman 2003) Another important thing to note is that this rare bough was not just growing on the tree but it was part of the tree.

From ancient literature we learn that the search for the Golden Bough was a great adventure, a dangerous mission, which few would undertake. Some of the main themes and elements of this quest conjure up scenes you might encounter in a Steven Spielberg movie such as the Underworld, the River Styx, the ferryman, the Triple Goddess and the Sybil, Tartarus, a talisman, the Gloomy grove and the Fateful Tree. In Virgil's classic poem it was the Sybil who commanded the quest and discovery of the sacred bough to be carried by Aeneas when he entered the Underworld, for without such a bough, from the wondrous tree sacred to infernal Juno, none could enter Pluto's realm. And when Charon, the ferryman, refused to carry Aeneas across the Stygian lake until the Sybil brought forth the Golden Bough from her bosom, it becomes clear enough, that the Bough is the passport to Hades. Charon, who guards the river Styx, refuses to take the unburied dead or living passengers until he is shown the Golden Bough. Thus we learn that one of the primary functions and importance of the Golden Bough was to enable the bearer to safely descend into the Otherworld and return with knowledge from the realms of the gods and the dead.

As we know from the Roman writer, Statius, Avernus in Italy, was a thick yew grove, where the Golden Bough was to be found close to the entrance to the Underworld. The grove of Persephone, daughter of Proserpina and herself associated with the Underworld, was near here. Although Aeneas can be pointed in the right direction to look for the Golden Bough, he must find it for himself and pluck it from the tree. However, the Bough cannot be taken from the tree unless it is his fate to do so. He is thus helped by the Sybil, prophetess, seer and the guardian of the sacred wood, to take this prize to the goddess Proserpina as a gift. Only in this way shall Aeneas be permitted to enter the realms of the dead. Once there our Trojan hero, Aeneas, must reach Proserpina's palace and plant the Golden Bough on her threshold.

Other Roman writers such as Ovid wrote about the Golden

Bough and we find there are common themes and factors to do with the character of this sacred branch. 'There is a shelving path, shaded with dismal Yew which leads through profound silence to the infernal abodes. Here languid Styx exhales vapours...' He also speaks of, 'the gloomy funeral yew which leads to the Underworld of Tartarus and the sluggish Styx'. In *Metamorphoses*, Ovid says 'He (Aeneas) besought leave to pass down to Averna (the Underworld) and meet his father's ghost. And she (the Sibyl) told him...You shall achieve your aim and with my guidance, you shall (visit the underworld)... She showed him in the glade of Juno Averna (Persephone), a gleaming golden bough and bade him break it from the trunk. Aeneas did her bidding and saw the riches of Orcus' (Hades) frightful realm and his own ancestors and the aged ghost of great-hearted Anchises.'

Since it is quite clear from these and other statements by writers such as Ovid and Statius that the yew plays a major role in the whole adventure of discovering the Golden Bough and entering the Underworld, it is a mystery as to why there has ever been any doubt as to what the Bough was or what type of tree it grew from. Further confirmation that the Golden Bough comes from the yew is presented by the fact that Persephone is depicted in ancient mythology as holding the yew bough! It is interesting to note a curiously related custom here. From Neolithic times up till the 18th or 19th century in Wales and the West Country, branches of yew were placed in graves to ensure the recently deceased a safe passage through the Underworld to the next world.

Statius elaborates on this procedure for safe passage through the Underworld, and in *Thebaid*, tells of Amphiaraus, King of Argos, who, in Greek mythology, also tried to gain admittance to the Underworld but who may not have been so successful as he omitted some of the necessary steps: 'Upon the Stygian shores... not yet had the Eumenis (Erinys or Furies) met and purified him (Amphiaraus) with a branch of Yew, not yet had Proserpine (Persephone) by the Golden Bough, gleaming on her door post, marked him, as admitted to the company of the dead.' Amphiaraus is depicted on an ancient vase dating from around 460 BCE which shows the Golden Fleece protected by the Yew goddess Athene, which speaks volumes! It seems obvious that the highly prized Golden Fleece which hangs on the bough of a sacred tree in the Colchis is the Golden Bough in its young state when it first appears.

Golden Fleece. Much Markle.

Later, one bough emerges and grows like any other branch (except, of course, for its colour) and at this point, the 'Fleece' disappears, giving way to the Golden Bough. In the epic journeys, the two things are sought after with the same single-minded determination.

Virgil writes of the dark abode of Tartarus, the underworld, in the following words taken from the *Aeneid*:-

> In the neighbouring grove
> There stands a tree; the queen of Stygian Jove
> Claims it her own; thick woods and gloomy night
> Conceal the happy plant from human sight.
> One bough it bears; but (wondrous to behold!)
> The ductile rind and leaves of radiant gold;
> This from the vulgar branches must be torn,
> And to fair Proserpina the present borne.
>
> Such was the glittering, such the ruddy rind,
> And dancing leaves, that wanton'd in the wind.
> He seized the shining bough with gripping hold.
> And rent away, with ease, the lingering gold

Referring to the Golden Bough, Virgil describes it as altogether golden, the stem as well as leaves. This is certainly an accurate description of the most developed present-day Golden Boughs with their bright, golden yellow leaves and copper-gold lustred branches. The description here of the 'ruddy rind', meaning reddish or golden bark, is a variation of the previous quote where the Bough bears the 'ductile rind'. Few trees have 'ruddy' or reddish bark, the Yew being one of them. 'Ductile' refers to a jewellery making process where gold is drawn out into pliant wires or threads of gold that resemble twigs. 'Rind' means bark. So here it is spelt out that the Golden Bough bears twigs like metal. The modern Golden Boughs vary from young small twigs to an entire branch or bough, an inch or more thick and, extraordinary as it sounds, the larger of today's boughs do indeed glitter and glisten with a kind of red-gold lustre, more reminiscent of metal than wood.

Another version of the Underworld described by the Roman writer Seneca, states 'In the Underworld the foul pool of Cocytus' sluggish stream...The leaves shudder, black with gloomy foliage, where sluggish Sopor (Hypnos), sleep, clings to the overhanging yew.' (Hypnos is depicted holding a yew branch). Yew foliage on a dismal winter's day in Wales can look black and the early classical writers when referring to a 'gloomy branch' connected with the Underworld were always describing a yew.

Golden Bough. Photo by Andrew MacLean.

But the Romans were not the only ones to pass down the legend of the Golden Bough. As we move north to colder climes, we come across the Norse legend of the World Tree Yggdrasil which strangely enough also refers to the Golden Bough. Here in Asgard, before the doors of Valhalla, there stands a grove called Glasir. The needles or leaves of Glasir are described as gold and the 12th century Icelandic poet, Snorri Sturluson, tells us that the old name for Asgard was Troy! So here is an extraordinary surprise connection with Aeneas, the Trojan hero and his Golden Bough!

From *A History of the Swedish People*, by Vilhelm Moberg (1898 - 1972) we learn that the Norse people had previously lived in Aeneas' part of the world but migrated from there as a result of war. One wonders if this could have been the Trojan War. There is also strong evidence that Swedish predecessors were migratory Thracians, aggressive refugee 'boat people', who first came from the ancient city of Troy. Located in North-West Asia Minor (present-day Turkey), the ruins of Troy were discovered in 1870. In the period beginning around 2500 BCE, Troy was populated by an 'invasion of peoples on the sea', users of ships, iron weapons and horses. Troy was known as a centre of ancient civilisations. Its inhabitants became known as Trojans but also Thracians (later called Dardanoi by Homer, Phrygians or Anatolians by others). Troy endured years of war specifically with Greek and Egyptian armies and was eventually reduced to ruins after ten years of fighting with the Greeks around 1194 - 1184 BCE. Thousands of Trojans left Troy. Some remained for thirty to fifty years after the Trojan War but eventually the Greeks sacked the city and after that those remaining emigrated. Many went to Italy where they established the Etruscan culture, while others went north across the Black Sea and into the Caucasus establishing a kingdom called Sicambria. The locals (nomadic Scythians) named these Trojan conquerors the 'Iron people' or the Aesir, who soon built their fortified city Asgard, described as 'Troy in the north'. Some historians suggest that Odin, later worshipped as a god by pagan Vikings, was a Thracian leader who reigned in the Sicambrian kingdom and lived in the city of Asgard in the first century BCE. Tradition knew the Sicambrians as ancient migrants from Troy, formidable warriors, who became the ancestors of the Vikings who inspired Norse mythology. They used the Don River as the main route to the north, where they dominated trade.

The other legend which may also have migrated north with

the Trojans is the Norse legend of Yggdrasil, the World Tree and the associated legend of Ragnarok, (the end of the world). This legend is so remarkably similar to the legend of Irkalla, the World Tree of ancient Babylonian mythology, that it cannot but derive from it. Long before Yggdrasil Irkalla was a huge legendary tree whose name translates as 'Great Earth Tree', and was known as a goddess that descended into the earth and sent down aerial roots to birth new trees (as yew trees do!). Irkalla has the same prophecies attached to it as Yggdrasil and like the Norse tree is the tree that stands at the end of the world. In early cuneiform writing it is said of the Babylonian tree, 'Irkalla will I shake and the heavens shall tremble' and we can compare this with the Norse legends of the universe trembling and the tree Yggdrasil, shaken but not brought down. It is obvious that the Norse culture has got Yggdrasil from Irkalla.

Snorri Sturluson, who was responsible in the 13th century for recording the legend of Yggdrasil from earlier sources, made an interesting comparison between the Viking Aesir gods and the people of Asia Minor in the Caucasus region and compared Ragnarok, (the Norse version of the first doom of the gods and men) with the fall of Troy, Troy itself with Asgard and Aeneas with Vidar, son of Odin and survivor of Ragnarok. Snorri describes 'a priest who carried a miniature palm tree with gold leaves.' (Those familiar with the yew's history know that the palm was often confused with the yew and yew branches were sometimes substituted in churches on Palm Sunday). As we might have expected, the Norse legend of the World Tree Yggdrasil also refers to the Golden Bough, whose story most likely migrated north from Troy. Here in Asgard, before the doors of Valhalla, there stands a grove which is called Glasir and Snorri asks 'Why is gold called the Needles or leaves of Glasir?' He describes the leafage or needles, (as yew leaves are often called), as all red gold (the colour and quality of the modern-day Golden Bough branches). Reference to the tree of Glasir with golden foliage standing beside Odin's abode in Valhalla can be found in Chapter 34 of the Norse prose entitled *Skáldskaparmal*. So, did the people from Troy perhaps take the Golden Bough with them, to be planted at their new home where it grew into a golden tree? Ancient peoples are known for taking their sacred trees with them.

In Valhalla, the special limb of the sacred tree in Valhalla was called Laeradr, which means 'giver of protection', i.e. acting as a talisman, just as Virgil's Golden Bough did. It is accepted that the World Tree of the Norse people, Yggdrasil, the 'needle ash', was a yew. In the Norse Vega of the Prose Edda, it is made very clear that Laeradr is a branch of Yggdrasil. We therefore must conclude that over a thousand years ago, a yew known as Yggdrasil had a branch which bore twigs of gold and that branch of Yggdrasil, known as Laeradr, was not singled out because it gave protection, because the whole tree did, but because Laeradr was the Golden Bough.

From the Hibbert Lectures 1886, we learn some further detail as to what kind of tree the tree of Glasir with golden foliage was. It was an evergreen tree with wide-spreading branches, said to have stood close to the temple of the gods in the ancient town of Uppsala. This mythic tree called Glass was described as standing with leaves of gold before the hall of Sig-tyr, the Norse Zeus. To those of us who know the yew so well the description of 'an evergreen tree with wide spreading branches' is an apt description of the yew tree.

There is one last thing to consider concerning the Trojans and the Golden Bough. It seems likely that the Golden Bough trees of Britain were brought here originally as cuttings or staffs taken from these legendary trees in ancient times, Brutus was the great-grandson of Aeneas and as such would doubtless have been told his great grandfather's story of the Golden Bough. Early writers, such as the 8th to 9th century Nennius, record the fact that Brutus, a Roman Consul, from whom the name of Britain derived, landed at Totnes (an old yew tree area) in Devonshire at the time when Eli was High Priest in Israel (c 1170 BCE). This was reiterated in Geoffrey of Monmouth's *History of the Kings of Britain* (*Historia Regum Brittaniae*) c 1136. Geoffrey was at pains in his introduction to disclaim direct authorship of the work, declaring himself to be merely the translator and editor of a very ancient book in the British (i.e. Welsh) tongue. He writes that Brutus conquered Britain, taking it from the giants who were hitherto resident and in fulfilment of a prophecy of the goddess Diana revealed to him in Greece, established a dynasty of Kings at their capital New Troy, later named Kaerlud (London). Aurelius Ambrosius and Uther Pendragon are said to be part of that royal line. According to this evidence then, some Britons would be grandchildren of Trojan warriors and others besides Brutus at the time would doubtless have known of the Golden Bough and possibly too, the White Tree. Janet and Stewart Farrar write in *The Witches' Goddess* 1987, that 'British legend says it was Diana who directed the Trojan Prince Brutus, the founder of the royal line of Britain, to take refuge here after the Fall of Troy'. It is, of course, to Devonshire that the Dunmonii tribe also came and so the ancient yews at Kenn (a Golden Bough tree) and Mamhead (in the same area), may well have come either with them or with Brutus.

The phenomenon of the Golden Bough does not end here. There are yet other things that link in. In some ways the idea of the Celtic Otherworld is similar to the Greek and Roman Hades and we can compare the silver branch of the Celtic realms, which is needed to enter the Otherworld, with the Golden Bough needed by Aeneas to enter the Underworld. In the Voyage of Bran this 'silver branch of the sacred apple-tree' (sacred apple tree being a medieval term used to describe the yew), is needed to enter the Otherworld before the appointed hour marked by death, as a passport, just as the Golden Bough is needed as a passport for Aeneas to enter the Underworld.

The cross-references and connections continue with one of

the mysteries of the yew discussed in the chapter on Fortingall, where is to be found in the 13th or 14th century Irish document, *The Settling of the Manor of Tara*, the story of the giant Trefuilngid Tre-eochair, who makes an appearance at a great assembly of Irish nobles. The giant carries the branch with the three fruits - nuts, apples and acorns (fruit of the tree of the thrice-blessed fruit - the yew) which is described as a 'golden, many coloured branch of Lebanon wood', a good description of a Golden Bough, (evidence for yews growing in Lebanon in ancient times is found in the chapter on Egypt). The giant would seem to be a sun god but may also have been an ancient yew tree and the story links the Golden Bough and the sun and the golden colour of both.

A golden rod may also be connected with the Golden Bough. From the Life of St. Beuno (7th century saint) comes a story of Cynan, Prince of Powys, who gave Bueno the golden rod and also granted him a place called Gwyddelwern in Denbighshire, on which he erected a church. A 16 foot girthed hollow yew with strikingly coloured bark, likely to have been planted by St Beuno, still grows there.

Yet another reference to the Golden Bough is mentioned by Fred Hageneder in *Yew: A History* where he says:

> At Diana's cult grove at Nemi, she was called Diana Nemorensis, which points to a fusion with Nemesis, a goddess of the greenwood...whose name in turn corresponds with the Celtic goddess Nemetona (from 'nemeton, sacred grove, sanctuary'). Nemesis is linked with the Fates and with the yew tree.

In the tradition of Nemorensis at Nemi, however, the sacred yew branch of the goddess is referred to as the 'Golden Bough'!

A final connection with the Golden Bough which is worth thinking about and which I offer without comment is pointed out in Gerald Massey's monumental work, *Ancient Egypt the*

Light of the World, 1907, where he talks about the burning bush of the book of Exodus in the Bible's Old Testament and equates it with the golden unbu of the *Egyptian Book of the Dead.* In the texts of the latter:

> the golden unbu is a symbol of the solar god. It is a figure of the radiating disk which is depicted raying all aflame at the summit of a sycamore-fig tree which thus appears to burn with fire and the tree is not consumed... This was the burning bush in which the sun god manifested as Tum, whose other name is Iu or Unbu, the burning bush being the solar 'unbu'.

The word 'Iu' means yew and was used also by the Saxons. 'Iu' appears again as part of the name of the yew island of Bernera in Scotland, discussed earlier. Massey goes on to say:

> In the story of the burning bush, it is an 'angel of the Lord' that appears 'in a flame of fire out of the midst of the bush'... The burning bush is identical with the 'golden unbu' of the *Egyptian Book of the Dead* and the 'golden unbu' of the *Pyramid Texts,* is literally the 'golden bough' of later legends, as in the English work of that name.

Massey also writes of Gilgamesh who is told that if he can lay hold of the immortal tree without his hand being torn, gather a branch and bear it away, it will secure for him eternal youth. 'The tree', Massey says, 'is identical with that which grew in the sacred grove of Nemi'.

The pair of ancient gold artefacts known as 'The Ram in the Thicket', excavated in Ur in Southern Iraq and dating to between 2600 and 2400 BCE I suspect may also be connected with the Golden Fleece.

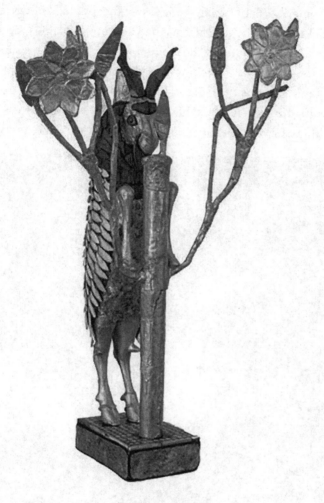

Ram in a thicket 2000 - 2400 BCE. Excavated in Ur.

These beautiful objects were named by the archaeologist who found them after the passage in Genesis where God orders Abraham to sacrifice his son Isaac but stops him at the last minute, substituting the ram caught in the thicket by his horns for Isaac. However, there is another possibility and a real reason for these artefacts most likely being produced as cult figurines as it is also thought that the Ram in the Thicket represents the Sumerian/Babylonian goddess Ningishzida, known as the goddess of Eternity and also as the Lady of the Magic Wand. The ram, of course, relates to the Golden Fleece which is produced in magnificent and eye-catching fashion on these artefacts. What if the magic wand is the Golden Bough? Ningishzida, the tree and serpent goddess, in all likelihood was a Golden Bough yew tree. This thing of great beauty could be both magic wand and Grail.

Golden Bough.

Attempts at a yew tree nursery to grow cuttings from a Golden Bough into trees failed, which may seem odd considering the vigour of the yew and the fact that the DNA is the same as the regular branches but the Golden Bough grows from a green tree that feeds it, and without green leaves, a tree cannot photosynthesise. However, the Golden Bough is a magical thing that cannot be commanded and one such cutting taken by a pagan who believes strongly in the yew has rooted and is growing into a healthy young yew tree with yellowish-green leaves. I hope that it will be planted for posterity on land to be decided on, which will never be disturbed.

None of the Golden Boughs which have appeared since the turn of the millennium have yet produced fruit. Perhaps they are, in the main, still too young to do so but one wonders if and when they do what colour the berries will be and whether they will turn out to be the colour of the magical 'golden apples'. Bearing in mind that the word 'apples' until medieval times was applied to the fruit of the yew, it is interesting that a certain Norse goddess, Idun, identified as a yew berry goddess and also a yew tree, is connected with golden apples and eternal youth, Spring and rejuvenation. Idun keeps the golden apples that are eaten by the gods to maintain their eternal youth. It is only the gods and not mere mortals who are allowed to eat them. Fred Hageneder in *Yew: A History* points out that Aphrodite is associated with 'apples' and says that 'Her underworld connection suggests that her apples could have been those of immortality'. These, of course, would be the sacred yew berries.

A recent discovery of the manifestation of a Golden Fleece type Golden Bough (which is often the way it grows when it first begins to sprout), is on an ancient yew in the churchyard at Llanelltyd. The significant thing about this is that Saint Illtyd, who the church at Llanelltyd is dedicated to, was one of three saints, along with Cadoc and Peredur, given the title of 'Keepers of the Secret of the Grail' in the *Welsh Triads* (a collection of folklore and history, the earliest surviving collection, dated to the 13th century). The earliest and most authentic statement left to us of what the grail actually was, is that of the 12th century writer Wolfram Von Eschenbach who disclosed it to be 'the perfection of Paradise, root and branch'; in other words, the Tree of Life, a very particular and special yew. It would be unlikely that the Keepers of the Grail secret would not know of the Golden Bough and also unlikely that the Tree of Life would not bear one. It is also remarkable that the three saints who bore the title all had connections with King Arthur and that, with the tales of this King, the one that stands out is the quest for the Holy Grail, portrayed as a golden cup. It reminds us of the 'acorn cup' of the fruit of the yew and the bearer of this cup, Ganymede, who bore it for the gods on Mount Olympus.

Illtyd, a 5th century saint of Druid descent, would certainly have carried a yew staff. Such early Celtic saints were known to have planted their staffs, some of which were brought from the Holy Lands and there are many stories of these staffs growing into trees. Illtyd was also one of the three Keepers of the Grail secret. In Wales, there is a tradition of 'Taxus Sanctus' (Saint's yews or sacred yew trees). The Golden Bough Yew at Llanelltyd is of an age and position in the churchyard which makes it likely it was one of these special trees, planted by Illtyd himself and placed here in order to preserve the lineage of the tree from Paradise. One can only speculate as to what properties such a tree would have and whether this yew is actually one of the Golden Bough trees of the Grail secret.

So, what are we to conclude from the fact that the Golden Bough has returned once more? This phenomenon is something sacred, magical and not of this world. The Golden Bough, 'unseen for many years', hangs between the sky and the earth, the world of the gods and the world of the humans. It is a thing of light and beauty that feels like a sign or an omen, a flame in the darkness, perhaps to warn us, a call to awake and act and change our ways before it is too late. The purpose of the Golden Bough 3,000 years ago was to act as a talisman, ensuring the safe passage of the querent in his descent into the darkness of the underworld, enabling him to return to our world with the knowledge he needed. Perhaps the Golden Bough is here once more, in our time, in just such a capacity for us, the human race, so besieged by darkness. There can be no doubt that it comes to claim our attention, for who can pass the golden flame of illumination without stopping, when it is seen among the dark branches of an ancient yew? Perhaps it comes to announce something, perhaps to wake us, who sleepwalk, to bring certain knowledge, a new consciousness, to enable us to change the way we live and reconnect us to the natural world and the sacred. Just lately I have noticed that a few of the boughs are changing. The leaves of some are going from golden yellow to greenish yellow and yellowish green. The golden sprigs on the ancient yew at Kenn have vanished without trace. Have they been removed by hand or does it mean the time of warning is coming to an end? We are on the verge of climate change tipping too far. The waters are rising, the ice melting and the fires are raging across the world. However, in the spirit of the Golden Bough there is hope that we will rise to the greatest challenge in the history of humanity and align ourselves with the ultimate power of the Tree of Life. Across the world there is a growing awareness that we and the sacred tree are one. We have tried to separate ourselves from Nature and visited the darkness of the Underworld. Now we must return and embrace the wisdom of our ancestors to renew and restore our world.

Chapter 19

The Golden Grove and the Gospel Pass

This chapter concerns unresolved work in progress and begs many questions but there are several intriguing things here, things of crucial importance to the yew story, mysteries which I cannot leave out. So far, due to an incomplete history, missing links and things being remembered and passed on in oral tradition rather than being written down (which was often the case with secret sacred knowledge), the picture of what took place in the Golden Grove and the Gospel Pass is obscured. Nevertheless, what is known could perhaps at some time in the future join up with other bits of the puzzle, crucial to our understanding of things of the past, that have a bearing on the mysteries of the yew. Hopefully, a more complete picture will eventually be restored.

For many years now I have been trying to figure out the significance of a Golden Grove, or a Gelli Aur, as it translates in the Welsh language. There are one or two places called by that name in Wales, one close to where I live in Carmarthenshire, where there appears to be ancient history in the form of two mounds, not unlike the Paps of Anu in Ireland, but on a smaller scale, set on the highest point of the ridge, with views for miles around. However, despite the name, there is no sign of a grove of golden trees. The poet Gerard Manley Hopkins was once moved to write about this Golden Grove, inspired by the appearance of the leaves in the autumn light, but lovely as it is, loveliness seems to be all that there is now, although, with such a significant name as this, the suggestion is that at one time it may have been a sacred site.

In the context of the Golden Boughs, the name is important and it would seem likely that a Golden Grove would mean Golden Bough Yews. There is no other plausible explanation other than a grove of entirely golden yew trees, as 'grove' indicates yews.

In present-day Herefordshire, however, on a large and private estate, a golden grove, not known by that name, lies hidden and well looked after. It is unique in having at least seven ancient yews, some of over 3,000 years and at least five of them carry Golden Boughs. Nowhere else have I seen so many together.

Kentchurch Yew Grove. (1)

Kentchurch Yew Grove. (2)

Lo and behold the evidence is that this is exactly where the significant Golden Grove was. It lies at the southern end of the

Golden Valley and the Gospel Pass, thus named according to legend, due to St Peter or St Paul or both, preaching the gospel while travelling along it, having been brought to Wales by Caradog's daughter, Eurgain. Peterchurch with its remarkable 3,000-year-old yew tree and its standing stone attests to the possible truth of this legend.

It is beyond reasonable doubt, as we have seen in the chapter on Llanilid, that St Paul came to Britain. As for St Peter, there is some suggestion if not exactly hard evidence that he also came here. In the English College in Rome there is a remarkable series of frescoes illustrating the history of Christianity since earliest times. The first fresco depicts St Peter, Prince of the Apostles, visiting Britain and consecrating the first Bishops for the British Church. The second Bishop of Rome (Peter's successor) was Linus of Llanilid, the place where St Paul stayed and it is therefore likely that St Peter would also have stayed there with his colleague when this title and office was conferred on Linus, whose home it was. Further, John Henry Newman, before converting to Catholicism, edited a series of *Lives of the British Saints*. In one of these volumes, the author (who was not Newman himself), referred to the apostolic visit to Britain, saying that although the story 'wanted historic evidence...yet it was received as a pious opinion by the Church at large'. Symeon Metaphrastes, a Byzantine theologian of Constantinople, who died in 978 CE, attested to St Peter having passed 23 years in Britain establishing several churches before returning to Rome in 65 CE. Ancient authors also claim this to be true and it is probable that St Peter passed the later years of his life in the western provinces of Rome, of which Britain was one. This would make his arrival in Britain to be 42 CE, around the time the Cor of Llanilid moved to Llanelltyd Fawr (Llantwit Major) and it leads one to ask whether the Gospel Pass was named after him or St Paul or both. The Pass itself is the highest road pass in Wales. It is at the head of the Vale of Ewyas in the Black Mountains of South East Wales.

I have been drawn to this area over and over again without

ever having begun to shed a single ray of light on what lies behind that word 'golden', in the context of this valley. The valley has plenty of allusions to the word, with place names such as Dorstone (French - 'D'or', meaning 'of gold') the golden spring and Abbeydore. The question is can it be a mere coincidence that the golden grove, important saints and also the Gospel Pass, St Peter and St Paul, all appear within this area. It seems they must be connected in some way but what is the connection? Perhaps it was as a result of a certain Golden Grove that this area was established since early times as being of religious or spiritual importance, perhaps to the Druids and as a result all these other connections formed and people were drawn here.

At one end of the valley near Orcop, lies Kentchurch. Unfortunately, the massive ancient 30 ft girth yew at Orcop was cut down some years ago. In the days before the Normans, who were probably the ones to rename this place, it was called by its Welsh name, Llanithog. There is still a house there of that name, probably the oldest habitation in the Kentchurch area and far older than the Court. Bards were associated with the Golden Grove of Llanithog and we know that St. Gildas the Wise (6th century) lived within the Golden Grove. Gildas' Celtic name means 'servant of God'. He was taught by Cadoc, one of the 'Keepers of the secret of the Grail', as described in the Mabinogion. It is more than likely that this secret involved the Golden Bough. The Italian name Gildas derived from the Germanic element 'gild', meaning 'sacrifice' but in Old English, the name means 'coated with gold; gilded'. Surely a fitting name for one who lived in the Golden Grove! There is some confusion as to whether Gildas had a brother called Aneurin the Bard, or whether Gildas and Aneurin were the same person but it seems more likely to be the latter. Perhaps St. Gildas, a monk who wrote the history of Britain before and during the coming of the Saxons, *De Excidioet Conquestu Brittaniae*, adopted a double identity to make his life and work easier as the work concerned what he called the 'Ruin' of Britain. He may then have been known as Aneurin when conducting Druidic matters and St. Gildas when in his role as Christian monk. However, the truth is that Gildas was both these things, both Druid and Christian, although like other saints of this period of overlap between the two religions it was perhaps not wise to say so. However, when setting up his abbey in Brittany at St. Gildas de Rhuys, Gildas the Christian monk, Gildas the Wise, as mentioned earlier, could not resist setting up a circle of flat standing stones inscribed with tree crosses, referencing an ancient grove, behind the altar there, where his body is buried.

Tree Cross and Staff at the Abbey St. Gildas de Rhuys, Brittany.

According to Taliesin's *Bardic Portraits*, although not a native of Wales, Aneurin spoke the old Cymry language. The Triads denote him 'Monarch of the Bards', the highest possible accolade and say he was 'privy to the Golden Grove' where Gildas lived. He was one of the Sons of Caw ab Geraint, a chief of the Ottadini of Northumberland. In *An Essay on the Welsh Saints of the Primitive Christians* by Rice Rees,1804 - 1839, we read,

It has however been suggested by two eminent antiquarians to whose researches the writer acknowledges himself greatly indebted, that Aneurin was none other than the celebrated Gildas. The reasons alleged are that Aneurin, as well as Gildas, is reckoned among the children of Caw in our old manuscripts but both do not occur as such in the same lists, for in those where Aneurin is said to be the Son of Caw, the other is omitted, and vice versa, where Gildas is inserted, the other is left out. Besides which, the name Gildas is a Saxon translation of Aneurin, according to practice not uncommon with ecclesiastical ways in which the names are written - 'Gilda, Gildas y Coed Aur, Aur y Coed Aur and Aneurin y Coed Aur' - all confirm their identity. Cenydd, a son and Ufelwyn, a grandson of Gildas, are sometimes called the son and grandson of Aneurin.

It seems therefore that the Welsh genealogists have always considered the names Gildas and Aneurin to be interchangeable. The father of Gildas and Aneurin was Caw, Lord or Chieftain of the Cwm Cawllwyd and sometimes styled Caw of Northern Brittanica. The Cawdors of this area and parts of Wales were associated with yew trees that appeared on their coat of arms. One medieval tradition is that Gildas had a brother who betrayed Arthur and was executed for his treachery. Although this event would have been likely to have caused a rift between the two it didn't and Gildas and Arthur were reconciled, proving the close connection between the two. Gildas is pictured with a book or a Celtic bell and like several other saints of this period, seems to have been a friend or relative of Arthur who renounced his royal lineage. He was educated by Illtyd, possibly also a relative. St. Illtyd was a warrior saint whose other name was Galahad, which is famously the name of one of Arthur's knights. Gildas attended the school in Wales founded by St. Illtyd and was therefore linked with one who was a 'Keeper of the Secret of the Grail' (explored in *The God Tree*), known as such in the Welsh Triads. Although this secret seems to have died out with its three Keepers - Illtyd, Cadoc and Peredur (the latter likely to have been Perceval of Arthurian legend), the fact that Gildas of the Golden Grove was so closely connected with Illtyd, who later spent time at his abbey in Brittany, suggests the Golden Grove and therefore the Golden Bough was involved in this secret. The three Keepers were also Bards of Britain a title that carried high status at that time and the fact that Aneurin, (likely to have been Gildas) was known as 'Monarch of the Bards', makes it obvious they were all closely connected, no doubt sharing the same secrets.

There are several stories about Gildas and his bell. He is often depicted with a bell and a book. In one story he is said to have sent a bell he had cast himself to Brigit in Ireland, a gift charged with significance in a culture where a bell was an emblem of the godhead. Even after Christianity came to Ireland and Brigit became St. Brigid, bells continued to be extremely important. Ollaves, the master poets of Ireland, second only to kings, carried golden branches with tinkling bells in honour of the triple goddess Brigit. This was noted recently in Gerelyn Hollingsworth's blog on St. Gildas in the National Catholic Reporter January 2010 and is interesting for several reasons. First Brigit is a triple goddess associated with the yew and also with holy springs and wells and apparently golden branches, which begs the question as to what Gildas was doing sending her a bell associated with the godhead and golden branches? We may never know but it seems like a secret message, probably known within a certain cult and it is yet another thing that adds to the intrigue of Gildas and the Golden Grove.

And so, the mystery and the possibilities begin, because if Gildas lived in the Golden Grove, then the grove must either have been golden at that time 1,500 years ago, or Gildas must have known of the ability of these trees of the grove to put out magical Golden Boughs. By its very nature, the Golden Grove would have been viewed as a special secret place. Although the central three Keepers of the Grail Secret would have been sworn to silence on the subject, Gildas must have been party to it, through his close friend Illtyd as well as through Cadoc and the fact that they were all Bards. As you will have read in the chapter on the Golden Bough, yew trees that carry such a thing are extremely rare and it seems they are likely to be connected to the Arthurian legend of the Grail and the Grail Secret which concerns the Tree of Life. Illtyd as a Knight of King Arthur was connected with this. There are those connected with the grove today who say the energy of the Golden Age will issue from these trees.

An essay on the Welsh saints of the Primitive Christians by Rev. Rees Rice, 1804 - 1839, says that Gildas was employed in Ireland, preaching the Gospel when he heard that his eldest brother Hueil, had been slain by Arthur, upon which he came to Britain and as a loyal subject of King Arthur, was able to forgive him and be reconciled to the King who had solicited his pardon and who also did penance for the deed. It was after this that Gildas taught at the school of St. Cadoc, who was another of the Keepers of the Grail Secret! So it, therefore, seems highly unlikely Gildas was not involved with it himself. The *Llancarfan Life* (of Gildas) contains some stories of him and Arthur including one of persuading Melvas to release Arthur's wife Guinevere (Welsh name Gwenhwyfar). Gildas himself claimed to have been born on the same day as the Battle of Baden, though officially he is thought to have been born sometime between 450 and 500.

The *Annales Cambria* put his death at about 572. At some point, he moved to Armorica, (Brittany), where he wrote his history of the Britons, a scathing attack on just about everyone, both Kings and clergy, except for Vortigern. It may have been as a result of this that he never returned to Britain but spent his last days in Brittany, died and was buried at Rhuys, a place which is something of an earthly Paradise with an ideal microclimate, where anything including bananas will grow.

Another 6th century saint - St Cwrdaf or Cawdaf, a disciple of Illtyd's, was connected with both the Golden Grove of Llanithog and a place called Caer Wyrd. He was a Celtic warrior chief. Alex Gibbon in writing *Jack of Kent* in 2004, mentions him as the warrior King of the Dark Ages of 500 CE based at Caer Wyard but connected to Llanithog. There seems to have been a connection between these two places, Caer Wyard and Llanithog which built up over the ages. We do not know what that connection was but the Welsh hero Owain Glyndwr, (c.1359 - c.1415) whose name was anglicised to Owen Glendower, was likewise linked to both places. It was said Glyndwr's influence extended north-east to Caer Wyard, which lay between Leominster and Worcester and was his main fortress or headquarters and that he summoned his Magi and went to Caer Wyard. Old traditions die hard and even at this late date, leaders like Glyndwr still had magicians, sorcerers, soothsayers, Druids and Bards with whom they consulted. These people worked between Caer Wyard and the Golden Grove at Llanithog. What they did we do not know but at the end of his days Glyndwr is thought to have been buried in the Park at Kentchurch close to Llanithog. One wonders if the ancient secret knowledge concerning the Grove was passed on to him and what he was doing between there and Caer Wyard, later known as Kyre Park. Kentchurch is where Owain Glyndwr went for safety and also where he was last heard of. A hundred or so acres of the Deer Park at Kentchurch were also at one time owned by the Knights' Hospitaller of the Commander of Dinmore. This Order of Knights was granted Garway, close to Kentchurch after the Order of the Knights Templar was dissolved. This is interesting from the perspective that the Templars held secret knowledge of the yew. It was after 1540 that the land was transferred to the Scudamores.

It was Aneurin, however, who we first hear of, travelling between the Golden Grove at Kentchurch (or rather Llanithog at that time) and what is now Kyre Park (Caer Wyard), where there are yew trees of over 2,000 years old which are mentioned in John Lowe's book *Yew trees of Great Britain and Ireland* 1897.

Kyre Park in Worcestershire is an earthwork, originally with two ancient yews growing on it. It was known as a Hundred Court meeting place where meetings took place beneath the Court Yew and its partner. One of the yews is known as The Parted Yew and has been in two halves for over a century. Massive yews such as these described by John Lowe over a century ago as having respectively 24, 26 and 32 foot girths, as measured three feet from the ground, are obviously of great antiquity. Both the 24 and 26 foot yews were described in 1895 as being split in two in Lowe's book, *The Yew trees of Great Britain and Ireland* published in 1897 and he offers a detailed description of the yews:

In the grounds... are two remarkably fine yews...In the shrubbery stands a very old tree, split in two parts; the portion on the lowest ground has fallen partly over and so slipped away from the upper half; the upright portion is now 30 feet in girth at the ground level, 24 feet in girth at 5 feet. The slanting portion is hollow, 36 feet at ground level, 32 feet at 5 feet. Total diameter of umbrage - 65 feet. Both parts show great vigour of growth. I think the yew was hollow before it was split and the interior shows fire action.

Lowe continues:

Outside the 'Wood-patch Grove' stands a yew tree 30 feet at

ground level, 26 feet at 5 feet, sound and growing; top not broken; with plenty of young growth. Forty or fifty years ago this tree was hollow and an old man remembers twelve persons standing inside it, but it is now filled. It stands by the River Kyre, which divides the counties of Worcestershire and Herefordshire and the Courts Leets were formerly held by the owners of Kyre Park under its shade.

John Lowe goes on to make another interesting remark: 'This tree affords another striking example... of the rapid growth of central roots, by means of which the trunk after being hollow again becomes solid.' He goes on to compare the yew tree to that of Fortingall and says that 'If it were broken away at the top and had young shoots springing up around, it would appear as one tree with a circumference exceeding that of Fortingall.' So here we have evidence of one of the all-time greats of the Yew tree world, a massive ancient yew, at Kyre Park, no doubt a holder of sacred knowledge, being the most likely reason why Gildas/Aneurin made frequent visits to Kyre Park/Caer Wyard. There is something else interesting here at Kyre Park. There is a place close by called Nineveh which gives rise to the question as to whether one of the almug trees (yews) grown in the so-called Hanging Gardens, which are now proved to have been at Nineveh rather than Babylon, may have been brought here and be the origin of the ancient yew which is reputed to carry a Golden Bough. Druids would doubtless have been based at this site and the name Wyard is strange and interesting. It seems likely it is from the same root as Wyardsbury, the old Saxon name for Wraysbury near Ankerwycke and Runnymede and would have a link with the Norse/Saxon Norns and wyrds and therefore be linked to the runes. 'Wyrd' is a concept in Anglo Saxon culture roughly corresponding to fate or personal destiny. The word is ancestral to the Modern English word 'weird' and in Old Norse is similar with a similar meaning and also personalized as one of the Norns, who correspond to the three Fates who sat beneath the Tree of Life.

As described earlier, places such as this evolved over time, adapting to current needs and may originally have been early places of settlement and occupation where people lived together as a village with a sanctuary which afforded some kind of protection; both physically, by way of the earthwork and spiritually through the yew trees. Later these may have evolved into fortified castles or burial sites like Merdon Castle near Winchester with its ancient yews. Eventually, of course, many of these places were no longer in use or were used rarely, as their importance and significance waned or was forgotten and by 1353, Caer Wyard had become known simply as a far-flung chapel where the Bishop of Herefordshire had appointed a curate. However, by the 1700s it was still said to have been 'filled with yew trees', suggesting perhaps its original purpose as some kind of grove or Druid site. The name Caer, which became 'Kyre', could have meant castle or Cor, i.e. a Druid temple and if the latter, would give some clue to the connection between it and Kentchurch.

On the modern map, on the other side of the road from Kyre Park is an area known as the Grove and the ponds, which are still there and which are associated with monasteries for their supply of fish, so Caer Wyard was likely an early Christian or Druidic monastery, or both at different times. In 1275 it was called Caer Wyard and was given in a grant by Edward 1st to John Wyard and presumably named after him but it is a bit odd that the name is the same. However, Caer Wydyr is mentioned in the Book of Taliesin, known as Preiddeu Annwyn, the Raid of Annwyn, the Raid of the Otherworld, involving King Arthur, written down around the same time 1275, although it is thought to have originated with the Bard Taliesin in the 6th century. This may be the same place with a different spelling as Caer Wyard or Caer Wyrdd. Spelling changes over time and was not set until recently. Part 30 of the

Book of Taliesin touches on certain mysteries related to the Caers. For instance in it is related that, except seven, none returned from Caer Sidi, Caer Pedrycan, Caer Vedwyd, Caer Rigor, Caer Wydyr, Caer Golud, Caer Vandwy and Caer Ochren. We can only speculate as to what is meant by this cryptic statement but it may be that Caer Wydyr is the same place as Caer Wyard. Perhaps too, there is some connection with the Saxon word for Wraysbury which was Wyardsbury and in the chapter on Ankerwycke you will see there may be a connection between this word, the yew runes and divination. The Arthurian legend of the Quest for the Grail, the warrior saints and the Keepers of the Grail Secret, are all inextricably linked as is Illtyd (Galahad) and Cadoc (also a warrior saint) with Gildas. The question is why was Gildas/ Aneurin travelling between these two important places, shrouded in mystery and connected with the Golden Bough? Could it be that Gildas/Aneurin guarded the Golden Grove with his life because within the identity and DNA of these trees lay something of such importance for the future of mankind, that it was inconceivable that it could be put at risk in any way?

To complicate matters, or at least to suggest more connections, it was also said that there was a Bard who visited an ancient yew grove and the golden yews in the land of Cydewen, which may well have been Kyre Park. However, golden yews do not exist there now, unless the yews there, as rumoured (I have not yet seen it personally), have produced such a bough in modern times as a link to evidence the past. The story of these yews and their visiting Bard rings similar bells to the Bard of the Golden Grove of Llanithog and maybe the place travelled to and between. If Kyre Park was the place of the golden yews of Cydewen, then we have the connection. Gildas the famous 5th or 6th century saint and scholar connected with Llanithog certainly had sacred knowledge of the yews as did his Grail friends Illtyd and Cadoc. St Patrick, it should be noted, was also very much part of the Yew Cult. Between them and no doubt others, these saints possessed long-forgotten secrets that seem to have died with them but I believe this sacred knowledge is of crucial importance for our future survival on this planet and must emerge again.

In ancient times, the Golden Grove of Cydewen or Cedewain was known as Powisland (from *The History of Powisland* Vol.1) and there is a reference to 'the golden yew trees in the land of Cydewen' in *The Triads of Bardism* (Iolo Morganwg 1747 - 1826). In the language of the ancient Britons, 'ked' was an old word for 'tree' (referred to by Nennius in 9th - 10th century history). In 1235 it was spelt 'Cedewen' or 'Cydewen' and in 1202 Ceri became Cydewen in Montgomeryshire. At Dolforwyn, home to an extraordinary ancient yew over a Holy Well below the castle, lay the central stronghold of Cydewen where the Lords of Cydewen resided. It was a legendary kingdom, known to have been passed on from the yew tribes and it would originally have stretched from Clun down to Abergavenny. Today this whole area is still rich in old yew trees. In the 12th century Cydewain, mentioned as being above Clun, was a medieval Cantref in the Kingdom of Powys. The name 'Cydewen', actually translates as 'Powisland of Yew trees' but Cydewen/Kedewen was originally a small kingdom in its own right which became part of Powisland. To add further to the intrigue, what was known as the 'four gates of olden times' included Arthur's Cydewen, Ceri and Chirbury. Arthur's territory included the ancient yew sites of Peterchurch, Bodcott Farm and Yazor. When this area became Powys, it was enlarged and stretched further north and south. St. Deiniol, brother of Aneurin the Bard, was also linked with Cydewen. The place named after him, Llandeiniolen, has ancient yew trees, one of which is known as 'The Chief'. One wonders why. I have not visited this tree for some time. Perhaps it too has sprouted a Golden Bough.

Chapter 20

The Legend of the White Tree

Moving on now to another Yew mystery, that of the White Tree, many readers will be familiar with and fascinated by this phenomenon through the work of J R R Tolkien's *The Lord of the Rings* 1968.

White Tree of Gondor.

But I wonder how many have realised it has its roots in ancient mythology with the legend of a White Tree on an island, a Tree of Life? As such, this iconic symbol lies deep in our psyche as something we carry which is highly significant, and which somehow, we know is deeply important. In *The Lord of the Rings* the tree is the White Tree of Gondor, the symbol of the realm of Gondor, reflecting the health of that Kingdom. At one point, as a seemingly dead tree, it comes back to life and flowers as if to announce the arrival of Aragorn, a Ranger of the North. It is one tree that is the elder of the two trees of Valinor. When it is destroyed it grows again, as a yew does and strangely enough as if to point to its origins, in the film this tree looks just like an ancient yew.

The Lord of the Rings provides a fascinating link with the otherworldly trees. We are all familiar with the 'Ents', and many of us 'tree people' can relate to them, the ancient trees that were able to move and fight and had been taught to speak. The most important of them is Treebeard who claims to be the oldest creature in Middle Earth. The Ents are portrayed as an old race of giants, sentient beings who have some human attributes and who are also strong, patient and cautious with a different, much slower sense of time to other races. They are the ancient shepherds of the forest who protect the trees from the Dwarves who are the first to cut them down and they march to war on Saruman, who cuts down large numbers of them. Unable to produce more of their kind with the loss of the Treewives, the Ents are under threat of extinction, knowing they will eventually die out and thus mirroring our own tree crisis.

Michael D C Drout (ed.), *J.R.R. Tolkien Encyclopedia* (New York: Routledge, 2007) writes about:

the Two Trees, which stood on a green mound outside Valmar, the city of the Valar, in Valinor. Sung into being at the beginning of the Elder Days by Yavanna, the Valië (Queen of the Valar) who was the Giver of Fruits, they were Telperion the White, Eldest of Trees, and Laurelin the Golden, younger of the two. (These two seem to mirror the White and the Yellow Haoma trees). The radiance of their flowers, silver and gold respectively, waxed and waned again every seven hours...beginning an hour apart; so the light of the one began to gather again an hour before the other ceased...

When the Eldar arrived in Eressea, a cutting of Telperion was given to them by the Valar to plant there. This became Galalithion, renowned for its beauty although it emitted no light. This tree and its heirs were to outlive their luminous forebear. Later in the First Age, a seed of Galalithion was taken to Numenor and became Nimloth the Fair. The White Trees of Gondor, first brought to Middle-earth by Elenedil and his sons at the end of the Second Age were its scion.

Unfortunately before fleeing Valinor, Morgoth fatally poisoned the Two Trees. Drout continues:

Just before they died, however, Telperion bore a last flower and Laurelin a final fruit. Of these (in Tolkien's original mythology) the grieving Valar made the Moon and Sun. But the light of the Two Trees also survived in what we now know as Venus; after Earendil voyaged to the West with the aid of a Silmaril - the only one to be recovered by the Eldar - it was eventually placed in the heavens as a beacon of hope by Elbereth or Varda. (This star was what we know as Venus, which is both the Morning and the Evening Star.)

Tolkien's account of the Two Trees and their place at the heart of events both in the Undying Lands and Middle-earth reveals the iconic status of trees in both his work and his life. In addition to his autobiographical remarks, this is also perceptible in his portrayal of the trees of Lothlórien and Fangorn, and indeed the Party Tree in Hobbiton, with which the story of *The Lord of the Rings* starts.

Tolkien's stories of the sacred trees of Middle Earth and the Undying Lands have parallels and resonance with our own ancient legends of tree gods and guardians and the descriptions of the White Tree and the Golden ones of our past.

Leaving Tolkien now and moving on to the ancient origins of the White Tree in our world, other legendary Trees of Life such as the Mes tree were described as White Trees and King Ur-Nammu, the founder of the Third Dynasty of Ur, is described as a White Mes tree growing in a pleasant spot in Ur. Just as many of the gods and goddesses were actually trees, kings too were described as being like, or as, the Tree of Life. The main tree to be known as the White Tree is the Gaokarena tree which grew in the land of this name in the Caucasus.

In *Zoroastrian Heritage* by KE Eduljee, we find information about the Gaokarena Tree of Life and the White Haoma. In the Middle Persian text known as the Bundahishn, we discover that:

The Tree of Many Seeds (Harawispa Tohma), having been produced from all those seeds of plants, grew up in the ocean Frakhvkart, where-from the seeds of all the species of plants are growing (on that tree). Near to that tree, the Goakaren (Gaokarena) tree was produced, in order to keep away ill-shaped decrepitude.

So this was a tree that preserved youth. Most importantly it is said that:

the complete exaltation of the world arose there-from. In different versions of this legend, there is confusion over whether this Tree of Life is one tree or two but here in this early version, it is two. The tree of immortality is a White Tree whose vivacity would certify the continuance of life in the universe. The Tree of Many Seeds, sometimes known as the Tree of All Seeds, is something of an ark that will preserve all life. It is a tree on which grow the seeds of all plants. The seeds are provided to keep away the ten thousand diseases that the evil spirit produced for the creatures. You could see this as being connected with the origins of herbal medicine and it can also be compared with the statement in Revelations 22:2, to the leaves of the Tree of Life being for the healing of the nations. It is said that from those ten thousand seeds have sprung the hundred thousand species of plants that are now in the world.

It is the Gaokarena Tree which produces the White Haoma, though there is sometimes confusion as to whether it is the Gaokarena tree that produced the Haoma or whether in this version from the *Bundahishn*, it is a plant that grows next to it:

And the white, healing, undefiled, Hom has grown next to that tree (the Tree of Many Seeds), in the stream of Ardvisur; whoever shall eat it will become immortal; they call it the Gaokarena tree; as one says, 'The death-dispelling Hom'; they prepare immortality therefrom at the renovation of the universe; it is the chief of plants.

So in the *Bundahishn*, the Gaokarena tree is the Tree of Life.

According to the Vendidad of the Avesta, the Gaoakarena is the source of the White Haoma that can prevent physical death and this Tree of Life in the Vourukasha Sea is a tree on which grows the seeds of plants of all kinds in their thousands and it is also the tree that contains all medications. So in this version, the Tree of All Seeds is also the Gaokarena Tree of the White Haoma, it is all one tree.

In the Vendidad, it is the goddess Ameretap, the goddess of long life and medicine who creates a garden in which grow thousands of health-giving plants. She creates the Tree of all Seeds which grows in the centre of the Vourukasha Sea or lake and the miraculous tree of Gaokarena, enemy of the malignant spirit and curer of all ills, the tree that gives immortality grows nearby. The Vourukasha Sea is now known as Lake Sevan.

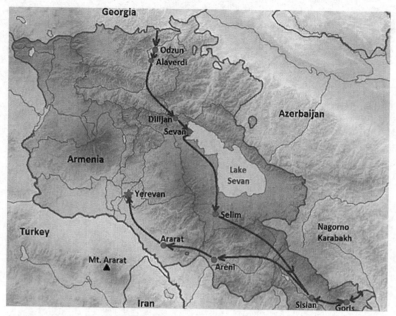

Map of Lake Sevan, Armenia.

In the *Greater Bundahishn* 24.1, it says:

> The White Hom which they call the Gaokarena Tree, which has grown in the ocean Frakhvkart, in the deep lake, is requisite for the performance of the renovation of the universe, as they will prepare immortality from it. 2. And the Evil Spirit, in opposition to it, has produced a lizard in that deep water, so that it may despoil the Hom. 3. And in order to restrain that lizard, Ohrmazd has there created two Kar fish, which are always encircling the Hom, so that the head of one of those fish is always towards [the] lizard. And these fish also have spiritual food, that is, they do not require food, and they will be contending up to the renovation of the universe. And there is a place where those fish are written off as the Araz of the water. 4. As one says, 'The greatest of the creatures [of] Ohrmazd are those fish, and the greatest of the [creatures] of the Evil Spirit is that lizard, in body and vigour... Those fish

are so sensitive that they comprehend a sensation as minute as a sharp needle in the deep water, whereby the water increases or decreases.'

This is a parallel to many other legends of the Tree of Life for the sacred tree always has its guardians. This time the guardians are hypersensitive fish, which will allow nothing to pass unnoticed but in the next version, in the *Lesser Bundahishn* 18.1, the two fish have increased to ten and we see that the Gaokarena tree is there at the beginning, at the creation of the world;

On the nature of the tree they call Gaokarena it says in revelation, that it was the first day when the tree they call Gaokarena grew in the deep mud within the wide-formed ocean; and it is necessary as a producer of the renovation of the universe, for they prepare its immortality there-from. 2. The evil spirit has formed therein, among those which enter as opponents, a lizard as an opponent in that deep water, so that it may injure the Haoma. 3. And for keeping away that lizard, Ohrmazd has created there ten Kar fish which, at all times, continually circle around the Haoma, so that the head of one of those fish is continually towards the lizard'. But also we see the fish beginning to become the serpents or dragons which in later myths are the main creatures who guard the sacred tree and we are given more information about the type of 'curing' the sacred tree is capable of. 6. This, too, is said, that those fish are so serpent-like in that clear water, they know the scratch of a needle's point by which the water shall increase, or by which it is diminishing. 9. The Tree of Many Seeds has grown amid the wide formed ocean and in its seed are all plants; some say it is the proper-curing, some the energetic-curing, some the all-curing.

It is interesting that together with the lizard those fish are spiritually fed, and till the renovation of the universe, they will remain in the sea and struggle with one another. It is something of a theme that the world is a place where a continual battle between good and evil goes on but that the Tree of Knowledge is there at the beginning to give humans knowledge of the difference between these two forces. According to the Bundahishn, there are two types of Haoma - the white and the golden. The White Haoma or Tree of Life guards the Tree of All Seeds while the Golden Haoma grants strength, good health and children. One wonders, in the light of the Golden Bough, which I would say has to be an essential part of the Tree of Life, whether the Golden Haoma is not the Golden Bough.

The Gokard (another name for Gaokarena) or White Tree is described as a luxuriant tree in whose branches a serpent dwells and there is more to this sacred tree. Irkalla as we have seen was a form of Ereshkigal, a serpent god/dess and translates as 'Great Earth Tree', known as a goddess that descends into the earth, and sends down aerial roots to birth new trees. This tree also carried the title the White One of Eridu, making it another legendary White Tree. Ningizzida, another serpent god/dess connected with the Tree of Life was also a special tree that had come from Anu, a very important, first ranking god/dess or mother tree, which must mean that Ningizzida is one of Anu's branches that descended to the ground, i.e. layered and grew into a separate tree. Ningizzida is known as the White Kiskanu tree, Kin-babbar, the Lady of the Tree of Life, which must mean she too is a White Tree.

Yet another god/dess Ninhursag is connected with all this. This time the goddess is connected with Lebanon, which name also derives from 'white' or 'whiteness' (the root verb 'laben' means to be or become white). This is probably from the snow which covers the summits of Lebanon's mountains for the greater part of the year and although this may simply be to do with this perpetual snow of the mountains, or perhaps with moral purity, there is another meaning which is to do with a particularly sacred tree connected with Haoma and the White Tree. Lebanon is a mountainous region that runs parallel to the Mediterranean coast not far north of Egypt, and the tree goddess, Ninhursag, was known as the 'Lady of the mountains' which may mean the mountain tree, a sacred tree that grew in the paradisial garden of Enki. In some versions, the source of the earthly White Haoma plant is a shining white tree that grows on a paradisial mountain, suggesting Lebanon as a possible location. Backing this up as a possible name source is the fact that the Hittite and Hurrite words for cypress and juniper are very similar to the words for Lebanon Mountains, so it is possible that the cedars and yews could have been the source of the name of both the mountain and the country. From the '*Theological Dictionary of the Old Testament*', Series Editors: G Johannes Botterweck, Helmer Ringgren, Heinz-Josef Fabry 1975, suggest another possible etymology may be found in the Hittite and Hurrian group of languages, Hittite 'lablana', Lebanon Mountains is identical with Hurrian 'lablahhi':

The appearance of these words in parallel with the words for cypress and juniper, suggests that they likewise refer primarily to some kind of tree.

In the Irish legend of Fintan, who himself is known as the 'White Ancient', the White Tree is linked with Lebanon and is discussed in depth in the chapter on the Fortingall Yew in this book but for clarity, I will repeat some essential points relating to the White Tree and Fortingall here, as it seems the two are very much related. Finn is the archetypal seer and poet, sometimes known as Fionn or Fintan. The name essentially means 'White Tree'. In the story related in *The Settling of the Manor of Tara*, Fintan tells of how he came to Ireland with the first invaders, who came from Egypt. A giant who also appears in the same story carries the branch with the three fruits - nuts, apples and acorns (fruit of the tree of the thrice-blessed fruit - the yew). This branch was described as a 'golden, many coloured branch of Lebanon wood', which sounds somewhat like a Golden Bough but most importantly, the branch comes from Lebanon, although Fintan himself is connected to Egypt. When the giant leaves, he gives Fintan some berries from the branch he carries, which Fintan plants and which then sprout and grow into the famous five sacred trees of Ireland. This legend must mean that the ancient yew at Fortingall, (Scotland was included in Ireland in earlier times) is a descendent of the White Tree along with the others of the five sacred trees of Ireland which are said to have grown from the berries given by the giant. They are all White Trees.

In Ireland, Mugna is a word for Augm or Haoma. Eo Mugna regarded as one of the most sacred trees in Ireland is also likely to have been a White Tree. Tragically these trees were cut down by the Danes but there may be other White Trees still growing in Britain. These trees are the most sacred trees of all. George Petrie in *The ecclesiastical architecture of Ireland,* 1845, writes of a sacred tree of Ireland called Crann-naomha. This is the same tree as the Persian Haoma tree, like the White Ancient (Fintan) which is also linked with Eo Mugna, one of the five sacred and legendary trees of Ireland. Petrie writes that a sacred fire near the tree was fed by wood from the tree. This is the same practice used by the Hittites! It was important to keep the smoke produced from the sacred tree pure and not pollute it. Charles Vallancey in *An Essay on the Primitive Inhabitants of Great Britain and Ireland* 1807 wrote that 'Om or Omna, a shortened version of Crann-naomha, was the sacred or celestial tree called such in the old laws'. He writes:

> To cut it down was punishable by death and if bees swarmed in it, they were the property of the priest of the adjoining temple. Once again, we are presented with another word (Omna) that has obvious links to Haoma. It is also interesting

to note that the sacred yew here was connected to and protected by a temple and also to bees which also occur in the stories of the sacred trees related to Cadoc and Illtyd, and considered holy creatures in many cultures.

With regard to ancient yews in Wales, I also wonder whether the Welsh word 'Ywen' actually originally meant 'white yew tree'! Its earliest spelling is 'Iwen'. The letter 'I' in all Indo-European languages originally represented Yew and the Welsh word 'wen' means 'white. So, could this possibly be a reference to the existence of these very sacred trees in Wales?

As already mentioned in Chapter 3, Ningishzida, as well as being a goddess is a special tree descended from one of the most important trees, if not the chief, Anu. *She is* known as the White Kiskanu tree, Kin-babbar, the Lady of the Tree of Life and is obviously also a White Tree of which there must have been several as stated in a legend of Eve, mentioned at the end of this chapter. Irkalla, a form of the goddess Ereshkigal whose name translates as 'Great Earth Tree' also carried the title 'The White One of Eridu' pointing to Irkalla being a legendary White Tree.

Rosemarie Taylor-Perry in *The God who Comes: Dionysian Mysteries Revisited* 2003 quotes, 'Thou shalt find to the left of the House of Hades, a spring, And by the side thereof standing a white cypress, To this spring approach not near'. The white cypress is doubtless a sacred White Tree. The deceased is directed to another spring which is what he requires as he is leaving one life and heading for heaven and that is the river of forgetfulness, which to drink from means to regain one's true primal and divine nature, before once more taking on a mortal life. This then leads us to wonder about the water coming from the white cypress and what its properties are and the implication is that it is the waters of life that issue from a White Tree of Life. The Dionysian Mysteries probably originated in Thracian or Phrygian culture and then entered Roman and Greek. A similar motif appears in the *Chandogya Upanishad* where the deceased, as he progresses on his after-life adventure, comes to the Brahma-world in the third heaven, where there is a lake with a tree showering soma (equivalent to haoma and which must, by definition, be the White Tree). In the Egyptian Book of the Dead, the deceased soul awakes in the 'underworld' in the sky and wanders into the area known as the Field of Reeds, the place where the Egyptians believed the Tree of Life grew.

In the course of examining yews over the last forty years, I have to admit I have referred to yews that are exceptionally old as 'white' or 'skeletal'. That is because their trunk and sometimes branches which are fairly depleted of leaves, resemble old bleached bones. On the cliffs at Llangollen where there are ancient yews, several of the trees, but one, in particular, stands out as greyish white against the skyline and another incredibly ancient yew on the mountain near Llanhamlach, where there are three ancient yews spread across the landscape, one of them being a yew at Ty Illtyd which appears to have changed sex from female to male. The

White Tree at North Fach near Llanhamlach.

white tree I want to draw attention to here is some distance away, perhaps a mile or so on a field boundary and is visible from afar. It is quite small, immeasurably old and white.

Other white trees are found from time to time like those at Kentchurch. They may have nothing to do with the sacred white trees. It may simply be a coincidence but nevertheless I want to show them here as I feel there is some connection.

Kentchurch White Tree. (1)

Kentchurch White Tree. (2)

One wonders whether the ancient yews at Fountains Abbey had any connections to the White Tree. The White Brotherhood, the Cistercian monks, an order founded by St, Bernard de Clairvaux in the 12th century (The White Monks) had shared kinship and many cooperative ventures with the Knights Templar, who had ancient knowledge of the yew and the Cistercians were also connected with yew trees. At Fountain's Abbey, the monks sheltered and lived under the yews while the abbey was rebuilt. There is some mystery surrounding them in terms of their connection to the Templars and their knowledge of and involvement with yews. Although Christian, there is no doubt the Cistercians were connected with nature, water and yew trees. St. Bernard's Fountain at Relec in Brittany is found in a yew wood and surrounded by these trees. Although there are thousands of Cistercian monasteries, and probably hundreds of Abbeys, I've found that in other Cistercian Abbeys I have visited, such as Strata Florida, Buckfast, Abbeydore, Newbattle, and Waverley, the yew trees are prominent, though I daresay they may have been destroyed in other places. The Cistercians also visited the Holy Lands and may have brought back yew cuttings. They certainly planted yews.

Finally, there are several references to the White Tree in *The God Tree*, but one in particular stands out as a most beautiful story. Starting on page 113, the story of 'The Legend of the Tree of Life', from *La Queste du Saint Graal*, reputed to have been written around 1230 and available in a Penguin Classic edition, is well worth reading for the full version. It is the story of Eve who plants the twig from her apple which she takes with her when thrown out of the Garden of Eden, which then grows into a White Tree, obviously a descendent of the Tree of Life in that garden and said to be as white as snow (as if a reference to the mountain tree) Eve then goes on to plant many other White Trees which grow easily from the twigs from her first tree but there comes a point when no others will grow. This may make the point that this tree is rare and only from a certain time long ago.

From the sacred book of the *Bundahishn* we have been given the information that the White Tree is requisite for carrying out the renovation and restoration of the universe. At this point in our history, this is something we are in dire need of and it may be the reason why the symbol of the White Tree is so strong an image and resonates so deeply within us, like a call from long ago to awake, for the time is now.

Chapter 21

The Elixir of Immortality - Haoma, Soma and the Tree Guardians

Yew and Elder. Photo by Alison Goulbourne.

The White Tree has some highly valued properties and purpose, to do with restoration and immortality and the question is how might these powers be released? The quest for immortality, the gift beyond price, has been searched for by many from Kings and Pharaohs to common people alike. The World Tree of the Iranians or Persians was considered to have been the Haoma Tree which bore the immortalising and life-giving juice of that name, the elixir of life, similar to the soma or amrita of the Hindus. The Avestan 'Haoma' and the Sanskrit 'Soma' were both derived from proto Indo-Iranian 'Sauma'. The physical attributes of Haoma, as described in the texts of the Avesta, are that the plant it derives from has stems, roots and branches and pliant twigs. It is fragrant and golden green, has golden blossom, can be pressed for its juice and grows on mountains. It aids and increases healing, physical strength, sexual arousal, alertness and awareness, is nourishing and is said by some to produce intoxicating effects. The legend of Haoma is that it is the elixir of life, the immortalising drink of the gods. Which plant or tree it came from is described but not really stated and there is much confusion over the nature of this legendary Haoma/Soma, as well as the identity of the plant it came from. There would appear to be at least two sacred elixirs, both called by this name and confused with each other. One, the White Haoma, most sacred of all, comes from the White Haoma tree and the other the Yellow Haoma, from which parahom/a (meaning 'before hom') comes is produced from the Ephedra plant.

This elixir of life is also known as nectar or ambrosia in other traditions, such as the Norse legend of Yggdrasil. A similar elixir is the Egyptian equivalent, described in *The Tree of Life* by Roger Cook, where our attention is drawn to a subject often painted on walls in the pyramids: the food and drink of immortality, the food and elixir offered by the tree goddess from the Egyptian celestial tree. It has been a major quest of many cultures as well as many people, to find such an elixir and it seems that two ancient sacred elixirs have been muddled together and share the same name. Like the legend of the Golden Bough, the ancient legend of an elixir of life would have come from an original story whose details have become lost, fragmented, distorted and substituted over time. As with the story of the Golden Bough, this one has several motifs in common with its variants, from several cultures across the world, such as a plant or tree, a bird, a cup, a lizard, dragon or serpent, a mountain, waters in the form of a fountain, sea or river and a quest to gain or steal the elixir from the gods whose property it was. The legend overlaps with the legend of the Tree of Life in the Garden of Eden.

Alexander Porteous in; *Forest Folklore, Mythology and Romance,* 1928, tells us that the Vedas mention a tree reminiscent of the Norse Yggdrasil, a tree whose foot is the earth and whose summit in heaven. A version of this tree, called the Tree of Abraham, holds the fire of lightning in its branches and through its leaves, it distils the elixir of life, the celestial soma or amrita as it is called in the Hindu religion, (from *The Migration of Symbols,* 1894, by Goblet d'Alviella).

Windischmann, writing on the Zend-Avesta says 'Haoma is the first of the trees planted by Ahura-Mazda in the fountain of life'. Ahura Mazda is said to be the eye of Mithra. He who drinks the Haoma juice never dies. There is a parallel in Norse mythology where Odin sacrifices an eye in exchange for a draught of the sacred Mead of Knowledge from Heimdall's horn.

Beyond the comparison of a common origin of Haoma and Soma, the elixir of life, derived from a plant, little has been done on the comparison of Vedic and Zoroastrian rituals. Also, as of 2003, as observed by Vincent J H Houben, there has been no significant comparative review of cultural/sacred haoma/soma extending beyond Alfred Hillebrandt's *Vedic Mythology,* 1891, comparison of the Vedic deity and the Zoroastrian divinity. However, in *Ancient Symbols in Modern Afghanistan,* 1957, by S Cammann, it states:

In the Zoroastrian tradition of Old Persia, the Tree of Life, Gaokarena, was also called the White Haoma, and it was the source from which the divine nectar was brought to earth by the divine bird, Saena, the sunbird prototype of the later Persian Simurgh.

The legends that surround the elixir of life have several similarities which point to the White Haoma being from a particular yew.

According to the *Bundehesh* the Gogard or Gaokarena Tree, investigated in *The God Tree*, bears the Haoma, which gives health and generative power and imparts life and resurrection. The Haoma plant according to S Cammann, 'does not decay, bears no fruit, resembles the vine, is knotty and has leaves like jessamin, yellow and white'. Cammann also says:

> From this, it appears that the White Haoma or the tree Gokard is the Tree of Life which grew in Paradise. The Zend-Avesta, actually, speaks of two trees, (as in the Genesis account of Paradise), the Haoma, and another one growing near it which is called the 'Impassive' or 'Inviolable'. The latter bears fruits containing the seeds of every kind of plant. The fountain of life in which these trees grow is called Vourukasha and a lizard under the direction of the Persian Satan is ever seeking to destroy the sacred Homa, like the serpent, who continually gnaws at the roots of Yggdrasil.

Soma is linked with Yggdrasil, for this tree according to Norse mythology contains inexhaustible mead, which the slain warriors of Valhalla drank to bring them back to life. AB Cook in *Zeus* 1914, writes about a bee nourishing dew named 'Honey fall' or Hydromel which came from Yggdrasil. In some legends, Haoma is said to have grown on Mount Elburz, north of the Vourukasha Sea and is known only to the immortals (those who could prolong life by taking this drug or elixir): 'on an island grew two sacred trees – the tree of all Remedies or Tree of all Seeds, guarded by a bird who roosts in its branches'.

The Vourukasha Sea seems to have its base in reality as Lake Van or Sevan which is situated to the south of Mount Elburz or Hara in Armenia. Mythologically, it was a huge expanse of water that supposedly covered one-third of the world and was the gathering point of all water. Andrew Collins in *From the Ashes of Angels*, says:

> In the centre of this inland sea, presumably on an island, were said to have been two divine trees – the first being the Tree of All Remedies, also known as the Tree of All Seeds or the Saena Tree (a reference to the bird associated with it which became Simurgh in later Persian)...Nearby this tree was the mighty Gaokarena tree, which possessed healing properties and bore fruit that provided immortality to those souls that achieved salvation, a reference once again to the Haoma plant. Together these two sacred trees equated respectively with the Tree of Knowledge of Good and Evil and the Tree of Life in the Book of Genesis.

The Vedas relate that the tree of the Soma was guarded by Gandharvas who were like centaurs. Agni, a swift sparrow hawk with golden wings, took flight one day from the summit, carrying the broken end of a branch. Hit by an arrow from a Gandharva, it let fall a feather and a claw. These produced the plants which resemble the bird of prey with their pennated leaves or thorns, and it was their sap that supplied the terrestrial Soma. The Persians placed two trees on the borders of a lake, each of which was guarded by a Gandharva. One of these trees was the White Haoma which according to the Yasna, wards off death and confers spiritual knowledge, the other according to the Bundehesh, is the Tree of All Seeds, also called the Eagle Tree. This reminds us of the two trees in Paradise also close to water. According to one version of the myth, when one of these birds flies away, a thousand branches grow on the tree and as soon as it returns to the nest, it breaks a thousand branches and causes a thousand seeds to fall. A legendary 'White Hom' grows at the junction of the 'great gathering place of the waters' and a mighty river. The sap of the Haoma, is the fertilising rain, like the Indian Soma and also the fermented liquor which was considered the drink of the gods. Soma, according to *Rig Veda* 10.943 is the branch of a ruddy tree (like a yew!) Other Vedic hymns describe Soma as having a 'ruddy radiance'.

The bird motif is present again with a bird called Simurgh or Simorgh who is associated with both Mithraism and Haoma. This is the bird of the Persian Tree of Life (or Tree of Seeds) that lives in the land of the sacred Haoma (Sanskrit Soma). A bird (eagle) is also associated with Yggdrasil and sits on the top of the tree. Simorgh goes by various names and is related to the Phoenix just as the tree it is associated with, has various names such as the Kazu Tree. This bird, connected with the Tree of Life, can heal wounds and return creatures to health from near death. It goes into a trance state before committing acts of healing and taking people to the magical tree. From Andrew Collins in *From the Ashes of Angels*, we learn that Rustum, one of those thus healed reveals that the healing was obtained through a noble vulture, who presents him with an elixir. The vulture may also have been used as a symbol of death and the transformation of the soul, which happened as a result of taking this elixir which was said to bestow wisdom through a ritualistic death. Moving to the Greek Odyssey, it is the very opposite sort of bird, the dove, who brings ambrosia, another word for the elixir of life, to the god Zeus.

This divine elixir is much sought after and was seen as a fabled super drug, believed to be able to rejuvenate the body and prolong life. It is collected in a cup or bowl and as Fred Hageneder says in *Yew: A History*, 'A number of Near Eastern traditions present the Tree of Life with a cup or bowl in its top'. Ganymede is the cupbearer of the gods on Olympus. The tree spirit appears as a bird and the drink in the acorn cup shows that the nectar is made from the tree itself. In the early stage of its development, the yew fruit is also called an acorn as the aril develops around the nut held within the acorn cup. Soma too is collected in a bowl from the tree 'showering nectar' and the bowl is also the crescent moon (*The Lunar Crescent and the Bowl* by EAS Butterworth, 1970). In Sumerian culture, Inanna, a Sumerian green goddess is the cupbearer of the essence of the grail otherwise known as the Tree of Life and in Hindu religion Garuda steals the moon goblet containing the ambrosia, amrita, nectar or soma which provides the Asura gods with supernatural power making them immortal. Garuda is able to revive the slain by outpourings of nectar from the goblet.

Although the nature of the reality of the elixir has forever been a matter of speculation, it has always been strongly linked with the sacred drug referred to in Iranian myth, a substance produced from a plant of unknown origin. The big question is what was the plant which produced this Haoma/Soma? As already said, the main group of plants widely believed to be its source is Ephedra, of which there are some thirty varieties. This Indian-Zoroastrian belief in Ephedra also manifests itself in the present-day Zoroastrian practice of administering a few drops of parahaoma made from Ephedra plants to the newborn or the dying. As Falk, recalling Auriel Stein's discovery of Ephedra plants interred at 1st century BCE Tarim Basin burial sites notes, it is 'an imperishable plant, representing or symbolising the continuity of life...most appropriate in burial rites'. Interestingly though, in *The Mysteries of Mithras* by Payam Nabarz, it is pointed out that Ephedra, is similar to ephedrine, a chemical contained by the yew, an alkaloid and a psychedelic drug that can cause hallucination and delirium, although this is hotly denied as a property of Haoma by adherents of Zoroastrianism. Another thing in common with the yew is that a bundle of twigs called a Barsom, said to have come from the Ephedra plant, acted like a lightning rod or magic wand or staff, as do yew staffs. This conducting power is also found in Sufism.

All the more recent studies have dealt with botanic identification of proto Indo-Iranian soma. Houben's workshop, in 2003, was the first of its kind to deal with the nature and identity of the Soma/Haoma plant and the juice pressed from it. The sap of the Persian Haoma, like Soma, was said to confer eternal life and cure all evils.

James Darmesteter, in his 1875 *Thesis on the mythology of the Avesta,* speculating on the Parsi belief that Ephedra twigs do not decay, wrote:

It comprises the power of life of all the vegetable kingdom... both Ved and the Avesta call it the king of healing herbs... the Zarathustra scriptures say that Haoma is of two kinds, the white Haoma and the painless tree. Could it be that Soma is the Tree of Life, the giver of immortality?

That tree is, of course, the yew and the 'painless tree' suggests a tree that was a healer or a source of a narcotic drug.

However, some believe the elixir to have been made from Fly Agaric, Latin name Amanita muscaria, the red mushroom with white spots, associated with fairies. This mushroom is hallucinogenic and may have aided shamans to take flight to the spirit world, usually to seek healing for someone. Mushrooms were doubtless used in rituals for 'out of body' experiences but according to Terence Mc. Kenna in, *The Food of Gods, The Search for the Original Tree of Knowledge: a Radical History of Plants, Drugs and Human Evolution,* 1993, the effects of Amanita muscaria contradict the properties described in the Rigveda. Another mushroom, Psilocybe, also contain a strong mind-altering drug and there are cultures and modern-day people who use these mushrooms for this reason. Amanita muscaria was finally dismissed, however, as being unable to produce a state of consciousness conducive to the development of a religion and to put the seal on it, an Indian herbologist and Vedic scholar of some authority, Vaidya Bhairavdutt, described as 'the only living authority on Soma', said that Soma was definitely not a mushroom.

In 1989 David Flattery concentrated on Iranian Haoma regarding the hallucinogenic properties which could be interpreted from the texts. He discounted Ephedra because he could not observe Zoroastrian priests becoming intoxicated and therefore concluded that Ephedra was a substitute for Sauma (or Haoma/Soma) but not the thing itself. Its main effect is as a stimulant similar to amphetamine, producing sleeplessness and high blood pressure. Ephedra does not grow in India and another plant Pegamun harmala was also proposed due to its being the only incense plant with hallucinogenic properties in Iran.

As many might guess, Cannabis Sativa has also been considered a possible candidate for Soma. This widely used hallucinogenic plant, claimed to have many healing properties, is known in Native American cultures as a 'teacher plant' which imparts wisdom. Ayahuasca and Ergot have also both been suggested along with Bella Donna, in fact just about all hallucinogenic plants have been considered. However, none of these plant-derived drugs seem to quite fit the bill and studies have been inconclusive. Fred Hageneder says 'The aim of the ritual libations was not to get out of one's mind but to attune to a higher reality than the personal'. This was part of the function of the elixir but there was more to it than that. The yew tree, the Tree of Life, Death, Resurrection and Immortality is, for many reasons, likely to be the source for one very powerful Elixir of Life. HP Blavatsky in *The Secret Doctrine,*1888, explicitly says 'Soma is the fruit of the Tree of Knowledge' and Fred Hageneder in *Yew: A History* agrees:

The notion of the Tree of Life producing divine ambrosia or

nectar is generally seen as a shared heritage of the peoples speaking Germanic, Persian and Indian languages (Indo European).

He goes on to state that:

Whether Soma is the extract from the fruits of the World Tree as the old Indian texts say, or the 'honey fall' dropping from Yggdrasil as the Scandinavians tell us, both can be related to Taxus.

There is certain knowledge that yew sap is used in modern-day Mithraism and it seems likely to have been the original substance used in ceremonies, perhaps mixed with other material, perhaps not, and used partly as a higher truth drug. There is no other possibility but that Haoma as the Elixir of Immortality is derived from the yew tree but a very particular yew tree, a White Tree. Such a drug prepared from the yew, probably originated from a much earlier, prehistoric, shamanistic culture, in which it may well have been used as part of a death-defying rite. The yew contains an alkaloid poison called taxine, a shamanistic drug. The toxin induces a near-death state enabling the soul to leave the body. Shamans inhaled the vapours of the sap to obtain visions and communicate with the dead. Some species of yew are not as poisonous as others but meditating near a yew in hot weather can produce trance as yew gives off a toxic vapour as discovered by Dr Layard.

Because of its enormous spiritual significance to the Iranian religion, Haoma became a healing god in its own right, which, because of the plant's obvious curative properties, could bestow health and strength on its worshippers. In some accounts, the bird Simorgh is seen as the guardian of the Haoma plant for as the *Encyclopaedia of Religion* by Michel de Salzmann 1986 explains:

In the traditions of the Indo Iranians, the drug is closely

connected with a mystical bird which took the Haoma from the place where it lay hidden and brought it to gods and men. The Avesta speaks of the bird Saena, which is the Simorgh of the Persian texts, who plays the same part.

The role of revealing the secrets of Haoma to both gods and men is a role played in early Hindu mythology by the half eagle, half-giant, called Garuda, who was the Indian equivalent of Simorgh.

In *Journal of Central Asia,* Vol. 9, from the Centre for the Study of Civilisations of Central Asia, 1986, the 'two Haomas, one Golden, the earthly king of healing plants, the other White Haoma or Gaokarena Tree' are discussed and the fact that they both grow in the middle of the sea is mentioned. (It is also said they both grow on mountains.)

The White Haoma, the chief of all plants, which confers immortality and rejuvenation, is the highest tree. It thus becomes possible to look upon Soma as the Indian Gokart or Gaokarena Tree. The Gokart tree functions as the agent of resurrection... the tree of immortality, by conferring everlasting life and becomes the best protector, for it keeps things in its charge everlasting.

When elevated to the position of a god, Haoma is called 'Golden Green eyed', which sounds like a tree god. The mention of the eye, as also in Ahura Mazda, the eye of Mitra, perhaps opened by the use of the sacred Haoma, may be an allusion to the third eye that sees into another world. It is only to be expected that the Haoma divinity is identified as having a priesthood and the Haoma plant becomes the central element in the legend surrounding the conception of Zoroaster where his mother and father drink some of the Haoma plant mixed with milk before conceiving Zoroaster, who is born instilled with the spirit of the sacred plant.

Zoroaster is said to have received his revelation while

preparing parahaoma to make good the damage done to water by humanity, by offering Haoma, 'possessed with milk, possessed with pomegranate' to water. Haoma is therefore established as a legendary plant with medicinal and spiritual properties which appears in ancient texts from both India and Persia. It is also the name of the spirit presiding over the Haoma plant, as the spirit was seen as a deity in its own right, a plant whose seeds can cure all evil. It had divine properties, enabling it to bestow immortality and give visions to priests and strength to soldiers. It is also very interestingly connected with pomegranate which gives another clue to Haoma being linked with yew. The Greek goddess, Persephone is a goddess of the underworld and her symbol is the pomegranate, which is the link between heaven and earth. The pomegranate, also connected with Judaism and Sufism, is thought to be the Tree of Life in some myths, although as was shown in *The God Tree* pomegranate seeds have been confused with yew seeds and Persephone is a triple goddess connected with yew. There is a difference in the Haoma used in the Zoroastrian Yasna ritual where Ephedra is used together with pomegranate twigs and leaves. This highlights the fact that at one time this elixir of life was made from a particular yew and is a different elixir altogether to the yellow Haoma made from Ephedra.

According to the Lesser Bundahishn 9.4, the White Haoma tree is the plant of eternal life called the Gokard/ Gokare/ Gaokarena tree (Vendidad 20.4). These legendary Trees of Life were examined in *The God Tree* and grow in the kingdom previously known as Gaokarena in the Caucasus. The yellow/ golden yellow/ or yellow-green Haoma is produced from pressing the twigs of a variety of Ephedra, a twiggy shrub that grows quite commonly on mountains across the east. Twigs from the Ephedra shrub were and still are pressed and pounded in a pestle and mortar to extract the juice. The twigs along with those of other plants are used for making the 'baresman' bundle carried by priests and used for healing and in ceremonies.

Ephedra is a scrubby shrub, which grows in the mountains in Eastern countries. It is quite prolific and not rare, or difficult to find and there are many different varieties of it, just one being slightly more tree-like than the others. In the Avesta of the Persian, Haoma is described as 'golden flowered, that grows on the heights, Haoma that restores us, that drives death afar'. It is described as 'nourishing' and 'most nutritious for the soul' (Yasna 9.16). Tiny amounts of the elixir are used and the substance possibly fermented. It is said to be harmful in excess. Of a Haoma-Soma workshop in Leiden in 1999, Jan E M Houben wrote in 2003 that:

> despite attempts to do away with Ephedra by those who are eager to see Sauma as a hallucinogen, its status as a serious candidate for the Rigveda Soma and Avestan Haoma still stands.

He also stated 'there is no need to look for a plant other than Ephedra, the one plant used today by the Parsis'. If this is the case then we must be talking about a quite different thing to the Haoma associated with the endurance of great trials and troubles on a quest to find and win this rare substance. On the subject of it being a mind-altering drug, Houben says, 'In the Avesta there is no indication whatsoever that Haoma was a hallucinogenic drug, and there is not a single instance of it ever having been used as such in Zoroastrian religious practice', but this Haoma is also described as 'righteous' and 'wise'. It is said to give 'insight' and it 'furthers righteousness'. In other words, it acts on the consciousness and spirituality of the person who partakes of it as do teacher plants such as cannabis, peyote and ayahuasca.

Looking to the *Zadspram* now, an ancient Zoroastrian book, a legendary 'White Hom' is described which grows at the junction of the 'great gathering place of the waters' and a mighty river. According to the *Zadspram*, at the end of time when Ormuzd triumphs over Ahriman, the followers of the good religion will share a parahom made from the 'White Hom' and so attain immortality for their resurrected bodies. (*Zadspram* 35.15) I think we can see we are talking about a completely different elixir here.

R W E Bunsen, a German chemist, wrote in 1887:

> The records about the Tree of Life are the sublimest proofs of the unity and continuity of tradition. The earliest records of the most ancient Oriental tradition refer to a Tree of Life which was guarded by spirits. The juice of the sacred tree, like the tree itself, was called Soma in Sanskrit and Haoma in Zend: it was revered as the life preserving essence.

Although both the elixir made from Ephedra (the Yellow Haoma) and that made from the Tree of Life (the White Haoma) are both life-enhancing, there is a difference between 'driving death afar' and offering 'immortality'. Clearly, the Yellow Haoma used quite regularly and frequently in rituals is not for the latter purpose and unlike the White Haoma, the Yellow Haoma doesn't come from a tree or have guardians.

Last but by no means least, as mentioned in *The God Tree*, it is said that Jesus was given Soma by Joseph of Arimathea and the physician Nicodemus as he hung dying on the tree. Nicodemus appears again after his death, bringing herbs and spices and assists Joseph of Arimathea with the body of Jesus (John 19:39-42). One wonders whether it was the elixir of the White Haoma that was given to Jesus and granted him immortality. Jesus, as shown in *The God Tree*, hung not just on any tree but on the Tree of Life, the tree planted on Adam's grave at the Place of the Skulls, in order to lift the original curse laid on Adam and Eve for taking and eating the fruit of the Tree of Knowledge. What happened was all deeply significant and it seems to me that Jesus, as well as his uncle Joseph of Arimathea and Nicodemus, was involved in the mysteries of the Yew Cult.

Chapter 22

Magic Fairy Trees

If the yew tree is a kind of god, it is also by definition an otherworldy tree of great mystery which we can never hope to know entirely. One of its functions is to act as a portal in time and space and another is to enable some to cross kingdoms, other realms and dimensions that run parallel to our own. Strange things can happen around yew trees. Once upon a time, there was a magic fairy tree, hidden deep in the forest in a place where people rarely went and the fairies were able to dance without fear of being seen. However, it happened one day that two labourers returning from work, accidentally crossed into the fairies' domain.

There are two versions of this fairy tale which took place in mid-Wales in the parish of Llanwrin. The second version concerns 'a lad and a lass' but other than that the story is essentially the same and centres around a great yew tree which still exists deep in the forest on a private estate, the location of which cannot be disclosed. This yew is 32 feet in girth over 40 feet in height and has a multiple layering from branches including a large fallen one, which has caused a small grove to develop over time. John Lowe recorded a girth of 30 feet at the ground of this tree in 1897 and a height of 52 feet and Terence Mc. Kenna in, *The Food of Gods, The Search for the Original Tree of Knowledge: a Radical History of Plants, Drugs and Human Evolution*, 1993, describing the yew's measurements as 32 feet girth at a height of 6 inches from the ground and with a height of 48 feet.

The story concerning Twm and Iago in Ffridd yr Ywen, ('The Forest of the Yew'), said to be in Powys, Wales but actually in Gwynedd, is told by Wirt Sikes around 1900 in two of his books *The Realm of Faerie - Fairy Life and Legend in Britain* and British Goblins, Welsh Folklore, Fairy Mythology, Legends and

Traditions. He tells of a magical yew tree as follows:

> A tradition is current in Mathavarn, in the parish of Llanwrin
> and the Cantref of Cyfeillioc, concerning a certain wood called
> Ffridd yr Ywen, 'The Forest of the Yew', that is so-called on
> account of a magical yew tree which grows exactly in the
> middle of the forest. Under that tree, there is a fairy circle
> called 'The Dancing Place of the Goblin'. There are several
> fairy circles in the Forest of the Yew, but the one in the middle
> under the yew has this legend connected with it.

The Fairy Yew Tree.

Twm and Iago at the Fairy Yew Tree.

He then goes on to tell of a time long ago when two farm servants called Twm and Iago, went out to work in the Forest of the Yew but went home early when a dense mist came down.

When they came to the yew tree in the middle of the forest, suddenly they found light all around them.

They lay down under the yew and fell asleep.

By and by Twm awoke, to find his companion gone. He was much surprised at this but concluded Iago had gone to the village on an errand of which they had been speaking before they fell asleep. So Twm went home and to all enquiries concerning Iago, he answered, 'Gone to the cobbler's in the village.' But Iago was still absent next morning.

Twm confessed that they had fallen asleep under the yew by the fairy circle and that was the last he saw of Iago. After many days searching:

Twm went to a 'gwr cyfarwydd' (conjurer) which the legend says was a common trade in those days. The conjurer gave him this advice: 'Go to the same place where you and the lad slept. Go there exactly a year after the boy was lost. Let it be on the same day of the year and at the same time of the day, but take care that you do not step inside the fairy ring. Stand on the border of the green circle you saw there and the boy will come out with many of the goblins to dance. When you see him so near to you, you may take hold of him, snatch him out of the ring as quickly as you can.' A year to the day later, these instructions were obeyed and Iago appeared, dancing in the ring with the Tylwyth Teg (Welsh fairy folk) and was promptly plucked forth. 'Duw! Duw!' (Oh god!) cried Twm, 'how wan and pale you look!

And don't you feel hungry too?' 'No', said the boy, 'and if I did, have I not here in my wallet the remains of my dinner that I had before I fell asleep?' But when he looked in his wallet, the food was not there. 'Well it must be time to go home', he said, with a sigh; for he did not know that a year had passed by. His look was like a skeleton and as soon as he had tasted food, he mouldered away.

One wonders if it was the fairies or the yew tree that caused the loss and distortion of time. The archaic address for this 'Forest of the Yew' is an authentic location, even if it may be a late addition to the tale: 'There is a village in Powys called Llanwrin, halfway between Machynlleth and Cemmaes'.

Another version of this legend describes the Forest of the Yew as an enchanted wood in the parish of Llanwrin:

As a lad and lass were strolling there one evening, they saw two elves come and draw a fairy ring round the yew tree. A troop of fairies then entered the ring with their musicians and began to dance. They danced so well that the lad joined them and went whirling round the fairy ring, while the lass sat and watched them. But hour after hour went by and the lad still danced and at daybreak, he and the fairies vanished together and the lass went home feeling lonely and broken-hearted.

One evening as she was looking for him in the forest, she met an old woman who told her to wait for a year and a day, and then return at night to the yew tree. The lass did so, and there she saw her sweetheart still dancing merrily with the fairies in the fairy ring, and tried to drag him out of it. 'Just let me dance another minute,' he cried, eagerly pushing her aside. 'No, you've danced long enough,' she said, and she seized him by the arm and pulled him away from the ring. 'I haven't been dancing five minutes!' he said, rather angrily. And it was not until he got back to Llanwrin that he believed that he had really danced for a year and a day.

Reverend Josiah Jones, minister of the Congregational Church of nearby Machynlleth said in 1911, that:

> A deacon in my church, John Evans, declared that he had seen the Tylwyth Teg (fairies) dancing in the day time, within two miles from here, and he pointed out the very spot where they had appeared. This was some twenty years ago. I think however that he saw only certain reflections and shadows because it was a hot and brilliant day.

It is to be noted that a deacon of a Christian church was not afraid to admit to seeing fairies and even at this date many people in Wales as well as Ireland, still believed in their existence.

The Tylwyth Teg (pronounced Tillowth Teg) were considered in Wales to be little people, supernatural beings, possibly from a bygone race before the Iron Age. One way of warding them off was apparently to show them iron as they were believed to disappear in its presence. Some say this is because the fairies existed up until the end of the Bronze Age when they began to disappear with the Iron Age and in some parts of Ireland, belief in the fairies still continues and they are thought to have simply retreated under the hills. The Tylwyth Teg could be helpful, mischievous or spiteful and were never to be underestimated. It was considered very dangerous to enter their realms for to do so meant that a person would become enchanted and held by a spell, subject to their power. Walking nine times around a fairy ring or fairy tree would let in the fairies. In *The Fairy Faith in Celtic Countries*, 1911, by WY Evans-Wentz, Mr Louis Foster Edwards of Harlech is reported as saying that the Tylwyth Teg lived by plundering at night and described them as having the power of invisibility and it was believed they could disappear like a spirit even as one happened to be observing them, in the twinkling of an eye. He said the world in which they lived was a world quite unlike ours, outside of our time and mortals taken to it by them were changed in nature and were rarely able to return to our world. Wentz also writes about people who have lengthy illness spending that time with the fairies. When they regain their health, they are sometimes gifted with the second sight. The belief in fairies, he said existed simultaneously with both Druidism and Christianity and still continues in certain parts of Britain. While the Otherworld is in many ways similar to Heaven, the ability to enter it and the conditions for doing so, despite its proximity to the mortal world, set it apart and only a few would ever go there. Rev. Josiah Jones said:

> As I recall the belief, the old people considered the Tylwyth Teg as living beings half way between something material and spiritual, who were rarely seen.

Joan of Arc was also associated with a magic fairy tree which she adored known as 'L'arbre fée de Bourlemont' (the fairy tree of Bourlemont). The yew is the national tree of France and although France does not have many ancient yews, most are in Normandy and Brittany where they are well looked after and seen as national monuments. Although it is not known what kind of tree this fairy tree was, Joan recollected that the children joined hands and danced around it. She said the fairies were still there when they were children but they never saw them because a hundred years before that, the priest of Domremy had held a religious function under the tree and barred them from redemption and warned them never to show themselves again on pain of perpetual banishment from that parish. It was obvious the priest believed the fairies existed and the Church did not try to obliterate the belief in fairies but over time the very nature of the fairies began to change within a Christian framework. At one time they were worshipped as gods but the integration of fairies is explained in one of WB Yeats theories on the origins of fairies and in the introduction to his work *Fairy and Folk Tales of Ireland*, he described them as 'fallen angels, not good enough to be saved, nor bad enough to be lost.'

Joan of Arc described a night when great misfortune befell. Edmond Aubrey's mother passed by the Fairy Tree and the fairies were stealing a dance, not thinking that anybody was by:

and they were so busy and so intoxicated with the wild happiness of it and with the bumpers of dew sharpened up with honey which they had been drinking, that they noticed nothing, so Dame Aubrey stood there astonished and admiring and saw the little fantastic atoms holding hands, as many as three hundred of them, tearing around in a great ring half as big as an ordinary bedroom and leaning away back and spreading their mouths with laughter and song, which she could hear quite distinctly and kicking their legs up as much as three inches from the ground in perfect abandon and hilarity - the very maddest and witchingest dance the woman ever saw but in a few minutes the fairies discovered her, began crying and disappeared.

The Dame went straight home and told the neighbours about it and when the priest, Pére Fronte found out, despite the crying and begging of the children and despite the fact that he was not without sympathy, he said he had warned the fairies not to return and that now he was forced to banish them.

Joan of Arc said the great tree was never quite the same to them again but that once a year she would sit under it and in her mind recall the lost playmates of her youth. The fairies' protection vanished as a result of the priest's banishing and the spring dried up somewhat and lost much of its freshness and coldness and the serpents and stinging nettles they'd banished, returned and multiplied and became a torment.

Sometime well before the 16th century, Scottish clans had adopted 'plant badges', to identify themselves as being a member of a certain clan. These plants were mostly trees. Before going into battle the Fraser clan wore sprigs of yew from their tribal tree, which grew on the hill of Tomnahuriach above Loch Ness. Tomnahuriach, 'the hill of the yews', just outside Inverness, is also associated with fairies and, this small steep hill was reputed to be the place where Thomas the Rhymer, the Scottish mystic and seer, disappeared into the Underworld or Faery realms. The culture of this area is altogether coloured with fairy legends. Today a large cemetery remains at the foot of this hill, where the famous Fraser yew grows and the hill is also known as the hill of the fairies. There is some confusion as to whether Thomas Rhymer or Sir Thomas Learmonth of Ercildourne, a 13th century Laird who is reputed to be buried there, is the same person as Thomas the Rhymer but it seems likely.

Legend tells us how Thomas the Rhymer went out walking one day and fell asleep beneath a tree on the side of the Eildon Hills. He awoke to find a shining woman, sitting on a grey horse at his side. This was the Queen of the Fairies who had set out to meet Thomas. Thomas was struck by her beauty and immediately fell under her spell and she asked him for a kiss, which he gave under the Eildon tree. The Fairy Queen then asked Thomas to go back with her to the Land of the Fairies to be her lover, which he did. As we saw in the previous story, time is different in the Land of the Fairies and while Thomas stayed with the fairies for what felt like three days, it was, in fact, seven years and when he left, the Queen gave Thomas the gift of poetry, (hence his name, 'the Rhymer'), of always speaking the truth (which Thomas protested against!) and the gift of prophecy with which he later predicted significant events that were to happen to Scotland. It was this story that formed the basis of the *Ballad of Tamlin*, though here Tamlin is held in Fairy Land by the Queen and has to be rescued.

Fairies and magic were and are associated with the yew but one wonders in the light of stories told of losing time at yew sites (see next chapter) and visiting different times (especially if walking around a yew in an anti-clockwise direction), whether the time loss was to do with the fairies or to do with the yew tree.

Chapter 23

The Burning Bush and Other Yew Mysteries

There will always be things about the yew that we will never understand. This is how it is but, in this chapter, I wanted to just touch on a few of these things which I have no answers to but find myself perennially contemplating.

The Eye of the Watcher

The book of Enoch is the first to mention the watchers. The Eye and the idea of it watching us is found in Mesopotamia tree cults, as well as in the eye of Ahura Mazda or Mitra, the bull cult deriving from the yew tree.

It is an ancient idea central to many cultures. The Eye of Horus in Egyptian culture protects and is a symbol of health, power and restoration. Funerary amulets depicting this symbol protected the Pharaoh from evil in the afterlife. The Eye of Ra in ancient Egyptian mythology was also protective and was connected with the sun disk. The sun is often referred to as the eye of the god. At other times the sun god is depicted inside the disk shape of the solar eye as if enclosed within it. The Egyptians often described the sun's movement across the sky as the movement of a barque carrying Ra and his entourage of other gods and the sun disk can either be equated with this solar barque or depicted containing the barque inside it. In Greek orthodox churches the eye watches from the ceiling. On Archaemenian seals of the First Persian Empire (around 6th century BCE), the solar disk is shown with the wings and tail of a powerful bird such as an eagle and is placed above the heads of gods and kings. The capital of this empire was Babylon and the religions were Mithraism and Zoroastrianism. Sometimes the king is shown within this winged disk leaning out from it as if to survey his subjects and sometimes this same disk with birds' wings and a tail is shown above the sacred tree. The winged globe or sun disk with the eagle was sometimes borne as a standard at the end of the staff in the manner of the Assyrian ensign, the Roman standard and Hitler's Germany. The eagle is an important part of this symbol too, representing wisdom, power and spirit. The symbol of the eagle and the serpent are typically reserved for powerful mythic figures, humans of unusual distinction or for royalty considered to be of divine origin. Shammuz was an Assyrian solar deity of justice who exercised the power of light over darkness and evil. He was the equivalent of the Sumerian Utu and was depicted within the solar disk with the wings and tail of an eagle.

When elevated to the position of a god, Haoma, the elixir of immortality is called 'Golden Green eyed', which sounds as if he was a tree god and the Haoma divinity is identified as having a priesthood, perhaps to watch over. The mention of the eye, in Ahura Mazda, the eye of Mitra may be an allusion to the third eye that sees into another world and this eye is perhaps opened by the use of the sacred Haoma.

Back to the seals and one Archaemenian seal dated between 6th and 9th centuries BCE, investigated previously in Chapter 2 where it is depicted, shows the Tree of the Sun with the eye within the disk and wings made from the needles of the tree, at the top of what is surely meant to be a depiction of a yew tree. Another cylinder seal, this time Mesopotamian Neo Assyrian (c. 746 - 609 BCE) of a tree with winged sun disk above shows much the same thing, so this was an important, enduring idea and may have originally been saying that the sacred tree is watching, as symbols found inside Laleham church near Ankerwycke suggest.

Assyrian Tree of Life. One of many carved images of this period showing a Deity or King above the tree within a circle or winged disk (bird wings and tail). The circle signifies either the sun or a watching eye and is connected with the Tree of Life. Compare with 'Tree of the Sun' from an Archaemenian seal in chapter 2 with yew-like needles.

*Assyrian Deity with sacred tree or Tree of Life
shown as an arch or portal.*

Laleham Church graffiti - Eye in the Tree. Photo by Lyndall Menzies.

Laleham Church graffiti - Pyramid and Sphinx.
Photo by Lyndall Menzies.

At Laleham, there is some strange graffiti on one of the church pillars. Although thought to be Norman and made of a stone called clunch, a kind of chalky limestone quite easy to carve, these small carvings, just a few inches high are reminiscent in style and size to the graffiti mentioned in the chapter on Jesus' Wand, which were drawn by the imprisoned Templars. Pillars are a valuable architectural feature that are recyclable parts of a building and often moved, so there is no way of knowing of the history of these pillars at Laleham but the graffiti clearly shows Mesopotamian, Assyrian or Sumerian images and features several things central to the religion of this culture including those symbols belonging to the goddess Inanna. Its relevance to this book is that it shows an open watching eye in what may be a yew tree with berries and in a place just a short distance away from the famous sacred yew of Ankerwycke. The graffiti also seems to show a pyramid and sphinx. One can only speculate as to whether this graffiti had any connection to that particular yew tree. The sketches may be showing it as an important sacred tree and may also be describing it as connected to the Eye of Ra. One wonders what it is doing there on a pillar in Laleham church and whether it was done in the last few hundred years or came from a previous time when the pillars were in a different and unknown location. The thing is, who nowadays would know these symbols and their possible relevance and why were they carved here? The images depicted by the graffiti are certainly not modern, Norman or Christian and from the size and height of them, it looks as if they have been done furtively, perhaps by a prisoner or at least by someone who wanted to leave the symbols secretly for others, perhaps to convey information that couldn't be put into words for fear of it falling into the wrong hands. I suspect they were done in the same way that the graffiti of the Knights Templar at the Chateau at Domme was done and for similar reasons.

The Burning Bush

It seems that holy fires play around certain sacred trees such as the burning bush out of which God spoke to Moses on his sacred mountain Horeb and sacred olive tree at Phoenician Tyre. The important thing is that the bush is said to burn with fire but is not consumed which, of course, suggests that either the fire is not a fire but a great light or it is a supernatural fire or that the bush has certain powers that prevent it from being burnt. If this was the case the question would be, what is fuelling the fire? Lucan describes a Druid grove where 'dead yews revived' and 'unconsumed trees were surrounded with flame'. True this may be poetic license but it concurs with the story of the burning bush and Colin Humphreys says that 'the book of Exodus suggests a long-lasting fire that Moses went to investigate, not a fire that flares up and then rapidly goes out.' The fire was coming from the bush but the book of Exodus has changed over many centuries and an early translation was 'appeared to be on fire', so perhaps it was something that looked like a fire but in fact wasn't. Exodus 3:3 states 'And Moses said I will now turn aside and see this great sight, why the bush is not burnt'. To me, this suggests two possibilities. First that the bush or tree was a Golden Bough tree in a dark place giving the appearance of yellow flames and second that there appeared to be a great deal of smoke suggesting a fire, due to clouds of male pollen which, as shown in *The God Tree*, is produced in great excess by the male yew to the extent that it obliterates the view and makes a person standing in the way of it disappear! In the story from Exodus the burning bush is the location where God appoints Moses to lead the Israelites out of Egypt. God tells Moses that the site is holy ground. When Moses asked God who he is the reply is 'Eya Asher Eya'. The phrase means 'I am that I am' but it should be noted that the Hittite word for Yew (Eya) is included here. God then tells Moses that 'I am' (Eya) is his name and that he should tell the Israelites "I am' has sent me unto you'. It would seem reasonable to think that God is saying he is the yew, he is the burning bush and in Pistis Sophia, a 1st or 2nd century Gnostic gospel, Jesus quite literally says 'Yew my father or 'The' father'. Yahweh then instructs Moses to take 'this staff' in his hands, in order to perform miracles with it, as if it is a staff which is being given to him, rather than it being originally his own. Staffs of power were often passed from one saint or holy man to another. Yahweh's staff is another connection to the sacred yew and a staff pertaining to be the Rod of Moses is still held at Birmingham Municipal Museum.

Another ancient story regarding light in trees occurs in the

Hittite document, where Gilgamesh and Enkidu take the axe which they have brought and fell the cedar and when the cedar is felled the glow in the forest fades and the brightness of the rays is no more. Enkidu has urged Gilgamesh to destroy the source of the rays' vitality! A further connection with burning or lighted trees or bushes is found in the story of Perceval (who may have been Peredur - one of the warrior saints who were Keepers of the Grail secret) in the Arthurian quest for the Holy Grail. Perceval sees afar off a tree, upon which burn many lights. In *The Christ Child in Medieval Culture: Alpha es et O!* 2012, by Mary Dizon and Theresa Kenney, they say that the author Rose Jeffries Peebles describes the lighted tree as the Tree of Life and other motifs in the story, such as the Cross and the children in the tree as pertaining to the Grail.

The Knights Templar who were connected with yew trees and knew something of its secrets held the 'Seal of the Golden Fleece' and a yew tree connected with them in Wales at Llanfihangel Aber Cywyn in Carmarthenshire was equated with the burning bush. It was set fire to and the fire was said to have burned for three days, after which the tree was not consumed. This yew is still alive and well today, though you can still see the scorch marks in the hollow tree if you look hard. This old site is a strange place with pilgrims' graves from around the 10th century with strange patterns and symbols inscribed on them, such as the chevron pattern, symbol of yew, a sun symbol and also Templar symbols such as two men on a horse. Inside one of the graves which were opened and investigated, were found scallop shells, a pilgrim symbol. The churchyard which is Celtic is along a serpentine river and is connected with serpents. The pilgrims promised to keep the churchyard free of serpents and venomous beasts as long as their graves were tended which was fine until the church and graveyard were abandoned in favour of a new church whereupon it became full of them. The congregation, however, still returned for an annual service but on one occasion the vicar found his way barred by the emergence of an enormous serpent from a hole by the churchyard. The following year as part of the service, the vicar set fire to the tree! It is apparent to me that the only reason for doing this was that the vicar thought the serpent lived in the tree. Other yews set on fire, some of which burnt for days but still survived, are at Linton, Gwytherin and Didcot. Not all were so lucky such as the large hollow yew at Llanelen in North Gower, an early church site dedicated to Helen the mother of Constantine. I can't rule out that the possibility that the burning bush is a phenomenon connected to the Golden Fleece or Bough. There are the remains of another yew which is just a large portion preserved in the porch of the derelict Templar abbey at Slebech where it has remained for many decades. Unfortunately, it was not recorded as to where this yew originally stood. Vaughan Cornish records it in his book on yew trees as 'Relic of a yew 13 ft 8ins in girth'. It was said to have been growing in the 12th century, 'straight and tall' near the water's edge and the knights built their church under its shadow but one wonders why it is in the porch or was taken down at all or whether it fell. I have found it remarkable that often yews associated with the Templars are of the same fluted type as if they may have been grown from cuttings taken from the same tree and there are some yews that are reputed to have come from Gethsemane and the Holy Lands of the same stock.

Yew staffs, wands and talismans

Staffs were often passed down from saint to saint and at one time there were hundreds of them in existence, some were ancient and some may have had less of a distant lineage but were also treated with great reverence, perhaps centuries old, given as a gift or passed on and made from a known or unknown sacred tree in Britain or other lands. Their main purpose was to act as a protector, both physically and spiritually, and they sometimes had certain other properties, individual character and miraculous powers. As described at length in *The God Tree*, there are many stories of how these staffs came to be planted and grew into remarkable trees

In the Hebrides, the nuts of the yew's thrice blessed fruit were called beans and were worn around the neck or kept in a pocket for protection. At St. Brieval in Gloucester, up until the 19th century, yew crosses made from two pieces of yew, were pinned to the rooves of cottages for protection. The cross or the cross in the circle was the symbol of the sacred yew tree in its enclosure, long before it became a Christian symbol. People knew about the yew and stillborn babies, too young to have been baptised, were given their souls protection, by being buried beneath the yew, a custom which still goes on in parts of Devon and places such as Burghill in Herefordshire, with its large yews known as the 12 Apostles. At the end of life, it was common practice, as it still is in parts of Wales, for sprigs of yew to be thrown into a grave, so the spirit of yew could accompany and protect the deceased on their journey into the afterlife.

Although we tend to think that Pagan practises were wiped out by the Church, they still exist in some places, particularly when it comes to belief in the yew. People resort to the healing trees in Wales at Pennant Melangell, for a miracle cure, (details in *The God Tree*) and planted protector yews on the southwest side of the house. Male yews were planted in Neolithic times on the north side of burial mounds as the dark forces and malevolent powers that were thought to threaten life were believed to come from the north, hence people have only been buried on the north side within the last three hundred years and that only because of lack of space in the churchyard.

Magic is often directed by a magic wand and as we have seen in this book, often the wands were made from the wood of the yew. The magic of the wand is, of course, primarily derived from the wood. There was a Frisian 'magic wand' found in Holland in 1906, called the Talisman of Britsum, which was dated to between 550 and 650 CE. The wand is made of yew, is inscribed with the yew rune Eihwaz and is about five inches long. The inscription on it roughly translates as 'Always carry this yew. There is power in it.' Fairies, fairy godmothers and Fairy Queens, as we all know from our childhood fairy tales, performed magic by waving a magic wand, sometimes accompanied by incantations or words of command. The power of the baculus or yew staff, which are simply magic wands by any other name, was well known. *The God Tree* explores this in great depth but here I just want to recap on one story of St. Padarn who was given a staff called Cyrwen, by the Archbishop of Jerusalem, with which he performed magic or more correctly in Christian times, 'miracles'. The staff was famous, had a will and character of its own and acted independently to bring peace in any dispute. Padarn, a direct descendent of Joseph of Arimathea, was called to Ireland when the country was devastated by the wars of the kings of the provinces of Ireland, as the Bishop of the two royal cities was told that peace could only be restored by Padarn and this peace was fulfilled in the 'gift of Cirguen' (meaning the staff). It was said that 'For so great is the service of that baculus, that if any two are at discord, they are made to agree by swearing on it'. The implication was that this saint, not from himself but through his staff, was a powerful instrument of peace. Padarn was seen as the keeper of the staff. Praise poems were written to Cyrwen, describing it as giving protection, 'Its holy power, reaching the limits of three continents'. It is likely that Padarn eventually planted his staff over his daughter's grave at Llanerfyl, where it became one of the most extraordinary yew trees ever to be seen, winding and twisting like four serpents around the churchyard. The yew tree is still there and this was by no means the only yew staff to be connected with wands and magic.

Druids

It is often said that Druids worshipped trees but this is a misconception. Druids didn't worship trees; they were one with the trees and spoke the same language. The Druid and the yew were intertwined and inseparable. The Druid was part of the yew. In Sanskrit, which was the international language for thousands of years before Latin, the name Deva Daru, the sacred tree, the tree of the god/dess, of divinity, meant both tree and truth, as it did in Saxon. The tree and the cross were indistinguishable and oaths were sworn by Celts and Saxons alike, under a sacred tree or on a yew staff and the Oath Super Bacculum, as it was known, was considered more binding than any other oath.

Druids didn't need to be near a yew to be able to communicate with them. The yew operates over time and space. When the yew spoke, the Druid could interpret it. They communicated telepathically. Nevertheless, Druids lived in the yew groves. They were time travellers but they could not travel without the co-operation of the yew. There was a time when I knew that the yew knew I had crossed a certain boundary and that I would be reprimanded for it when I reached home, hundreds of miles away. The yew is primaeval and can be ruthless in its punishments and has a way of letting you know beyond doubt that nothing is hidden from it, the Watcher. We are all different and, as a visual person, the yew communicates with me through images and symbols, while others hear a voice. It also organises events and meetings which has meant that the right person, seemingly miraculously, has contacted me out of the blue when a yew tree needed help. The yew is looking for servants. If you let it know you are interested and sympathetic, your life will no longer be your own but you may not mind if you decide to set foot on a great unfolding adventure.

'Merlin's Oak'

Merlin's Oak (actually a Yew) on the shores of Llyn Tegid (Lake Bala).

In the mythology of early times, oak and yew were confused. There is plenty of evidence of this pointed out in *The God Tree*. So, when I was trying to find a tree known as 'Merlin's Oak' I had it in mind that this tree I was looking for was actually more likely to have been a yew. It was described as being located between two lakes. Merlin was connected with the yew and at the end of his life he was said to have lived his life backwards in an ancient yew. Merlin, the great magician was associated with the Druids whose principle tree of life, death and rebirth was the yew, the tree of time and eternity.

In Nikolai Tolstoy's *Merlin* there is the following:

'Math and Gwydion. Gwydion created me, great magic from the staff of enchantment'
'An oak tree grows between two lakes,

435

Darkly overspreading shy and vale:

If I do not speak falsely,

These are the limbs of Lleu'. (limbs may be branches)

Lleu/Lug, a goddess, was one of the 'crimson stained ones' of Britain which may be so named after the red staining yew berries. As Gwydion's incantatory verses make plain, this is no ordinary oak (or yew) but the World-Tree itself. It is also described as 'darkly overspreading', a good description of a yew not an oak. The tree is compared to the Norse World Tree Yggdraṣil and possesses Otherworldly characteristics.

A photograph by the tree writer and photographer Julian Hight of a very ancient and decrepit yew drew my attention. It was said to grow on the shores of Lake Tegid near Bala. It was an extraordinary looking tree, extraordinarily old, gnarled and twisted but not very big or tall, indicating a yew that had at one time in earlier life been larger and more vigorous but which had shrunk, which ancient yews often do, falling into decay before regenerating. This particular tree, no more than ten or twelve feet tall, looked as if it was hanging onto life, refusing to give up. It was interesting to find out that the name Bala means 'a sliver of land or isthmus between two lakes'. It took us a while to find this tree. It had been something of a quest and for decades while searching for Merlin's Oak (yew) the only yew that could be found in the area of Bala was at Llangower on the south side of the lake but the tree here is not particularly old, perhaps some 1,400 years at most. The location for the ancient yew tree of Julian's photo was given as Glan Llyn on the north of the lake. Eventually we (myself and two friends) found the Glan Llyn Outdoor Activities Centre run by the Urdd and here the staff who knew of the whereabouts of the yew tree below the Centre on the shore of the lake, were intrigued and good enough to take us across the lake by boat to see the ancient yew.

We were struck by the obviously extraordinary age of the

yew. It was on very low lying land and Geraint at the Centre said that in the thirteen years that he had worked there, he had seen the waters rise and that quite likely there had been a strip of land there originally, like an extension of the land where the tree grows. This would have originally extended parallel to the present shore across to where that shore meanders out into the lake, just some two hundred yards away. This strip, believed to be now underwater, would then have made the two lakes, written about by Tolstoy. There are only a small handful of trees of this age and I know of no other site like this with an ancient yew. The closest would be the Runnymede Yew. Ancient yews are normally sited on high ground. This tree is immeasurably old, several thousand years old. It was hard to tell its age as we were unable to find any decayed wood samples within the tree and therefore couldn't get any ring counts but this is a rare and very special yew. It is so old it has almost petrified, although it is still alive. The wood is hard as iron and almost polished and the root and trunk run into each other in a way I've not really seen before, making the tree seems almost lifted off the ground. Yews can become dormant for many years and then resume growing. It seems this one is one of those. It was also impossible to tell whether the tree was male or female with no fruits, nuts or acorns visible or remains of male flowers. The grey green foliage holds fast to the tree, which was inundated by rising lake waters last winter to a depth of four feet and this would probably have washed away any nuts that may have lain on the ground, along with any samples of decayed wood.

I am concerned that it is inevitable that this tree will die eventually from climate change which will cause it to be drowned as the waters rise. In normal circumstances such trees are immortal but being regularly inundated by the lake waters will kill the tree. However, in the interests of Welsh culture and history, I wonder if someone could be found to instigate a unique project. Ancient yews have sometimes been moved, such as the one at Buckland-in-Dover which was moved 60 feet from one side of the churchyard to another in 1880 and survived. The Bala Lake or Llyn Tegid Yew is planted on a mound, which such ancient yew trees often were but considering the size of the mound, I would say this is not the usual grave of a chieftain. It may well be the last resting place of several warriors and contain grave artefacts. Connected as it is to Merlin and Taliesin and adjacent to an Urdd Centre, it should be recognised as important to Welsh culture. It presents a unique opportunity as it might be possible to turn the situation here to advantage and move the yew tree to a higher position up on the hill where the Centre is located, at the same time making an archaeological investigation of the mound before it is lost to the lake waters.

Time loss, time distortion

These things can happen at a yew tree. A friend disappeared from view when he walked anti-clockwise around an ancient yew, seeing the railings disappear and the voices, sights and sounds of another time appear. On his return, walking around the other way and thinking just ten minutes had elapsed, those he had been with, said he'd disappeared for two hours and they'd been looking everywhere for him. He was hidden in the same space but in another time. There are other similar stories of enchanted circles around yew trees. In fact, many people have experienced strange happenings around yew trees and during the Yew campaign launched by David Bellamy at the Conservation Foundation in the 80s and 90s, the Foundation received many letters recounting odd and weird experiences that had taken place at yew trees. On a personal level, I have experienced a kind of rapid downloading of information and visions of things from times past at ancient yew sites.

We are living in a time now when the knowledge and wisdom of the yew are thankfully returning like a beacon of light, at a time when spiritual darkness and climate change threaten life on earth. With it comes the return of hope for the future. As time travellers, the Druids were capable of passing into the future, as well as the past and with the yew, were capable of passing on knowledge to anyone in time and space, often choosing the least likely people. The Druids are still alive through other people, through those around us, who may not call themselves such, to enable ancient and forgotten knowledge, needed now, to return. We are at a crisis, a turning point in human history, where our survival along with all life on this planet is at stake. The yew speaks to those who can hear, and whose minds are open and do not dismiss ideas they cannot understand as rubbish.

It is possible that you can find a particular yew, perhaps one you can climb inside of, which can arrange time travel. You may not always know that such a thing has happened, or perhaps you will. You may think you have lost time or that time has become elastic, or you may wonder how certain things could have happened in the time available, you may be transported in dreams and sleep. The time has come for us to set aside our fixed ideas, suspend our disbelief, renew our connection with yew and return it to our consciousness.

The ancient hollow yew

is nothing less than a portal to other worlds, a time lord that can take us back or forwards and this is what it may have been intended to convey with all the Mesopotamian images mainly on cylinder seals of the goddess standing within a bower or winged gate. In the pyramid paintings, the Pharaoh stands on the boat which takes him on a journey passing through several gates which he has to pass successfully through before morning when he will have completed his journey and arrived in the next world. On the boat, the Pharaoh stands within this same arch, not unlike the portal to eternity or the next world which the tree goddesses stand within or as depicted on the Atropos stone at Gresford. Like a tunnel, it is a way through to another dimension. As a yew portal it offers protection during a change of consciousness.

Pennant Melangell

I cannot leave these mysteries without another story to follow the one I told in *The God Tree* of the miraculous healing of a friend of mine at Pennant Melangell which above all demonstrates the extraordinary power of the yew. Whatever else the yew is, and it is many things, it has the power to bestow life, death and transformation.

I have taken several people to Pennant Melagell for healing. Some recovered, others did not. All received some insight or resolution. It is a place of pilgrimage, contemplation and of truth and beauty. Miracles are never guaranteed but this sacred place with roots in early times has a reputation for that possibility. Pennant Melangell holds the only Romanesque shrine in Britain and is dedicated to Melangell whose name appears to mean 'Sweet angel' or 'Honey angel' who was given the site by Prince Brochwel of Powys after a hare hid beneath her skirt and was saved from his hunting party.

Ten years or more ago I was due to take two people with cancer there. The day came and snow was forecast in that area but here down south it dawned bright and clear with no sign of any such thing and we decided to go. At the last minute one person decided not to come. We set off and as we got closer, I thought how wrong weather forecasts can be but when we turned off the main road at Llangynog to head towards the mountains at the end of the valley, travelling down the two mile track to the church, it began to snow. I prayed that it might stop and give us at least half an hour there. Immediately the snow ceased and as we got out of the car a powerful sunbeam suddenly and dramatically struck the top of the breast-shaped mountain above the church and the yews and poured down its side like golden honey, echoing Melangell's name.

We quietly entered the church yard and went to the male and female yews on the right. The first, the female, resembles a shrine with a womb like cavern in its trunk. We spent a half hour there between the two yews asking for the healing of the trees and felt refreshed and blessed. My friend felt something significant had happened. Then just as suddenly as it had stopped the snow started again and fell relentlessly and silently quickly blurring the features of the landscape and we drove as fast as the conditions would allow as the snow got heavier. I thought we would have to find somewhere to stay the night, although I didn't want to as I had to go to work the next day but the mountain lay between us and home. As we came towards Newtown the place was deserted with no sign of life and no cars on the road but ahead at a roundabout a snow plough pulled in front of us and we followed it as it cleared a path for us. The seemingly heaven-sent vehicle drove in front of us, leading the way and taking the same road that we were. At the top of the mountain we saw three cars that had spun around and been abandoned but we and the snow plough kept going over the mountain and down, where the plough turned back and we travelled on. My friend recovered and still lives, though sadly not so the person who didn't come. Perhaps it was pure coincidence but our pilgrimage felt very precious and meaningful and it was one of the adventures that enriched my life and spoke to my soul as so many things on my journey with the Yew do. To me it is important to be as open as I can to new and perhaps strange experiences, even if they seem impossible or threaten what we hold as our sanity. Often it is these things that deepen our understanding, put us on the right path and help re-sanctify our lives, for in our time we have grown up with ideas about life that are simply wrong. Ideas for instance which tell us that trees do not have consciousness, or that we are above Nature, or are not subject to the same things as other animals. Often things make sense only in the processing of an experience. Some things can't be explained or put into words but can only be felt and held as a certain knowing. The Yew's ability to communicate and affect things makes no sense if we rely on logic. The mind has its place but Spirit and the Heart can defy the mind, bypass it and lead to the truth. I have been truly blessed with a life that has been one long, mysterious and magical adventure with the Eternal Yew which operates beyond time and space. I wouldn't have missed it for the world.

Last Words

From Cyfraith Hywel or The Laws of Hywel Dda
Hywel Dda, 880 to 950 King of Wales

A consecrated yew, its value is a pound.
A mistletoe branch, three score pence.
An oak six score pence.
Principal branch of an oak, thirty pence.
A yew tree (not consecrated) fifteen pence.
A sweet apple, three score pence.
A sour apple, thirty pence.
A thorn tree, seven pence halfpenny
Every tree after that, four pence.

Yew-Trees by William Wordsworth

There is a Yew-tree, pride of Lorton Vale,
Which to this day stands single, in the midst
Of its own darkness, as it stood of yore:
Not loathe to furnish weapons for the Bands
Of Umfraville or Percy ere they marched
To Scotland's heaths; or those that crossed the sea
And drew their sounding bows at Agincour,
Perhaps at earlier Crecy, or Poitiers.
Of vast circumference and gloom profound,
This solitary Tree! -a living thing
Produced too slowly ever to decay;
Of form and aspect too magnificent
To be destroyed. But worthier still of note
Are those Fraternal Four of Borrowdale,
Joined in one solemn and capacious grove;
Huge trunks! -and each particular trunk a growth

Of intertwisted fibres serpentine.
Up-coiling, and inverateley convolved, -
Nor uninformed with Fantasy, and looks
That threaten the profane; - a pillared shade,
Upon whose grassless floor of red-brown hue,
By sheddings from the pining umbrage tinged
Perennially - beneath whose sable roof
Of boughs, as if for festal purpose decked
With unrejoicing berries - ghostly Shapes
May meet at noontide: Fear and trembling Hope,
Silence and Foresight, Death the Skeleton
And Time the Shadow; there to celebrate,
As in a natural temple scattered o'er
With altars undisturbed of mossy stone,
United worship; or in mute repose
To lie, and listen to the mountain flood
Murmuring from Glaramara's inmost caves.

Elegy Written in a Country Churchyard by Thomas Grey

Beneath those rugged elms, that yew tree's shade,
Where heaves the turf in many a mouldering heap,
Each in his narrow cell for ever laid.

The Yew Tree by Brian Mc. Neil

My bonnie yew tree
Tell me what did you see...

A mile frae Pentcaitland, on the road to the sea
Stands a yew tree a thousand years old,
And the old women swear by the grey o' their hair
That it knows what the future will hold.
For the shadows of Scotland stand round it

444

'Mid the kail and the corn and the kye
All the hopes and the fears of a thousand long years
Under the Lothian sky...

But a wee bird flew out from your branches
And sang out as never before,
And the words o' the song were a thousand years long
And to learn them's a long thousand more.

From: The Fields of Runnymede by Jehanne Mehta

There stands a tree but more than tree,
Beneath a dusky canopy,
The home of runes and mystery,
By rush and sedge and reed;
And those who would true counsel seek,
From far and near their journey make,
To the ancient yew of Ankerwycke,
In the fields of Runnymede.

The Yew Tree by Sylvia Plath

The yew tree points up, it has a Gothic shape.
The eyes lift after it and find the moon.
The moon is my mother. She is not sweet like Mary.
...The moon sees nothing of this. She is bald and wild.
And the message of the yew tree is blackness - blackness and
silence

Ode to an Old Soul by Charlotte Smith

O magnificent Yew,
In your majesty you reign supreme.
The sunlight filters through your swaying branches,

Your dark green needles tremble in the wind,
Your trunk with its reddish, flaking bark is
so distinctive against the blue of the sky.
From early morning till night, your massive, squat
form is a unique sight.
Standing so alone, without any of your kind for
companionship or sharing of illumined thoughts -
Was it always so?
Tell me of the time when you once held court over
growing saplings, teaching them the ways of the
ancient trees.
I watch you through the changing seasons,
and my heart glows.

Spring, Summer, Autumn, Winter:
yet you are evergreen and as solid and dependable as
Nature made you.
Wise, wise Yew,
What divine power guides your very lifeforce?
For there is a spiritual intelligence within you
that is so alive and omnipotent.
I will leave you now but I will return again soon,
for Old Souls need love and compassion to match
their years.
I can never give you all you deserve, but I can give
you all I have and so I shall,
as long as we are friends in this life and the next.

The Burning Perch by Louis Mac Neice

The wind, that cannot rest,
Soothed and then waked the darkness of the yew
Until the tree was restless too.

Of all the winds I knew
I thought, and how they muttered in the yew,

Lines left upon a seat in a Yew-Tree
by William Wordsworth

...Who he was that piled these stones and with the mossy sod
First covered o'er and taught this aged tree
Now wild, to bend its arms in circling shade,
I well remember. He was one who own'd
No common soul.

Voices from Things Growing in a Churchyard
by Thomas Hardy

Hardy's heart is buried in the shade of Stinsford Churchyard's ancient yew tree, not far from the grave of Thomas Voss, whose disembodied voice is heard here:

I, these berries of juice and gloss,
Sir or Madam,
Am clean forgotten as Thomas Voss;
Thin-urned, I have burrowed away from the moss
That covers my sod, and have entered the yew,
And turned to clusters ruddy of view,
All day cheerily,
All night eerily!

We who remain by Robert M Macefield

The flowers of spring, hilltops full with morning dew,
Remembered songs, dancing in groves of Oak and Yew
Precious, most sacred, Avalon,
All these years long gone.

We who travel through Time, following streams of love that
flow.
A Royal Court built with the powers of Merlin's rhyme,
Mirrors to contain, a Grail to find.
Many paths we follow, sent that day to this,
From Ceridwen's hollow, Camelot we miss.

So many knights have fallen, lost their way,
Half remembered paths to steer, this world in which we stay.
Few left who dream here with us now.
Along side us still, unseen, the Table Round
Our spiral wheel.

Enemies we confound, ancient Grail they cannot steal.
Hold in your heart this noble band,
For we travel still, through Ancestral lands.

And if you know those, who would blame,
In anger, fear or controlling shame,
Send us your prayers, we hear them clear
Dispelling the fog of many a year.

So I sit before the sacred yew and well,
Knowing this rhyme
My last farewell,
Losing reason, mind, and ties that bind,
The Grail, I someday hope to find.

Returning back, through hollowed hills,
To where I know, and feel,
The centre, my Medicine Wheel.

So wish us well, no sad refrain,
The Knights of Old...

Some still remain.

Merlin's Prophecy Lines attributed to Merlin

When...root and branch shall change place,
And the newness of the thing shall seem a miracle,
At last the healing maiden will return, her footsteps bursting
into flame.
She will weep tears of compassion for the people of the land,
Dry up polluted rivers with her breath,
Carry the forest in her right hand, the city in her left,
And nourish the creatures of the deep.

With her blessing man will become like a god
Waking as if from a dream;
Heart open and filled with light,
Radiant face, glowing like the rising sun,
Shining eyes, like twin silver moons,
Radiant ears, shimmering with song.
Shining lips, that dance over words,
Words of magic that burst into the air, becoming swallows.
The soul shall walk out; the mind of fire shall burn.
And in the twinkling of an eye the dust of the ancients shall
be restored.

Ode à l'If by Sandrine Perkins

Toi qui est éternel
Toi qui peut grandir, mourir et renaitre.

Tu es le père et la mère
Le ciel et la terre
Solide et puissant
Dans ta grandeur.

Mystérieux et mystique
Le messager de l'univers
L'origine, le plus ancien des anciens.

Tu étais là avant nous
et tu le seras après nous.

Translation
Ode to the Yew

You who are eternal,
You who can grow to adulthood, die and be reborn,

You are the father and the mother
The sky and the earth,
Solid and powerful
In your grandeur

Mysterious and mystical
The messenger of the Universe
The origin, the most ancient of ancients

You were there before us
And you will be there after us.

'Heart of Yew' Painting by Janis Fry.

About the Author

Janis Fry studied Theology and English Literature at Bangor University in North Wales and Art at Swansea College of Art. She is considered a leading authority on ancient yew trees. Her interest began in 1974 while exploring the grounds of a derelict country house where she tripped and fell through a hole in the undergrowth and found herself in the magical twilight world of an ancient yew tunnel. From then on yew trees started to show up in her life. In the 1980s Janis contributed to the first book on yews for 100 years, *The Sacred Yew* by Anand Chetan and Diana Brueton, which began the revival of interest in yews and was the forerunner for all other books on yew. She also contributed yew research to David Bellamy's organisation, The Conservation Foundation. In 2014 Janis put the Defynnog Yew on the map as the oldest tree in Britain and in recent years set up the Campaign for Legal Protection of Ancient Yews on change.org which has gained 266,000 signatures.

Self-Published Books

The Defynnog Yew, Britain's Oldest Tree
The Ankerwycke Yew, Living Witness to the Magna Carta

Bibliography

Allcroft A H *The Circle and the Cross* 1927

Amar Annus *The God Ninurta* 2002

Anderson G and P A *Guide to the Highlands and Islands of Scotland, Including Orkney and Zetland* 1842

Baert B *A Heritage of Holy Wood* 2004

Bailey H *The Lost Language of Symbolism* 1912

Bancroft H *The Book of Wealth, a Study of the Achievements of Architecture* 2015

Bardwell S *Walking in Scotland* 2001

Barrington D *Philosophical Transactions* 1769

Bevan Jones R *The Ancient Yew* 2002

Black J, Cunningham G, Robson E and Zolyomi G *Inanna and Dumuzid* 2004

Black J *The Literature of Ancient Sumer* 2004

Blavatsky H P *The Secret Doctrine* 1888

Boulay R A *Flying Serpents and Dragons: The Story of Mankind's Reptilian Past* 1990

Brash R R *The Ogam Inscribed Monuments of the Gaedhil in the British Isles* 1879

Butler N M Butler *Magna Carta* 1915

Busatta S *The Tree of Life Design* 2015

Butterworth E A S *The Lunar Crescent and the Bowl* 1970

Cammann S *Ancient Symbols in Modern Afghanistan* 1957

Chetan A and Brueton D *The Sacred Yew* 1994

Christisons Sir R *Trans Botanical Society Edinburgh* 1870

Clark D and Roberts A *Twilight of the Celtic Gods* 1996

Coles F *Report on Stone Circles Surveyed in Perthshire. The Northern Antiquarian* 1910

Collins A *From the Ashes of Angels* 1996

Collins B J *Masters of the Animals in Old World Iconography* 2010

Cook A B *Zeus* 1914

Cook R *The Tree of Life Symbol of the Centre* 1974

Cornish V *The Churchyard Yew and Immortality* 1946

Cox E H M *New Flora and Sylva* c.1930

Cripps H W *Laws Relating to the Church and Clergy* 1886

Cunliffe B *Facing the Ocean – The Atlantic and its Peoples* 2001

Darmesteter J *Thesis on the mythology of the Avesta* 1875

Dowden K *Technology, Statues, Shrines and Temples* 2013

Dowden K *European Paganism* 2000

Dizon M and Kennedy T *The Christ Child in Medieval Culture* 2012

Edgar J G *From Runnymede and Lincoln Fair* 1866

Eduljee K E *Zoroastrian Heritage* 2005

Ekwall, *English River Names* 1928

Eliade M, *The Sacred and the Profane* 1957

Ellis R *Eden in Egypt* 2004

Ellis R *Scota, Egyptian Queen of the Scots* 2006

Eugène Goblet d'Alviella *The Migration of Symbols* 1894

Evans D Rev. *The Churchyard Yews of Gwent* 1988

Evans-Wentz W Y *The Fairy Faith in Celtic Countries* 1911

Fry J and Meredith A *The God Tree* 2012

Gardener L *Genesis of the Grail Kings* 1999

Gardiner H *The Beginning of Christianity* 1930s

George A R *The Babylonian Gilgamesh Epic* 2003

Giorgio de Santillana and Hertha von Dechend *Hamlet's Mill* 1969

Gilbert A, Wilson A and Blackett B *The Holy Kingdom* 1998

Green J R *A Short History of the English People* 1874

Grimm J *Teutonic Mythology* 1880

Gyll G *History of Wraysbury* 1861

Hageneder F *Yew, A History* 2007

Hall T *The Immortal Yew* 2018

Harper R F *Assyrian and Babylonian Letters* 1893

Harris R *Egypt in Britain* 1927

Hayman R *Trees* 2003

Henslow G Professor *Plants of the Bible* 1895

Hight J *World Tree Story* 2015

Hillebrandt A *Vedic Mythology* 1891

Hooke D FSA *Trees in Anglo Saxon England* 2011

Hunter F *Guide to Perthshire; Evidence of Roman Intrusions in the Fortingall Area* 2000

Hutchison R FRSA *The Old and Remarkable Yew Trees in Scotland* 1890

Ingram H Dr. *Dragging down Heaven: Jesus as Magician and Manipulator of Spirits in the Gospels* 2007

Gardener L *Genesis of the Grail Kings* 1999

Jastrow M *The Religion of Babylonia and Assyria* 2007

Jefferson L M *The Staff of Jesus in Early Christian Art* 2010

Jefferson L M *Christ the Miracle Worker in Early Christian Art* 2014

Johnson W *Byways of British Archaeology* 1912

Jones F *The Holy Wells of Wales* 1954

Kuniholm, P I Newton M W, Griggs C B, and Sullivan P J *The Functional Use of Wood* at *Phrygian Gordion through Charcoal Analysis* 2005

Lewington A and Parker E *Ancient Trees; Trees that Live for a Thousand Years* 1999

Loudon J C *Arboretum Fructicetum Brittanicum (The Trees and Shrubs of Britain)* 1838

Lowe J Yew *Trees of Great Britain and Ireland* 1897

Mabey R *The Cabaret of Plants* 2015

Macdonald R Rev. *The Topographical Statistical and Historical Gazetteer of Scotland* 1841

Maclagan R C *The Perth Incident of 1396 from a Folklore Point of View* 1905

Malcor L A *The Hittite Sword in the Stone: The Sword God and his Twelve Companions* 2012

Massey G *The Light of the World* 1907

Mattfield W *The Garden of Eden Myth* 2010

Matthews T F *The Clash of Gods A Reinterpretation of Early Christian Art* 1993

Mee A *King's England* 1930

Mc. Kenna T *The Food of the Gods, The Search for the Original Tree of Knowledge: a Radical History of Plants, Drugs and Human Evolution* 1993

Moberg V *A History of the Swedish People* 1898 - 1972

Moffat A *The Sea Kingdoms* 2001

Monmouth Geoffrey *The History of the Kings of Britain* (*Historia Regum Brittaniae*) 1136

Morgan Rev W *St Paul in Britain: or the Origin of British as Opposed to Papal Christianity* 1861

Morganwg I *The Triads of Bardism* 1747 - 1826

Nabarz P *The Mysteries of Mithras* 2005

Neil Dr P *Edinburgh Philosophical Transactions Journal* 1833

Newman D *The Lives and the Deaths of the Holy Apostles* 1685

O'Grady S H *Silva Gadelica* (translation) 1892

Owen Rev. E *Old Stone Crosses* 1886

Parpola S *The Ideology of Assyrian Kingship: Sons of God* 2000

Pennant T *A Tour in Scotland* 1771

Petrie G *The Ecclesiastical Architecture of Ireland* 1845

Philpot Mrs *The Sacred Tree* 1897

Polwhele R *Historical Views of Devonshire* 1793

Porteous A *Forest Folklore, Mythology and Romance* 1928

Price D *The Missing Years of Jesus* 2010

Prideaux C G *Practical Guide to the Duties of Churchwardens* 1895

Prince C and Picknett L *The Templar Revelation* 1997

Rahtz Dr, and Watts L *Glastonbury, Myth and Archaeology* 2009

Regardie I *The Tree of Life, a Study in Magic* 1932

Rice Rees *An Essay on the Welsh Saints of the Primitive Christians* 1804 - 1839

Rotherham I D, Handley C, Agnoletti M *Trees beyond the Word* 2013

Sayce Prof. A H *The Hittites* 1888

Soulier. E Andriveau Goujon J *Ancient Empires* 1838

Schema S *The Verdant Cross* 1995

Sharkey J *Pilgrim Ways, The Grand Pilgrimage to St. David's* 1994

Sikes W *The Realm of Faerie - Fairy Life and Legend in Britain'* and *'British Goblins: Welsh Folklore, Fairy Mythology, Legends and Traditions* c.1900

Sitchin Z *Earth Chronicles* 2004

Stedman Davies Rev. *Yew Trees in Churchyards* 1945

Stirling S A *The King Arthur Conspiracy* 2013

Strabo W *Homily of the Credo* AD 800

Strutt J G *Sylva Brittanica* 1882

Swanton E W *The Yew Trees of England* 1958

Taylor B *Exploring* the Supernatural 1986,

Taylor S and WJ Watson W J *Celtic Place Names of Scotland* 1926

Taylor-Perry R *The God who Comes: Dionysian Mysteries* 2003

Thompson R *Illustrations of the History of Great Britain* Vol. 1 1828

Tolkien J R R *The Lord of the Rings* 1968

Tranter Nigel *Columba* 1987

Tyack Rev. G S *Lore and Legend of the English Church* 1899

Urantia Foundation *The Urantia Book* 1955

van Buren E D *Symbols of the Gods in Mesopotamian Art* 1945

Vallancey C *An Essay on the Primitive Inhabitants of Great Britain and Ireland* 1807

Westwood J O *Lapidarium Walliae: The Early Inscribed and Sculptured Stones of Wales, Delineated and Described* 1876

Widengren G *The King and the Tree of Life in Ancient Near Eastern Religion* 1996

Williams T *The Doom of Colyn Dolphyn* pre-1923

Williams N *The Early Christian Monuments of Wales* 1950

Wurts J S *Pedigrees of the Barons* 1942

MOON
BOOKS

PAGANISM & SHAMANISM

What is Paganism? A religion, a spirituality, an alternative belief system, nature worship? You can find support for all these definitions (and many more) in dictionaries, encyclopaedias, and text books of religion, but subscribe to any one and the truth will evade you. Above all Paganism is a creative pursuit, an encounter with reality, an exploration of meaning and an expression of the soul. Druids, Heathens, Wiccans and others, all contribute their insights and literary riches to the Pagan tradition. Moon Books invites you to begin or to deepen your own encounter, right here, right now.

If you have enjoyed this book, why not tell other readers by posting a review on your preferred book site.

Recent bestsellers from Moon Books are:

Journey to the Dark Goddess
How to Return to Your Soul
Jane Meredith
Discover the powerful secrets of the Dark Goddess and
transform your depression, grief and pain into healing
and integration.
Paperback: 978-1-84694-677-6 ebook: 978-1-78099-223-5

Shamanic Reiki
Expanded Ways of Working with Universal Life Force Energy
Llyn Roberts, Robert Levy
Shamanism and Reiki are each powerful ways of healing; together,
their power multiplies. *Shamanic Reiki* introduces techniques to
help healers and Reiki practitioners tap ancient healing wisdom.
Paperback: 978-1-84694-037-8 ebook: 978-1-84694-650-9

Pagan Portals – The Awen Alone
Walking the Path of the Solitary Druid
Joanna van der Hoeven
An introductory guide for the solitary Druid, *The Awen Alone* will
accompany you as you explore, and seek out your own place
within the natural world.
Paperback: 978-1-78279-547-6 ebook: 978-1-78279-546-9

A Kitchen Witch's World of Magical Herbs & Plants
Rachel Patterson
A journey into the magical world of herbs and plants, filled with
magical uses, folklore, history and practical magic. By popular
writer, blogger and kitchen witch, Tansy Firedragon.
Paperback: 978-1-78279-621-3 ebook: 978-1-78279-620-6

Medicine for the Soul
The Complete Book of Shamanic Healing
Ross Heaven
All you will ever need to know about shamanic healing and how to
become your own shaman…
Paperback: 978-1-78099-419-2 ebook: 978-1-78099-420-8

Shaman Pathways – The Druid Shaman
Exploring the Celtic Otherworld
Danu Forest
A practical guide to Celtic shamanism with exercises and
techniques as well as traditional lore for exploring the Celtic
Otherworld.
Paperback: 978-1-78099-615-8 ebook: 978-1-78099-616-5

Traditional Witchcraft for the Woods and Forests
A Witch's Guide to the Woodland with Guided Meditations and
Pathworking
Mélusine Draco
A Witch's guide to walking alone in the woods, with guided
meditations and pathworking.
Paperback: 978-1-84694-803-9 ebook: 978-1-84694-804-6

Wild Earth, Wild Soul
A Manual for an Ecstatic Culture
Bill Pfeiffer
Imagine a nature-based culture so alive and so connected,
spreading like wildfire. This book is the first flame…
Paperback: 978-1-78099-187-0 ebook: 978-1-78099-188-7

Naming the Goddess
Trevor Greenfield

Naming the Goddess is written by over eighty adherents and scholars of Goddess and Goddess Spirituality.

Paperback: 978-1-78279-476-9 ebook: 978-1-78279-475-2

Shapeshifting into Higher Consciousness
Heal and Transform Yourself and Our World with Ancient Shamanic and Modern Methods

Llyn Roberts

Ancient and modern methods that you can use every day to transform yourself and make a positive difference in the world.

Paperback: 978-1-84694-843-5 ebook: 978-1-84694-844-2

Readers of ebooks can buy or view any of these bestsellers by clicking on the live link in the title. Most titles are published in paperback and as an ebook. Paperbacks are available in traditional bookshops. Both print and ebook formats are available online.

Find more titles and sign up to our readers' newsletter at
http://www.johnhuntpublishing.com/paganism
Follow us on Facebook at https://www.facebook.com/MoonBooks
and Twitter at https://twitter.com/MoonBooksJHP